THE CONTROL OF
AMERICAN FOREIGN RELATIONS

THE MACMILLAN COMPANY
NEW YORK · BOSTON · CHICAGO · DALLAS
ATLANTA · SAN FRANCISCO

MACMILLAN & CO., LIMITED
LONDON · BOMBAY · CALCUTTA
MELBOURNE

THE MACMILLAN CO. OF CANADA, LTD.
TORONTO

THE CONTROL OF
AMERICAN FOREIGN RELATIONS

BY

QUINCY WRIGHT, Ph.D.

PROFESSOR OF INTERNATIONAL LAW
IN THE UNIVERSITY OF MINNESOTA

"The qualities indispensable in the management of foreign negotiations point out the Executive as the most fit agent in those transactions; while the vast importance of the trust, and the operation of treaties as laws, plead strongly for the participation of the whole or a portion of the legislative body in the office of making them."
—*The Federalist*

NEW YORK
THE MACMILLAN COMPANY
1922

PRINTED IN THE UNITED STATES OF AMERICA

Copyright 1922
By The American Philosophical Society

Copyright 1922
By The Macmillan Company

Set up and electrotyped. Published August, 1922

To

Louise Leonard

χωρὶς γὰρ ταύτης (αἰτίας) οὔτε τῶν κατὰ λόγον οὔτε τῶν παρὰ λόγον εἶναι δοκούντων οὐδὲν οἷόν τε συντελεσθῆναι.—*Polybius*.

The Crowned Essay
for which the Henry M. Phillips Prize of
two thousand dollars was awarded on April 23, 1921,
by the American Philosophical Society.

PREFACE.

For some years a small group of the writer's colleagues at the University of Minnesota have dined together periodically in order to listen to discussions or papers in the widely different fields of scholarship which the group represents. In the winter of 1920, with the Treaty of Versailles still unratified and unrejected by the Senate, the writer discussed before this group a subject then in the front of everyone's mind—the American system or lack of system for controlling foreign relations. The same material presented in a paper read before the American Political Science Association, December, 1920, was published in the American Political Science Review of February, 1921, and reprinted in Spanish in Inter-America, November, 1921.

The writer utilized his investigations in connection with this brief article to prepare an essay in accordance with the regulations governing the award of the Henry M. Phillips Prize offered by the American Philosophical Society in 1921 for an essay on "The Control of the Foreign Relations of the United States: The Relative Rights, Duties and Responsibilities of the President, of the Senate and the House, and of the Judiciary, in Theory and in Practice." This essay has been expanded and revised up to January, 1922, for the present publication.

The essay seeks to draw particular attention to a difficulty in the control of foreign relations found in every government, but especially in a government with powers defined in a judicially enforced written constitution. This is the difficulty which arises from the fact that the organs conducting foreign relations have their responsibilities defined by international law, while their powers are defined by constitutional law. Since the sources of these two bodies of law are different, a lack of coordination between the powers and the responsibilities of these organs is to be expected. To avoid confusion the writer has considered the subject from the international point of view and from the constitutional point of view in separate parts of the book, even at the risk of some repetition. Part II is devoted to the former—parts III and IV to the latter.

Throughout the book the writer has tried to indicate his reasons for thinking that the difficulty referred to can be solved only by the development of and adherence to constitutional understandings, supplementing the law of the constitution and indicating how the organs entrusted with the control of foreign relations ought to exercise their discretionary powers to avoid friction. Part V seeks to develop this thought systematically.

Primary use has been made of the sources: court reports; acts of Congress; Treaties; Presidential messages; diplomatic correspondence and Congressional debates, reports and documents, particularly the reports of the Senate Foreign Relations Committee. The classified extracts from this material in Moore's Digest of International Law have been of great assistance. The unofficial writings of American statesmen have been utilized, particularly Cleveland's Presidential Problems, Roosevelt's Autobiography, Taft's Our Chief Magistrate and His Powers, Wilson's Constitutional Government in the United States and Sutherland's Constitutional Powers and World Affairs. Of special studies in the field, the writer feels especially indebted to Corwin's The President's Control of Foreign Relations, Crandall's Treaties, Their Making and Enforcement, and Hayden's The Senate and Treaties. Numerous secondary works have been examined, reference to which is made in the footnotes. The writer has made use of his own articles published in the American Journal of International Law, the American Political Science Review, The Columbia Law Review, and the Minnesota Law Review. He thanks the publishers of these periodicals for their courteous consent to such use. Finally he wishes to thank his colleague and friend, Robert E. Cushman, for many helpful suggestions made during the progress of the work. For the plan of the work, for the conclusions, for the errors and omissions, no one but the writer is responsible.

QUINCY WRIGHT.

MINNEAPOLIS, MINNESOTA
May, 1922.

ANALYTICAL TABLE OF CONTENTS.

PART I.

CHAPTER I. THE NATURE OF THE FOREIGN RELATIONS POWER

1. Difficulty in Developing a Legal Theory of the Subject............ 3
2. Dual Position of the Foreign Relations Power.................... 4
3. The International Point of View................................. 4
4. The Constitutional Point of View................................ 6
5. Methods of Reconciling These Points of View.................... 7
6. Relation of Law and Understandings.............................. 7
7. Constitutional Understandings................................... 8
8. International Understandings.................................... 8

PART II.

THE POSITION OF THE FOREIGN RELATIONS POWER UNDER INTERNATIONAL LAW.

CHAPTER II. THE REPRESENTATIVE ORGAN OF GOVERNMENT.

9. The Nature of International Law................................. 13
10. Independence of States... 14
11. The Representative Authority under International Law........... 15
12. The President is the Representative Authority in the United States. 21

CHAPTER III. ATTRIBUTES OF THE NATIONAL REPRESENTATIVE ORGAN UNDER INTERNATIONAL LAW.

A. Sole Agency for Foreign Communication.

13. Foreign Representatives May Officially Communicate with the Nation Only Through the President or His Representatives...... 28
14. National Organs of Government other than the President or His Representatives May Not Communicate......................... 30
15. National and State Laws Subject to International Cognizance...... 30
16. Legislative Expressions of Opinion, not of International Cognizance. 33
17. Self-constituted Missions, Forbidden............................ 34
18. Missions of *de facto* Governments, Unofficially Received........... 35

B. All Acts of the President Subject to International Cognizance.

19. Communications of the President to Congress..................... 35
20. President Presumed to Speak for the Nation...................... 36

xi

ANALYTICAL TABLE OF CONTENTS.

CHAPTER IV. CONCLUSIVENESS OF THE ACTS AND UTTERANCES OF NATIONAL ORGANS UNDER INTERNATIONAL LAW.

A. With Reference to the Making of National Decisions.

21. Acts of the President... 38
22. National and State Statutes...................................... 40
23. Acts of Subordinates to the President........................... 40

B. With Reference to the Making of International Agreements.

24. Foreign Nations Presumed to Know the Constitution.............. 41
25. Signature under Authority of the Treaty Power.................. 41
26. Signature under Authority of the President..................... 44
27. Reservations Expressly Consented to............................ 45
28. Reservations Tacitly Consented to.............................. 48
29. Exchange of Ratifications under Authority of the President..... 52
30. Treaty Provisions *ultra vires* from Lack of Original Authority.... 53
31. Treaty Provisions *ultra vires* from Operation of Constitutional Limitations 55
32. Treaty Made Under Necessity.................................... 57

C. With Reference to the Meeting of International Responsibilities.

33. United States Bound by International Law and Treaties.......... 58
34. Decisions by the President..................................... 59
35. Decisions by Subordinates to the President..................... 60
36. Decisions of International Organs Authorized by the President.. 61
37. Meeting Responsibilities Distinguished from Making Agreements.. 62
38. Interpretation of Treaties..................................... 63
39. Understandings do not Require Forbearance in Pressing International Claims... 66

PART III

CONSTITUTIONAL LIMITATIONS UPON THE FOREIGN RELATIONS POWER.

CHAPTER V. LIMITATIONS UPON STATE POWERS.

40. Position of the Foreign Relations Power under Constitutional Law. 71
41. Relation Between State and National Powers..................... 72
42. Constitutional Prohibitions of State Power..................... 73
43. Action of National Organs Limiting State Powers................ 74

ANALYTICAL TABLE OF CONTENTS. xiii

CHAPTER VI. LIMITATIONS UPON NATIONAL POWERS: PRIVATE RIGHTS AND STATES' RIGHTS.

A. Private Rights.
44. Nature of Prohibitions... 76
45. Effect upon Power to Meet International Responsibilities........... 78
46. Effect upon Power to Make International Agreements............... 80
47. Effect upon Power to Make Decisions on National Policy.......... 82

B. States' Rights.
48. Nature of Prohibition.. 86
49. Effect upon Power to Meet International Responsibilities........... 87
50. Effect upon Power to Make International Agreements............... 88
51. Effect upon Power to Make Decisions on National Policy.......... 93

CHAPTER VII. LIMITATIONS UPON NATIONAL POWERS: THE SEPARATION OF POWERS.

52. Nature of the Theory.. 95
53. Protection of Independence of Departments........................ 96
54. Protection of Delegated Powers of Departments................... 97
55. Prohibition upon Exercise of Uncharacteristic Powers by any Department 98

A. Effect on the Power to Meet International Responsibilities.
56. Government as a Whole Competent to Meet Responsibilities...... 99
57. Power of President and Courts to Meet Responsibilities............ 100

B. Effect on the Power to Make International Agreements.
58. Limitations upon the Government as a Whole..................... 101
59. Limitations Derived from Powers of Congress..................... 101
60. The Delegation of Legislative Power.............................. 103
61. Congressional Delegation of Power to Make International Agreements 105
62. Treaty Delegation of Power to National Organs................... 106
63. Treaty Delegation of Power to International Organs............... 110
64. Limitations Derived from Powers of the Judiciary................. 115
65. Limitations Derived from Powers of the President................. 119

C. Effect on the Power to Make National Decisions.
66. Alleged Encroachments.. 120

CHAPTER VIII. CONCLUSION ON CONSTITUTIONAL LIMITATIONS.
67. Traditional Statements of Limitations upon the Treaty-power...... 121
68. Most Limitations Unimportant in Practice......................... 124
69. Important Limitations from Separation of Powers.................. 125

PART IV.

THE POWER TO CONDUCT FOREIGN RELATIONS UNDER THE CONSTITUTION.

CHAPTER IX. THE POSITION OF THE FOREIGN RELATIONS POWER IN THE CONSTITUTIONAL SYSTEM.

A. Source of National Powers.

70. Distribution of Powers between States and National Government... 129
71. Theory of Sovereign Powers.................................... 130
72. Theory of National Sovereignty in Foreign Relations.............. 131
73. Theory of Resultant Powers..................................... 132

B. Essential Nature of the Foreign Relations Power.

74. Controversy as to Nature of Foreign Relations Power............. 134
75. Foreign Relations Power not Essentially Judicial................ 135
76. Theory of Essentially Executive Nature: Early Opinion.......... 135
77. Essentially Executive Nature: Practice......................... 136
78. Essentially Executive Nature: Recent Opinion................... 136
79. Theory of Essentially Legislative Nature: Early Opinion........ 137
80. Essentially Legislative Nature: Practice....................... 139
81. Essentially Legislative Nature: Recent Opinion................. 139
82. Theory of a Fourth Department Different from Either Executive or Legislative... 140
83. A Fourth Department: Opinion of Theoretical Writers............ 141
84. A Fourth Department: British and Colonial Precedents........... 143
85. A Fourth Department: Opinion of the Constitutional Fathers..... 145
86. A Fourth Department: Functional Classification................. 148
87. A Fourth Department: Practice.................................. 148
88. The Foreign Relations Department............................... 150

CHAPTER X. THE POWER TO MEET INTERNATIONAL RESPONSIBILITIES.

89. The Law of International Responsibility........................ 151
90. State Power to Meet International Responsibilities............. 153
91. National Power to Meet International Responsibilities.......... 154
92. Theory of Inherent Executive Power to Meet International Responsibilities 155
93. President's Duty to Execute the Laws 157
94. Power of the Courts to Meet International Responsibilities..... 158
95. Power of Congress to Meet International Responsibilities....... 159
96. Power to Meet International Responsibilities by Treaty......... 160

ANALYTICAL TABLE OF CONTENTS.

CHAPTER XI. THE POWER TO MEET INTERNATIONAL RESPONSIBILITIES THROUGH THE OBSERVANCE OF INTERNATIONAL LAW.

97. Conditions Favoring the Observance of International Law........ 161
98. Observance of International Law by the States.................... 161
99. Observance of International Law by the Constitution............. 162
100. Observance of International Law by Congress...................... 162
101. Checks upon Congressional Disregard of International Law...... 164
102. Observance of International Law by the Treaty-making Power.... 166
103. Observance of International Law by the President................. 166
104. Observance of International Law by Military and Civil Services.... 167
105. Observance of International Law by the Courts.................... 170
106. Courts Apply International Law and Treaties as Part of the Law of the Land.. 171
107. This Principle not Applicable to Political Questions.............. 172
108. This Principle not Applicable to Cases Covered by Written Law... 174

CHAPTER XII. THE POWER TO MEET INTERNATIONAL RESPONSIBILITIES THROUGH THE ENFORCEMENT OF INTERNATIONAL LAW.

109. Due Diligence... 176
110. Enforcement by the States....................................... 177
111. Enforcement under the National Constitution..................... 179

A. Enforcement by Legislative Action.

112. Congressional Resolutions Before the Constitution................ 179
113. Offenses Against Persons Protected by International Law......... 180
114. Offenses Committed on the High Seas............................ 180
115. Offenses Against Neutrality...................................... 181
116. Offenses Against Foreign Governments............................ 182
117. Offenses Relating to International Boundaries.................... 183
118. Offenses Against Treaties.. 184
119. General Empowering Statutes.................................... 186
120. Sufficiency of Existing Legislation to Protect Resident Aliens...... 186
121. Sufficiency of Existing Legislation for Punishing Offenses Against Foreign Governments.. 187
122. Sufficiency of Existing Legislation in Aid of Foreign Criminal Justice 189

B. Enforcement by Action of the Treaty Power.

123. Treaties as a Basis for Executive and Judicial Action............ 190
124. Treaties as a Basis for Congressional Action..................... 191

C. Enforcement by the President.

125. Enforcement by the President.................................... 192
126. President's Use of Military Forces............................... 193
127. President's Direction of Administrative Action.................... 194

D. *Enforcement by the Courts.*

128. Early Assumptions of Common Law Criminal Jurisdiction by Federal Courts... 196
129. Federal Courts have no Common Law Jurisdiction................ 197
130. Federal Courts have no Criminal Jurisdiction from Treaties Alone. 198
131. Statutory Criminal Jurisdiction of Federal Courts................ 199
132. Admiralty Jurisdiction of Federal Courts......................... 200
133. Civil Jurisdiction of Federal Courts in Cases Affecting Aliens...... 201
134. Conclusion 203

CHAPTER XIII. THE POWER TO MEET INTERNATIONAL RESPONSIBILITIES THROUGH PERFORMANCE OF NATIONAL OBLIGATIONS.

135. Nature of This Responsibility.................................... 205
136. Performance of Obligations by the States......................... 205

A. *The Nature of National Obligations.*

137. Obligations Founded on International Agreement.................. 206
138. Obligations Founded on General International Law................ 208
139. The Determination of Obligations............................... 209
140. Justiciable and Non-justiciable Questions......................... 211
141. The Obligation of Treaties and International Law................. 212
142. Practice in Submitting Disputes to Arbitration.................... 214

B. *Power to Interpret National Obligations.*

143. By National Political Organs: Congress........................... 215
144. By National Political Organs: The Senate........................ 216
145. By National Political Organs: The President..................... 217
146. By International Political Organs................................ 218
147. By National Courts.. 220
148. By International Courts... 222

C. *Power to Perform National Obligations.*

149. Appropriations 225
150. Cession of Territory... 226
151. Guarantees and Use of Military Force............................ 227
152. Conclusion of Subsequent Treaties................................ 227
153. Participation in International Organization....................... 228
154. Commerce and Revenue Laws.................................... 228
155. Formal Amends in Reparation.................................... 229

CHAPTER XIV. THE POWER TO MAKE INTERNATIONAL AGREEMENTS.

156. Power of the States to Make Agreements with Consent of Congress. 230
157. Power of the States to Make Agreements Independently.......... 231
158. Power of the National Government to Make Agreements.......... 233
159. Congress cannot make International Agreements.................. 233
160. The Courts cannot make International Agreements................ 234

ANALYTICAL TABLE OF CONTENTS. xvii

A. *The Power to Make Executive Agreements.*

161. The Obligation of Executive Agreements.......................... 234
162. Administrative Agreements under Authority of Act of Congress.... 235
163. Administrative Agreements under Authority of Treaty........... 236
164. Independent Administrative Agreements........................ 237
165. Recent Practice... 237
166. The Validity of Administrative Agreements..................... 239
167. The Power to Make Military Agreements....................... 240
168. Armistices and Preliminaries of Peace........................... 241
169. Validity of Military Agreements................................ 242
170. Power to Make Diplomatic Agreements........................ 243
171. Diplomatic Agreements Settling Controversies................... 244
172. Validity of Diplomatic Agreements............................. 245

B. *The Power to Make Treaties.*

173. The Subject Matter of Treaties................................. 246
174. The Initiation of Treaties...................................... 248
175. The Appointment of Negotiators............................... 249
176. The Negotiation and Signature of Treaties...................... 249
177. Consent to the Ratification of Treaties.......................... 252
178. The Ratification of Treaties.................................... 254
179. The Exchange of Ratifications.................................. 254
180. The Proclamation of Treaties................................... 255

C. *The Power to Terminate Treaties.*

181. Change in Conditions.. 256
182. Violation of Treaty by One Party............................... 256
183. Conclusion of New Treaty...................................... 257
184. Denunciation by Congress...................................... 258
185. Denunciation by the Treaty-making Power...................... 259
186. Denunciation by the President.................................. 259
187. Legislative Abrogation... 260
188. Conclusion 261

CHAPTER XV. THE POWER TO MAKE POLITICAL DECISIONS IN FOREIGN AFFAIRS: RECOGNITION, ANNEXATION, CITIZENSHIP AND THE DETERMINATION OF POLICY.

189. Distinction Between Domestic and Foreign Affairs................ 263
190. State Power to Make Political Decisions in Foreign Affairs........ 264
191. National Power to Make Political Decisions in Foreign Affairs.... 265

A. *The Power to Recognize Foreign States, Governments and Belligerency.*

192. The Power of Recognition...................................... 268
193. Limits of Recognition Power................................... 269
194. Exclusiveness of President's Recognition Power.................. 270
195. Claim of Congress to Recognition Power........................ 271

B. The Power to Determine National Territory and Citizenship.
196. Judicial Recognition of Territorial Limits........................... 273
197. Recognition of Territorial Limits by the President................. 274
198. Power to Annex Territory by Treaty and Executive Agreement... 274
199. Power of Congress to Annex Territory............................. 275
200. Power of Congress to Naturalize Aliens and Establish Criteria of Citizenship... 276
201. Power of Executive to Recognize Citizenship...................... 277

C. Power to Determine Foreign Policy.
202. Congressional Resolutions on Incidents in Foreign Affairs........ 278
203. President not Bound by Congressional Resolutions on Foreign Affairs 279
204. Congressional Declarations of General Policy...................... 281
205. Power of the President to Determine Foreign Policy.............. 282

CHAPTER XVI. THE POWER TO MAKE POLITICAL DECISIONS IN FOREIGN AFFAIRS: WAR AND THE USE OF FORCE.

A. The Power to Make War.
206. The Power to Make War... 284
207. The Causation of War.. 284
208. The Recognition of War by Congress............................. 286
209. The Recognition of War by the President........................ 286
210. The Power to Recognize War.................................... 289
211. The Power to Declare War....................................... 290
212. The Power to Terminate War.................................... 290
213. The Power to Recognize the Termination of War................ 291

B. The Power to Use Force in Foreign Affairs.
214. Diplomatic Pressure... 293
215. Display of Force.. 294
216. Occupation and Administration of Territory...................... 296
217. Capture and Destruction of Foreign Military Forces.............. 297
218. Seizure and Destruction of Private Property...................... 298
219. Commercial Pressure and Retaliation.............................. 301
220. Exclusion, Expulsion and Internment of Aliens.................... 303
221. Power to Employ Various Methods of Coercion................... 304
222. Purposes for Which the President May Employ Force under the Constitution 305
223. Purposes for Which the President May Employ Force under Statute. 308
224. Conclusion 309

ANALYTICAL TABLE OF CONTENTS.   xix

CHAPTER XVII.   THE POWER TO ESTABLISH INSTRUMENTALITIES
FOR CONDUCTING FOREIGN RELATIONS.

A. Constitutional Principles.

225. The Power of Congress to Create Offices and Agencies............. 311
226. The Power to Create Offices and Agencies by Treaty.............. 312
227. The Power of the President to Create Offices and Agencies........ 313
228. The Appointment of Officers and Agents.......................... 314
229. Limitations upon the Appointing Power........................... 315
230. Powers of Removing and Directing Officers and Agents............ 316

B. Application of Principles to Foreign Affairs.

231. The Types of Agencies Conducting Foreign Relations.............. 317
232. National Military, Naval and Administrative Offices................ 320
233. Appointment of Military and Naval Officers........................ 321
234. Organization of the Department of State.......................... 322
235. National and International Political Officers and Agents.......... 323
236. Power to Determine Grades in the Foreign Service................. 324
237. Power to Determine Occasion for Appointments in Foreign Service. 326
238. Power of President to Appoint Diplomatic Agents.................. 328
239. Practice of Sending Presidential Agents........................... 329
240. Controversies with Respect to Presidential Agents................. 330
241. Presidential Agent not an Officer................................. 333
242. International Administrative and Judicial Agencies................ 334
243. Conclusion on Power to Conduct Foreign Relations................ 335

PART V.

THE UNDERSTANDINGS OF THE CONSTITUTION.

CHAPTER XVIII.   UNDERSTANDINGS CONCERNING THE RELATIONS
OF THE INDEPENDENT ORGANS.

244. Reason for Constitutional Understandings......................... 339

A. The Overlapping of Powers of Independent Departments.

245. Constitutional Understanding Respecting the Overlapping of Powers. 340
246. Concurrent Powers of President and Congress..................... 340
247. Concurrent Powers of President and Courts....................... 342
248. Concurrent Powers of Treaty Power and Congress................. 344

B. Cooperation of Independent Organs.

249. Constitutional Understanding Respecting the Cooperation of Independent Organs... 346
250. Decisions by the Courts.. 346
251. Acts of the President.. 348
252. Acts of Congress... 350

253. Acts of the Treaty-making Power: Obligation of the Courts...... 351
254. Acts of the Treaty-making Power: Obligation of the President.... 352
255. Obligation of the Treaty-making Power Itself as to Future Action 352
256. Acts of the Treaty-making Power: Obligation of Congress........ 353

C. Duty of the Departments to Act.

257. Constitutional Understanding respecting the Establishment of Necessary Instrumentalities... 357
258. Duty of all Organs to Aid in Meeting International Responsibilities. 357

CHAPTER XIX. THE CONTROL OF FOREIGN RELATIONS IN PRACTICE.

259. The Position of the President...................................... 360
260. Friction in the American System.................................. 360
261. Criticisms of the American System................................ 361
262. Need of Popular Control in Foreign Relations..................... 362
263. Need of Centralization of Authority.............................. 363
264. Practice in American History..................................... 364
265. Constitutional Changes not Necessary............................. 368
266. Need of Constitutional Understandings............................ 368

APPENDIX A. Congressional Delegation of Power to Make International Agreements.................................. 375

APPENDIX B. Constitutional Understandings................ 376

INDEX 377

TABLE OF CASES.

Abrams v. U. S., 250 U. S. 616, (1919) 188
Ah Fong, In re, 3 Sawyer 144.. 90
Alleganean, The, Alabama Claims Commission, 1885, Moore, Int. Arb., 4333, 4675, 32 Albana L. J. 484 274
American Banana Co. v. United Fruit Co., 219 U. S. 347, (1909) 165
American Insurance Co. v. Canter, 1 Pet. 511........116, 130, 275, 312
Amiable Isabella, The, 6 Wheat. 1, (1821)..................218, 234
Anderson v. Dunn, 6 Wheat. 204.. 96
Anna, The, 5 C. Rob. 373, (1805). 274
Antelope, The, 10 Wheat. 66, (1825) 169
Appam, The, 243 U. S. 124, (1916)................48, 172, 200
Applicants for License, In re, 143 N. C. 1...................... 97
Appollon, The, 9 Wheat. 362.... 172
Argun, The, Takahashi, Russo-Japanese War, 761........... 290

Baiz, In re, 135 U. S. 403....172, 242
Baldwin v. Franks, 120 U. S. 678....................79, 88, 187
Baker v. Portland, 5 Sawyer 566, (1879) 90
Bartram v. Robertson, 122 U. S. 116 228
Belgenland, The, 114 U. S. 355 ....201, 203
Bermuda, The, 3 Wall. 514..... 295
Betsey, The, (U. S.) v. Great Britain, Moore, Int Arb. 3208.. 18
Blythe v. Hinckley, 180 U. S. 333 88
Bolcher v. Darrell, Fed. Cas. 1607, (1795) 166
Bollman, Ex parte, 4 Cranch 75.. 197
Brig Aurora, 7 Cr. 382.......... 302

British Prisoners, Case of the, 1 Wood and Min. 66, (1845), 78, 191, 194, 198
Brown v. Turner, 70 N. C. 93... 340
Brown v. U. S., 8 Cranch 110, (1814)............85, 86, 169, 300
Buttfield v. Stranahan, 192 U. S. 470, (1904)................... 303

Carneal v. Banks, 10 Wheat. 259, (1825) 90
Carter v. Virginia, 96 Va. 971.. 96
Cary v. South Dakota, 250 U. S. 118 88
Chapman, In re, 166 U. S. 661.. 96
Charkieh, The, L. R. 4 A. and E. 59, (1873) 173
Charlton v. Kelly, 229 U. S. 447 257
Charming Betsey, The. (See Murray v. The Charming Betsey.)
Cherokee Nation v. Georgia, 5 Pet. 1, (1831) 173, 206
Cherokee Tobacco Case, 11 Wall. 616, (1870) 82, 260
Chile v. United States. (See Trumbull Case.)
Chinese Exclusion Cases, 130 U. S. 581, (1889)....17, 130, 133 159, 163, 260, 263, 304, 307, 344
Chirac v. Chirac, 2 Wheat. 259, (1817).....73, 88, 90, 91, 265, 277
City of London v. Wood, 12 Mod. 669, (1701) 210
Cohens v. Virginia, 6 Wheat. 264 133
Collector v. Day, 11 Wall. 113.. 86
Comancho, Case of Venezuelan Minister, Moore, Int. Law Digest, 4: 644 ....79, 162
Comegys v. Vasse, 1 Pet. 193, (1828), ...82, 116, 224, 235

xxi

Commonwealth v. Kosloff, 5 Serg. and Rawle 545................ 198
Compagnie Francaise v. State Board of Health, 186 U. S. 380, (1902) 91
Cooley v. Board of Port Wardens, 13 How. 294....73, 153, 265
Cooper, In re, 138 U. S. 404.. 172
Cooper, In re, 143 U. S. 472, (1892), ...173, 174, 343
Cooper, Matter of, 22 N. Y. 67.. 97
Cotesworth and Powell, (Great Britain) v. Colombia, Moore, Int. Arb., 2081 19
Cross v. Harrison, 16 How. 164 ....116, 297, 314
Cuba v. North Carolina, 242 U. S. 665, (1917) 206
Cushing, Adm., v. U. S., 22 Ct. of Cl. 1, (1886) 19, 82

Davisson v. Sealskins, 2 Paine 324 169
Day, In re, 181 Ill. 73 97
Day v. Savadge, Hob. 85 (1610). 210
Debs, In re, 158 U. S. 564....96, 193
Dillon, In re, 7 Sawyer 561, Fed. Cas. No. 3914, (1854),........ 124
Dillon Case, Moore, Int. Law Digest, 5: 80, 167.........40, 116
Divina Pastora, The, 4 Wheat. 52 ....83, 172, 272
Dobbins v. Erie County, 16 Pet. 435 73
107a, 114a, (1600) 210
Doe v. Bradon, 16 How. 635, (1853) 49, 173, 257
Dalby v. Wolf, 14 Iowa 228, (1862) 104
Dorr v. U. S., 195 U. S. 138..80, 84
Downes v. Bidwell, 182 U. S. 244, (1901) 80, 89
Dr. Bonham's Case, 8 Co. Rep.
Duskin Case, Cleveland, Presidential Problems, 56............. 341
Dubois, Case of Dutch Minister, 1856, Moore, Int. Law Digest, 4: 643 ....79, 162
Durand v. Hollins, 4 Blatch. 451 ....21, 306

Durousseau v. U. S., 6 Cranch 307 340
Dynes v. Hoover, 26 How. 65.. 85

Ekaterinoslav, The, Takahashi, Russo-Japanese War, 573..... 290
Elkinson v. Deliesseline, Leg. Doc. Mass. 1845, (Sen. No. 31), p. 39, (1823) 90, 91
Epstein v. State, 128 N. F. 353, (Ind. 1920) 97
Estrella, The, 4 Wheat. 298
191, 200, 201
Exchange, The, Schooner, v. McFaddon, 7 Cr. 116,
159, 172, 208, 242

Fairfax v. Hunter, 7 Cr. 603, (1813) 90, 91
Field v. Clark, 143 U. S. 649, (1892) 30, 99, 103, 104, 106, 110, 233, 236, 302
Fleming v. Page, 9 How. 603 ....130, 169, 276, 297
Fong Yue Ting v. U. S., 149 U. S. 698, (1893),
83, 130, 133, 195, 266, 304
Ford v. Surget, 97 U. S. 594.... 85
Fort Leavenworth Railroad v. Lowe, 114 U. S. 525........89, 232
Foster v. Neilson, 2 Pet. 253, (1829) 124, 172, 207, 274, 353
Fourteen Diamond Rings v. U. S., 183 U. S. 176, (1901),
34, 46, 253, 254
Fox v. Ohio, 5 How. 416, (1847) 178
Fredericksen v. Louisiana, 23 How. 443, (1860) 91

Geofroy v. Riggs, 133 U. S. 258, (1890) 82, 88, 89, 92, 121, 248
Glass v. The Betsey, 3 Dall. 6.. 200
Gordon v. U. S., 2 Wall. 561, 117 U. S. 697, (1864),
98, 117, 118, 312
Grange, The, Att. Gen. Randolph, 1 Op. 32 274
Grapeshot, The, 9 Wall. 129..... 314
Gray v. U. S., 21 Ct. Cl. 340.... 82

TABLE OF CASES. xxiii

Great Britain v. Colombia. (See Cotesworth and Powell Case.)
Green v. Biddle, 8 Wheat. 1.... 231

Hamilton v. Kentucky Distilleries and Warehouse Co., 251 U. S. 146 84
Hauenstein v. Lynham, 100 U. S. 483, (1879) 88, 91, 92, 207
Haver v. Yaker, 9 Wall. 32, 31, 52, 253, 255
Hawaii v. Mankichi, 190 U. S. 197 80
Hayburn's Case, 2 Dall. 409.... 98
Head Money Cases, 112 U. S. 580 ....260, 344, 384
Heim v. McCall, 239 U. S. 175, (1915) 90, 91
Henderson v. New York, 92 U. S. 259, (1875) 90
Henfield, In re, Fed. Cas., No. 6360 197
Hennen, Ex parte, 13 Pet. 230, (1839) 317
Hilton v. Guyot, 159 U. S. 113, (1895) 189
Ho Ah Kow v. Nunan, 5 Sawyer 532, (1879) 90
Holmes v. Jennison, 14 Pet. 540, (1840) 91, 134, 153, 178, 230
Hopkirk v. Bell, 3 Cranch 454 ....88, 91
Houston v. Moore, 5 Wheat. 1 312
Hudson v. Guestier, 6 Cranch 281, (1810) 169

Indiana v. Kentucky, 136 U. S. 479, (1880) 274
Insular Cases. (See Downes v. Bidwell.)

Jane, The, 37 Ct. Cl. 24 295
Jecker v. Montgomery, 13 How. 498 ....116, 221, 314
Jones v. U. S., 137 U. S. 202, (1890) 83, 130, 133, 172, 173, 274, 343
Jones v. Walker, 2 Paine 688 .. 257

Kansas v. Colorado, 206 U. S. 46 ....96, 131

Kaine, In re, 14 How. 103, (1852) 195
Kawananako v. Polyblank, 205 U. S. 349, (1907) 210
Kennett v. Chambers, 14 How. 38 172
Kentucky v. Dennison, 24 How. 66 312
Kilbourne v. Thompson, 103 U. S. 168 ....95, 96, 98
Killock, Ex parte, 165 U. S. 526 104
King of Prussia v. Kupper, 22 Mo. 550, (1856) 23
King of Spain v. Oliver, 1 Pet. C. C. 217, (1810) 23
Kneedler v. Lane, 45 Pa. 238, (1863) 94
Königin Luise, 184 Fed. 170, (1910) 104, 116

La Abra Silver Mining Co. v. U. S., 175 U. S. 423, (1899).... 223
La Jeune Eugenie, 2 Mason 409, (1822) 80, 169
La Ninfa, 49 Fed. 575, (1891).... 174
La Ninfa, 75 Fed. 513, (1896), 110, 116, 164, 169, 174, 207, 224, 227, 345
Lattimer v. Poteet, 14 Pet. 14, (1840) 89
Legal Tender Cases, 12 Wall. 457 133
License Cases, 5 How. 504...... 91
Lindo v. Rodney, 2 Doug. 613, (1781) 15
Little v. Barreme, 2 Cranch 170, 169, 299
Little v. Watson, 32 Maine 214, (1850) 227
Lottawana, The, 21 Wall. 558.... 181

McCardle, Ex parte, 7 Wall. 506 ....99, 202, 312, 340
McCulloch v. Maryland, 4 Wheat. 316 ....73, 80, 103, 311
McVeigh v. U. S., 11 Wall. 259, (1870) 169, 172
Manchester v. Massachusetts, 139 U. S. 240 274

Marbury v. Madison, 1 Cranch
  137 314
Marianna Flora, The, 11 Wheat.
  1, (1826) 169
Marie Glaeser, The, L. R. (1914),
  P. 218 48
Martin v. Hunter, 1 Wheat. 304,
  (1816) 357
Martin v. Mott, 12 Wheat. 19,
            104, 193, 216, 309
Matthews v. McStea, 91 U. S. 7,
  (1875) 288
Mighell v. Sultan of Johore,
  (1894), 1 Q. B. 149 173
Montalet v. Murray, 4 Cranch
  46 203
Morrill v. Jones, 106 U. S. 466.. 104
Murray v. The Charming Betsey,
  2 Cranch 64 ....165, 175
Meade v. U. S., 9 Wall. 691,
            82, 116, 235
Merryman, Ex parte, Taney Reports, 246 131
Metzger, (U. S.) v. Haiti, U. S.
  For. Rel., 1899, p. 262 ....27, 41
Metzger, In re, 5 How. 176,
            190, 194
Metzger, In re, 1 Barb. 248,
  (N. Y., 1847) 194
Mexico v. Arrangoiz, 11 How.
  Prac. 1, (N. Y., 1855) 202
Miller v. U. S., 11 Wall. 268,
            85, 169, 300
Milligan, Ex parte, 4 Wall. 2,
  (1866)....85, 98, 124, 305, 307,
            311, 317, 322
Minor v. Happersett, 21 Wall.
  162 72
Mississippi v. Johnson, 4 Wall.
  475 97
Missouri v. Holland, 252 U. S.
  416, (1920) 57, 87, 90, 91, 186
Mitchell v. Harmony, 13 How.
  115, (1851) 85, 169, 299

Neagle, In re, 135 U. S. 1,
          157, 193, 305, 307, 313
Neeley v. Henkel, 180 U. S. 109,
  (1901) 78, 84, 85, 116, 173, 185
Nereide, The, 9 Cranch 388,
  (1815) 169, 171, 173, 221

New York Indians v. U. S., 170
  U. S. 1, (1898) 34, 46, 254
Ocean City Association v. Shriver,
  46, Atl. 690, (N. J., 1900).... 274
Oetjen v. Central Leather Co.,
  246 U. S. 207, (1917) 172
Opinions of Attorney General of
  United States 327
  Berrien, 20 Op. 431, (1831).. 90
  Cushing, 6 Op. 148, 209, 291,
    (1854) 5, 18, 63, 195, 257
  Cushing, 7 Op. 186, 214, 453.
    (1855) 14, 317, 324, 341
  Cushing, 8 Op. 175, 390,
    (1856), ...116, 274
  Griggs, 22 Op. 214, (1898),
            90, 123
  Knox, 23 Op. 533, (1901).... 334
  Lee, 1 Op. 74, (1797)...... 22
  Randolph, 1 Op. 32.......... 274
  Randolph, Fed. Cas. No. 6360,
    p. 1116.................... 197
  Richards, Acting, 22 Op. 13,
            302, 341
  Wickersham, 29, Op. 322,
    (1912) 308
  Wickersham, 32 Op. 322.... 94
  Wirt, 10 Op. 661, (1824).... 90

Paquette Habana, 175 U. S. 677,
            169, 171, 208, 221
Parsons v. U. S., 167 U. S. 324,
            96, 317, 341
Passenger Cases, The, 7 How.
  283, (1849) 90, 91, 265
Patsone v. Pennsylvania, 232 U. S.
  138 ....90, 91
Pearcy v. Stranahan, 205 U. S.
  257, (1907) 173, 343
Pensacola Telegraph Co. v. Western Union Telegraph Co., 96 U.
  S. 1, (1878) 302
People v. Gerke, 5 Cal. 381,
  (1855) 91, 92
People v. Noglee, 1 Cal. 232,
  (1850) 90
Peggy, The, 1 Cranch 103 ..344, 345
Phoebe Ann, The, 3 Dall. 319,
            166, 207
Pious Fund, The, (U. S. v.
  Mexico), Wilson, Hague Arbitration Cases, 1 65

TABLE OF CASES.

Prevost v. Greenaux, 10 How. 1, (1856) 91
Prize Cases, The, 2 Black 635, 39, 83, 124, 172, 284, 288, 348, 350
Protector, The, 12 Wall. 700, (1871) 173, 291, 293

Res Publica v. De Longchamps, 1 Dall. 111 177
Rhode Island v. Massachusetts, 4 How. 591, (1846)............ 274
Ricaud v. American Metal Co., 246 U. S. 304, (1917) 172
Robertson v. Baldwin, 165 U. S. 275, (1897) 84
Rocca v. Thompson, 232 U. S. 318 91
Rose, The, 37 Ct. Cl. 240 295
Rose v. Himeley, 4 Cranch 241 .. 169
Ross, In re, 140 U. S. 453, (1890), 84, 88, 104, 116, 124, 312, 313
Ruppert v. Caffey, 251 U. S. 264. 84

Sanborn, In re, 148 U. S. 226 .. 221
Sandberg v. McDonald, 248 U. S. 185 165
Santiago v. Nogueras, 214 U. S. 260 .... 297, 314, 320, 341
Santissima Trinidad, The, 7 Wheat. 283 172
Sapphire, The, 11 Wall. 164, (1870) 24, 172
Schooner Exchange, The. (See Exchange v. McFaddon.)
Scotia, The, 14 Wall. 170, (1871) 181
Sea Lion, The, 5 Wall. 630, (1866) 240
Selective Draft Cases, 245 U. S. 366 ....85, 94
Shepherd v. Insurance Co., 40 Fed. 341 ....52, 254
Ship Richmond v. U. S., 9 Cranch 102, (1815) 169
Shurtleff v. U. S., 189 U. S. 311.. 317
Slaughter House Cases, 16 Wall. 36 306
Society for the Propagation of the Gospel v. New Haven, 8 Wheat. 464, (1823) 90, 256
South Dakota v. North Carolina, 192 U. S. 286, (1904) 233

Southern Pacific v. Jensen, 244 U. S. 205, (1917) 64
Splane, In re, 123 Pa. 527 97
Spooner v. McConnell, 1 McLean 347 72
State v. Noyes, 30 N. H. 279.. 104

Talbot v. Jensen, 3 Dall. 133 200
Tennessee v. Davis, 100 U. S. 257 198
Terlinden v. Ames, 184 U. S. 270, (1902) 78, 173, 190, 257
Texas v. White, 7 Wall. 700, (1860) 73, 89, 124
Thomas, In re, 12 Blatch. 370... 257
Three Friends, The, 166 U. S. 1, (1897) 172, 173, 182, 200, 269, 284
Tiburcio Parrott, In re, 6 Sawyer 349, (1880) 90, 91
Toscano, Ex parte, 208 Fed. 938, (1913) 182, 190, 196, 207
Trade Mark Cases, 100 U. S. 82.. 105
Truax v. Raich, 239 U. S. 33, (1915) 90, 91
Trumbull, (Chile) v. U. S., Moore, Int. Arb. 3569, (1892), 27, 41
Tucker v. Alexandroff, 183 U. S. 424, (1902) 78, 242
Turner v. American Baptist Missionary Union, 5 McLean 347, (1852) 9, 66, 339

Underhill v. Hernandez, 168 U. S. 250 172
U. S. v. Arjona, 120 U. S. 479, 15, 87, 154, 182
U. S. v. Coolidge, Fed. Cas. No. 14, 857 198
U. S. v. Coolidge, 1 Wheat. 415, (1816) 198
U. S. v. Gettysburg Electric Ry. Co., 160 U. S. 668 133
U. S. v. Great Britain. (See The Betsey.)
U. S. v. Haiti. (See Metzger Case.)
U. S. v. Holmes, 5 Wheat. 412 .. 165
U. S. v. Hudson, 7 Cranch 32 .. 197

U. S. v. Ju Toy, 198 U. S. 253, (1905) 83, 99, 278, 304
U. S. v. Klintock, 5 Wheat. 144, 165, 180
U. S. v. La Jeune Eugenie. (See La Jeune Eugenie.)
U. S. v. La Ninfa. (See La Ninfa.)
U. S. v. McCullagh, 227 Fed. 288 87
U. S. v. Moore, 3 Cranch 159.. 340
U. S. v. New York, 160 U. S. 615 221
U. S. v. Palmer, 5 Wheat. 610, (1818) 165, 172, 180
U. S. v. The Peggy. (See The Peggy.)
U. S. v. Percheman, 7 Pet. 51, (1833) 172, 353
U. S. v. Perkins, 116 U. S. 143.. 317
U. S. v. Pirates, 5 Wheat. 184, (1820) 165
U. S. v. Ravara, 2 Dall. 297, Fed. Cas. No. 6122 ....197, 198
U. S. v. Rauscher, 119 U. S. 407, 178, 230
U. S. v. Reynes, 9 How. 127.... 172
U. S. v. Repentigny, 5 Wall. 211, (1866) 222
U. S. v. Robbins, Fed. Cas. No. 16, 175, Bees. Adm. 266, 78, 190, 194
U. S. v. Shauves, 214 Fed. 154.. 87
U. S. v. Smith, 5 Wheat. 153, (1820) 181, 201
U. S. v. Trumbull, 48 Fed. 99, (1891) 182
U. S. v. The William, 28 Fed. Cas. 614, (1808) 302

U. S. v. Wong Kim Ark, 169 U. S. 649 277
U. S. v. Worrall, 2 Dall. 384 .. 197

Villas v. City of Manilla, 220 U. S. 345, (1911) 172
Virginia v. Tennessee, 148 U. S. 503, (1893) 227, 232, 274

Ware v. Hylton, 3 Dall. 199, (1796) 18, 58, 88, 91, 162, 175, 256, 257
Watts v. Unione Austriaca de Navigazione, 248 U. S. 9, (1918) 172
Watts v. U. S., 1 Wash. Terr. 288, (1870) 239
Weber v. Freed, 239 U. S. 325.. 303
Whitney v. Robertson, 124 U. S. 190 228
Wildenhus Case, 120 U. S. 1.... 88
Williams v. Suffolk Ins. Co., 13 Pet. 415 ....83, 172, 268
Williams v. U. S., 23 Ct. Cl. 46.. 325
Wilson v. Shaw, 204 U. S. 24 (1907) 83
Wilson v. Wall, 73 U. S. 83, (1867) 210
Worcester v. Georgia, 6 Pet. 515, (1832) 89
Wynan's Petitioner, 191 Mass. 276 91

Yick Wo v. Hopkins, 118 U. S. 356, (1886) 91

Zamora, The, L. R. (1916) 2 A. C. 77 170

PART I.

The Nature of the Foreign Relations Power.

THE CONTROL OF AMERICAN FOREIGN RELATIONS.

CHAPTER I.

THE NATURE OF THE FOREIGN RELATIONS POWER.

1. *Difficulty in Developing Legal Theory of Subject.*

There is no phase of American constitutional law on which commentators have found it more difficult to procure a logical and consistent theory than the control of foreign relations. Not only have opinions differed as to the relative powers of President, Senate and House of Representatives, but also as to the limitations imposed upon the national foreign relations power as a whole by the guaranteed rights of individuals, "reserved powers" of the states and the doctrine of separation of powers. Discussion has dealt particularly with the treaty-making power but similar differences have developed in considering the power to make national decisions such as the recognition of foreign states and governments, and the declaration of war, and the power to meet international responsibilities, all of which are here included under the general term, the foreign relations power.

For this difficulty several reasons may be assigned, as for instance, vagueness in the terms of the constitution on this subject, inconsistency in the interpretations acted upon by the political organs of government at different periods of history, and the comparative lack of judicial interpretation, due to the tendency of the courts to regard questions involving foreign relations as political and so beyond their consideration.[1] There is, however, a more fundamental reason for this difficulty, a reason which lies back of those mentioned and which explains the existence of a similar difficulty in all other constitutional states. This reason is the

[1] *Infra*, secs. 107, 247.

4   THE CONTROL OF AMERICAN FOREIGN RELATIONS.

dual position necessarily occupied by the authority controlling foreign relations.

2. *Dual Position of Foreign Relations Power.*

This authority is on the one hand an agency of the national constitution. It is created by that instrument and subject to all the limitations of power and procedure therein expressed or implied. But on the other hand it is the representative of the nation before other nations and is expected by them to meet international responsibilities according to the standard of international law and treaty. Thus its activity is governed at the same time by constitutional law and international law, its powers by one, its responsibilities by the other. Conflicts may occur in the application of these two laws. For example, international law requires that all validly concluded treaties be executed, but constitutional law may make it difficult if not impossible to execute particular treaty provisions because of certain constitutional limitations. This problem has arisen in the United States in connection with the police power of the states and the exclusive power of Congress to appropriate money. It has been alleged that under constitutional law the states and congress are entitled to an unlimited discretion in exercising these powers irrespective of treaty provisions.[2] Commentators have differed in their views as to the scope of the powers belonging to the various organs controlling foreign relations, according as they have approached the subject from the constitutional or from the international point of view.

3. *The International Point of View.*

If the international point of view were adopted in full it would result that an international commitment made by the proper constitutional authority would bind all organs of the government. Thus Secretary of State Livingston wrote the French government in 1833:

---

[2] *Infra,* secs. 50, 59.

"The government of the United States presumes that whenever a treaty has been concluded and ratified by the acknowledged authorities competent for that purpose, an obligation is thereby imposed upon each and every department of the government to carry it into complete effect, according to its terms, and that on the performance of this obligation consists the due observance of good faith among nations." [3]

But constitutions, acting by tradition and convenience, if indeed not practical necessity, have ordinarily vested the power of international negotiation in a single individual, the chief executive, acting with or without the advice of a council.[4] Now the international commitments of this individual might radically alter the constitution. They might impair national independence. They might establish autocracy. Were these commitments fundamental law, obligatory upon all organs of the government, the achievements of centuries of battling for constitutionalism and popular sovereignty might be sacrificed by the stroke of a pen.[5]

---

[3] Wharton, Int. Law Digest, 2: 67. See also Cushing, At. Gen. 1854, 6 Op. 291; Duer, Outlines of Constitutional Jurisprudence, 138; Wheaton, Elements of Int. Law, Dana ed. Sec. 543; Moore, Int. Law Digest, 5: 230, 370; Willoughby, Constitutional Law, 1: 515, *infra*, sec. 37. This doctrine seems to be an implication of Art. VI, sec. 2 of the Constitution of the United States—"all treaties made, or which shall be made, under the authority of the United States, shall be the supreme Law of the Land"—but it must be admitted that the United States has been more insistent upon applying it to other nations than to itself. (*Infra*, sec. 39.) Nations usually adopt the international point of view in discussing the powers and responsibilities of other nations, the constitutional point of view in discussing their own powers and responsibilities.

[4] "The necessity of such caution and secrecy was one cogent reason for vesting the power of making treaties in the President, with the advice and consent of the Senate, the principle on which that body was formed confining it to a small number of members." Washington, Message to House of Representatives, March 30, 1796, Richardson, Messages and Papers of the President, 1: 195. "The reason why we trust one man, rather than many, is because one man can negotiate and many men can't. Two masses of people have no way of dealing directly with each other. . . . The very qualities which are needed for negotiation—quickness of mind, direct contact, adaptiveness, invention, the right proportion of give and take—are the very qualities which masses of people do not possess." Lippmann, The Stakes of Diplomacy, N. Y., 1915, pp. 26, 29.

[5] "Applying the principle broadly, the contention that one department of the Government may in any way coerce another is a repudiation of the very

4. *The Constitutional Point of View.*

If, on the other hand, the constitutional point of view is adopted in full, the situation seems even less promising. Yet illustrations are not wanting. The House of Representatives resolved in 1796 and again in 1871 that:

"When a treaty stipulates regulations on any of the subjects submitted by the Constitution to the power of Congress, it must depend for its execution as to such stipulations on a law or laws to be passed by Congress; and it is in the constitutional right and duty of the House of Representatives in all such cases to deliberate on the *expediency* or *inexpediency* of carrying such treaty into effect and to determine and act thereon, as in their judgment may be most conducive to the public good." [6]

Should a general opinion develop that national commitments made by the proper constitutional authority and solemnized with due formality might be ignored or repudiated by other organs of the government because of some obscure constitutional limitation, unknown to a foreign nation, the authority conducting foreign relations could no longer command a hearing as the representative of the nation, international negotiation would be unfruitful and international anarchy would prevail.[7]

---

purpose of the division of power, and would result in the destruction of that freedom under law which the Constitution aims to establish. If such an attempt were for any reason successful, it would result in the establishing of an autocratic form of government. Absolutism, which the Constitution was intended to prevent, might thus creep in through the usurpation of power by a single department, or even by a single officer of the Government. There could be no greater offense against the Constitution than this, and public opinion should unite in condemning even the suggestion of it." D. J. Hill, Present Problems in Foreign Policy, N. Y., 1919, p. 163.

[6] Annals, 4th Cong., 1st Sess., p. 771; *Cong. Globe,* 42d Cong., 1st Sess., p. 835; Wharton, Int. Law Digest, 2: 19.

[7] "Others, though consenting that treaties should be made in the mode proposed, are averse to their being the *supreme* law of the land. They insist and profess to believe that treaties, like acts of assembly, should be repealable at pleasure. This idea seems to be new and peculiar to this country, but new errors as well as new truths often appear. These gentlemen would do well to reflect that a treaty is only another name for a bargain, and that it would be impossible to find a nation who would make any bargain with us which should be binding on them absolutely, but on us only so long and so far as we may think proper to be bound by it." Jay, Federalist No. 64, Ford ed., p. 431. See also Washington, message cited *supra*, note 4.

5. *Methods of Reconciling these Points of View.*

In practice modern states have avoided both alternatives by compromises, partly of a legal and partly of a conventional character.[8] There has been a tendency for constitutions to multiply the organs whose concurrence is necessary to bring foreign negotiations to a valid conclusion. Thus many constitutions now vest power to make the most important decision in foreign affairs, such as declarations of war and the ratification of treaties, in the legislative body.[9] So far as this is done, there is no difficulty in giving international commitments the force of law. However, a practical difficulty is here met. The legislative body is usually large, slow moving and ill informed on foreign relations. Many international situations must, under present conditions, be met by personal negotiation and immediate decision for which such a body is ill adapted.[10] Consequently many types of international commitment are still made by executive authority. In these cases, and in fact they are still the majority, the difficulty is solved either by *constitutional understandings,* whereby the executive power is in fact if not in law expected to act in such a way that the other organs of government will approve its action; or by *international understandings* whereby the other states of the world consider commitments formally concluded by the executive authority merely provisional until they have been endorsed by other organs of the government, whose cooperation is necessary for their execution.[11]

6. *Relation of Law and Understandings.*

The writer believes that a comprehensive legal theory of the control of foreign relations must give equal weight to the powers and responsibilities derived from both constitutional law and international law. But in constructing such a theory, he has found

---

[8] See Dicey, The Law of the Constitution, 8th ed., p. 23, for this distinction.

[9] Wright, The Legal Nature of Treaties, *Am. Jl. of Int. Law,* 10: 711 et seq.

[10] *Supra,* note 4.

[11] Wright, *Am. Jl. of Int. Law,* 10: 710; and *infra,* sec. 39.

himself forced to take account of understandings of the kind mentioned. He believes these understandings furnish the true explanation of the functioning of all systems for controlling foreign relations and especially of that in the United States. Without them a constitutional deadlock or an international breach of faith would be probable at every important international transaction.

7. *Constitutional Understandings.*

The constitutional understandings are based on the distinction between the possession of a power and discretion in the exercise of that power. The law of the constitution decides what organs of the government possess the power to perform acts of international significance and to make valid international commitments, but the understandings of the constitution decide how the discretion or judgment, implied from the possession of power, ought to be exercised in given circumstances.[12] The powers given by law to various organs often overlap. Even more often, two or more organs must exercise their powers in cooperation in order to achieve a desired end. In such circumstances, were it not for understandings, deadlocks would be chronic. The law is the mechanism, the understandings the oil that permit it to run smoothly.

8. *International Understandings.*

International understandings are based on the same distinction as constitutional understandings and are often referred to as comity or imperfect rights under international law. " Our obligations to others," says Vattel, "are always imperfect when the decision as to how we are to act rests with us."[13] They are observed on the principle of reciprocity and are of two kinds. Thus states are accustomed to exchange certain courtesies and favors, not required by strict law. They also sometimes withhold

---

[12] Dicey, *op. cit.,* p. 418.

[13] Vattel, The Law of Nations, Introduction, sec. 17; see also Phillimore, Commentaries on Int. Law, 1: 161, sec. 163; Hall, Int. Law, 7th ed. (Higgins), pp. 14, 56; Woolsey, Int. Law, sec. 24; Davis, Elements of Int. Law, 4th ed. (Sherman), pp. 92, 116; Wright, The Understandings of Int. Law, *Am. Jl. of Int. Law,* 14: 568 (Oct., 1920).

NATURE OF THE FOREIGN RELATIONS POWER.

pressure when others fail to meet the responsibilities imposed by strict law. It is with the latter kind that we are especially concerned here. As an example, international law requires that commitments to be valid be made by the proper constitutional authority, and therefore assumes that all governments are informed of the authority in foreign states with which they deal, competent to make various sorts of international commitments. International law, however, considers that commitments once made must be carried out.[14] It knows nothing of constitutional restrictions making execution difficult or impossible, consequently governments are not required to know the agencies in foreign states for executing international commitments and are entitled to protest if execution fails, whatever the cause. If such protests are withheld it is by virtue of an international understanding.[15]

Constitutional understandings suggest modes of exercising constitutional powers out of respect for international responsibilities. International understandings suggest a tolerant attitude toward certain deficiencies in the meeting of international responsibilities out of respect for constitutional limitations.

---

[14] Wright, *Columbia Law Rev.,* 20: 121–122; and *infra,* sec. 39.
[15] Turner *v.* Am. Baptist Union, 5 McLean 347 (1852). See also Wright, *Am. Jl. of Int. Law,* 10: 709, 716, and *infra,* sec. 39.

PART II.

THE POSITION OF THE FOREIGN RELATIONS POWER UNDER INTERNATIONAL LAW.

CHAPTER II.

The Representative Organ of Government.

9. *The Nature of International Law.*

International law has developed in a society based upon the assumption of the complete independence of territorial states.[1] This independence is commonly said to imply that the state has power to form a constitution and organize a government as it sees fit; to formulate law and administer justice within its territory according to its own notions; to formulate and pursue foreign policies and to be the sole judge of its international responsibilities.[2] However, the contemporary and contiguous existence of many states, each with an equal independence, practically requires limitations in the exercise of these powers and the practice and usage defining these limitations constitute international law. The formulation, however, of a body of practice as law implies responsibility for its observance. Thus we may define international law as the body of rules and principles of conduct, observed within the society of independent states, for the violation of which states are habitually held responsible, by diplomatic protest, intervention, reprisals, war or other means.[3]

[1] "In the fifteenth century international life was fast resolving itself into a struggle for existence in its barest form. In such condition of things no law could be established which was unable to recognize absolute independence as a fact prior to itself." W. E. Hall, Int. Law, 7th ed. (Higgins), 1917, p. 18.

[2] Wilson, Handbook of Int. Law, 1910, p. 56; Hershey, The Essentials of Int. Pub. Law, 1912, p. 147; Bonfils, Manuel de droit international public, 6th ed. (Fauchille), 1912, sec. 58, p. 119; Borchard, The Diplomatic Protection of Citizens Abroad, 1915, p. 177; Wright, *Am. Pol. Sci. Rev.*, 13: 563; *Columbia Law Rev.*, 20: 146.

[3] For justification of this definition and comparison with other definitions see Wright, Enforcement of Int. Law through Municipal Law in U. S., U. of Ill., Studies in the Social Sciences, 5: 12–13 and Borchard, *op. cit.*, p. 177 *et seq.*

10. *The Independence of States.*

Of the various fields to which the independence of a state extends, it is clear that other states would be less affected by a state's constitution and form of organization than by the legislation and administration of justice in its territory. Furthermore, each of these would affect other states less than the course of its foreign policy and the interpretation of its international responsibilities. However, history has shown that the constitution and form of organization of states is not a matter of total indifference to their neighbors [4] and international law does limit the exercise of independence even in this field, but as a corollary to limitations upon the state's external and internal activity. Acts and omissions, not institutions are the primary concern of international law, but the interrelation of the two cannot be ignored.

For example, international law requires that states, desiring to enter into relations with other states, do so through diplomatic officers exercising powers and enjoying rights and privileges fixed by international law or treaty.[5] So also states admitting foreigners to their territory are required by international law to maintain courts acting under a procedure calculated to assure substantial justice.[6] Where they have not been able to do this, foreign states

---

[4] Note for example the sympathy of the Holy Alliance for absolute governments and of the United States for popular governments since its foundation. (See Greene, Am. Interest in Popular Government, War Information Series, Sept., 1917, No. 8.) "A steadfast concert for peace can never be maintained except by a partnership of democratic nations. No autocratic government could be trusted to keep faith within it or observe its covenants. . . . We are accepting the challenge of hostile purpose because we know that in such a government following such methods, we can never have a friend, and that in the presence of its organized power, always lying in wait to accomplish we know not what purpose, there can be no assured security for the democratic governments of the world. . . . The world must be made safe for democracy." President Wilson, War Message, April 2, 1917.

[5] The classification of these officers as fixed by the treaty of Vienna 1815 has been generally accepted. Wilson and Tucker, Int. Law, 7th ed., p. 162. It is recognized that Article II, sec. 2, cl. 2 of the Constitution of the U. S., relating to the appointment of ambassadors and other public ministers, is to be interpreted according to international law. Cushing, Attorney General, 7 Op. 190, 192. *Infra,* sec. 236.

[6] "Nations are bound to maintain respectable tribunals to which the subjects of states at peace may have recourse for the redress of injuries and

have habitually exercised diplomatic protection of their nationals or have insisted that permission be given them to establish extra-territorial courts for deciding cases in which their nationals are defendant.[7]

11. *The Representative Authority Under International Law.*

More important for our purposes, however, is the requirement of international law that states maintain a definite authority to which foreign states may complain of violations of international law and from which they may expect satisfaction on the basis of that law alone. This requirement appears to be a necessary deduction from the accepted principle that under international law states are responsible as units[8] and that this responsibility is unaffected by

---

the maintenance of their rights." Mr. Webster, Secretary of State, to Chevalier d'Argaiz, Spanish Minister, June 2, 1842, Moore, Digest, 2: 5. See also Borchard, Diplomatic Protection of Citizens Abroad, 1915, p. 213, 335; Moore, Digest, 6: 695. The obligation to establish courts punishing offenses against international law was recognized by Congress before the Constitution (See Wright, Enforcement of Int. Law, p. 221) and is recognized in the Constitution (Art. 1, sec. 2, cl. 10). The obligation of a belligerent to establish prize courts is especially well recognized. "Neutral states have a right to demand *ex debito juditiæ* that there be courts for the administration of international law sitting in the belligerent countries." (Phillimore, Int. Law, 1: 55.) See also report of British Commission on Silesian Loan controversy, 1753, American State Papers, For. Rel., 1: 494; Moore, Digest, 7: 603; Lord Mansfield in Lindo *v.* Rodney 2 Doug. 613, 616 (1781); Lord Stowell in the Recovery, Rob. 348 (1807). Diplomatic discussion, however, is not necessarily excluded until such judicial remedies are exhausted (*infra,* note 13).

[7] Borchard, *op. cit.,* p. 346.

[8] Borchard, *op. cit.,* pp. 199–201. Hall, Int. Law, 7th ed., p. 54. Wilson and Tucker, *op. cit.,* p. 45, defines a state for purposes of international law as "a sovereign political unity." The Supreme Court has said: "the National Government is . . . responsible to foreign nations for all violations by the United States of their international obligations," U. S. *v.* Arizona, 120 U. S. 479, 483. Apparent exceptions to this unity of responsibility such as federal states whose constitutions permit a limited diplomatic power to the member states (Germany and Switzerland) and imperial commonwealths which in practice permit their self-governing colonies to exercise considerable diplomatic power (British Empire) (See Moore, Digest, 1: 25; Wright, *Am. Jl. of Int. Law,* 13: 265) prove not to be on inspection. In these cases the *power of making commitments* is to some extent distributed but *responsibility for their execution* continues unified. Thus the German Constitution

16   THE CONTROL OF AMERICAN FOREIGN RELATIONS.

domestic law.[9]   States have uniformly refused to accept con-

---

of 1871 made it the duty of "the Emperor to represent the Empire among nations" and foreign nations have held the imperial government responsible for the execution of treaties made by the member states. "Unquestionably," wrote Secretary of State Bryan to Ambassador Gerard on April 28, 1915, "the destruction of this vessel (William P. Frye) was a violation of the obligations imposed upon the *Imperial German Government* under existing treaty stipulations between the United States and *Prussia,* and the United States government, by virtue of its treaty rights, has presented to the Imperial German Government a claim for indemnity on account of the resulting damages suffered by American citizens." (U. S. White Book, European War No. 1, p. 88.) Germany had admitted its responsibility under the treaty in an earlier note. (*Ibid.*) Under the German Constitution of 1919 "The Commonwealth has *exclusive* jurisdiction over foreign relations" (Art. 6) and though "the states may conclude treaties with foreign countries in matters subject to their jurisdiction, such treaties require the assent of the commonwealth." (Art. 78.)

The responsibility of the British government for acts of the self-governing dominions has never been questioned and apparently remains even though these dominions are given independent representation in the League of Nations. "Disputes," said President Wilson before the Senate Foreign Relations Committee, "can rise only through the Governments which have international representation. In other words, diplomatically speaking, there is only one 'British Empire.' The parts of it are but pieces of the whole. The dispute, therefore, in the case you have supposed (dispute between the United States and the *United Kingdom*) would be between the United States as a diplomatic unit and the *British Empire* as a diplomatic unit." David Hunter Miller, technical expert at the Peace Conference, testified to the same effect:

"Senator Hitchcock: 'So that any dispute that could arise between the United States and the Dominion of Canada involves the whole British Empire?'

"Mr. Miller: 'It seems so to me, Senator.'"   (66th Cong., 1st Sess., Senate Doc. No. 106, pp. 540, 422.)

[9] Moore, Digest, 6: 309–324, especially pp. 317, 321. This ineffectiveness of municipal law extends both to the right and the remedy. Thus municipal law cannot alter the international law principles of responsibility. (*Supra*, sec. 89.) In a few matters, as for instance, the protection of resident aliens, international law has to a limited extent adopted the municipal responsibility of a state as the measure of its international responsibility. In such cases the principles of municipal responsibility become indirectly subject to international discussion. This, however, does not vitiate the principle stated. (Borchard, *op. cit.*, 116, 178, 179.) Nor can municipal law deprive foreign states of remedies such as diplomatic intervention or the use of force recognized by international law, though South American States have frequently asserted the contrary. (*Ibid.*, p. 836.)

stitutional limitations,[10] legislative acts[11] or omissions,[12] or judicial

---

[10] "The contention of Mr. Marcy in the case of M. Dillon, French consul at San Francisco, that the sixth amendment to the Constitution of the United States, which provides that an accused party shall have compulsory process for obtaining witnesses in his favor, should be considered as qualifying the general and absolute terms of the consular convention with France, 'was not acquiesced in by the French government, which required their flag, when raised to the mastheads of certain of their men-of-war at San Francisco, to be saluted as a reparation for the alleged indignity to their consul.'" Mr. Fish, Secretary of State, to Mr. Bassett, Oct. 18, 1872, Moore, Digest, 5: 81. See also Borchard, *op. cit.*, p. 201, 226, 839, 845. *Infra*, sec. 31.

[11] Borchard, *op. cit.*, pp. 181, 838 *et seq.*, Moore, Digest, 6: 309–324. There have been numerous cases in which the legislative abrogation of a treaty or the passage of laws in conflict with international law or treaty, though valid in municipal law, have proved no defense to international protests. See Moore, Digest, 5: 357, 365. For principles of municipal law governing the application of constitutions, statutes and ordinances in violation of international law, see Wright, *Am. Jl. Int. Law*, 11: 1, 566. China refused to accept the exclusion acts as an excuse for violations of her treaties (For references to her protests, see Moore, Digest, 4: 198, 202, 213, 235) and the U. S. Supreme Court recognized that these laws though valid in municipal law were no defense in international law. "It must be conceded that the act of 1888 is in contravention of express stipulations of the treaty of 1868 and of the supplementary treaty of 1880, but it is not on that account invalid or to be restricted in its enforcement (in municipal law). . . . The question whether our government was justified in disregarding its engagements with another nation is not one for the determination of this court. . . . This court is not a censor of the morals of the other departments of the government." (Chinese Exclusion Cases, 130 U. S. 589, 600.) President Hayes by vetoing an earlier act (1879) had recognized the impossibility of avoiding international responsibility by legislation. " Were such delay fraught with more inconveniences than have ever been suggested by the interests most earnest in promoting this legislation, I cannot but regard the summary disturbance of our existing treaties with China as greatly more inconvenient to much wider and more permanent interests of the country. I have no occasion to insist upon the more general considerations of interest and duty which sacredly guard the faith of the nation, in whatever form of obligation it may have been given." (Message, March 1, 1879, Richardson, Messages and Papers of the Presidents, 7: 519.) The matter was succinctly explained by Secretary of State Fish in 1876. "Of course, in speaking of the effect of subsequent legislation upon the provisions of a prior treaty, I refer only to the effect in the country where the legislation is enacted, and upon the officers and people of that country. The foreign nation, whose rights are invaded thereby, has no less cause of complaint and no less right to decline to recognize any internal legislation which presumes to limit or curtail rights accorded by treaty." Moore, Digest, 5: 365. Wharton, Digest, 1: 35.

decisions[13] as mitigations of international responsibility. It fol-

[12] Borchard, *op. cit.*, p. 214. The lack of legislation to give effect to international law was not thought by Great Britain to absolve the United States from responsibility for its failure to secure the release of Alexander McLeod from state jurisdiction in 1841. (Lord Ashburton, British Minister, to Secretary of State Webster, July 28, 1842, Moore, Digest, 2: 28.) Italy was not deterred from pressing her claims on account of the Louisiana lynchings during the nineties by the plea that the United States had not passed legislation necessary to give effect to treaties. (Moore, Digest, 6: 848, United States Foreign Relations, 1901, 283–299.) The United States saw no merit in the British contention that lack of legislation excused its failure to prevent departure of the Alabama in 1862 and the Geneva Arbitration of 1871 upheld the American position saying, "The government of Her Britannic Majesty cannot justify itself for failure in due diligence on the plea of insufficiency of the legal means of action which it possessed." (Moore, Digest, 6: 1061; Malloy, Treaties of the United States, 1: 719; Moore, International Arbitrations, 4: 4101–4109; Digest, 7: 878.) The American Continental Congress recognized this need of legislation in order to meet many international responsibilities and urged the passage of suitable laws by the states (Journ. Congress, 7: 181; Ford ed., 21: 1137). The Constitution authorizes such legislation (Art. 1, sec. 8, cl. 10) and Congress has enacted many statutes for this purpose. (Wright, Enforcement of Int. Law through Municipal Law, pp. 221–223; *infra*, secs. 112–122.) Presidents have repeatedly urged further legislation of this character, especially legislation giving federal courts jurisdiction adequate to protect the treaty rights of aliens. (Pres. Harrison, Message, Dec. 9, 1891; Pres. McKinley, Messages, Dec. 5, 1899, Dec. 3, 1900; Pres. Roosevelt, Message, Dec., 1906; Pres. Taft, The United States and Peace, N. Y., 1914, pp. 64–68.) The courts, attorneys general and text writers have insisted that the passage of such legislation is a constitutional duty of Congress. (Iredall, J., in Ware *v.* Hylton (1796), 1 Dall, 199; Cushing, Att. Gen. 6 Op. 291 (1854), Moore, 5: 370; Willoughby, Constitutional Law, 1: 487; Wheaton, Elements of International Law, sec. 266, Dana's note, pp. 339, 715.) We may agree with Mr. Root: "It is to be hoped that our government will never again attempt to shelter itself from responsibility for the enforcement of its treaty obligations to protect foreigners, by alleging its own failure to enact the laws necessary to the discharge of those obligations." (*Proc. American Society of Int. Law,* 4: 25.) See also excellent article by C. C. Hyde, *Proc. Acad. of Pol. Sci.,* 7: 558.

[13] "This department has contested and denied the doctrine that a government may set up the judgment of one of its own courts as a bar to an international claim, when such judgment is shown to have been unjust or in violation of the principles of international law." (Report of Mr. Bayard, Sec. of State, to the President, Feb. 26, 1887. Sen. Ex. Doc. 109, 49th Cong., 2d Sess., Moore, Digest, 6: 667.) See also The Betsey, U. S. *v.* Great Britain, adjudicated by the mixed commission formed under Article 7 of the Jay treaty of 1794, Moore, Int. Arb., 3: 3208, especially Commissioner

lows that discussions of international responsibility can hardly be fruitful unless the organ for discussing is itself free of municipal restrictions. Thus, in a protest to Great Britain against alleged violations of neutral rights at sea, Secretary of State Lansing answered the British contention, that American citizens deeming themselves aggrieved could get relief in the prize courts, by calling attention to the restrictions placed upon these courts by orders in Council:

"The United States government feels," he wrote, "that it cannot reasonably be expected to advise its citizens to seek redress before tribunals which are, in its opinion, unauthorized by the unrestricted application of international law to grant reparation, nor to refrain from presenting their claims directly to the British government through diplomatic channels." [14]

This requirement that states maintain a definite representative authority is, however, specifically evidenced by the authority of text

---

Pinckney's opinion (*Ibid.*, 3: 3182); Wheaton's argument in the Danish claims arbitration, Moore, Int. Arb., 5: 4555; Hale's Report of Commission formed under Article 12 of the Treaty of Washington, 6: 88, Moore, Int. Arb. 3: 3209; Wharton, Digest, 2: 672; Moore, Digest, 6: 695–697; Cotesworth and Powell Case, Great Britain *v.* Colombia, Moore, Int. Arb., 2: 2081; Justice Davis in Cushing, Administrator, *v.* U. S., 22 Ct. cl. 1, 1886; Ralston, International Arbitral Law and Procedure, pp. 29, 310; Borchard, *op. cit.*, pp. 197, 342; Dana's Wheaton, sec. 391 *et seq.*, note, p. 483; Bluntschli, Le Droit International Codifie, 4th ed., Paris, 1886, sec. 851; Oppenheim, Int. Law, 2d ed., London, 1912, 2: 557; Lawrence, Principles of Int. Law, 4th ed., p. 479; Earl Grey to Mr. Page, Ambassador to Great Britain, July 31, 1915, United States White Book, European War, No. 2, p. 182, par. 9. See also *supra*, note 30.

[14] U. S. White Book, European War No. 3, p. 37. The force of Secretary Lansing's argument was evidently felt by the British prize courts, for a few months later the Judicial Committee of the Privy Council handed down the decision of the Zamora which held prize courts competent to apply international law irrespective of conflicting orders in council. "It is obvious, however, that the reason for this rule of diplomacy (that an aggrieved neutral should exhaust his remedies in belligerent prize courts before appealing to the diplomatic intervention of his own government) would entirely vanish if a Court of Prize, while nominally administering a law of international obligation, were in reality acting under the direction of the Executive of the belligerent Power." (L. R. 1916, 2 A. C. 77.) The difficulty arising from the fact that even the representative organ is necessarily restricted by the Constitution has been referred to (sec. 4), but this organ must be free of other municipal law restrictions.

writers[15] and by practice. Thus where no such representative authority exists, or where it exists but its control is so ineffective that it cannot in fact represent the state recognition has usually been withheld or regular diplomatic relations have been broken. "No power," says Westlake, "would willingly try to weave ties with a rope of sand."[16]

---

[15] " As a state is an abstraction from the fact that a multitude of individuals live in a country under a sovereign Government, every State must have a head as its highest organ, which represents it, within and without its borders, in the totality of its relations. . . . The Law of Nations prescribes no rules as regards the kind of head a State may have. . . . Some kind or other of a head of the State is, however, necessary according to International Law, as without a head there is no State in existence, but anarchy." (Oppenheim, International Law, vol. 1, sec. 341.) " Sovereigns as the universal representatives of states can be considered as having independently a personality under the law of nations." (Rivier, Principes du droit des gens, 1: 51, Moore, Digest, 1: 17.) See also Phillimore, Int. Law, 3d ed., 1: 81; Sec. of State Fish, Feb. 21, 1877, Moore, Digest, 1: 250.

[16] Recognition and the maintenance of diplomatic intercourse are discretionary with each state, but by examining the conditions under which recognition has been accorded or relations broken we can discover what perfection of organization modern states actually regard as prerequisite to entry into international intercourse.

In recognizing new *states,* the primary consideration has been the actual state of independence of a community of people occupying a definite territory, but as Westlake points out, " The recognizing powers must respectively be satisfied that the new state gives sufficient promise of stability in its government. No power would willingly try to weave ties with a rope of sand." (Int. Law, 1: 50.) (For practice in recognizing new states see Moore, Digest, 1: 74–119.)

Thus the possession of a stable government is a prerequisite to recognition of a state. Does it follow that if the government of a recognized state dissolves or undergoes convulsions the state departs from the family of nations? Publicists say not—but in practice its membership is in abeyance until a new government is recognized. The nature of the recognition of a new government has been much discussed, some asserting that it has no place in international relations (Hall, *op. cit.,* p. 20; Woolsey, Int. Law, p. 39; Twiss, Int. Law, 1: 21) or is a mere formality (Goebel, Recognition Policy of the U. S., Columbia University Studies in History, Economics and Public Law, 66: 67) but in practice the recognition or non-recognition of a government may have important results, as witness the American policy toward the governments of Huerta in Mexico (1914), Tinoca in Costa Rica (1916) and Lenin in Russia (1917). Practice shows that a radical change in a state's constitution is a matter of international consideration and that the new government must present prospects of reasonable

12. *The President is the Representative Authority in the United States.*

In the United States, the President, acting through the Department of State, is this representative authority.

"The president," said John Marshall while in Congress, "is the sole organ of the nation in its external relations, and its sole representative with foreign nations. Of consequence, the demand of a foreign nation can only be made of him." [17]

"The Executive," reported the Senate Foreign Relations Committee in 1897, "is the sole mouthpiece of the nation in communication with foreign sovereignties." [18]

The same has been reiterated by courts,[19] by commentators,[20]

---

stability and responsibility before the state can again enter into official international relations. The various criteria which have been followed at different times for judging of such stability and responsibility such as (1) *defacto* control, (2) legal continuity or legitimacy, or (3) consent of the members of the state need not detain us here. (For American practice in recognition of new governments see Moore, 1: 119–164.)

Finally even when a recognized state has a recognized government it may still be unable to maintain international relations if that government presents no definite authority able to meet international responsibilities. Because of this lack the United States under the Articles of Confederation had difficulty in exchanging diplomatic officers with other states. Thus Hamilton said of the Confederation, "The treaties of the United States, under the present constitution, are liable to the infractions of thirteen different legislatures, and as many different courts of final jurisdiction, acting under the authority of those legislatures. . . . Is it possible that foreign nations can either respect or confide in such a government?" (Federalist, No. 22, Ford ed., p. 141.) See also remarks of James Wilson and Madison in the Federal Convention of 1787, Farrand, Records of the Federal Convention of 1787, 1: 426, 513. Even after the Constitution was in effect the apparent irresponsibility of the President for acts committed within the states violative of international rights of foreigners caused Italy to withdraw its minister. (Moore, Digest, 6: 837–841.) Practice seems to show that states must maintain a stable government with a single definite representative organ under penalty of international ostracism.

[17] Benton, Abridgment of Debates of Congress, 2: 466.

[18] 54th Cong., 2d Sess., Sen. Doc., No. 56, p. 21.

[19] "As the Executive head of the nation, the President is made the only legitimate organ of the General Government, to open and carry on correspondence or negotiations with foreign nations, in matters concerning the interests of the country or of its citizens." Nelson, J., in Durand *v.* Hollins, 4 Blatch, 451, 454.

[20] "Official communications involving international relations and general international negotiations are within the exclusive province of the Depart-

22 THE CONTROL OF AMERICAN FOREIGN RELATIONS.

by Congress[21] and by the President himself in official communications to Congress[22] and to foreign nations.[23] The President's position as the exclusive organ for communication with foreign nations

---

ment of State, at the head of which stands the Secretary of State." (Wilson and Tucker, *op. cit.*, p. 187.) " A foreign minister here is to correspond with the Secretary of State on matters which interest his nation, and ought not to be permitted to resort to the press. He has no authority to communicate his sentiments to the people by publications, either in manuscript or in print, and any attempt to do so is contempt of this Government. His intercourse is to be with the executive of the United States only, upon matters that concern his mission or trust." (Lee, Attorney General, 1 Op. 74, 1797, Moore, Digest, 4: 682.) See also *supra*, notes 17, 18.

[21] " In 1874, Congress declared that claims of aliens cannot properly be examined by a committee of Congress, there being a Department of this Government in which most questions of an international character may be considered—that which has charge of foreign affairs: that Congress cannot safely and by piecemeal surrender the advantage which may result from diplomatic arrangements; that this has been the general policy of the Government, and Congress has not generally entertained the claims of aliens and certainly should not unless on the request of the Secretary of State (See Report No. 498, Committee on War Claims, 1st Sess., 43d Cong., May 2, 1874)," Moore, Digest, 6: 608; Senate Report, *supra*, note 18. Apparently attempts to negotiate with foreign governments except under authority of the President is a criminal offense under the Logan Act, Jan. 30, 1799, Rev. Stat., sec. 5335, Criminal Code of 1909, Art. 5, Moore, Digest, 4: 449. See also *infra*, sec. 17.

[22] " The Constitution of the United States, following the established usage of nations, has indicated the President as the agent to represent the national sovereignty in its intercourse with foreign powers, and to receive all official communications from them, . . . making him, in the language of one of the most eminent writers on constitutional law, 'the constitutional organ of communication with foreign states.'" (President Grant, Message vetoing two joint resolutions in response to congratulations of foreign states on the occasion of the Centennial exposition, Richardson, *op. cit.*, 7: 431.)

[23] "'But,' said he (Citizen Genet), 'at least, Congress are bound to see that the treaties are observed.' I told him no; there were very few cases indeed arising out of treaties, which they could take notice of; that the President is to see that treaties are observed. 'If he decides against the treaty, to whom is a nation to appeal?' I told him the Constitution had made the President the last appeal. He made me a bow, and said, that indeed he would not make me his compliments on such a Constitution, expressed the utmost astonishment at it, and seemed never before to have had such an idea." (Sec. of State Jefferson, Moore, Digest, 4: 680.) " I do not refer to this for the purpose of calling the attention of the Imperial

is a well-established implication from the powers expressly delegated to him by the constitution to receive and to commission diplomatic officers.[24] But this position is not founded merely on the constitution. It has apparently acquired a certain foundation in international law through recognition by foreign nations. Thus foreign nations have habitually presented their claims to the President through the Department of State.

"All foreign powers recognize it (the Department of State)," wrote Secretary of State Seward, "and transmit their communications to it, through the dispatches of our ministers abroad, or their own diplomatic representatives residing near this Government. These communications are submitted to the President, and, when proper, are replied to under his direction by the Secretary of State. This mutual correspondence is recorded and preserved in the archives of this Department. This is, I believe, the same system which prevails in the governments of civilized states everywhere." [25]

The only exception to this rule appears to be in matters of a private law nature litigated before the courts.[26] In matters of international law foreign nations have sometimes been willing to

German Government at this time to the surprising irregularity of a communication from the Imperial German Embassy at Washington addressed to the people of the United States through the newspapers, but only, etc." (Secretary of State Bryan to Mr. Gerard, American Ambassador at Berlin, May 13, 1915, White Book, European War No. 1, p. 76.) See also *infra*, sec. 13.

[24] "The President is the organ of diplomatic intercourse of the Government of the United States, first, because of his powers in connection with the reception and dispatch of diplomatic agents and with treaty making; secondly, because of the tradition of executive power adherent to his office." (Corwin, The President's Control of Foreign Relations, p. 33.) See also Wright, *Columbia Law Rev.,* 20: 131.

[25] Mr. Seward, Secretary of State, to Mr. Dayton, Minister to France, June 27, 1862, Moore, Digest, 4: 781. See also Borchard, *op. cit.,* p. 355. Congressional Committees may not hear such claims, *supra,* note 22. "The Department of State has explained that claims against the Government can be presented only in one of two ways: (1) Either by the claimant's availing himself directly of such judicial or administrative remedy as the domestic law might prescribe; or (2) in the absence of such remedy, if the claimant was an alien, by his government 'formally presenting the claim as an international demand to be adjusted through the diplomatic channel.'" (Acting Secretary of State Davis to Baron de Fava, Italian Minister, July 9, 1884, Moore, 6: 608.)

[26] Foreign states are entitled to bring suit in United States courts, state or federal (Mexico *v.* Arrangoiz, 11 How. Prac. 1, N. Y. 1855; King of Prussia *v.* Kupper, 22 Mo. 550, 1856; King of Spain *v.* Oliver, 1 Peter's

permit trial of the issue in the courts first,[27] but they have always reserved the right to carry the case before the President (through the Department of State) later, if they think the decision unjust.[28] In important matters foreign governments have refused to follow a suggestion for settlement in the courts.[29] They have been equally

---

C. C. 217, 276, 1810; The Sapphire, 11 Wall. 164, 1870), and the United States Court of Claims has a limited jurisdiction of claims against the government. (Borchard, *op. cit.*, 164.)   See also Westlake, *op. cit.*, 1: 250.

[27] *Supra*, note 6.

[28] *Supra*, note 13.

[29] See suggestions for judicial settlement of the California-Japanese School and Land Ownership questions. (Corwin, *op. cit.*, p. 108; H. M. Dilla, Mich. L. R., 12: 583.) In a note of March 16, 1916, with reference to the Appam, a British vessel captured by Germany and brought to a United States port, the German government said: "The opinion of the Department of State that the American courts must decide about the claims of the British Shipping Company is incompatible with the treaty stipulations. It is, therefore, respectfully requested that the legal steps before an American court should be suspended."   The American answer of April 7, 1916, "holding the view that Article 19 is not applicable to the case of the Appam, this Government does not consider it necessary to discuss the contention of the Imperial Government that under Article 19 American courts are without jurisdiction to interfere with the prize," appears satisfactory. It is, therefore, unfortunate that the note added the following inadmissible argument. "Moreover, inasmuch as the Appam has been libeled in the United States District Court by the alleged owners, this Government, under the American system of government, in which the judicial and executive branches are entirely separate and independent, could not vouch for a continuance of the *status quo* of the prize during the progress of the arbitration proposed by the Imperial Government. The United States Court, having taken jurisdiction of the vessel, that jurisdiction can only be dissolved by judicial proceedings leading to a decision of the court discharging the case—a procedure which the executive cannot summarily terminate."   However correct this may be from the standpoint of constitutional law it could not justify a failure to meet international responsibilities. (*Supra,* note 13. White Book, European War, No. 3, pp. 340, 343.)

The United States has been similarly reluctant to leave important matters of international law to foreign courts. In a note of June 24, 1915, with reference to indemnity for destruction of the United States vessel William P. Frye, by Germany, Secretary Lansing wrote, "The Government of the United States, therefore, suggests that the Imperial German Government reconsider the subject in the light of these considerations, and because of the objections against resorting to the Prize Court the government of the United States renews its former suggestion that an effort be made to settle this claim by direct diplomatic negotiations." (*Op. cit.*, No. 2, p. 187; see also note of April 28, 1915, *op. cit.*, No. 1, p. 88.)

unresponsive to suggestions for a discussion of international claims with the state governments within the United States.[30] They have insisted upon discussion with the President, through the Department of State,[31] have accepted the President's interpretation of the responsibilities as the voice of the nation[32] and the United States has acquiesced.[33]

Thus, though the Presidency is primarily an office under the constitution, it is also an office with distinctive functions and, it may be added, enjoying privileges[34] under international law. Does

---

[30] See Louisiana Lynching Cases, U. S. For. Rel., 1891, pp. 665–667, 671–672, 674–686, 712–713, *Ibid.*, 1901, p. 253; Moore, Digest, 6: 837. "We should not be obliged to refer those who complain of a breach of such an obligation to governors of states and county prosecutors to take up the procedure of vindicating the rights of aliens which have been violated on American soil." (Taft, *Proc. Am. Soc. of Int. Law*, 4: 44.) The United States has taken a similar attitude as to claims against foreign states. "This government cannot with propriety apply to the authorities of Yucatan for redress, that province constituting only a part of the Republic of Mexico, which is responsible in the last resort for all injuries which the judicial tribunals may have neglected or may have been incompetent to redress." (Mr. Calhoun, Secretary of State to Mr. Holmes, Nov. 20, 1844, Moore, Digest, 4: 682.)

[31] *Supra*, note 26. If some international organ of settlement is utilized it must of course be on the basis of express agreement. In the absence of treaty, arbitration is voluntary. See Wright, *Columbia Law Rev.*, 20: 146.

[32] Foreign states have insisted that executive interpretations of treaties are binding even though not submitted to the Senate (See controversies with reference to notes explaining Mexican Peace Treaty of 1848 and Clayton-Bulwer treaty with England, 1850, Moore, Digest, 3: 138; 5: 205; Wright, *Minn. Law Rev.*, 4: 22; Crandall, Treaties, their Making and Enforcement, 1916, pp. 85, 381) and that the President's messages to Congress are subject to international cognizance. (See President Jackson's threat of reprisals against France, Dec., 1834, and President Taylor's comments on the Hungarian revolt of 1848, Message, March 18, 1850, and protests thereat, Moore, Digest, 7: 125; 1: 222. See also *infra*, secs. 19, 20.

[33] In the various lynchings of aliens, especially Italians, the government has paid the indemnities demanded. Though expressly stated to be gratuities, the uniform practice seems to indicate a sense of responsibility. (Moore, Digest, 6: 837.) The United States has sometimes refused to accept presidential interpretations of responsibility. *Infra*, secs. 34–38.

[34] The President apparently enjoys sovereign's immunities under international law. See Satow, Diplomatic Practice, 1917, 1: 6; Willoughby, Constitutional Law, 2: 1300, *et seq.*; Oppenheim, *op. cit.*, sec. 356.

it follow that an attempt to alter the international functions of the office by constitutional amendment would involve a violation of international law? We believe not. Such an amendment would be a matter for international cognizance but no complaint would be justified if a new organ capable of performing the international functions of the president were substituted. International law is concerned only with the existence of a definite organ capable of giving satisfaction to demands based on international law or treaty, not with its precise form.[35] Doubtless the authority might be a council or a congress though there is an unquestionable tendency for international law to favor organs for international communication of the traditional form, that is the Chief Executive acting through a foreign minister.[36] However, until the constitution has been amended to this effect, and the change has been recognized by foreign nations, they will be entitled to look to the President as the authority to whom they may present their claims and from whom they may expect satisfaction according to the standard of international law and treaty.

Now there is danger of misunderstanding. This does not mean that foreign nations are entitled to consider the President competent to commit the United States to all sorts of international responsibilities. A treaty or any other international obligation is valid only when the consent of the state is tacitly or expressly given,[37] and to determine the reality of consent the constitutional law of the state must be appealed to. Only the organs there designated, each within its constitutional competence,[38] can bind

---

[35] Hall, *op. cit.*, p. 20, *supra*, note 15.

[36] *Supra*, notes 22, 25.

[37] Wilson and Tucker, *op. cit.*, p. 213; Hall, *op. cit.*, sec. 108; Wright, *Minn. Law Rev.*, 4: 17.

[38] Crandall, *op. cit.*, sec. 1, 2: Wheaton, Dana ed., sec. 265; Borchard, *op. cit.*, pp. 183–184, says, "The power of officers of the government, superior and inferior, to bind the government is limited by their legal authority to enter into such obligations. This authority is generally strictly construed. The President of a country cannot legally grant or alter the terms of concessions to foreigners, if the constitutional law of the country requires the approval of Congress for such acts. Those dealing with agents of the

the nation. But once the treaty or other commitment is made by the proper constitutional authority, the President is, in the absence of express treaty provision to the contrary,[39] the authority to whom they may look for its execution.

---

state are ordinarily bound by their actual authority, and not, as in private law, by their ostensible authority. But in the Trumbull case (Chile v. U. S., Aug. 7, 1892, Moore, Int. Arb. 3569) the apparent authority of a diplomatic officer to contract was held sufficient to bind his government, and in the Metzger case (U. S. v. Haiti, Oct. 18, 1899, For. Rel. 262) Judge Day expressed the opinion that the 'limitations upon official authority, undisclosed at the time to the other government,' do not 'prevent the enforcement of a diplomatic agreement.'" See also Wright, *Columbia Law Rev.*, 20: 121-122. *Infra*, sec. 24.

[39] For treaty provisions designating other organs of government as responsible, see Wright, *Columbia Law Rev.*, 20: 123-124.

CHAPTER III.

Attributes of the National Representative Organ under International Law.

A. Sole Agency for Foreign Communication.

13. *Foreign Representatives may officially communicate with the nation only through the President or his Representatives.*

The position of the President as the representative organ implies that foreign nations are entitled to present their claims to him but it also implies: (*a*) that they can communicate with the nation through him alone and (*b*) that they may take cognizance of all his official acts. Efforts of foreign governments to communicate with organs of the United States other than the President or his representatives, with private American citizens or with the American people directly have been protested by the President, while efforts of American organs of government or self-constituted missions to communicate with foreign nations have been vetoed or prohibited by law. Thus in 1793 when Citizen Genet sought to obtain an exequatur for a consul whose commission was addressed to the "Congress of the United States," Secretary of State Jefferson told him that "the President was the only channel of communication between the United States and foreign nations" and refused to issue an exequatur until the commission was correctly addressed.[1] In 1833 Secretary of State Livingston sent letters to the Chargés of the United States in various capitals instructing them to notify the foreign minister that "all communication made directly to the head of our Executive Government should be addressed 'to the President of the United States of America' without any other addition." He referred to the fact that the style of address "to the President and Congress of the United States" which had

[1] Moore, Digest, 4: 680.

been continued since the old Confederation was no longer proper.[2] In 1874 Congress itself passed a resolution refusing to consider foreign claims, "there being a department of the government in which most questions of an international character may be considered."[3] Political correspondence with American citizens by the resident diplomatic representative of a foreign nation has usually resulted in a demand for the recall or in the dismissal of the representative as in the case of the British Minister Lord Sackville who was led to communicate his views of the impending presidential election to an American correspondent.[4] Foreign ministers who have tried to talk over the head of the government directly to the people have been sharply rebuked. The government requested the recall of Citizen Genet whose misconduct in that direction became notorious[5] and in the later case of the Spanish minister Yrujo, Attorney General Lee said:[6]

"A foreign minister here is to correspond with the Secretary of State on matters which interest his nation and ought not to be permitted to resort to the press. He has no authority to communicate his sentiments to the people by publications, either in manuscript or in print, and any attempt to do so is contempt of this government. His intercourse is to be with the executive of the United States only upon matters that concern his mission or trust."

More recently Ambassador Bernstorff's newspaper warning to American citizens to keep off of the Lusitania was referred to by Secretary of State Lansing as "the surprising irregularity of a communication from the Imperial German Embassy at Washington addressed to the people of the United States through the newspapers."[7]

---

[2] Corwin, *op. cit.*, p. 48, citing 54th Cong., 2d Sess., Sen. Doc. No. 56, p. 9, footnote, and J. Q. Adams, Memoirs, 4: 17–18.

[3] Magoon, Reports, 1902, p. 340, Moore, Digest, 6: 608. See also *supra*, Chap. II, note 21.

[4] Pres. Cleveland, Annual Message, Dec. 3, 1888, Richardson, Messages of the Presidents, 8: 780, Moore, Digest, 4: 537–548.

[5] Moore, Digest, 4: 487.

[6] Lee, Att. Gen., 1 Op. 74 (1797), Moore, Digest, 4: 682.

[7] Mr. Bryan, Sec. of State, to Mr. Gerard, Ambassador to Germany, May 13, 1915, U. S. White Book, European War, No. 1, p. 76.

14. *National Organs of Government other than the President or his Representatives may not communicate.*

The United States has likewise taken steps to prevent its organs of government other than the President, from communicating with foreign governments. President Grant's veto of two resolutions passed by Congress in response to congratulations on the Centennial Exposition of 1876 is typical of the fate of such resolutions of Congress. "The Constitution of the United States," wrote President Grant, "following the established usage of nations, has indicated the President as the agent to represent the national sovereignty in its intercourse with foreign powers."[8]

15. *National and State Laws subject to International Cognizance.*

There appears, however, to be an exception to this rule in the cognizance which foreign nations take of state or national laws. In the states, statutes usually become effective upon signature by the governor, or if passed over his veto, upon signature by the Clerk of the last House of the Legislature to act. Sometimes there is provision for official publication, sometimes not, but there is never requirement for formal communication to foreign nations through the President of the United States.[9] Yet foreign nations have taken cognizance of such statutes deemed to be in violation of their rights under international law or treaty, as illustrated by Japanese protests at anti-alien legislation in California and other states.[10] The United States has itself recognized that state laws are subject to international cognizance by occasionally concluding treaties, the operation of certain clauses of which is made dependent upon state law. Thus article VII of the treaty of 1853 with France allowed French citizens to possess land on an equality

---

[8] Richardson, *op. cit.*, 7: 431; *supra*, sec. 12, *infra*, sec. 202.

[9] Field *v.* Clark, 143 U. S. 649 (1892), appended note. Finley and Sanderson, The Am. Executive and Executive Methods, N. Y., 1908, p. 81; Reinsch, Am. Legislatures and Legislative Methods, N. Y., 1913, p. 142.

[10] On controversy as to the rights of Japanese School Children in California, 1906, see E. Root, *Am. Jl. of Int. Law,* 1: 273 and editorials, 1: 150, 449; Corwin, National Supremacy, 1913, p. 217. On controversy as to Japanese right to hold land, 1913, and since, see Editorial, *Am. Jl. Int. Law,* 8: 571, Moore, Principles of Am. Dip., p. 191, and Corwin, *op. cit.,* p. 232, Am. Year Book, 1917, p. 48.

NATIONAL REPRESENTATIVE ORGAN.   31

with citizens " in all states of the Union where existing laws permit it, so long and to the same extent as the said laws shall remain in force." [11]

Acts or resolutions of Congress become effective upon signature by the President, or if passed over his veto, upon signature by the Clerk of the last House of Congress to act.[12] Amendments to the Federal Constitution become effective upon proclamation by the Secretary of State.[13] Treaties become effective as domestic law upon proclamation by the President, but as between nations they are effective from signature if ratifications are subsequently exchanged.[14] Only in the case of treaties is there any official proc-

---

[11] See also Art. IV of the treaty of 1854 with Great Britain by which "the Government of the United States further engages to urge upon the state governments to secure to the subjects of Her Britannic Majesty the use of the several state canals on terms of equality with the inhabitants of the United States." By Art. V of the treaty of peace with Great Britain of 1783 it is agreed that "Congress shall earnestly recommend it to the legislatures of the respective states, to provide for the restitution of the estates," etc., of the Loyalists.

[12] Rev. Stat., sec. 204, amended Dec. 28, 1874, 18 Stat., 294, sec. 2, Comp. Stat., sec. 302, and *supra,* note 9. The Secretary of State is required to furnish copies of valid resolutions and acts of Congress and treaties to the Congressional Printer "as soon as possible" after they have become "law." Rev. Stat., sec. 308.

[13] Rev. Stat., sec. 205, Comp. Stat., sec. 303.

[14] Rev. Stat., sec. 210, Comp. Stat., sec. 308. Treaties must be published in one newspaper in the District of Columbia to be designated by the Secretary of State, Act July 31, 1876, 19 Stat., 105, Comp. Stat., sec. 7184. "It is undoubtedly true as a principle of international law, that, as respects the rights of either government under it, a treaty is considered as concluded and binding from the date of its signature. In this regard the exchange of ratifications has a retroactive effect, confirming the treaty from its date. (Wheat, Int. Law, by Dana, 336.) But a different rule prevails where the treaty operates on individual rights. . . . In so far as it affects them it is not considered as concluded until there is an exchange of ratifications. . . . In this country a treaty is something more than a contract, for the federal constitution declares it to be the law of the land. If so, before it can become a law, the Senate, in whom rests the authority to ratify it, must agree to it. But the Senate are not required to adopt or reject it as a whole, but may modify or amend it, as was done with the Treaty under consideration. As the individual citizen, on whose rights of property it operates, has no means of knowing anything of it while before the Senate, it would be wrong in principle to hold him bound by it, as the law of the land, until it was ratified and proclaimed." Haver *v.* Yaker, 9 Wall., 32.

lamation by the President, yet all of these instruments, declared supreme law by article VI of the Constitution, are subject to international cognizance immediately upon becoming effective.[15] Foreign nations, in fact, always taken cognizance of acts of Congress deemed to be in violation of their rights under international law or treaty as did China of the exclusion acts[16] and Great Britain of the Panama Canal tolls act of 1911.[17] In the latter case Secretary of State Knox maintained that such protest was not proper until action under the statute had actually impaired British rights or as least until executive proclamation to give effect to the statute had issued but his view does not seem to have been accepted. The British ambassador replied:[18]

"His Majesty's government feel bound to express their dissent. They conceive that international law or usage does not support the doctrine that the passing of a statute in contravention of a treaty right affords no ground of complaint for the infraction of that right, and that the nation which holds that its treaty rights have been so infringed or brought into question by a denial that they exist, must, before protesting and seeking a means of determining the point at issue, wait until some further action violating those rights in a concrete instance has been taken."

So also foreign nations enjoying most favored nation commercial privileges by treaty with the United States, have always applied for the advantages assured by such treaties upon the taking effect of any act or treaty which gives a favor to other nations. Thus Germany and other countries applied under most favored nation clauses for a reduction of the tonnage dues on their vessels upon passage of the act of 1884 which reduced tonnage dues upon vessels from specified ports in the western hemisphere,[19] and

---

[15] *Infra*, sec. 22.

[16] Chinese Protests against Act of Oct. 1, 1888, see U. S. For. Rel., 1889, 115–150, *Ibid.*, 1890, 177, 206, 210–219, 228–230; against Act of May 5, 1892, see *Ibid.*, 1892, 106, 118, 119, 123, 126, 134–138, 145, 147–155, 158, cited Moore, Digest, 4: 198, 202.

[17] Mr. Innes, Chargé d'Affaires of Great Britain, to Secretary of State Knox, July 8 and Aug. 27, 1912, Diplomatic History of the Panama Canal, 63d Cong., 2d Sess., Sen. Doc., No. 474, pp. 82–83.

[18] *Ibid.*, p. 101.

[19] Report of Mr. Bayard, Sec. of State, to the President, Jan. 14, 1889, 50 Cong., 2d Sess., H. Ex. Doc., No. 74, Moore, Digest, 5: 289.

Switzerland gained recognition of her claim for an application of the most favored nation clause in her treaty of 1855 upon the conclusion of a treaty in 1898 by which the United States had given commercial favors to France.[20]

16. *Legislative Expressions of Opinion, not of International Cognizance.*

Though all acts, *prima facie* law, are subject to international cognizance without transmission through the President, whether they originate in state constitutional or legislative provisions or in national constitutional, legislative or treaty provisions, this is not true of legislative resolutions not law. Thus resolutions of a single house of congress or concurrent resolutions not submitted to the President are not law according to the Constitution and have not been noticed by foreign nations.[21] This has been expressly held by the courts with reference to such resolutions purporting to interpret treaties.[22] Thus the houses of Congress have been able

---

[20] Moore, Digest, 5: 283–285.

[21] Secretary of State Seward wrote Mr. Dayton, the minister to France, with reference to a House Resolution declaring "that it does not accord with the policy of the United States to acknowledge a monarchical government erected on the ruins of any Republican government in America, under the auspices of any European power," reference being to the Maximilian government in Mexico: "This is a practical and purely Executive question, and the decision of it constitutionally belongs not to the House of Representatives, nor even to Congress, but to the President of the United States. . . . While the President receives the declaration of the House of Representatives with the profound respect to which it is entitled, as an exposition of its sentiments upon a grave and important subject, he directs that you inform the government of France that he does not at present contemplate any departure from the policy which this government has hitherto pursued in regard to the war which exists between France and Mexico. It is hardly necessary to say that the proceeding of the House of Representatives was adopted upon suggestions arising within itself, and not upon any communication of the Executive department; and that the French Government would be seasonably appraised of any change of policy upon this subject which the President might at any future time think it proper to adopt." Corwin, *op. cit.*, p. 42, citing McPherson's History of the Rebellion, pp. 349–350.

[22] "There is," said the Supreme Court in refusing to apply an amendment to which the Indians had not consented, "something which shocks the conscience in the idea that a treaty can be put forth as embodying the

34   THE CONTROL OF AMERICAN FOREIGN RELATIONS.

to pass resolutions on such questions as Irish independence without arousing international controversy.[23] So also a concurrent resolution could not be made effective to denounce a treaty. The effect of the Senate to incorporate a reservation in the Peace treaty of 1919 giving a concurrent resolution, this effect would have proved futile. The treaty, not being able to amend the Constitution, could not make a concurrent resolution a law of either international or domestic effect.[24]

17. *Self-Constituted Missions Forbidden.*

To prevent private negotiations with foreign nations, the Logan Act of 1799 was passed, after the attempt to make peace with France of the self-constituted mission of Dr. George Logan, a Philadelphia Quaker, had annoyed the government. The statute provides a fine of up to $5,000 and imprisonment up to six months for every citizen of the United States:[25]

> "Who without the permission or authority of the government, directly or indirectly, commences or carries on any verbal or written correspondence or intercourse with any foreign government, or an officer or agent thereof, with an intent to influence the measures or conduct of any foreign government, or of any officer or agent thereof, in relation to any disputes or controversies with the United States, or to defeat the measures of the government of the United States; and every person, being a citizen of, or resident within the United States, and not duly authorized, who counsels, advises or assists in any such correspondence with such intent."

---

terms of an arrangement with a foreign power or an Indian tribe, a material provision of which is unknown to one of the contracting parties, and is kept in the background to be used by the other only when the exigency of a particular case may demand it." N. Y. Indians *v.* U. S., 170 U. S. 1 (1898). The Supreme Court said in reference to a joint resolution passed by a majority of the Senate stating the purpose of the Senate in ratifying the treaty annexing the Philippines: "We need not consider the force and effect of a resolution of this sort. . . . The meaning of the treaty cannot be controlled by subsequent explanations of some of those who may have voted to ratify it." Justice Brown concurring said: "It cannot be regarded as part of the treaty since it received neither the approval of the President nor the consent of the other contracting power." Fourteen Diamond Rings *v.* U. S., 183 U. S. 176 (1901), Moore, Digest, 5: 210.

[23] See House Resolution on Ireland, March 4, 1919, Senate Resolution, June 6, 1919, and proposed 15th reservation to the Treaty of Versailles, passed by a majority of the Senate March 18, 1920. *Infra*, sec. 190.

[24] *Infra*, sec. 62.

[25] Rev. Stat., sec. 5335, Moore, Digest, 4: 449.

This act expressly excepts application by American citizens to foreign government for redress of injuries, and in general presentation of claims by an individual is not considered a violation of the principle that the representative organs of government communicate officially only with the representative organs of other governments. However, in practice the department of state in the United States and the foreign office in other states generally refuse to consider claims not officially presented by the claimant's government.[26]

18. *Missions of De Facto Governments, Unofficially Received.*

One other exception is recognized in the unofficial reception of agents of belligerent communities. Thus the British foreign Secretary communicated unofficially with Mason and Slidell, the Confederate emissaries in England,[27] and the President of the United States communicated unofficially with representatives from South Africa after the proclamation of annexation by Great Britain had made the status of that country one of rebellion.[28] Such unofficial communication with representatives of *de facto* governments is justified by the right of foreign states to take measures for protecting their citizens in a region outside the actual control of the *de jure* government, and is not a real exception to the rule.[29]

B. All Acts of the President Subject to International Cognizance.

19. *Communications of the President to Congress.*

The President's representative character also implies that foreign nations are entitled to take cognizance of all his official utter-

---

[26] Moore, Digest, 6: 607–610, *supra,* note 3.

[27] Moore, Digest, 1: 209.

[28] The proclamation of annexation was issued July 1, 1900. On May 21 and 22, 1900, the South African delegates were received by the Department of State and President McKinley, and they were received by President Roosevelt on March 14, 1902. The war ended with the treaty of Vereeniging, May 31, 1902. Moore, Digest, 1: 213.

[29] See Earl Russell, British Foreign Secretary, to Mr. Adams, U. S. Minister, Nov. 26, Moore, Digest, 1: 209.

ances whether communicated by diplomatic note, public proclamation or public communication to Congress. Presidents have always maintained that communications of the latter character are not subject to the cognizance of foreign states, but in fact they have often been noticed, as when France protested against the threatening language of President Jackson's message of December, 1834, suggesting reprisals[30] and Austria protested against President Taylor's comments on Kossuth's revolution of 1848.[31] In the former case President Jackson seems to have admitted the French demand for retraction by explanations in a later message.[32] In the last year of the World War Executive messages to the legislature became the regular medium of communication between Germany and the United States.[33]

20. *President Presumed to Speak for the Nation.*

Finally, from the President's representative character, foreign nations are entitled to presume that his voice is the voice of the nation. Secretary of State Jefferson told French minister Genet that whatever the President communicated as such, foreign nations had a right and were bound to consider "as the expression of the nation's will" and that no foreign agent could be "allowed to question it."[34] As we shall see, this presumption becomes absolute with reference to the fact of action taken by national organs in the United States and practically so with reference to decisions of fact and policy by the nation,[35] but with reference to the constitu-

---

[30] Moore, Digest, 7: 124–125.

[31] "The publicity which has been given to that document has placed the Imperial Government under the necessity of entering a formal protest, through its official representatives, against the proceedings of the American Government, lest that Government should construe our silence into approbation, or toleration even, of the principles which appear to have guided its action and the means it has adopted." Moore, Digest, 1: 222.

[32] Message, Dec. 7, 1835, Moore, Digest, 7: 125.

[33] See speeches of President Wilson, Premier Lloyd George of Great Britain, Count Czernin of Austria and Count Hertling of Germany before their respective legislative bodies in 1918, printed in Dickinson, ed., Documents and Statements relating to Peace Proposals and War Aims, London, 1919.

[34] Moore, Digest, 4: 680; Corwin, *op. cit*, p. 47.

[35] *Infra*, sec. 21.

tional law governing the treaty-making power, the foreign nation may in certain cases have to go back of the President's assertions.[36]

We thus find that, aside from their cognizance of state and national laws, foreign nations can officially communicate with the United States only through the President. Communication of governments with private individuals on claims and with representatives of *de facto* or belligerent governments are of an unofficial character. Furthermore, all official utterances of the President are of international cognizance and are presumed to be authoritative.

---

[36] *Infra*, sec. 24 *et seq.*

CHAPTER IV.

Conclusiveness of the Acts and Utterances of National Organs Under International Law.

To how great an extent are foreign governments expected to know American constitutional law defining the competence of governmental organs? The answer varies according as the issue relates to (*a*) the making of a national decision on fact or policy, (*b*) the making of a treaty or agreement, (*c*) the meeting of an international responsibility.

A. With Reference to the Making of National Decisions.

21. *Acts of the President.*

Foreign nations need not know and they are not entitled to discuss the constitutional competence of organs of the United States making national decisions on fact or policy. They must accept the assertion of the President as final. Thus in a conversation with Citizen Genet in 1793, Secretary of State Jefferson refused to discuss the question of whether it belonged to the President under the constitution to admit or exclude foreign agents. "I inform you of the fact," he said, " by authority of the President."[1] This principle was also illustrated by the prompt acceptance by foreign nations of President Lincoln's proclamation of blockade on April 19, 1861, as a proclamation that war existed.[2] The power of the President to thus proclaim war without authority of Congress was questioned in the United States and in the decision finally given by the Supreme Court sustaining the President's act, three justices

---

[1] Moore, Digest, 4: 680.

[2] "It was, on the contrary, your own government which, in assuming the belligerent right of blockade, recognized the Southern States as Belligerents. Had they not been belligerents the armed ships of the United States would have had no right to stop a single British ship upon the high seas." Earl Russell, British Foreign Minister, note, May 4, 1865. Moore, Digest, 1: 190.

ACTS AND UTTERANCES OF NATIONAL ORGANS. 39

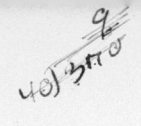

out of seven vigorously dissented.[3] However, since the fact of war was a matter subject to foreign cognizance, foreign nations would doubtless have been justified in issuing neutrality proclamations, even had they not been obliged to consider the President's act conclusive.[4]

Aside from declarations of war and recognitions of new states, governments and neutrality,[5] the President's assertions may be considered authoritative by foreign nations when they relate to the termination of war, the termination of a treaty, or the existence of a national sentiment or policy.[6] Thus Great Britain officially recognized the President's proclamation of the termination of the Civil War,[7] and Mr. C. F. Adams, the American Minister to Great Britain, insisted that the British government was incompetent to inquire into the competence of the Secretary of State to give notice of the denunciation of the Great Lakes disarmament treaty of 1817 or to withdraw that notice.[8]

"It could," he said, "only accept and respect the withdrawal as a fact." The question of competency, "being a matter of domestic administration affecting the internal relations of the executive and legislative powers," in no wise concerned Great Britain. The raising by her of a question as to "the authority of the executive power" in the matter, would have constituted "an unprecedented and inadmissible step in the international relations of governments."

---

[3] The Prize Cases, 2 Black 635; Moore, Digest, 1: 190, 7: 172; Willoughby, Constitutional Law, 2: 1210.

[4] Dana, note to Wheaton, pp. 37–38; Willoughby, *op. cit.*, p. 1212; Moore, Digest, 1: 189.

[5] The recognition power is vested in the President. See Moore, Digest, 1: 243–248, and "Memorandum on the method of recognition of foreign governments and foreign states by the government of the United States, 1789–1892. 54th Cong., 2 Sess., Sen. Docs. 40, 56; The Divina Pastora, 4 Wheat, 52; Corwin, *op. cit.*, p. 71. See also *infra*, sec. 192.

[6] Lord Salisbury considered the interpretation of the Monroe Doctrine given by President Cleveland and Secretary of State Olney as subject to international cognizance as an official expression of American opinion. See Moore, Digest, 6: 560. See also *supra*, sec. 20.

[7] U. S. Dip. Correspondence, 1865, 1: 409; Moore, Digest, 1: 187.

[8] Report of Mr. Foster, Sec. of State, to the President, Dec. 7, 1892, H. Doc. 471, 56th Cong., 1st Sess., pp. 4, 36; Moore, Digest, 5: 169–170.

22. *National and State Statutes.*

Thus statements of a decision on fact or policy, authorized by the President, must be accepted by foreign nations as the will of the United States. We have noticed that acts *prima facie* law are subject to international cognizance whether issuing from state or national organs.[9] They may not be accepted as definitive however, if their validity is denied by the President. Thus state constitutional or legislative provisions are not really law if in conflict with the national constitution, laws, or treaties; and acts of congress or treaty provisions are not law if in conflict with the Constitution. If the President discovers such a conflict and denies the validity of the purported law his interpretation is conclusive for foreign nations, even though it differs from the view of the court.[10]

23. *Acts of Subordinates to the President.*

An act by a subordinate, purporting to be under authority of the President, may not be accepted by foreign nations as the will of the United States if promptly repudiated. Thus the salute to the insurgent Brazilian navy in the harbor of Rio Janeiro, authorized by Commodore Stanton in 1893, could not be considered a recognition of that party as the government of Brazil in view of the President's prompt repudiation of this act.[11]

With reference to the making of national decisions, foreign nations may accept the voice of the President as authoritative. Purported national or state laws and the acts or utterances of subordinates to the President, presumably subject to his instructions, are the only other pronouncements on this subject which may be considered authoritative, and they cannot, if their validity is promptly denied by the President. On this subject foreign nations are not expected to know the constitutional provisions defining the competence of national organs.

---

[9] *Supra,* sec. 15.
[10] See discussion of the Dillon Case, Moore, 5: 80, 167, and *infra,* sec. 46.
[11] Moore, Digest, 1: 24.

B. *With Reference to the Making of International Agreements.*

24. *Foreign Nations Presumed to know the Constitution.*

In making international agreements, however, foreign nations must look back of the President's assertions to the constitution itself.[12] They are presumed to know, and if they do not, are entitled to demand proof of the constitutional competence of all organs or agents assuming to make agreements for the United States, before exchanging ratifications. " *Qui cum alio contrahit, vel est vel debet esse non ignarus condicienis eius,*" said Ulpian.[13] Furthermore, the authority of agents of the state is usually strictly construed. " Those dealing with them are ordinarily bound by their actual authority and not as in private law by their ostensible authority." [14] This, however, is subject to certain exceptions. The international court of arbitration in the Metzger case held that " limitations upon official authority, undisclosed at the time to the other government," do not " prevent the enforcement of a diplomatic agreement." [15]

25. *Signature under Authority of the Treaty Power.*

The first step[16] in the making of international agreements, if of a

---

[12] " The Constitution of the United States, like the Constitution of Brazil, points out the way in which treaties may be made and the faith of the nation duly pledged. . . . Of such provisions in each other's constitutions governments are assumed to take notice." Mr. Gresham, Secretary of State, to Mr. Mendonça, Brazilian Minister, October 26, 1894, Moore, Digest, 5: 361.

[13] Digest of Justinian, Lib. L, Tit. xvii, cited by Crandall, Treaties, Their Making and Enforcement, p. 2, who adds: " To know the power of him with whom negotiations are conducted requires a knowledge not only of his special mandate and powers, the exhibition of which may always be demanded before the opening of negotiations, but also of the fundamental law or constitution of the state which he professes to represent, and of any limitations which may result from an incomplete sovereignty." Geffcken, in a note to Heffter, Das Europaische Völkerrecht der gegenwart, p. 201, says: " Without doubt a government should know the various phases that the project must follow at the hands of the other contractant; it is not able to raise reclamations if the treaty fails in one of these phases."

[14] Borchard, Diplomatic Protection of Citizens Abroad, p. 184.

[15] Metzger (U. S.) *v.* Haiti, Oct. 18, 1899, U. S. For. Rel., p. 262, cited Borchard, *loc. cit.* See also Trumbull (Chile) *v.* U. S., Aug. 7, 1892, Moore, International Arbitrations, p. 3569.

formal and permanent character, is exchange of "full powers" by the negotiators. Although these, if satisfactory, originally signified an actual full power of the negotiators to bind the state within the limits of their instructions, at present they are understood to mean that the negotiator is vested merely with the powers of the organ under whose authority he acts, usually in practice the representative organ.[17] Suppose the organ giving "full powers" to the negotiator is the full treaty-making power of the state. It was held by early publicists that in such cases the document when signed bound the state and ratification became a mere form which could not be refused except for the most cogent reasons.[18] Though recent opinion is less definite, yet it holds that a strong obligation to ratify exists[19] and this has been the view of the United States. Thus in 1804 and in 1819 the Secretary of State insisted that the Spanish crown was under an absolute obligation to ratify the treaties which had been made within the instructions of the negotiators acting

---

[16] The conclusion of a treaty involves three steps: (1) exchange of full powers, negotiation and signature, (2) consent to ratification with or without reservations and ratification, (3) exchange of ratifications. Often legislation must be passed before the treaty becomes executable and "putting into effect" may be considered a fourth step in the conclusion of a treaty. In the United States legislation is not needed for self-executing treaties which are executable after proclamation by the President. However, under international law, the treaty is complete and binding after exchange of ratifications and the parties are responsible for a failure to take measures necessary to put them into effect. See Wright, *Am. Jl. of Int. Law*, 10: 710 (Oct., 1916), Crandall, *op. cit.*, p. 345; Anson, The Law and Custom of the Constitution, 3d ed., Oxford, 1907, vol. 2, pt. 1, p. 54.

[17] Wheaton, International Law (Dana, ed.), pp. 337, 338; Crandall, *op. cit.*, p. 2; Moore, Digest, 5: 184, 362; Satow, Diplomatic Practice, London, 1917, 2: 273; Harley, *Am. Jl. Int. Law*, 13: 389 (July, 1919), Wright, *Minn. Law Rev.*, 4: 18.

[18] Grotius, *De Jure Belli ac Pacis*, c. 11, sec. 12; Vattel, *Le Droit des Gens*, 2, c. 12, sec. 156; Martens, *Précis des Droit de Gens*, c. 1, sec. 36.

[19] After citing five authorities supporting an absolute obligation to ratify, thirteen for a moral obligation, eight for no obligation at all, and the circumstances of ten *causes célèbres* in which ratification was refused, Harley, *loc. cit.*, concludes, "It would seem that the weight of opinion holds that a moral obligation to ratify exists." See also Moore, Digest, 5: 187; Scott, The Reports of the Hague Conferences of 1899 and 1907, London, 1917, introduction, p. xxvii; Hall, International Law (Higgins, ed.), p. 341.

under full powers of the Crown.[20] The United States has also admitted the same principle with reference to its own ratification when instructions have been given by the full treaty power. Thus in 1790 two-thirds of the Senate joined with the President in instructing the negotiation of a treaty with the Cherokees. When the treaty was submitted for ratification, the Senate committee found that it conformed to these instructions and consequently ratification became obligatory.[21] The same was true of the consular convention with France signed in 1788 according to instructions of Congress which had power to make treaties under the Articles of Confederation. The treaty was submitted to the Senate for ratification after organization of the new government under the Constitution. On his advice being asked, John Jay, who continued in charge of foreign affairs, replied that "while he apprehended that the new convention would prove more inconvenient than beneficial to the United States, the circumstances under which it had been negotiated made,

---

[20] A claims convention signed with Spain in 1802 was rejected by the Senate but on new evidence being presented, the Senate changed its mind. Now, however, Spain refused to ratify. "Were it necessary," replied Secretary Madison, "to enforce these observations by an inquiry into the right of His Catholic Majesty to withhold his ratification in this case, it would not be difficult to show that it is neither supported by the principles of public law, nor countenanced by the examples which have been cited." Madison to Yrujo, Oct. 15, 1804, Am. St. Pap., For. Rel., 2: 625. The convention was finally ratified by Spain in 1818. Almost immediately a similar controversy arose over the Florida cession treaty. Secretary Adams said, "The President considers the treaty of 22d February last as obligatory upon the honor and good faith of Spain, not as a perfect treaty, ratification being an essential formality to that, but as a compact which Spain was bound to ratify." He then drew an analogy between an unratified treaty and a covenant to convey land, asserting that "the United States have a perfect right to do what a court of chancery would do in a transaction of similar character between individuals, namely, to compel the performance of the engagement as far as compulsion can accomplish it, and to indemnify themselves for all the damages and charges incident to the necessity of using compulsion." It should be noted that in the full powers of his plenipotentiary, the Spanish monarch had expressly promised to ratify "whatsoever may be stipulated and signed by you." 5 Moore, Digest, 189–190. In both of these cases the United States distinguished its own position, in which the recognized constitutional rights of the Senate precluded an obligation to ratify.

[21] Crandall, *op. cit.*, p. 79. The question might be raised whether such a delegation is not an unconstitutional delegation of legislative power. See *infra*, sec. 60.

in his opinion, its ratification by the Senate indispensable." The Senate immediately proceeded to ratify.[22]

26. *Signature under Authority of the President.*

In case the agreement is of a character which the President has authority to make on his own responsibility, such as protocols, truces and armistices, he is bound by the act of his agents acting within their instructions. In such cases where the agent acts beyond his instructions, as did General Sherman in concluding an armistice with General Johnston in 1865, the President may repudiate the agreement as did President Lincoln on this occasion.[23]

In the case of treaties, full powers and instructions are generally from the President alone, although ratification requires the consent of the Senate. Consequently the latter retains full discretion to refuse ratification of the signed instrument.[24] The Senate has often rejected treaties and the practice was thus justified by Secretary of State Clay:[25]

"The government of his Britannic Majesty is well acquainted with the provision of the Constitution of the United States, by which the Senate is a component part of the treaty making power, and that the consent and advice of that branch of Congress are indispensable in the formation of treaties. According to the practice of this government the Senate is not ordinarily consulted in the initiatory state of a negotiation, but its consent and advice are only invoked after a treaty is concluded under the direction of the President and submitted to its consideration."

Foreign nations have acquiesced in the practice though occasionally exception has been taken to the practice of amendment or reservation by the Senate on the ground that such amendments present a virtual ultimatum to the foreign government to accept or reject, leaving no opportunity for negotiation.[26]

---

[22] Crandall, *loc. cit.;* Hayden, The Senate and Treaties, 1789–1817, N. Y., 1920, p. 7.

[23] Halleck, International Law, 4th ed. (Baker), 2: 356, *infra,* sec. 167.

[24] *Supra,* note 17.

[25] Moore, Digest, 5: 200. See also Foster, Practice of Diplomacy, N. Y., 1906, p. 276.

[26] Willoughby, Constitutional Law, p. 465. See also Crandall, *op. cit.,* p. 82, Moore, Digest, 5: 201; Satow, *op. cit.,* 2: 274. See the vigorous denunciation of the Senate amendment to the proposed King-Hawkesbury treaty of 1803 by Great Britain, Am. St. Pap., For. Rel., 3: 92–94; Hayden, *op. cit.,* p. 150.

"His Majesty's Government," wrote Lord Lansdowne, refusing to accept the first Hay-Pauncefote treaty as amended by the Senate, "find themselves confronted with a proposal communicated to them by the United States Government, without any previous attempt to ascertain their views, for the abrogation of the Clayton-Bulwer treaty."

Objection is here taken to a breach of diplomatic etiquette in method but the full power of the United States under international law to refuse ratification or to consent only if certain alterations are made, is not denied.

27. *Reservations Expressly Consented to.*

Though the United States can not be reproached with violation of international law if it refuses to ratify or qualifies its ratification of a treaty signed by authority of the President alone, yet a qualified ratification is of no effect unless consented to by both signatories. How may this consent be evidenced? Express consent to reservations by statement in the act of ratification or by exchange of notes would of course by sufficient,[27] as would acceptance without objec-

---

[27] The Senate advised ratification of the treaty with France of Feb. 3, 1801, provided a new article be substituted for article II. Bonaparte ratified with this modification but added a new proviso. Ratifications were exchanged at Paris, but before proclamation President Jefferson resubmitted the treaty to the Senate which accepted Bonaparte's proviso. Malloy, Treaties, etc., p. 505. Hayden, *op. cit.*, p. 124. After consenting to ratification of the General Act for the suppression of the African Slave Trade (1890), the Senate "Resolved further, That the Senate advise and consent to the acceptance of the partial ratification of the said General Act on the part of the French Republic, and to the stipulations relative thereto, as set forth in the protocol signed at Brussels, January 2, 1892." It then made a reservation on its own behalf. The protocol of deposit of ratifications of Feb. 2, 1892, provided for in Article 99 of the treaty, recites the Senate's resolution and states: "This resolution of the Senate of the United States having been preparatively and textually conveyed by the Government of His Majesty the King of the Belgians to the knowledge of all the signatory powers of the General Act, the latter have given their assent to its insertion in the present Protocol which will remain annexed to the Protocol of January 2d, 1892." Malloy, Treaties, etc., p. 1992. In the treaty of 1911, Japan gave express assent to an "understanding" and tacit assent to an "amendment." The proclamation of President Taft reads: "And whereas, the advice and consent of the Senate of the United States to the ratification of the said Treaty was given with the understanding 'that the treaty shall not be deemed to repeal or affect any of the provisions of the Act of Congress entitled "An Act to regulate the Immigration of Aliens into the United States," approved February 20th, 1907;'

tion of an official note stating such reservations.[28] The terms of such a note must be consented to by all the organs constituting the treaty power of each state. Thus, as is the case with the treaty itself, unless the President and Senate have each consented to amendments, reservations or interpretations, the United States is not bound. Attempts of either to act separately have been unavailing. The Supreme Court said in reference to a joint resolution passed by a majority of the Senate, stating the purpose of the Senate in ratifying the treaty annexing the Philippines:[29]

"We need not consider the force and effect of a resolution of this sort. . . . The meaning of the treaty can not be controlled by subsequent

"And whereas, the said Treaty, as amended by the Senate of the United States, has been duly ratified on both parts, and the ratifications of the two Governments were exchanged in the City of Tokyo, on the fourth day of April, one thousand nine hundred and eleven;
"Now, therefore, be it known that I, William Howard Taft, President of the United States of America, have caused the said Treaty, as amended and the said understanding to be made public, to the end that the same and every article and clause thereof may be observed and fulfilled with good faith by the United States and the citizens thereof. In testimony whereof, etc." Charles, Treaties, etc., p. 82. An interpretation proposed by the Senate to the treaty of 1868 with the North German Confederation was duly communicated to that government and accepted as the true interpretation of the article. It was, however, omitted in the exchange copy given by that government. This omission being noticed later, a special protocol was signed in 1871, recognizing the interpretation. Crandall, *op. cit.*, p. 88.

[28] In negotiating the treaty of 1850 with Switzerland, the American negotiator agreed that the unqualified most-favored-nation clause of article 10 should be interpreted absolutely. In 1898, Switzerland claimed under this clause, the benefits offered to France under a reciprocity agreement of May 30, 1898. At first the United States objected that to admit the claim would be contrary to her accepted interpretation of identical most-favored-nation clauses, but "It was found upon an examination of the original correspondence that the President of the United States was advised of the same understanding and that the dispatch in which it was expressed was communicated to the Senate when the treaty was submitted for its approval," consequently customs officials were directed to admit Swiss importations at the reduced rate. Moore, Digest, 5: 284.

[29] Fourteen Diamond Rings v. United States (1901), 183 U. S. 176. "The power to make treaties is vested by the Constitution in the President and Senate, and while this proviso was adopted by the Senate, there is no evidence that it ever received the sanction or approval of the President." N. Y. Indians v. U. S. (1898), 170 U. S. 1. See also Moore, Digest, 5: 210; Crandall, *op. cit.*, p. 88.

explanations of some of those who may have voted to ratify it." Justice Brown, concurring, said:

"It can not be regarded as part of the treaty, since it received neither the approval of the President nor the consent of the other contracting power. . . . The Senate has no right to ratify the treaty and introduce new terms into it, which shall be obligatory upon the other power, although it may refuse its ratificatiton, or make such ratification conditional upon the adoption of amendments to the treaty."

A similar fate has met interpretations or reservations made by the President without consent of the Senate, even when accepted by the other signatory. Thus explanatory notes signed by the plenipotentiaries on exchange of ratifications to the Mexican peace treaty of 1848 and the Clayton-Bulwer treaty with Great Britain of 1850 were considered of doubtful validity,[30] and on other occasions the President has submitted such explanatory documents to the Senate before proclaiming the treaty.[31]

Thus, if in fact the note has not received consent of the full treaty-making power, the United States is not bound unless the foreign nation can show that it had reason to suppose the note had been constitutionally accepted. There would certainly be such a

---

[30] Moore, Digest, 5: 205–206; Crandall, *op. cit.*, pp. 85, 381. Bigelow, Breaches of Anglo-American Treaties, pp. 116–149, discusses at length the effectiveness of these and other documents alleged to be explanatory of the Clayton-Bulwer treaty. Secretary Root agreed by exchange of notes with Mr. Bryce, British Ambassador, as to the meaning of Art. II of the arbitration convention of 1908. These documents were submitted to the Senate for its information but apparently not for its approval. Crandall, *op. cit.*, p. 89; D. H. Miller, Reservations to Treaties, 1919, p. 89.

[31] Jefferson thought it necessary to submit an interpretation offered by Napoleon of the treaty of 1801 to the Senate before exchange of ratifications. Charles Francis Adams said that the British interpretation of the Declaration of Paris, to which the United States desired to accede, would have to be submitted to the Senate. Secretary Fish declared the exchange of ratifications of a treaty with Turkey in 1874 was invalid because accompanied by an explanation of the American plenipotentiary which rendered a Senate amendment nugatory. Secretary Bayard refused to give an explanation of a Senate amendment to the treaty with Hawaii of 1884 and to authorize a protocol explaining the submarine cable convention of 1886 without Senate approval. Crandall, *op. cit.*, pp. 86–89; Moore, Digest, 5: 207. Although protocols prolonging the time for exchange of ratifications have not always been submitted to the Senate, this has usually been done. Crandall, *op. cit.*, pp. 89–92.

presumption where the exchange of notes took place before the Senate had acted. Thus intrepretive agreements relating to the treaties with Mexico (1848) and Great Britain (1850) not having been exchanged until after ratification, though considered valid by foreign nations,[32] were questioned by the United States.[33] On the other hand, the interpretive notes exchanged *before* the Senate had acted on the Swiss treaty of 1855 were considered valid. In this case the notes in question had been submitted to the Senate but had not been formally acted on by that body.[34]

28. *Reservations Tacitly Consented to.*

Tacit consent to reservatons is also possible, but it seems doubtful whether the United States would be bound by a reservation submitted by a foreign power unless the Senate has had an opportunity to object. The signature and exchange of ratifications of treaties are formal ceremonies offering suitable opportunities for the proposal of reservations. It would appear that if such proposals are stated as conditions of consent by the proposing power, on either of these occasions, lack of protest within a reasonable time by others could be construed as tacit consent. At the Hague Conferences, the numerous reservations offered upon signature of the Conventions and maintained by the power upon ratification were accorded tacit consent in this manner.[35] Other signatories are,

---

[32] Mexico and Great Britain respectively asserted the validity of these agreements. Moore, 5: 205; Lord Clarendon to Mr. Buchanan, May 2, 1854, Br. and For. St. Pap., 46: 267, Moore, 3: 138. The Mexican agreement is printed after the Treaty in Malloy, Treaties, etc., p. 1119.

[33] *Supra,* note 30.

[34] *Supra,* note 28.

[35] The Marie Glaeser, L. R. (1914), P. 218; The Appam (1916), 243 U. S. 124, *infra,* note 38. In most cases reservations were offered at signature and affirmed at ratification though sometimes they were offered for the first time at ratification. Thus the Senate resolution advising ratification of the 1907 Hague Convention for the Pacific Settlement of International Disputes affirmed the declaration made by the American plenipotentiaries on signature and added a new reservation. Malloy, Treaties, etc., p. 2247. See discussion, Scott, Reports of the Hague Conference, xxviii, and D. H. Miller, Reservations to Treaties (p. 145), who considers silent acquiescence at exchange of ratifications, " express acceptance." *Ibid.,* pp. 141, 145, 160. For reservations with statement of the method of presentment see Carnegie Endowment edition of the Hague Conventions.

however, at liberty to object to reservations. Thus the powers objected to a reservation to the treaty of Versailles proposed by China upon signature and, as a result, China refused to sign the treaty.[36] Sometimes the treaty itself has stated that it is not subject to reservation. Thus article 65 of the Declaration of London provided "The provisions of the present Declaration form an indivisible whole." [37]

The United States Senate is presumed to be aware of reservations made by foreign powers on signature, *before* it consents to ratification, consequently the United States is bound by such reservations. Thus, said the Supreme Court of a reservation attached by the King of Spain to his ratification of the Florida cession treaty of 1819: [38]

"It is too plain for argument that where one of the parties to a treaty at the time of its ratification annexes a written declaration explaining ambiguous language in the instrument or adding a new and distinct stipulation

---

[36] *Am. Year Book*, 1919, p. 93.

[37] Upon this, the drafting committee, of which M. Renault was chairman, commented as follows: "This Article is of great importance, and is in conformity with that which was adopted in the Declaration at Paris. The rules contained in the present Declaration relate to matters of great importance and great diversity. They have not all been accepted with the same degree of eagerness by all the Delegations; some concessions have been made on one point in consideration of concessions obtained on another. The whole, all things considered, has been recognized as satisfactory. A legitimate expectation would be defeated if one Power might make reservations on a rule to which another Power attached particular importance." Naval War College, Int. Law Topics, 1909, p. 155. Protocol No. 24 of the Paris Congress of 1856 provided with reference to the Declaration of Paris, "On the proposition of Count Walewski, and recognizing that it is for the general interest to maintain the indivisibility of the four principles mentioned in the declaration signed this day, the plenipotentiaries agree that the powers which shall have signed it, or which shall have acceded to it, can not hereafter enter into any arrangement in regard to the application of the right of neutrals in time of war, which does not at the same time rest on the four principles which are the object of the said declaration." This was recognized as a binding obligation on the powers and as a result the United States being unwilling to accept one provision of the Declaration was excluded from the treaty, a situation which proved most disadvantageous upon the outbreak of the Civil War five years later. *Ibid.*, 1905, p. 110.

[38] Doe *v.* Braden, 16 How. 635, 656 (1853). See also Crandall, p. 88, and *supra*, note 28.

and the treaty is *afterwards ratified by the other party* with the declaration attached to it, and the ratifications duly exchanged—the declaration thus annexed is a part of the treaty and as binding as if it were inserted in the body of the instrument. The intention of the parties is to be gathered from the whole instrument as it stood when the ratifications were exchanged."

In case foreign reservations are proposed upon exchange of ratifications, the Senate has no opportunity to object unless the reservations are especially submitted to it by the President. President Jefferson thus submitted Napoleon's reservation to the treaty of 1801 after exchange of ratifications and the Senate consented.[39] Doubtless, prompt notification of Senatorial objection, had it been given, would have relieved the United States of responsibility under the treaty, in spite of the fact that ratifications had been exchanged.

In multi-partite treaties a formal exchange of ratifications is often dispensed with and provision is made for deposit of ratifications at a central bureau. This was provided in the African Slave Trade, Algeciras, Hague, Versailles and other Conventions.[40] With such provisions, qualified ratifications may be deposited in the

---

[39] Crandall, *op. cit.*, p. 86, and *supra*, note 27.

[40] Article 440 of the Treaty of Versailles reads:

"The present Treaty of which the French and English texts are both authentic, shall be ratified.

"The deposit of ratifications shall be made at Paris as soon as possible.

"Powers of which the seat of the Government is outside Europe, will be entitled merely to inform the Government of the French Republic through their diplomatic representative at Paris that their ratification has been given; in that case they must transmit the instrument of ratification as soon as possible.

"A first procès-verbal of the deposit of ratifications will be drawn up as soon as the Treaty has been ratified by Germany on the one hand, and by three of the Principal Allied and Associated Powers on the other hand.

"From the date of this first procès-verbal the Treaty will come into force between the High Contracting Parties who have ratified it. For the determination of all periods of time provided for in the present Treaty this date will be the date of the coming into force of the Treaty.

"In all other respects the Treaty will enter into force for each Power at the date of the deposit of its ratification.

"The French Government will transmit to all the signatory Powers a certified copy of the procès-verbaux of the deposit of ratifications."

ACTS AND UTTERANCES OF NATIONAL ORGANS. 51

method provided, but if upon receipt of the procès-verbal of the deposit of such qualified ratification, any signatory objects to the reservations, the treaty will not be in effect as between those signatories. As to signatories offering no objection the reservations will be regarded as tacitly accepted, and the treaty will be in effect as from the date of deposit of ratifications. Undoubtedly, when foreign states make reservations the Senate ought to be given an opportunity to object to such reservations[41] and that was done in the French reservation to the African Slave Trade Convention of 1890.[42] It does not appear that all reservations attached to deposit of ratifications of the Hague Convention were submitted to the

---

[41] "It is believed that it is immaterial whether the reservation be made before, at, or after signing, as until a Power has ratified and deposited ratifications of the Convention it is not bound. But good faith requires that objections to any article be stated either before or at the time of signing, so that nations may know the nature and extent of the obligations they are assuming with other nations. International conventions are often compromises, and the price of a compromise to a nation may be the very article which another nation excludes from the convention or interprets in a special sense in the act of ratification." Scott, *op. cit.*, p. xxviii. See also *supra*, note 37.

[42] The following draft of a Protocol of Jan. 2, 1892, is printed in Malloy, Treaties, etc., p. 1990, following the African Slave Trade General act of 1890:

"The undersigned . . . met at the Ministry of Foreign Affairs at Brussels, in pursuance of Article XCIX of the General Act of July 2, 1890, and in execution of the Protocol of July 2, 1891, with a view to preparing a certificate of the deposit of the ratifications of such of the signatory powers as were unable to make such deposit at the meeting of July 2, 1891.

"His Excellency the Minister of France declared that the President of the Republic, in his ratification of the Brussels General Act had provisionally reserved, until a subsequent understanding should be reached, Articles XXI, XXII, XXIII, and XLII to LXI. The representatives . . ., acknowledged to the Minister of France the deposit of the ratifications of the President of the French Republic, as well as of the exception bearing upon Articles XXI, XXII, XXIII, and XLII to LXI.

"It is understood that the powers which have ratified the General Act in its entirety, acknowledge that they are reciprocally bound as regards all its clauses.

"It is likewise understood that these powers shall not be bound toward those which shall have ratified it partially, save within the limits of the engagements assumed by the latter powers.

Senate and question might arise as to their validity, though undoubtedly, after a considerable lapse of time, the foreign nation would be entitled to assume tacit acceptance of its reservation.[43]

29. *Exchange of Ratifications under Authority of the President.*

Even after the treaty has been ratified[44] by both parties and interpretations, reservations or amendments properly consented to, the foreign nation can not hold the United States bound until ratifications have been exchanged.[45] This act, performed under authority of the President,[46] gives the treaty complete international validity, which, so far as international obligations are concerned, is then held to date back to the time of signature unless expressly stated otherwise in the treaty itself.[47]

"Finally, it is understood that, as regards the powers that have partially ratified, the matters forming the subject of Articles XLII to LXI, shall continue, until a subsequent agreement is adopted to be governed by the stipulations and arrangements now in force."

The United States Senate resolution of ratification expressly accepted the French reservation and made another which was consented to by the powers prior to deposit of ratification. *Supra,* note 27.

[43] It does not appear that the Senate had an opportunity to consider the reservation to the Sanitary Convention of 1903 made by Persia on deposit of ratifications. (Malloy, p. 2129.) The Procès-verbal of ratification contains reservations by Great Britain and the United States also but these were proposed at signature. (Miller, *op. cit.,* pp. 112–117.) In its resolution of ratification the Senate failed to note the reservations made at signature either by the American or foreign plenipotentiaries. President Roosevelt hesitated to ratify the convention but did so when informed by the French Government that reservations attached to signature became part of the treaty and so had been in reality accepted by the Senate. (*Ibid.,* pp. 117–119.)

[44] Ratification in the United States is under authority of the President alone and he may refuse to ratify treaties after the Senate has consented. Shepherd *v.* Insurance Co., 40 Fed. 341; Taft, Our Chief Magistrate, and His Powers, p. 106; Crandall, *op. cit.,* pp. 81, 94, 97; Willoughby, *op. cit.,* 1: 466; Black, Constitutional Law, p. 124; Foster, Practice of Diplomacy, p. 279; Spooner, Sen. from Wis., *Cong. Rec.,* 59th Cong., 1st Sess., p. 1419, quoted Corwin, *op. cit.,* p. 175. See also colloquy Senators Reed, Mo., and Brandegee, Conn., March 2, 1920, *Cong. Rec.,* 59: 4032.

[45] Scott, *op. cit.,* p. xxvii; Foster, *op. cit.,* p. 280; Crandall, *op. cit.,* p. 6.
[46] Crandall, *op. cit.,* p. 93.
[47] Haver *v.* Yaker, 9 Wall. 32; Crandall, *op. cit.,* p. 343; Willoughby, *op. cit.,* 1: 517; Hall (Higgins ed.), *op. cit.,* 343, *supra,* sec. 15, note 14; *infra,* secs. 179, 180.

It thus appears that foreign nations recognize their duty to know the organization of the full treaty power under the Constitution. They recognize that the United States is not responsible for any instrument beyond the instructions of the negotiators and is not bound by a treaty, signed or ratified merely under authority of the President without advice and consent of the Senate. They have likewise recognized that reservations or amendments, not consented to by the whole treaty power, do not bind the United States unless there is reason to suppose that such action had taken place.

30. *Treaty Provisions Ultra Vires from Lack of Original Authority.*

Difficulties, however, arise in cases where the constitutional law defining the competence of the organ for making agreements is obscure. In such cases, is the foreign nation justified in accepting the President's interpretation of the Constitution? We must recall that the President is for them the only official source of information about the Constitution of the United States.[48] Following practice, the answer seems to depend upon whether the alleged want of competence arises (1) from a lack of original authority or (2) from operation of obscure constitutional limitations.

Foreign nations are supposed to know what organs the Constitution designates for concluding various types of international agreements. Thus they are supposed to know that in England power to make treaties is vested in the Crown in Council,[49] that in France:[50]

"The President of the Republic shall negotiate and ratify treaties. Treaties of peace and of commerce, treaties which involve the finances or the state, those relating to the person and property of French citizens in foreign countries, shall be ratified only after having been voted by the two chambers."

That in the United States. "The President shall have power, by and with the advice and consent of the Senate, to make treaties, provided two-thirds of the Senators present concur."[51] Until these organs have authorized ratification, foreign nations can not hold

---
[48] *Supra,* sec. 13.
[49] Anson, *op. cit.,* vol. 2, pt. 1, p. 54; pt. 2, p. 108.
[50] Constitutional Law of July 16, 1875, art. 8.
[51] Const. Art. II, sec. 2.

the nation bound even though the authority conducting negotiations neglected to inform them or informed them erroneously as to the organs with constitutional competence. However, all agreements are not treaties. Certain military agreements, such as armistices, are usually within the inherent power of the Commander-in-Chief. Others such as protocols and agreements of temporary effect are within the inherent power of the representative organ.[52] The President has often concluded such agreements, notably the preliminaries of peace to end the Spanish and World Wars. If he permits the other nation to understand that such action is within his constitutional authority, is the United States bound, even though the Senate subsequently take a contrary view? Opinions have differed in the United States[53] but foreign nations have actually held the United States bound.[54] We believe that in such cases the United States is bound only if the President actually is within the scope of his constitutional powers. However, the extent of these powers is so obscure that the foreign nation is justified in accepting the President's own view of his powers and holding the United States

[52] Crandall, *op. cit.*, p. 111; Willoughby, *op. cit.*, 1: 200–202, *infra*, secs. 161–172.

[53] President Wilson took the position that the agreement of Nov. 5, 1918, and earlier exchanges of notes, upon the basis of which the armistice of November 11, 1918, was concluded with Germany, rendered ratification of a treaty in accordance with those terms obligatory upon the United States. "I am ready," he said in a speech at Spokane, Washington, Sept. 12, 1919, "to fight from now until all the fight has been taken out of me by death to redeem the faith and promises of the United States." (Sen. Doc. No. 120, 66th Cong., 1st Sess., p. 173.) President Wilson and the German delegation agreed as to the obligation of the preliminary agreement but differed as to the concurrence of the treaty therewith. See also Wright, *Minn. Law Rev.*, 4: 35. The Senate appears to have paid little attention to arguments derived from the obligation of the preliminary agreements, in considering either the Spanish treaty of 1898 or the German treaty of 1919.

[54] Thus Spain insisted that the preliminaries of peace of Aug. 12, 1898, were a binding obligation and protested against proposed terms of the definitive treaty on the ground of conflict (Benton, Int. Law and Diplomacy of Spanish-American War, Baltimore, 1908, p. 244) and Germany protested against proposed terms of the treaty of Versailles on the ground of conflict with the preliminary exchange of notes of Nov. 5, 1918. (See Text of German note of May 29, 1919, Int. Conciliation, 1919, p. 1203, and Official Summary, 66th Cong., 1st Sess., Senate Doc. No. 149, p. 83.)

ACTS AND UTTERANCES OF NATIONAL ORGANS. 55

accordingly unless that view is very obviously erroneous, *i.e.,* unless the agreement in question is obviously of sufficient permanence and importance to constitute a "treaty."

31. *Treaty Provisions Ultra Vires from Operation of Constitutional Limitations.*

When an alleged want of constitutional competence in the agreement-making power arises from the operation of an obscure constitutional limitation, the foreign nation would seem entitled to accept the ostensible competence of the agreement-making authority absolutely and to hold the nation accordingly. Thus in England, if the Crown in Council ratifies a treaty on its own responsibility, the other party is entitled to insist upon its validity, even though the treaty is of a character which, according to the law of the Constitution, should have been submitted to parliament before ratification, if indeed there are any such.[55] So the United States is bound by all agreements ratified by the treaty-making power, even though it may subsequently appear that the treaty-making power acted in disregard of limitations imposed by the guarantees of the Constitution in favor of individual, state or other rights.[56]

Thus in negotiation of the Webster-Ashburton treaty involving a fixing of the Maine boundary and the cession to Great Britain of land claimed by that state, the British government was aware of the doubt which existed as to the competence of the United States treaty-making power to cede territory belonging to the state without that state's consent. They, therefore, refused to negotiate until assured by authority of the President that the constitutional difficulty had been eliminated, an assurance which was made possible by Maine's consent to the cession.[57] So also, in 1854 France

---

[55] *Supra,* note 49.

[56] "The fundamental laws of a state may withhold from the executive department the power of transferring what belongs to the state; but if there be no express provision of that kind, the inference is, that it has confided to the department charged with the power of making treaties, a discretion commensurate with all the great interests, and wants, and necessities of the nation. (Kent, Commentaries, 1: 166.)

[57] "The negotiations for a convention to settle the boundary question can hardly be said to have made any positive progress, since last year. . . . The interest of both parties, undoubtedly, requires a compromise, and I have

contended that the United States continued bound by the provision of the treaty of 1852 granting consuls immunity from compulsory process to serve as witnesses, in spite of the American contention that the provision was in violation of the guarantee of compulsory process for obtaining witnesses to persons accused of crime in the Fifth Amendment of the Constitution, and thus beyond the competence of the treaty-making power. The United States acquiesced after a considerable controversy and made amends for the arrest of the French consul which had actually occurred, although instructions were issued to avoid the inclusion of such provisions in future treaties.[58]

It appears that foreign nations are expected to know what organs are authorized by the Constitution to conclude international agreements of various kinds, but with respect to constitutional limitations upon the power of these organs, they are entitled to infer from the statements or silence of the President at the time, that the Constitution has been followed.

"It is a principle of international law," says Willoughby, "that one Nation in its dealings with another Nation is not required to know, and, therefore, is not held to be bound by, the peculiar constitutional structure of

---

no doubt that the position which Maine has assumed is the only obstacle to bringing such a compromise about. The English government can not treat with us about a compromise, unless we say we have authority to consummate what we agree to; and although I entertain not the slightest doubt of the just authority of this government to settle this question by compromise, as well as in any other way, yet in the present position of affairs, I suppose it will not be prudent to stir, in the direction of compromise without the consent of Maine." (Mr. Webster, Sec. of State, to Mr. Kent, Gov. of Maine, Dec. 21, 1841, Moore, Digest, 5: 174, *infra*, sec. 50.) The terms of the agreement with Maine and Massachusetts were included in article 5 of the treaty with Great Britain. The same principle doubtless applies to constitutional limitation upon the treaty power arising from rights guaranteed to individuals and the rights and privileges of departments of the national government as well as rights guaranteed the states. The tendency, however, has been to minimize the application of these limitations and where necessity presses as in treaties of peace to end a disastrous war, doubtless the ostensible authority of the executive even of a de facto government would fully bind the nation. (Kent, *op. cit.*, 1: 166-167, Wright, Am. Jl. Int. Law, 13: 249-250, *infra*, sec. 32.)

[58] Moore, Digest, 5: 80, 167. *Infra*, secs. 45, 46.

that other Nation. It is required, indeed, to know what is the governmental organ through which treaties are to be ratified." [59]

32. *Treaty Made under Necessity.*

One general exception to this rule may be noticed. In case of necessity any treaty whatever, even if made under mere *de facto* authority, is valid under international law. While international law recognizes coercion of the negotiators of a treaty as grounds for voiding a treaty, it does not so recognize coercion of the state.[60] All commentators agree that in case an unfortunate war necessitated, the treaty power might cede state territory without state consent or impair the Republican form of government in a state by accepting a monarchical protectorate.[61] This would be valid even though the government under the Constitution were overthrown and a *de facto* government with neither President nor Senate set up in its stead were the only authority concerned in making the treaty. It has been suggested that the phraseology of Article VI, whereby treaties are supreme law if made "under the authority of the United States" and need not, as statutes, "be made in pursuance" of the Constitution, gives authority for this plenary power of treaty making.[62] If that were accepted, however, it would free the treaty power of constitutional restrictions in times of tranquility as well as of necessity, a view which is not accepted. The better view seems to admit that such a treaty would be unconstitutional in its origin but would be valid under international law upon the principle of self-preservation.

---

[59] Willoughby, *op. cit.*, 1: 515.
[60] Crandall, *op. cit.*, p. 4.
[61] Crandall, *op. cit.*, pp. 227–229; Wright, *Am. Jl. Int. Law,* 13: 250.
[62] See Congressman D. J. Lewis, Feb. 17, 1917, *Cong. Rec.,* 64th Cong., 2d Sess., p 4205, quoted, Wright, *Am. Jl. Int. Law,* 13: 249, and Holmes, J. in Mo. *v.* Holland, U. S. Sup. Ct., April 19, 1920: "Acts of Congress are the supreme law of the land only when made in pursuance of the Constitution, while treaties are declared to be so when made under the authority of the United States. It is open to question whether the authority of the United States means more than the formal acts prescribed to make the convention." See also Kent, Commentaries, 1: 166, 176. The different phraseology was actually introduced to assure the validity of treaties concluded by the United States before 1789. Rawle, On the Constitution, p. 60; Farrand, *op. cit.*, 2: 417.

C. *With Reference to the Meeting of International Responsibilities.*

33. *United States Bound by International Law and Treaties.*

Are foreign nations entitled to consider the President's interpretation of the international responsibilities of the United States as authoritative? We have noticed that the United States as a sovereign nation, is under international responsibilities, only in so far as such responsibilities have been accepted by organs acting within their apparent constitutional powers.[63] General international law is presumed to have been tacitly accepted by the United States on becoming a member of the family of nations.[64] Treaties are formal

---

[63] *Supra,* sec. 24.

[64] Maine, International Law, N. Y., 1888, p. 37, *infra,* sec. 258. Duponceau, Jurisdiction of the Courts of the U. S., Philadelphia, 1824, p. 3, has expressed the same view: "The law of nations, being the common law of the civilized world, may be said indeed to be a part of the law of every civilized nation; but it stands on other and higher grounds than municipal customs, statutes, edicts or ordinances. It is binding on every people and on every government. It is to be carried into effect at all times under the penalty of being thrown out of the pale of civilization or involving the country in war. Every branch of the national administration, each within its district and its particular jurisdiction, is bound to administer it. It defines offenses and affixes punishments and acts everywhere *propria vigore,* whenever it is not altered or modified by particular national statutes or usages not inconsistent with its great and fundamental principles. Whether there is or not a national common law in other respects, this *universal common law* can never cease to be the rule of executive and judicial proceedings until mankind shall return to the savage state." The Supreme Court said in Ware *v.* Hylton, through Wilson, J.: "When the United States declared their independence, they were bound to receive the law of nations in its modern state of purity and refinement." (3 Dall. 199, 281, 1796.) So also Secretary of State Webster: "Every nation, on being received, at her own request, into the circle of civilized governments, must understand that she not only attains rights of sovereignty and the dignity of national character, but that she binds herself also to the strict and faithful observance of all those principles, laws and usages which have obtained currency among civilized states and which have for their object the mitigation of the miseries of war." (Letter to Mr. Thompson, Minister to Mexico, April 15, 1842, Moore, Digest, 1: 5.) Willoughby calls attention to the evidence that the United States actually has accepted general international law: "The federal constitution provides that Congress shall have the power to define and punish offenses against the law of nations, and to make rules concerning captures on land and water. Furthermore, it is declared that treaties made under the authority of the United States shall be the supreme law of

ACTS AND UTTERANCES OF NATIONAL ORGANS. 59

modifications of the general law of nations with respect to the parties, and are only valid when *expressly* accepted through ratification by the proper constitutional process. But when consent has been given whether tacitly or expressly, foreign nations can hold the United States bound for the future.

34. *Decisions by the President.*

We have noticed that international law requires that every independent government maintain a representative organ able to discuss with and give satisfaction to foreign nations for demands based on international law and treaty.[65] We have seen that foreign nations have recognized the President acting through the Department of State as the representative organ of the United States.[66] It follows that, with respect to the meeting of international responsibilities, foreign nations are entitled to accept the President's opinion as the authoritative voice of the United States. Thus if the President admits that international law or treaty requires the payment of a sum of money, the cession of territory, the dispatch of military forces, the delivery of a fugitive, or the release of an alien held in custody, the foreign nation can hold the United States bound to perform such an act, even though Congress, or the states or whatever other organ may be endowed with the necessary legal power to act has not been consulted.

In practice foreign nations have acted on this theory. Where the President has given an opinion against the contention of a foreign nation, that nation may of course continue discussion until a decision has been reached satisfactory to it or authorized by an arbitration court or other body by whose decision it has agreed to be bound. Where, however, the President has acknowledged the justice of a foreign claim, the foreign nation has held the United States bound. Thus in the McLeod case, the Italian lynching cases

---

the land. The effect of these clauses which recognize the existence of a body of international laws and the granting to Congress of the power to punish offenses against them, the courts have repeatedly held is to adopt these laws into our municipal law *en bloc* except where Congress or the treaty-making power has expressly changed them." (*Op. cit.*, p. 1018.)

[65] *Supra,* sec. 11.
[66] *Supra,* sec. 12.

and the Panama Canal tolls controversy the ultimate acknowledgment by the President of an obligation to return McLeod,[67] to pay damages[68] and to charge equal tolls upon American vessels using the Canal[69] made the cases *res adjudicata*.

In many cases it would doubtless be expedient, in some it is required by constitutional law,[70] and in others it is required by constitutional understanding,[71] that the President assure himself of the needed cooperation of other departments before interpreting an international responsibility or acknowledging a specific obligation flowing therefrom, but the foreign nation is not obliged to concern itself with such questions. It is entitled to present all international claims to the President and to hold his voice as the voice of the nation with respect to their settlement.

35. *Decisions by Subordinates to the President.*

This is true of agents acting under authority of the President unless their action is promptly repudiated by the President. Thus if a representative of the President should sit in the Council of the League of Nations and admit that a guarantee undertaken by treaty by the United States required the use of armed forces in a specific manner under existing circumstances, the United States would be bound to carry out the treaty in that precise manner.[72] The proposed Hitchcock reservation to Article X of the Covenant, while not impairing the obligation of the United States to fulfill

---

[67] Moore, Digest, 6: 261.

[68] Moore, Digest, 6: 839, 849.

[69] "In my own judgment, very fully considered and maturely formed, that exemption . . . is in plain contravention of the treaty with Great Britain concerning the canal, concluded on November 18, 1901." (President Wilson, Message to Congress, March 5, 1914, *Cong. Rec.*, 51: 4313.)

[70] *Infra*, secs. 143–145.

[71] *Infra*, sec. 251.

[72] This interpretation of the Covenant is contained in the Swiss official commentary. "The Council may formulate *obligatory* advice unanimously only and solely for its own members and for other states invited in the specific instance to be represented on the Council, Art. 4, par. 5." This implies that for states whose representatives have consented, the advice is obligatory. See the League of Nations, published by the World Peace Foundation, III, No. 3, p. 125.

ACTS AND UTTERANCES OF NATIONAL ORGANS.   61

the guarantee, transferred the representative powers of the President to Congress in this respect, by indicating that the representative on the Council was not competent to acknowledge an obligation owed by the United States and expressly stating that Congress remained free to interpret the obligation according to its own "conscience and judgment."[73] The same result could of course be obtained by transferring control of the American representative in the Council to the Congress, but this, as proved by the experience of congressional control of diplomats during the revolutionary period, would hardly be expedient.[74]

36. *Decisions by International Organs Authorized by the President.*

The same binding obligation flows from the decisions of international courts of justice or arbitration acting on cases submitted by the President. As the President can himself interpret the obligations of the United States, or do so through agents in conference with the representatives of other nations, so he can do so through

---

[73] Article X reads: "The members of the League undertake to respect and preserve as against external aggression the territorial integrity and existing political independence of all Members of the League. In case of any such aggression the Council shall advise upon the means by which this obligation shall be fulfilled." The proposed Hitchcock reservation reads: "That the advice, mentioned in Article X of the Covenant of the League, which the Council may give to the member nations as to the employment of their naval and military forces, is merely advice, which each member nation is free to accept or reject, according to the conscience and judgment of its then existing government, and in the United States this advice can be accepted only by action of the Congress at the time, it being Congress alone, under the Constitution of the United States, having the power to declare war." The proposed Lodge reservation to Article X did not affect merely the authority to interpret Article X, but under it the United States refused to accept the guarantee of Article X altogether. For text of these reservations and notes upon the votes received in the Senate, see The League of Nations, III, No. 4 (August, 1920).

[74] See Hamilton, The Federalist, No. 22, Ford ed., p. 141; and Fish, American Diplomacy, N. Y., 1916, pp. 60, 77; "The experience of the Continental Congress was most useful to the country. . . . It had made it clear that a most serious defect was in the absence of an executive, clothed with sufficient power and dignity to properly conduct intercourse with foreign sovereigns. . . . An attempt had been made to supply these wants by the creation of various committees or boards. . . . The experience of the confederation with its various boards was most unsatisfactory and sometimes pathetic." Foster, Century of Am. Diplomacy, N. Y., 1901, pp. 103-104.

submission to an international court. It is true that under the contitution, such submissions must, if involving national claims or claims against the United States, be by general or special treaty to which the Senate has consented,[75] but since the function of a court of arbitration is to decide on obligations and not to make agreements, the foreign nation is not obliged to take cognizance of such constitutional provisions. It can hold the arbitrated case *res adjudicata* even though the President exceeded his powers in submitting it.[76]

37. *Meeting Responsibilities Distinguished from Making Agreements.*

It will be observed that while foreign nations are entitled to accept the President's statements absolutely with respect to meeting international responsibilities, it can only accept them presumptively with respect to making international agreements. It is, therefore, important to distinguish between these two acts. Usually the line is clear enough. In the case of treaties, steps up to and including the exchange of ratifications are making the treaty steps afterward are meeting the responsibility. Thus the Senate has a part in the making of treaties as it must give its advice and consent before ratification. The House of Representatives, however, is concerned only with meeting responsibilities under them as pointed out by President Washington in the controversy over the Jay treaty.[77] One hundred and twenty-five years later Former Secretary of State Root explained the same point.[78]

" The making of a treaty . . . is a solemn assurance to all the nations that (the subject matter) is within the treaty making power and that the promise to make war binds Congress as fully as it binds all other members

---

[75] *Infra*, sec. 148.

[76] " Recourse to arbitration implies an engagement to submit in good faith to the award." I Hague Conventions, 1907, act. 37. See also *infra*, sec. 62.

[77] Message to House of Rep., March 30, 1796. Richardson, Messages, 1: 195, Moore, Digest, 5: 225.

[78] Telegram to Governor Cox, October 21, 1920. See also Hamilton, Pacificus Paper, quoted Corwin, The President's Control of Foreign Relations, p. 14; Taft, *op. cit.*, p. 115.

ACTS AND UTTERANCES OF NATIONAL ORGANS.   63

of our government to maintain the plighted faith of the United States. In all governments the power to declare war rests somewhere, and an agreement to make war is an agreement that that power shall be so exercised by the officers in whom it rests. A refusal of Congress to pass the necessary resolution would simply be a breach of the treaty."

Consequently though failure of the Senate to consent can be offered to foreign nations as a valid excuse for non-ratification,[79] failure of the House of Representatives to pass an appropriation, declare war or take other measures necessary to give effect to a ratified treaty can not be offered as an excuse for avoiding the responsibility.[80]

"If a treaty," says Dana, "requires the payment of money, or any other special act, which cannot be done without legislation, the treaty is still binding on the nation; and it is the duty of the nation to pass the necessary laws. If that duty is not performed, the result is a breach of the treaty by the nation, just as much as if the breach had been an affirmative act by any other department of the government. Each nation is responsible for the right working of the internal system, by which it distributes its sovereign functions; and, as foreign nations dealing with it cannot be permitted to interfere with or control these, so they are not to be affected or concluded by them to their own injury."

38. *Interpretation of Treaties.*

But what of the interpretation of a treaty? Is interpretation a step in the making, or in the execution of the treaty? Interpretation is essentially a judicial function but there has been a long controversy as to whether judges make law or merely apply it. The familiar saying of Bishop Hoadley, "Whoever hath an absolute authority to interpret any written or spoken laws, it is he who is truly the law giver to all intents and purposes," points to the former

---

[79] *Supra,* secs. 24–26.

[80] Dana, note to Wheaton, Int. Law, sec. 543, p. 715. See also Willoughby, *op. cit.,* p. 515; Moore, Digest, 5: 230. "A treaty though complete in itself, and the unquestioned law of the land, may be inexecutable without the aid of an act of Congress. But it is the constitutional duty of Congress to pass the requisite laws. But the need of further legislation, however, does not affect the question of the legal force of the treaty per se." Cushing, Att. Gen., 6 Op. 291, 1854; Moore, Digest, 5: 226, 370.

view.[81] The true distinction seems to depend upon the *generality* or *concreteness* of the interpretation. Where judicial interpretations of the law extend to merely the case before them, judges do not make law. Where their opinions furnish precedents for the future they do. Thus if an interpretation of law merely renders the controversy *res adjudicata,* it is not law-making. If, on the other hand, the principle *stare decisis* is applied the interpretation assumes a legislative character.[82]

The same distinction exists in the decision of international controversies. A decision upon the applicability of a treaty, or a principle of international law *to a particular case,* and the determination of the obligation resulting therefrom, has to do with the meeting of the responsibility and not with the making of the treaty or the principle of law. Consequently foreign nations are entitled to hold a controversy upon which decision has been made under authority of the President, *res adjudicata.* But can they regard such a decision and the interpretation of international law or treaty upon which it is based as going farther than this and as binding the United States when similar controversies arise in the future.[83]

"The President," says ex-President Taft, "carries on the correspondence through the State Department with all foreign countries. He is bound in such correspondence to discuss the proper construction of treaties. He must state our attitude upon questions constantly arising. While strictly he may not bind our government as a treaty would bind it, to a definition of its rights, still in future discussions foreign Secretaries of other countries are wont to look for support of their contentions to the declarations and admissions of our Secretaries of State in other controversies as in a sense binding upon us. There is thus much practical framing of our foreign policies in the executive conduct of our foreign relations.

---

[81] Sermon preached before the King, 1717, Works, 15th ed., p. 12, Gray, Nature and Sources of the Law, pp. 100, 120. "Statutory construction is practically one of the greatest of executive powers. . . . One might say, . . . Let any one make the laws of the country if I can construe them." (Taft, Our Chief Magistrate, p. 78.) "I recognize that judges do and must legislate. But they can do so only interstitially: they are confined from molar to molecular motions." (Holmes, J., dissent in Southern Pacific *v.* Jensen, 244, U. S. 205, 1917.)

[82] See Gray, *op. cit.,* chap. IX, and especially sec. 498; Cooley, Constitutional Limitations, 6th ed., pp. 61-68.

[83] Taft, *op. cit.,* p. 113, see also *infra,* sec. 172.

"Whenever our American citizens have claims to present against a foreign nation, they do it through the President by the State Department and when foreign citizens have claims to present against us, they present them through their diplomatic representatives to our State Department, and the formulation and the discussion of the merits of those claims create an important body of precedents in our foreign policy."

As President Taft points out, it is inevitable that the principle of *stare decisis* will be of weight in the settlement of future controversies and consequently that executive practice will in fact establish an interpretation of responsibilities from which it will be difficult for future Presidents to escape. In theory, however, it is believed that foreign nations can not hold the United States absolutely bound by decisions or interpretations under authority of the President alone, except with reference to the specific controversy under discussion.[84] Thus explanatory or interpretive notes, designed to control the general application of a treaty in the future, are part of its making, whether they precede, accompany, or follow exchange of ratifications and do not internationally bind the United States unless foreign nations had reason to suppose that the full treaty power had consented to them.[85]

---

[84] In the Pious Fund Arbitration Case (U. S. *v.* Mexico), 1903, the court held that while the principle *stare decisis* was not wholly applicable to arbitration, the principle of *res adjudicata* was:

"Considering that all the parts of the judgment or the decree concerning the points debated in the litigation enlighten and mutually supplement each other, and that they all serve to render precise the meaning and the bearing of the dispositif (decisory part of the judgment) and to determine the points upon which there is *res judicata* and which thereafter can not be put in question;

"Considering that this rule applies not only to the judgments of tribunals created by the State, but equally to arbitral sentences rendered within the limits of the jurisdiction fixed by the compromise;

"Considering that this same principle should for a still stronger reason be applied to international arbitration, etc." (Wilson, Hague Arbitration Cases, Boston, 1915, p. 9.)

[85] The United States refused to consider itself bound by explanatory notes exchanged prior to exchange of ratification of the Mexican peace treaty of 1848 and the Clayton-Bulwer treaty of 1850 though Mexico and Great Britain protested. See Moore, Digest, 5: 205–206; Crandall, *op. cit.,* pp. 85, 381; Wright, *Minn. Law Rev.,* 4: 16; *supra*, secs. 27, 28. It has been the usual practice to submit such explanatory notes to the Senate. See Crandall, *op. cit.,* pp. 86–89; Moore, Digest, 5: 207, 284.

39. *Understandings do not Require Forbearance in Pressing International Claims.*

The distribution of constitutional powers among various organs in the national and state governments of the United States often makes it very difficult for the President actually to satisfy claims which he has admitted to be valid under international law. In fact these constitutional limitations are well known to foreign nations. The United States has sometimes urged such difficulties as an excuse for failure to meet the obligation promptly. While such a plea has no validity whatever, under international law[86] it remains to be seen whether there is an international understanding whereby nations withhold pressure on just claims in view of constitutional difficulties in the delinquent state.

> "Every nation," said Justice McLean, "may be presumed to know that, so far as the treaty stipulates to pay money, the legislative sanction is required. . . . And in such a case the representative of the people and the States exercise their own judgment in granting or withholding the money. They act upon their own responsibility and not upon the responsibility of the treaty-making power." [87]

The theory is attractive for delinquent states. Unfortunately for them it is not practiced. No such understanding of international law exists. The United States did not withhold pressure from France when she pleaded the refusal of her legislature to appropriate for carrying out the claims treaty of 1831.[88] Nor have European nations withheld pressure from the United States in similar circumstances. Congress has always, though generally with much protestation by the House of its untrammeled discretion, appropriated money where treaty or international law has required,[89] but the states have often failed in performing essential acts. Thus Louisiana failed to take sufficient interest in apprehending those

---

[86] See *supra*, sec. 33 *et seq.*

[87] Turner *v.* Am. Baptist Missionary Union, 5 McLean, 347, 1852, paraphrased in Wharton, Digest, 2: 73; Moore, Digest, 5: 222.

[88] President Jackson recommended reprisals on this occasion. (Moore, Digest, 7: 123–126.) See also note of Secretary of State Livingston to the French government, *supra*, chap. 1, note 3, and of Mr. Wheaton, Minister to Copenhagen, to Mr. Butler, Attorney General, Jan. 20, 1835. Wharton, Digest, 1: 36.

[89] *Infra*, secs. 149, 256.

ACTS AND UTTERANCES OF NATIONAL ORGANS. 67

guilty of lynching Italians in the nineties, nor did she take measures adequate to prevent the frequent repetition of these gross violations of the Italian treaty of 1871. In the state of congressional legislation the power of the national government to act within the states was not adequate and Italy was so informed but there was no abatement of diplomatic pressure. In fact, Italy at length withdrew her ambassador and the United States was forced to pay the indemnity demanded.[90]

Experience seems to show that it is unwise to assume the existence of such international understandings. Nations are wont to demand the pound of flesh. "To calculate upon real favors from nation to nation," said Washington, "is an illusion which experience must cure, which a just pride ought to discard." [91] Such understanding may be well to follow in pressing claims against others but to expect that others will observe them in pressing claims against us is unwise.[92] The United States should so modify its laws and the understandings of its own constitution that acknowledged obligations of the nation under international law and treaty will be promptly executed.

Thus from the standpoint of international law, the national authority for meeting international responsibilities is the important element in the control of foreign relations, and in the United States this authority is the President acting through the Secretary of State. Foreign nations are entitled to bring their grievances to him and to expect from him redress according to the standard of international law and treaty. Constitutional limitations upon his power to effect the redress are to them unknown, either by law or understanding. With the making of international agreements on the other hand

---

[90] Moore, Digest, 6: 838 *et seq.* See also *infra, secs.* 120, 149.

[91] Farewell Address, Sept. 17, 1796, Richardson, *op. cit.,* 1: 223.

[92] Vattel makes a similar distinction: " Since the *necessary* (natural or moral) law is at all times obligatory upon the conscience, a Nation must never lose sight of it when deliberating upon the course it must pursue to fulfill its duty; but when there is a question of what it can demand from other states, it must consult the *voluntary* (positive) law whose rules are devoted to the welfare and advancement of the universal society," *op. cit.,* Introduction, sec. 28.

foreign nations are entitled to assume no such Presidential omnipotence. The United States cannot be bound by new engagements until the organs designated by the Constitution have acted. In the *meeting* of international responsibilities, international law is prior, in the *making* of international engagements the Constitution is prior.

PART III.

Constitutional Limitations upon the Foreign Relations Power.

CHAPTER V.

LIMITATIONS UPON STATE POWERS.

40. *Position of the Foreign Relations Power under Constitutional Law.*

From the standpoint of international law the essential element in the foreign relations power of any state is the authority recognized by foreign states as representing the state and competent to meet its international responsibilities. We have seen that in the United States this authority is the President acting through the Department of State. Foreign states with claims or complaints need know nothing of constitutional powers or limitations. They are entitled to present their cases to the President through the State Department and to demand of him satisfaction according to the measure of international law and treaty. If he is unable to obtain it the United States is liable to such measures of redress as international law may permit the claimant state.

In sharp contrast, is the position of the foreign relations power under constitutional law. The question is not of responsibility but of power. Under constitutional law the foreign relations power consists of those organs of government competent to perform the various acts connected with the conduct of foreign relations. These acts may be classified as (1) the meeting of international responsibilities, (2) the making of international agreements (3) the making of national decisions of international importance. The first includes the observance and enforcement of international law and treaty. The second includes the settlement of international controversies and the making of treaties. The third includes the recognition of facts and the declaration of policies of international significance. Before considering the constitutional authority for performing these acts, however, it will be well to recall certain fundamental principles of the Constitution.

41. *Relation Between State and National Powers.*

Under American constitutional law the legal competence of any organ is determined by two factors, the authorization of power and restrictions upon the exercise of power. With one hand the people are supposed to have granted certain powers expressed in written constitutions, to be exercised by governmental organs, for the general welfare,[1] but with the other hand they are supposed to have taken away in part the powers thus granted through restrictions upon their exercise expressed in bills of rights, guarantees and prohibitions for the protection of private individuals, subordinate governmental areas and particular organs of the government.[2] The authority for all powers exercised by organs of the national government comes from the federal Constitution either by express or implied delegation. The authority for all powers exercised by state governments comes from their own Constitutions and may include all governmental powers the exercise of which does not conflict with the full exercise of its delegated powers by the national government, and is not expressly prohibited by the federal Constitution. This theory of the division of governmental authority between national and state governments is set forth in the tenth amendment and the sixth article of the federal Constitution.

---

[1] "The theory of our political system is that the ultimate sovereignty is in the people, from whom springs all legislative authority." Cooley, Constitutional Limitations, 6th ed., p. 39, citing McLean, J., in Spooner *v.* McConnell, 1 McLean 347, Waite, C. J., in Minor *v.* Happersett, 21 Wall. 162, 172, etc. For influence of the theories of popular sovereignty and the social contract on the constitutional fathers, see Merriam, Am. Political Theories, N. Y., 1903, p. 38; Willoughby, Am. Constitutional System, N. Y., 1904, p. 23 *et seq.*

[2] The theory of constitutional limitations derived from the dogma of separation of powers and from the supposed division of sovereignty between the state and nation was prominent in the federal convention, but the Federalist (No. 84) thought a bill of rights unimportant. The Jeffersonian Republicans took a different view and succeeded in having the first ten amendments attached to the Constitution, thereby following the usual custom in state constitutions. See Cooley, *op. cit.*, chap. ix, p. 311 *et seq.* For influence of theories of separation of powers, divided sovereignty, and natural rights upon the constitutional fathers, see Merriam, *op. cit.*, pp. 107, 146, and Willoughby, *loc. cit.*

LIMITATIONS UPON STATE POWERS.

"The powers not delegated to the United States by the Constitution, nor prohibited by it to the States, are reserved to the States respectively or to the people.

"This Constitution, and the Laws of the United States which shall be made in Pursuance thereof; and all Treaties made, or which shall be made, under the Authority of the United States, shall be the supreme law of the Land; and the Judges in every State shall be bound thereby, any Thing in the Constitution or Laws of any State to the Contrary notwithstanding."

The system may be characterized by the three phrases: national delegated powers, state residual powers, and national supremacy.[3]

42. *Constitutional Prohibitions of State Power.*

Restrictions upon the exercise of state power may exist by virtue of (1) express or implied constitutional prohibitions or (2) as a result of action taken by national governmental organs. Constitutional restrictions may be expressed in the state's own Constitution or in the federal Constitution. In the latter are several express restrictions upon the exercise of state power. Some are for the protection of private rights such as the prohibition of laws impairing the obligation of contracts, *ex post facto* laws and laws depriving persons of life, liberty and property without due process of law.[4] Others are intended to insure the centralization of power in matters of national interest, especially in the control of foreign relations. Such are the prohibitions against treaty making, war making, import, export and tonnage duties.[5] In addition are several prohibitions implied from the nature of the federal union such as the prohibitions against secession[6] and the taxation of agencies of the national government.[7] Other prohibitions have been implied from the necessarily exclusive character of certain powers delegated to the national government such as the power to regulate foreign commerce, except purely local regulations, and to provide for the naturalization of aliens.[8]

---

[3] See Willoughby, Const. Law, pp. 53, 78.
[4] Constitution, Art. I, sec. 10, cl. 1, Amendment XIV.
[5] *Ibid.*, Art. I, sec. 10.
[6] Texas *v.* White, 7 Wall. 700 (1868).
[7] McCulloch *v.* Md., 4 Wheat. 316, 432; Dobbins *v.* Erie County, 16 Pet. 435.
[8] Willoughby, *op. cit.*, pp. 73-74; J. P. Hall, Constitutional Law, pp. 254, 288; Cooley *v.* Port Wardens, 12 How. 299; Chirac *v.* Chirac, 2 Wheat. 259.

74   THE CONTROL OF AMERICAN FOREIGN RELATIONS.

43. *Action of National Organs Limiting State Powers.*

State powers may also be restricted in their exercise by the principle of national supremacy. As national organs exercise more and more of their concurrent powers, state powers are correspondingly reduced. For example when Congress passes bankruptcy statutes or statutes fixing standards of weights and measures, the state's power in these fields is lost and state statutes on the subject automatically cease to operate though if the national statute is repealed they automatically come into force again.[9]

The state police power has been greatly restricted by the more complete exercise by the national government of its powers to regulate interstate commerce, to establish postoffices and post roads and to tax.[10] No less remarkable, however, has been the reduction of state powers through the exercise of national powers relating to foreign relations. Thus wars have justified legislation by Congress such as recently illustrated by the draft acts, acts authorizing railroad, telegraph, food and fuel control, and acts punishing espionage and disloyal conduct. These have all entered fields ordinarily within state control. Similar reductions of state power but in less degree have resulted from a state of neutrality and the consequent operation of laws punishing offenses against neutrality, authorizing national censorship of telegraph and radio communication and a closer supervision of commercial transactions. Even in time of peace the exercise of foreign relations powers has shown a tendency to narrow state power. Thus Congress has extended the jurisdiction of federal courts over many cases involving treaty interpretation, over numerous controversies where aliens or persons especially protected by international law are parties, and over many offenses against international law and treaty. Congress has also given national officers authority to enforce such treaties as those protecting migratory birds, and fish in boundary waters, and those requiring extradition of criminals and prohibition of the white slave traffic. Many self-executing treaties have limited state power

---

[9] Willoughby, *op. cit.,* pp. 74, 779.

[10] See Cushman, The Police Power of the National Government, 1920, reprinted from the *Minn. Law Rev.,* vols. 3, 4.

without congressional action such as those according property and personal rights to aliens.[11]

Although this limitation of state powers by action of national organs has been a patent phenomenon, its constitutionality has been questioned, especially so far as effected through exercise by the national government of its power over foreign relations. Thus it has been alleged that all state powers are not merely residual but that some, for instance the police power, are "reserved" powers incapable of limitation by any exercise of its delegated powers by the national government. It will readily be seen that this notion is wholly incompatible with the principle of national supremacy and while it has great historic importance, it never commanded wholehearted support from the courts and at present enjoys no legal recognition.[12] The concept of "reserved" powers is, however, of importance as an "understanding" of the Constitution. In practice both Congress and the treaty-making power have sometimes refrained from fully exercising their powers out of respect for state susceptibilities, and the courts have sometimes given rather strained interpretations to treaties for the same reason.[13]

We may conclude that state exercises of power in the field of foreign relations have been so restricted that such powers hardly exist at all.

---

[11] See Corwin, National Supremacy, N. Y., 1913; Sutherland, Constitutional Power and World Affairs, N. Y., 1919.

[12] *Infra.*, secs. 48–51.

[13] *Infra,* sec. 50.

CHAPTER VI.

Limitations upon National Powers: Private Rights and States' Rights.

A. Private Rights.

44. *Nature of Prohibitions*.

Restriction upon the exercise of power by national organs may be expressed in the federal Constitution or implied from the rights guaranteed the states and individuals and the independence guaranteed the departments of government by the federal Constitution. Whether stated in the negative form of a prohibition against the national government or in the positive form of a right or privilege guaranteed the individual, state, or particular organ of government, the effect is the same.

These restrictions fall into three groups. (1) Some are in behalf of the states, as those prohibiting anti-slave-trade laws before 1808 and the freeing of fugitive slaves;[1] those prohibiting direct taxes except in proportion to population, export taxes and discriminatory commercial or revenue regulations or tariffs;[2] those prohibiting the formation of new states within the jurisdiction of existing states or the junction of states without their consent;[3] and those implied from the guarantee to the states of territorial integrity, a Republican form of government and immunity of their necessary governmental organs from taxation.[4] (2) A second class of restrictions is in behalf of the separation of powers as that prohibiting members of the House or Senate from holding any office under the United States,[5] that prohibiting appropriations except by "law,"[6] and those implied from the privileges expressly guaranteed

---
[1] Constitution, I, sec. 9, cl. 1; IV, sec. 2, cl. 3.
[2] *Ibid.*, I, sec. 9, cl. 4–6; sec. 8, cl. 1.
[3] *Ibid.*, IV, sec. 3, cl. 1, 2.
[4] *Ibid.*, IV, sec. 4. See also *infra*, sec. 48.
[5] *Ibid.*, I, sec. 6, cl. 2.
[6] *Ibid.*, I, sec. 9, cl. 7.

certain organs or from the separation of the legislative, executive and judicial departments.[7] (3) The most numerous prohibitions are in behalf of individual rights and interests. Thus the individual's supposed interest in democratic government, Puritanic morals, and the general welfare are protected by prohibitions against titles of nobility, the acceptance by officers of foreign presents, the abridgment of the voting privilege on account of race, color, previous condition of servitude, or sex;[8] by prohibitions against slavery and intoxicating beverages,[9] and by the implied prohibition against taxes not for the "general welfare."[10] The individual's interest in life, liberty and property are especially protected by prohibitions against suspension of the privilege of habeas corpus except in emergency, bills of attainder and ex post facto laws;[11] prohibitions against religious tests for officers, against the establishment of religion, the abridgment of the freedom of speech, press, assembly, petition and the bearing of arms;[12] prohibitions against compulsory quartering of troops in time of peace, unreasonable searches and seizures, the taking of life, liberty or property without due process of law and the taking of private property for public use without just compensation,[13] and finally prohibitions designed to assure a fair trial, especially in criminal cases, as the requirement of jury trial and compulsory process to obtain witnesses and the prohibition against excessive bail, double jeopardy, cruel and unusual punishments.[14] Prohibitions for the protection of individual interests have seldom affected the power of national organs in the conduct of foreign relations.

---

[7] See *infra*, secs. 52–55.
[8] *Ibid.*, I, sec. 9, cl. 8; Amendments XV, XIX.
[9] *Ibid.*, Amendments XIII, XVIII.
[10] *Ibid.*, I, sec. 8, cl. 1. See also Willoughby, *op. cit.*, p. 39; J. P. Hall, Constitutional Law, pp. 173–174.
[11] *Ibid.*, I, sec. 9, cl. 2, 3.
[12] *Ibid.*, VI, sec. 3, Amendments I–II.
[13] *Ibid.*, Amendments III–V.
[14] *Ibid.*, III, sec. 2, cl. 3; sec. 3; Amendments V–VIII.

45. *Effect upon Power to Meet International Responsibilities.*

Such guarantees have not interfered with the meeting of responsibilities imposed by international law or treaty.[15] They are not applicable exterritorially, thus do not interfere with the carrying out of treaties giving American consular courts jurisdiction over crimes committed by American citizens abroad. It was held that such a consular court in Japan was not obliged to accord jury trial in criminal cases.[16] Nor have constitutional guarantees interfered with the execution of treaties for the internment of belligerent troops entering the territory when the United States is neutral, the return of seamen deserting from foreign vessels, and the extradition of criminals found within the United States. Compliance with the terms of the treaty has been held to accord the person subject to internment,[17] return[18] or extradition[19] the " due process of law " required by the Vth Amendment. It is, however, doubtful whether an extradition authorized by the President in the absence of treaty would be legal though one Arguelles was thus extradited to Spain under authority of President Lincoln in 1864.[20]

Doubt has been expressed as to the power of the United States to execute treaties requiring the punishment of persons for certain acts, such as the acceptance of letters of marque, therein described

---

[15] Most Constitutional Limitations cannot affect the power *to execute* treaties, because they apply to the treaty-making power as well as other organs of government. Consequently if an apparent treaty proved inexecutable by virtue of a constitutional limitation, it would really be no treaty at all, but *ultra vires* and void from the start. See *Infra*, sec. 46. As we have noticed, however, the United States would be bound by such an obligation because the foreign government cannot be presumed to know of obscure constitutional limitations. *Supra,* sec. 31. See also Willoughby, *op. cit.,* p. 515.

[16] *In re Ross,* 140 U. S. 453 (1890).

[17] *Ex Parte Toscano,* 208 Fed. Rept. 938.

[18] Tucker *v.* Alexandroff, 183 U. S. 424 (1902); Moore, Digest, 6, 423.

[19] U. S. *v.* Jonathan Robbins, Bees Adm., 266; The British Prisoners, 1 Wood and Min. 66; Neeley *v.* Henkel, 180 U. S. 109 (1901), Moore, Digest, 6: 267, 270.

[20] Dicta in Terlinden *v.* Ames, 184 U. S. 271, 289 (1902), and Tucker *v.* Alexandroff, 183 U. S. 424, 431 (1902); Moore, Digest, 6: 247-253; Willoughby, *op. cit.,* p. 479.

PRIVATE RIGHTS AND STATES' RIGHTS. 79

as crimes.[21] There has also been doubt of its ability to punish those violating rights guaranteed by treaty or international law to resident aliens.[22] In these cases, however, the difficulty has arisen from the strictly statutory character of the jurisdiction of federal courts and not from constitutional guarantees. Congress is competent[23] and in fact has provided for the punishment of offenses of the first though not of the second character in federal courts.[24]

Constitutional guarantees do not seem to interfere with a due observance of the immunities guaranteed to foreign sovereigns, diplomats, naval and military forces, consuls, etc., by international law or treaty. Thus foreign diplomatic officers have been considered immune from compulsory attendance as witnesses.[25] In a case where the accused claimed a constitutional right to have a French consul subpoenaed as a witness in a criminal trial, the California court upheld the consul's claim of treaty immunity on the ground that the guarantee of the VIth Amendment of the Constitution gave the accused only the same rights as the prosecution and not an absolute right " to have compulsory process for obtaining witnesses in his favor." [26] It also appears that the prohibition amendment does not interfere with the exemption from inspection enjoyed by the baggage of diplomatic officers.[27]

---

[21] See Marcy, Sec. of State, to Mr. Aspuria, Nov. 15, 1854, Moore, Digest, 2: 978; 5: 169; Livingston, J., in the Bello Corrunes, 6 Wheat. 152, and discussion by Wright, *Am. Jl. Int. Law*, 12: 79. The objection in these cases, however, was based on a supposed encroachment by the treaty upon the power of Congress to " punish . . . offenses against the law of nations."

[22] Objection has been made in Congress on the score of encroachment upon state reserved powers. See Taft, U. S. and Peace, N. Y., 1914, p. 74.

[23] Baldwin *v.* Franks, 120 U. S. 678.

[24] U. S. Rev. Stat., secs. 5373-5374; Criminal Code of 1910, secs. 304-305; *infra*, chap. XII.

[25] See case of the Dutch minister Dubois, 1856, who refused to appear in a criminal trial, and case of the Venezuelan minister, Comancho, who with consent of his government waived his privilege and appeared as a witness in the Guiteau trial for murder of President Garfield. Moore, Digest, 4: 643-645.

[26] *In re* Dillon, Sawyer 561, Fed. Case No. 3914 (1854); Moore, Digest, 5: 78.

[27] The papers of October 22, 1920, reported a controversy on this subject between the State and Treasury departments at Washington. See Hyde, International Law, 1922, 1: 759.

Finally, constitutional guarantees have not impaired the government's ability to follow the custom of international law whereby the succeeding government continues the existing system of civil and criminal law in newly acquired territory. In the insular cases the Supreme Court held that constitutional guarantees did not apply to unincorporated territory *ex propria vigore* and hence the pre-existing system of law in the Philippines, Porto Rico, etc., although not providing for jury trial and other methods guaranteed by the Constitution, might be continued.[28] The court, however, suggested that certain "natural rights" among these guarantees, such as that requiring "due process of law," might apply even in these territories.[29] Clearly the prohibition of slavery stated in amendment XIII to extend to "any place subject to the jurisdiction" of the United States would so apply. However, there is no international custom favoring the continuance of institutions disapproved by the usual standards of justice and morality.[30]

46. *Effect upon Power to Make International Agreements.*

The power to make international agreements, likewise, seems almost unaffected by constitutional guarantees of private right. Many of these guarantees apply to all organs of the government, and hence in theory limit the treaty-making power, but a treaty has never been held void in consequence.[31] The courts have shown an inclination to reconcile such guarantees to treaty provisions where a conflict has been alleged. The various cases we have considered in which the power of the government to meet responsibilities founded on treaty has been sustained likewise indicates the competence of the treaty power. According to American constitutional theory and the terms of the " necessary and proper clause" the national government is competent to carry into effect all of its constitutional powers.[32] Hence if the courts had

---

[28] Hawaii *v.* Mankichi, 190 U. S. 197; Dorr *v.* U. S., 195 U. S. 138.

[29] Dicta of Brown, J., in Downes *v.* Bidwell, 182 U. S. 244, 282; Dorr *v.* U. S., 195 U. S. 138.

[30] As to the attitude of international law on slavery see Story, J., in U. S. *v.* La Jeune Eugenie, 2 Mason 409 (1822).

[31] Willoughby, *op. cit.,* p. 493; Corwin, National Supremacy, p. 5; Anderson, *Am. Jl. Int. Law,* 1: 647; Wright, *ibid.,* 13: 248, *infra,* sec. 173.

[32] Marshall, C. J., in McCulloch *v.* Md., 4 Wheat. 316.

PRIVATE RIGHTS AND STATES' RIGHTS. 81

held the execution of treaties for extradition, internment, or the return of deserting seamen to be in violation of constitutional guarantees, they would in reality have been holding the treaty itself void as beyond the competence of the treaty power.[33] This issue was definitely raised in the case of the French consul referred to. In this case as we have seen the California court upheld the consul's claim to immunity by an interpretation reconciling the treaty clause and the constitutional guarantee in question.[33a] However, in a diplomatic controversy resulting from a French protest against the original arrest of the consul for refusal to obey the *subpoena,* Secretary of State Marcy took a less favorable view of the treaty:[34]

"The Constitution is to prevail over a treaty where the provisions of the one come in conflict with the other. It would be difficult to find a reputable lawyer in this country who would not yield a ready assent to this proposition. Mr. Dillon's counsel admitted it in his argument for the consul's privilege before the court in California. The sixth amendment to the United States Constitution gives, in general and comprehensive language, the right to a defendant in criminal prosecutions to have compulsory process to procure the attendance of witnesses in his favor. Neither Congress nor the treaty-making power are competent to put any restriction on this constitutional provision. . . . As the law of evidence stood when the Constitution went into effect, ambassadors and ministers could not be served with compulsory process to appear as witnesses, and the clause in the Constitution referred to did not give the defendant in criminal prosecutions the right to compel their attendance in court. But what was the case in this respect as to the consuls? They had not the diplomatic privileges of ambassadors and ministers. After the adoption of the Constitution the defendant in a criminal prosecution had the right to compulsory process to bring into court as a witness in his behalf any foreign consul whatsoever. If he then had it, and has it not now, when and how has this constitutional right been taken from him? Congress could not take it away, neither could the treaty-making power, for it is not within the competence of either to modify or restrict the operation of any provision of the Constitution of the United States."

Though with his interpretation of the VIth Amendment, Secretary Marcy was doubtless correct from a constitutional point of view,[35]

---

[33] *Supra,* note 15.

[33a] *Supra,* note 26. This interpretation is supported by J. B. Moore, Proc. Am. Phil. Soc., Minutes, 60: xv; Digest, 5: 168.

[34] Moore, Digest, 5: 167.

[35] To the same effect, see Mr. Marcy to Mr. Aspuria, Nov. 15, 1854; Mr. Blaine, Sec. of State, to Mr. Chen Lan Pin, March 25, 1881; Mr. Cass to

yet in the international discussion he found it necessary to acquiesce in the French view and make amends for the arrest.[36] Since France could not be presumed to know of the constitutional limitation when the treaty was made she was entitled to hold the United States bound.[37] However, the state department has adhered to Secretary Marcy's position and instructed negotiators to exclude such provisions from future treaties.[38]

Finally it has been held that the treaty power violates no constitutional guarantee when it refuses to press the claims of American citizens against foreign governments or settles them unjustly by compromise.[39] Conventions of the latter effect cannot be said to deprive an individual of a guaranteed right, because the constitution can guarantee no more than the government can obtain.[40] Where valid private claims are bartered for national advantage, as were the French Spoliation claims in 1801, a moral duty of the government to compensate undoubtedly exists and was acted on in this case after the lapse of a century.[41] The constitutionality of the treaty, however, was not questioned.

47. *Effect upon Power to Make Decisions on National Policy.*

Although important decisions on foreign policy such as the

Lord Napier, Feb. 7, 1859; Moore, Digest, 5: 169, 177; Cherokee Tobacco Case, 11 Wall. 616 (1870); Geofroy v. Riggs, 133 U. S. 258 (1890); Corwin, National Supremacy, p. 5; Crandall, *op. cit.*, p. 266; VonHolst, Constitutional Law of U. S., Chicago, 1887, p. 202.

[36] Moore, Digest, 5: 80.

[37] *Supra*, sec. 31.

[38] Mr. Fish, Sec. of State, to Mr. Bassett, Oct. 18, 1872, Moore, Digest, 5: 81. This provision is omitted in consular treaties with Greece and Spain, 1902, Malloy, Treaties, pp. 855, 1701; Corwin, National Supremacy, p. 15; Wright, *Am. Jl. Int. Law*, 13: 260.

[39] Comegys v. Vasse, 1 Pet. 193 (1828). "In as much as the government is under no legal obligation to any citizen to prosecute his claim against a foreign country, but is guided solely by the public interest, considerations of public policy and upright dealing between states may warrant the abandonment of a claim." Borchard, *op. cit.*, p. 367.

[40] Corwin, National Supremacy, p. 16, and Borchard, *op. cit.*, p. 366 *et seq.*

[41] Gray v. U. S., 21 Ct. Cl. 340, and Cushing v. U. S., 22 Ct. Cl. 1. Meade's claim, however, though generally admitted to have been unjustly settled by the Spanish treaty of 1819, has never been liquidated by the United States. See Borchard, *op. cit.*, pp. 377, 380.

recognition of foreign states, governments and belligerency, the annexation of territory and the declaration of war and intervention may have important effects upon the life, liberty or property of individuals, such acts are considered "political questions" not reviewable by the courts and are not affected by constitutional guarantees.[42] The court refused to enjoin the Secretary of the Treasury from disbursing funds for construction of the Panama Canal on suit of one Wilson, a tax-payer, on the ground that Panama was not properly a state and the United States had no authority. The recognition of Panama by the President and acceptance of his act by Congress were held conclusive by the court.[43]

"For the courts to interfere," said Justice Brewer, "and at the instance of a citizen, who does not disclose the amount of his interest, stay the work of construction by stopping the payment of money from the Treasury of the United States therefore, would be an exercise of judicial power which, to say the least, is novel and extraordinary. . . . In the case at bar it is clear not only that the plaintiff is not entitled to an injunction, but also that he presents no ground for any relief."

In the carrying out of foreign policies and decisions in peace and war the national government has been very little impeded by constitutional guarantees. It may exclude or expel aliens without judicial hearing, even when they allege citizenship, the courts holding that in such cases administrative hearing is "due process of law."[44] It may annex territory and subject it to military[45]

---

[42] Williams v. Suffolk Ins. Co., 13 Pet. 415; The Divina Pastora, 4 Wheat. 52; Jones v. U. S., 137 U. S. 202; The Prize Cases, 2 Black 635; Willoughby, op. cit., pp. 999-1008.

[43] Wilson v. Shaw, 204 U. S. 24 (1907).

[44] U. S. v. Ju Toy, 198 U. S. 253 (1905). Holmes, J., also suggested that the constitutional guarantee might not apply to an immigrant because "although physically within our boundaries (he) is to be regarded as if he had been stopped at the limit of our jurisdiction and kept there while his right to enter was under debate." On power to expel see Fong Yue Ting v. U. S., 149 U. S. 698 (1893). The immigration act of Feb. 5, 1917, art. 19, provides for return of immigrants illegally entering within a period of 5 years, on warrant of the Secretary of Labor, and the act of Oct. 16, 1918, provides for the expulsion of any alien within enumerated classes, on warrant of the Secretary of Labor. Rule 19 of May 1, 1917, gives the procedure of enforcement. See Dept. of Labor, Bureau of Immigration, ed. of Immigration Laws, 1919, and compiled statutes, secs. 4289 1/4 jj. 4289 1/4 b(2). For Chinese exclusion and deportation provisions see acts, May 6, 1882, secs.

or civil government[46] untrammeled by constitutional guarantees. The constitutional guarantees do not extend to annexed territory until it has been incorporated by act of Congress.[47]

The government may give its consuls, diplomatic and naval officers authority over American citizens abroad, even to the extent of criminal convictions without jury or other constitutional requirements.[48] By a recognized custom at the time the XIIIth Amendment was adopted, seamen may be compelled to fulfill their contracts against their will and by force without violation of the prohibition against slavery and involuntary servitude.[49]

Though the Supreme Court has said,[50] " The war power of the United States, like its other powers . . . is subject to applicable constitutional limitations," practice indicates that few such limitations are applicable.[51] Military discipline may be enforced within the army and navy by courts martial exempt from constitutional restrictions and subject only to the articles of war enacted by

---

1, 12 (22 stat. 58, 61), as amended July 5, 1884 (23 stat. 115, 117), Sept. 13, 1888, sec. 13 (28 stat. 1210). For finality of decisions of immigration and customs officials see act, Aug. 18, 1894, sec. 1 (28 stat. 390). See Comp. Statutes, sec. 4290 et seq.; J. P. Hall, Const. Law, pp. 124, 325; Willoughby, op. cit., pp. 1286-1293.

[45] Neeley v. Henkel, 180 U. S. 109 (1901).

[46] Dorr v. U. S., 195 U. S. 138.

[47] Ibid.

[48] In re Ross, 140 U. S. 453 (1890).

[49] Robertson v. Baldwin, 165 U. S. 275 (1897). This rule was altered by the La Follette Seaman's act of 1915, sec. 16, 38 Stat. 1184, Comp. Stat., sec. 8382a.

[50] Brandeis, J., in Hamilton v. Ky. Distilleries and Warehouse Co., 251 U. S. 146, 156. See also Ruppert v. Caffey, 251 U. S. 264.

[51] " In my judgment, the power exists without any restrictions whatsoever, save those which are imposed by such express prohibitions of the Constitution, and such fundamental restraints upon governmental action, as are obviously and clearly intended to apply at all times and under all conditions. There is, in this field of governmental activity therefore, little, if any occasion to employ those niceties of logical analysis which have crystallized into canons of statutory and constitutional construction, the application of which tends to elucidate the meaning of language otherwise obscure." Sutherland, Constitutional Power and World Affairs, N. Y., 1919, p. 94. Senator Sutherland's language doubtless elucidates the obscurities connected with the limitations of the war power.

Congress.[52] Armies may be raised by draft without violation of constitutional guarantees,[53] and by express exception of the Vth Amendment persons in the service may be held to answer for infamous crimes without presentment or indictment of grand jury. Foreign territory, or even domestic territory in rebellion may be occupied and governed without observance of the guarantees.[54] Within any territory of the United States the privilege of the writ of habeas corpus may be suspended by Congress when in case of rebellion or invasion the public safety may demand it. Though such a suspension of the writ does not mean a suspension of the other guarantees and a rule of martial law except in so far as "necessity," due to public disturbance and an actual closure of the courts, may demand, yet the practice of the Civil War indicates that an actual rule of martial law may be established in territory not the scene of immediate violence.[55] In pursuance of war, Congress may provide for the confiscation of property in enemy territory (even though American territory in rebellion)[56] or property belonging to enemy persons wherever found[57] without following the guarantees of the Vth and VIth Amendments. Such confiscations are authorized under the power of Congress to make rules concerning captures and not under its power of criminal legislation, hence the guarantees for criminal trial do not apply.[58] Under military necessity executive authority alone will justify the confiscation of property.[59] Congress may also provide for the internment and expulsion of alien enemies by administrative process.[60]

---

[52] Dynes v. Hoover, 26 How. 65.

[53] Selective Draft Cases, 245 U. S. 366.

[54] Neeley v. Henkel, 180 U. S. 109 (1901), Ford v. Surget, 97 U. S. 594.

[55] Ex parte Milligan, 4 Wall. 2, and dissent by Chase, C. J., which Winthrop (Military Law, 2: 38) regards as the "sounder and more reasonable" view.

[56] Miller v. U. S., 11 Wall. 268.

[57] Brown v. U. S., 8 Cranch 110. See Trading with the Enemy Act, Oct. 6, 1917. Property of loyal citizens may be taken under necessity but must be paid for as required by the Vth Amendment, U. S. v. Russell, 13 Wall. 623; Willoughby, op. cit., p. 1243.

[58] Miller v. U. S., 11 Wall. 268.

[59] Mitchell v. Harmony, 13 How. 115. It has been held that the rights of the President as commander-in-chief, though not limited by the Constitu-

We may conclude that constitutional guarantees of individual rights restrict the foreign relations power very little whether acting to meet international responsibilities, to make international agreements or to make and carry out national decisions and policies.

B. States' Rights.

48. *Nature of Prohibition.*

Restrictions upon the exercise of power by national organs may be implied from the guarantee of certain rights to the states. Territorial integrity,[61] a republican form of government[62] and the independence of their governmental organs from taxation or other burdening[63] appear to be genuine "states' rights" and must be distinguished from the so-called "reserved powers" of the states. The former constitute definite limitations upon the exercise of national power, the latter if they restrict the exercise of national powers at all, do so simply by virtue of constitutional understandings.

---

tion, are limited by the international law of war and consequently confiscation of property beyond those allowed by the law of war can only be justified by act of Congress. Brown *v.* U. S., 8 Cranch 110, thus held that enemy property on land was not subject to confiscation except by express act of Congress. See also Lieber's Instructions for the Government of the Armies in the Field, Gen. Order, 100, April 24, 1863, arts. 4, 11; and Sutherland, *op. cit.,* pp. 75, 77. Willoughby thinks the President may even go beyond the law of war (*op. cit.,* 1212) and, regarding the Emancipation Proclamation of Jan. 1, 1863, as a confiscation of enemy property on land, President Lincoln probably did so by that proclamation. For criticism see Burgess, The Civil War and the Constitution, 2: 117; Rhodes, History of U. S., 4: 70. See also *infra,* sec. 218.

[60] See Alien Enemy Act, July 6, 1798 (1 stat. 577), amended July 6, 1812 (1 stat. 781, rev. stat., secs. 4067, 4068), and April 16, 1918, making it applicable to women, which authorizes internment and expulsion. The President issued proclamations under them April 6, Nov. 16, Dec. 11, 1917, and April 19, 1918. See Comp. Stat., secs. 7615–18. See also Brown *v.* U. S., 8 Cranch 110.

[61] Constitution, IV, sec. 3, cl. 1; sec. 4.

[62] *Ibid.,* IV, sec. 4.

[63] Collector *v.* Day, 11 Wall. 113; Willoughby, *op. cit.,* pp. 110–114; Willoughby, The American Constitutional System, pp. 123, 129. For express prohibitions upon the national government in behalf of the states, see *supra,* sec. 44.

49. *Effect upon Power to Meet International Responsibilities.*

The power to meet international responsibilities does not seem to be limited by any states' rights. The power to define and punish offenses against the law of nations and the necessary and proper clause of the Constitution[64] confer upon Congress ample power to provide for carrying out all treaties and all responsibilities under international law. Legislation of Congress punishing offenses against neutrality, offenses against foreign diplomatic officers, and the counterfeiting of foreign securities have been held to violate no guaranteed states' rights[65] and many acts for the carrying out of treaties have been sustained.[66] Of this character are acts providing for extradition and for the return of deserting seamen. The conclusion of treaties may unquestionably extend the power of Congress to provide for the exercise of police power within the states. Thus although the court held unconstitutional an act of 1907 rendering persons criminally liable for harboring immigrant women as prostitutes within a period of three years of landing, it indicated that if the law had been in pursuance of a treaty it would have been valid.[67] The Mann White Slave Act of 1910[68] actually includes provisions in pursuance of the International White Slave Convention of 1904. So also an act for the protection of migratory birds was held unconstitutional[69] but the court has sustained a similar act passed in pursuance of a treaty with Great Britain.[70]

"The treaty in question," says Mr. Justice Holmes, "does not contravene any prohibitory words to be found in the Constitution. The only question is whether it is forbidden by some invisible radiation from the general terms of the 10th Amendment. We must consider what this country has become in deciding what that amendment has reserved. . . . Valid treaties, of course, 'are as binding within the territorial limits of the states as they are effective throughout the dominion of the United States.'"

---

[64] Constitution, I, sec. 8, cl. 10, 18.
[65] U. S. *v.* Arjona, 120 U. S. 479.
[66] Mo. *v.* Holland, 252 U. S. 416 (1920).
[67] Ullman *v.* U. S., 213 U. S. 138 (1909), declaring act of Feb. 20, 1907, sec. 3 (34 stat. 898), void.
[68] Act, June 25, 1910, sec. 6, 36 stat. 825.
[69] U. S. *v.* Shauves, 214 Fed. 154; U. S. *v.* McCullagh, 227 Fed. 288.
[70] Mo. *v.* Holland, 252 U. S. 416 (1920).

Baldwin v. Franks, 120 U. S. 678, 683. No doubt the great body of private relations usually falls within the control of the state, but a treaty may override its power. We do not have to invoke the later developments of constitutional law for this proposition; it was recognized as early as Hopkirk v. Bell, 3 Cranch 454, with regard to statutes of limitation, and even earlier as to confiscation, in Ware v. Hylton, 3 Dall. 199. It was assumed by Chief Justice Marshall with regard to the escheat of land to the state in Chirac v. Chirac, 2 Wheat. 259, 275; Hauenstein v. Lynham, 100 U. S. 483; Geofroy v. Riggs, 133 U. S. 258; Blythe v. Hinckley, 180 U. S. 333, 340. So, as to a limited jurisdiction of foreign consuls within a state. Wildenhus Case, 120 U. S. 1. See Re Ross, 140 U. S. 453. Further illustration seems unnecessary, and it only remains to consider the application of established rules to the present case.

"Here a national interest of very nearly the first magnitude is involved. It can be protected only by national action in concert with that of another power. The subject matter is only transitorily within the state, and has no permanent habitat therein. But for the treaty and the statute, there soon might be no birds for any powers to deal with. We see nothing in the Constitution that compels the government to sit by while a food supply is cut off and the protectors of our forests and of our crops are destroyed. It is not sufficient to rely upon the states. The reliance is vain, and were it otherwise, the question is whether the United States is forbidden to act. We are of opinion that the treaty and statute must be upheld. Cary v. South Dakota, 250 U. S. 118."

The present inability of federal courts to prosecute persons within the states guilty of violating the rights of aliens guaranteed by international law or treaty is not due to a limitation upon national power but to an insufficiency of congressional legislation.[71]

50. *Effect upon Power to Make International Agreements.*

The national guarantee of territorial integrity and a republican form of government to the states limits the treaty power. The capacity of the treaty power to cede state territory was discussed in Washington's cabinet. Secretary of State Jefferson maintained that "the United States had no right to alienate one inch of the territory of any state" while Secretary of the Treasury Hamilton took the opposite view.[72] While admission of the supremacy of

---

[71] Willoughby, Am. Constitutional System, p. 108; Pomeroy, Const. Law, 9th ed., p. 571; Corwin, National Supremacy, pp. 288–289; Taft, U. S. and Peace, 40 *et seq.*, Gammons, *Am. Jl. Int. Law*, 11: 6; Moore, Digest, 6: 839 *et seq.*

[72] Jefferson's Anas, March 11, 1792, Wharton, Digest, 2: 66.

PRIVATE RIGHTS AND STATES' RIGHTS. 89

treaties granting Indian tribes an exclusive right in reservations within the states[73] seems to go far toward admitting the right of the treaty power to alienate state territory, an actual cession was not here in question. In the only case of foreign cession of state territory that has arisen, the adjustment of the Maine boundary by the Webster-Ashburton treaty of 1842, the political expediency if not the constitutional necessity of obtaining the state's consent was admitted. The compensation to be paid Maine and Massachusettes was especially referred to in the treaty.[74] The better opinion seems to hold that state consent must be obtained,[75] though in case of necessity, as to end an unfortunate war, a treaty cession without such consent would doubtless stand.[76]

The interpretation of the guarantee of a " Republican Form of Government " was held by the courts a political question in a case recognizing the legitimacy of the military government set up in Texas after the Civil War.[77] Doubtless a treaty putting a state under a protectorate or otherwise subverting its government could be equally well reconciled with the guarantee. Legally, however, the guarantee unquestionably restricts the treaty power.

The "reserved powers" of the states, however, do not limit the treaty-making power. Powers often claimed to be "reserved powers" may be classified as (1) the power to regulate exclusively state land and natural resources; (2) the power to exercise exclusive control over public services supported by state taxation; (3) the power to exercise police control over classes of persons and businesses within the state in behalf of public safety, health, morals and economic welfare. Treaty provisions often guarantee to aliens rights of entry, residence landholding, inheritance, etc.,

---

[73] Worcester v. Ga., 6 Pet. 515 (1832).

[74] Art. V of treaty. See Moore, 5: 172–174, *supra,* sec. 31. This incident is discussed in Fort Leavenworth Railroad Co. v. Lowe, 114 U. S. 525, 541, quoting Webster's Works, 5: 99, 6: 273.

[75] Dicta in Lattimer v. Poteet, 14 Pet. 14 (1840); Geofroy v. Riggs, 133 U. S. 267 (1890); Insular Cases, 182 U. S. 316 (1901); Fort Leavenworth Railroad Co. v. Lowe, 114 U. S. 525, 541; Moore, Digest, 5: 171–175; Butler, The Treaty Making Power, 1902, 1: 411–413, 2: 238, 287–294; Corwin, National Supremacy, 130–134; Wright, *Am. Jl. Int. Law,* 13: 253.

[76] *Supra,* sec. 32.

[77] Texas v. White, 7 Wall. 700.

90   THE CONTROL OF AMERICAN FOREIGN RELATIONS.

equal to that of citizens or subjects of the most-favored nation.[78] It has been alleged that such provisions are void in so far as they conflict with the exercise by the States of these "reserved" powers. The issue has been judicially considered in reference to state statutes discriminating against aliens, or aliens of a particular race or nationality (1) in the privilege of owning land,[79] operating mines,[80] and taking fish[81] and game;[82] (2) in the use of public schools[83] and the right to labor on public works;[84] (3) and in the freedom of immigration,[85] labor,[86] personal habits,[87] and

[78] Art. XI of the Treaty of 1778 with France and Art. I of the Treaty of 1894 with Japan, superseded by Art. I of the Treaty of 1911, are examples of this type of provision.

[79] Fairfax v. Hunter, 7 Cr. 603; Chirac v. Chirac, 2 Wheat. 259 (1817); Society for the Propagation of the Gospel v. New Haven, 8 Wheat. 464 (1823); Carneal v. Banks, 10 Wheat. 259 (1825); California-Japanese controversy, 1913, Corwin, *op. cit.*, p. 232. Art. VII of the treaty of 1853 with France made concessions to this "states' right." It allowed Frenchmen to possess land on an equality with citizens "in all the states of the Union where existing laws permit it, so long and to the same extent as the said laws shall remain in force." As to the other states "the President engages to recommend to them the passage of such laws as may be necessary for the purpose of conferring the right."

[80] People v. Noglee, 1 Cal. 232 (1850).

[81] Griggs, Att. Gen., 1898, 22 Op. 214.

[82] Patsone v. Pa., 232 U. S. 138, 145, Mo. v. Holland, 252 U. S. 416 (1920).

[83] California-Japanese school children controversy, 1906, Corwin, *op. cit.*, p. 217; E. Root, *Am. Jl. Int. Law*, 1: 273, and editorials, *ibid.*, 1: 150, 449. Art. IV of the Treaty of 1854 with Great Britain indicates that the United States doubted its right to control a state established utility without state consent. "The government of the United States further engages to urge upon the state government to secure to the subjects of Her Britannic Majesty the use of the several State Canals on terms of equality with the inhabitants of the United States."

[84] Baker v. Portland, 5 Sawyer 566 (1879); Heim v. McCall, 239 U. S. 175 (1915), *Am. Jl. Int. Law*, 10: 162.

[85] Elkinson v. Deliesseline, Leg. Doc. Mass. 1845 (Senate), No. 31, p. 39 (1823), Thayer, Cases in Constitutional Law, p. 1849, Corwin, *op. cit.*, p. 125; Wirt, Att. Gen., 10: 661 (1824); Berrien, Att. Gen., 20: 431 (1831) The Passenger Cases, 7 How. 283 (1849); *in re* Ah Fong, 3 Sawyer 144; Henderson v. N. Y., 92 U. S. 259 (1875).

[86] *In re* Tiburcio Parrott, 6 Sawyer 349 (1880); Truax v. Raich, 239 U. S. 33, 43 (1915), *Am. Jl. Int. Law*, 10: 158.

[87] Ho Ah Kow v. Nunan, 5 Sawyer 532 (1879).

PRIVATE RIGHTS AND STATES' RIGHTS. 91

conduct of business.[88] In a few cases dicta damaging to the treaty power have been uttered;[89] sometimes the treaty has been subjected to a strained interpretation to save the State's power;[90] but in no case has a clear treaty provision been superseded by the state law. On the contrary, state statutes of this character have frequently been declared void when conflicting with clear treaty provisions.[91] With respect to statutes relating to the control of natural resources and state-supported services, the attitude of the courts has been cautious, with a decided tendency in recent cases to compromise by adopting interpretations of the treaty favorable to the state power.[92] The question, however, has been on the applicability of the treaty, not upon its validity.

A more extreme extension of the "reserved powers" doctrine has been put forward in the claim that unlimited discretion in the regulation and taxation of property and inheritances is a state power exempt from interference by the treaty-making power. Treaties of the character mentioned have sometimes conflicted with the alleged exclusive right of the state to regulate the ownership, transmission and inheritance of property within its limits.[93] An historical view of the many cases bearing upon this point shows that in the days of Marshall[94] and since the Civil War[95] the Supreme

---

[88] Yick Wo v. Hopkins, 118 U. S. 356 (1886); Compagnie Francaise v. State Board of Health, 186 U. S. 380 (1902). Frequently in these cases the XIV Amendment as well as treaties have been in opposition to the exercise of state powers. See also Rocca v. Thompson, 232 U. S. 318.

[89] Taney, C. J., in Holmes v. Jennison, 14 Pet. 540 (1840); The Passenger Cases, 7 How. 283, 465 (1849); Daniels, J., in The License Cases, 5 How. 504, 613; Grier, J., in The Passenger Cases, 7 How. 283 (1849).

[90] Compagnie Francaise v. State Board of Health, 186 U. S. 380 (1902).

[91] Chirac v. Chirac, 2 Wheat. 259 (1817); Elkinson v. Deliesseline, supra, note 42; in re Tiburcio Parrott, 6 Sawyer 349 (1880); Truax v. Raich, 239 U. S. 33, 43 (1915), Am. Jl. Int. Law, 10: 158.

[92] Patsone v. Pa., 232 U. S. 138, 145; Heim v. McCall, 239 U. S. 175, 193 (1915). Am. Jl. Int. Law, 10: 162. But see Mo. v. Holland, supra, sec. 49.

[93] Ware v. Hylton, 3 Dall. 199 (1796); Hopkirk v. Bell, 3 Cranch 454; Prevost v. Greenaux, 10 How. 1 (1856); Fredricksen v. La. 23 How. 443 (1860); Hauenstein v. Lynham, 100 U. S. 483 (1879); Wynans Petitioner, 191 Mass. 276; People v. Gerke, 5 Cal. 381 (1855).

[94] Fairfax v. Hunter, 7 Cr. 603 (1813); Chirac v. Chirac, 3 Wheat. 259 (1817).

Court has uniformly and in no uncertain voice sustained the treaty power as against these alleged states' reserved powers. Only during the period preceding the Civil War was there a wavering, even then confined to dicta.[96]

Statesmen and text writers with few exceptions have taken a similar attitude in support of a broad treaty power.[97] We may accept the view of a California judge in a case involving the state intestacy laws.[98]

"One of the arguments at the bar against the extent of this power of treaty is, that it permits the Federal Government to control the internal policy of the States, and, in the present case, to alter materially the statutes

---

[95] Hauenstein v. Lynham, 100 U. S. 483 (1879) ; Geofroy v. Riggs, 133 U. S. 258 (1890).

[96] *Supra,* note 89.

[97] For supremacy of treaty power over state powers:
Anderson, C., *Am. Jl. Int. Law,* 1 : 636;
Burr, Treaty Making Power of U. S., 1912;
Butler, The Treaty Making Power of the U. S., 1902;
Calhoun, Discourse, Works, ed. 1853, 1 : 202; Elliot's Debates, 4 : 463;
Corwin, National Supremacy, 1913;
Crandall, Treaties, their Making and Enforcement, 1916;
Devlin, Treaty Power under the Constitution of U. S., San Francisco, 1908;
Elliott, E. C., The Treaty Making Power, with reference to the Reserved Powers of the States, Case and Comment, 22 : 77 (1913) ;
Hall, J. P., State Interference with the Enforcement of Treaties, *Proc. Acad. Pol. Sci.,* 7 : 24;
Livingston, Sec. of State, Wharton, 2 : 67;
Moore, J. B., *Pol. Sci. Quar.,* 32 : 320;
Pomeroy, Introduction to the Constitutional Law of U. S., 9th ed., 1886, sec. 674;
Root, *Am. Jl. Int. Law,* 1 : 273;
Story, Commentaries on the Constitution;
Willoughby, W. W., Constitutional Law of U. S., 2 vols., 1910.
Against supremacy of treaty power over state powers:
Hayden, *Am. Hist. Rev.,* 22: 566 (takes a historical view showing that the political check has sometimes preserved states' rights from adverse treaties) ;
Jefferson, Manual of Parliamentary Practice, p. 110;
Mikell, *University of Pa. Law Rev.* 57; 435, 528;
Tucker, H. S., Limitations on the Treaty Making Power under the Constitution of U. S., Boston, 1915;
Tucker, J. R., Constitution of U. S., 2 vols., 1899.

[98] People v. Gerke, 5 Cal. 381 (1855).

of distribution. If this was so to the full extent claimed, it might be a sufficient answer to say, that it is one of the results of the compact, and, if the grant be considered too improvident for the safety of the States, the evil can be remedied by the Constitution-making power."

Thus any respect that is shown by the treaty-making power to "reserved powers" of the states is merely by virtue of an understanding of the Constitution. In fact such respect has often been shown and it was thus to safeguard the interests of the states that the Senate was made such an important element in treaty-making.[99] This function the Senate has recognized, and, especially in the period before the Civil War, has frequently exercised a veto upon treaties thought to violate states' rights, or redrafted them so as to permit of state consent before the treaty became effective within its territory.[100] The practice of the Senate, the opinions of statesmen and dicta of the courts indicate that, except for the most cogent reasons, the treaty power ought to exercise its powers in such way as not to interfere with the control by the states of their own land, natural resources, and public services and not to interfere unnecessarily with the enforcement by the state of its own policy with reference to the protection of public safety, health, morals and economic welfare.

51. *Effect upon Power to Make Decisions upon National Policy.*

States' Rights have not interfered with the making and carrying out of national decisions. Such decisions as the declaration of war, recognition of foreign states and governments, annexation of territory, etc., being of external application, have never been alleged to conflict with states' rights, unless the protests of the Hartford Convention against the War of 1812 be so considered.[101] The

---

[99] Ralston Hayden, The States' Rights Doctrine and the Treaty Making Power, *Am. Hist. Rev.*, 22: 56; Corwin, National Supremacy, 141, 302. The fathers seem to have considered the Senate a special bulwark of states' rights, Farrand, *op. cit.*, 2: 393; The Federalist, No. 64 (Jay), Ford ed., p. 432; Elliot, Debates, 4: 137.

[100] Hayden, *op. cit., Am. Hist. Rev.*, 22: 56. For example see *supra*, note 79.

[101] See proposed amendment to the Constitution requiring two-thirds vote of both houses to declare war, MacDonald, Select Documents in American History, N. Y., 1898, p. 206.

exercise of war powers, has conflicted with alleged states' reserved powers. Thus the drafting of armies was attacked as an impairment of the states' reserved power over its militia.[102] Though the contention at first received some judicial support in Civil War cases,[103] it was thoroughly demolished during the World War.[104]

Apparently the only legal limitation upon the exercise of powers in foreign relations imposed by states' rights is that upon the power to cede state territory by treaty, which is acknowledged to evaporate before necessity.

[102] Constitution, Art. I, sec. 8, cl. 15, 16. The national government can call forth the militia, as such, only "to execute the laws of the Union, suppress insurrections and repel invasions," which does not permit of use outside the territory (Wickersham, Att. Gen., 29 Op. 322), but under present law the militia are not used as such but are reenlisted in the national army when called out for national service. (Act June 3, 1916, 39 stat. 200, 211, secs. 70, 71, 73, 111.) The power to raise armies (Constitution, I, sec. 8, cl. 12) is wholly distinct from the power over the militia and is not limited by the state's right to its militia. (Selective Draft Cases, 245 U. S. 366.) See Wright, Military Administration, Report of Efficiency and Economy Committee of Illinois, 1915, p. 903.

[103] Kneedler v. Lane, 45 Pa. 238 (1863), Thayer, Cases on Constitutional Law, p. 2316. Lowrie, J., supported by Justices Woodward and Thompson, with Justices Strong and Read in dissent, granted a preliminary injunction on November 9, 1863. On December 12, 1863, Justice Lowrie's term expired. He was succeeded by Justice Agnew, who sided with the two former dissenting justices, thus making Justice Strong's opinion dissolving the injunction the opinion of the court.

[104] Selective Draft Cases, 245 U. S. 366; Sutherland, *op. cit.*, p. 108.

CHAPTER VII.

Limitations upon National Powers: The Separation of Powers.

52. *Nature of the Theory.*

The doctrine of separation of powers means that the legislative, executive, and judicial powers of government ought to be exercised by separate and independent departments.

"It is also essential," says the Supreme Court, "to the successful working of the system that the persons intrusted with power in any one of these branches shall not be permitted to encroach upon the powers confided to the others, but that each shall by the law of its creation be limited to the exercise of the powers appropriate to its own department and no others."[1]

The doctrine is implied by three clauses of the Constitution:

"All legislative power herein granted shall be vested in a Congress of the United States." (Art. I, sec. 1.)

"The executive power shall be vested in a President of the United States of America." (Art. II, sec. 1.)

"The judicial power of the United States shall be vested in one Supreme Court and in such inferior courts as the Congress may from time to time ordain and establish." (Art. III, sec. 1.)

It will be noticed that the Congress is vested merely with "all legislative powers herein granted" while the President and the courts are vested respectively with "the executive power" and "the judicial power of the United States." The mere fact that a power is legislative in character does not, therefore, indicate its possession by Congress unless it is specifically granted to that body elsewhere in the Constitution. It has been urged, however, that all powers by nature executive belong inherently to the Pres-

---

[1] Kilbourn v. Thompson, 103 U. S. 168. On impossibility of so defining the functions of the departments as to make an actually complete separation, see Goodnow, The Principles of the Administrative Law of U. S., N. Y., 1905, p. 26, and Willoughby, *op. cit.,* p. 1262.

[2] Hamilton, "Pacificus" Letter, June 29, 1793, and Roosevelt, Autobiography, pp. 388–389, quoted, Corwin, The President's Control of Foreign Relations, pp. 11, 168. See also *infra,* sec. 92.

ident[2] and all powers by nature judicial to the courts.[3] Doubtless certain inherent executive and judicial powers and privileges, necessary for the functioning of the organ, and for the preservation of its independence, such as the executive power to remove officials[4] and the judicial power to punish for contempts,[5] exist aside from express delegation, but so also do inherent legislative powers, such as the power to subpoena witnesses necessary to give information essential to intelligent legislation.[6] The general vesting of executive and judicial power cannot, therefore, be made the basis of powers other than essentially inherent power. To do so would render the subsequent express delegations of power to the President and the courts useless verbiage. *Expressis unius exclusis alteris* applies to the executive and judicial powers as well as the legislative.[7]

Aside, therefore, from its assurance of certain necessary and inherent powers to each department, the theory of separation of power is a limitation rather than a source of power for each department. We may express the doctrine in three principles.[8]

53. *Protection of Independence of Departments.*

Each department is endowed with such rights, privileges and inherent powers as will assure its independence of the others.[9] Thus members of Congress are immune from arrest during the session, each house is given exclusive authority to judge the qualifications of its own members, to make its own rules of procedure, to discipline and expel its own members and to subpoena witnesses and commit for contempt when necessary for performing its

---

[3] Kansas v. Colorado, 206 U. S. 46, 81–83, Corwin, *op. cit.*, p. 31.

[4] Parsons v. U. S., 167 U. S. 324; Willoughby, *op. cit.*, pp. 1181–1184, and Congressional debate of 1789 on the question there cited. *Infra*, sec. 230. The removal power is not, however, regarded as an inherent executive power in the states. Goodnow, *op. cit.*, p. 311.

[5] *In re* Debs, 158 U. S. 595; Carter v. Va., 96 Va. 791; Willoughby, *op. cit.*, pp. 1268–1270; J. P. Hall, Constitutional Law, p. 19.

[6] Anderson v. Dunn, 6 Wheat. 204; Kilbourn v. Thompson, 103 U. S. 168; *In re* Chapman, 166 U. S. 661; Willoughby, *op. cit.*, p. 1272.

[7] See Taft, Our Chief Magistrate, pp. 73, 140, 144; Senate debate of 1831 quoted Corwin, *op. cit.*, p. 59; and *infra*, sec. 92.

[8] *Infra*, secs. 53–55.

[9] Goodnow, *op. cit.*, p. 38.

SEPARATION OF POWERS.

legislative functions.[10] The President is immune from judicial process except trial of impeachment and holds himself entitled to exclusive control of the personnel of the national civil and military service through the power to commission and remove officials.[11] The Federal Justices are assured permanence of tenure and compensation and the courts hold themselves to enjoy certain inherent privileges such as the power to commit for contempt and perhaps to control admissions to the bar and rules of practice.[12] These rights, privileges and inherent powers cannot be impaired by action of the organ itself or by that of other organs.

54. Protection of Delegated Powers of Departments.

Each department is entitled to exercise the powers delegated to it by the Constitution. Two interpretations of this guarantee of quite divergent effect must be distinguished. Thus it is generally recognized that one organ cannot, unless the Constitution expressly provides otherwise, take away a power specifically or impliedly delegated to another organ or give away a power so delegated to itself.[13] But it is sometimes contended, that in addition, one organ cannot so exercise its own powers as to limit the discretion of another organ or of itself in the future exercise of its powers. These two interpretations are very different and much misconception has arisen from their confusion. Thus for the treaty power to provide that in defined circumstances the United States would automatically be at war, would be a clear invasion of the power

---

[10] Constitution, I, secs. 5, 6, and *supra,* note 6.

[11] Mississippi *v.* Johnson, 4 Wall. 475; Willoughby, *op. cit.,* 1300–1304; Constitution, II, sec. 3, and *supra,* note 4.

[12] Constitution, III, sec. 1, *supra,* note 5. Illinois and Pennsylvania hold the setting of standards for admission to the bar is an inherent judicial power (*In re* Day, 181 III, 73, *In re* Splane, 123 Pa. 527), while New York and North Carolina hold the contrary (Matter of Cooper, 22 N. Y. 67, *Re* applicants for license, 143 N. C. 1). Indiana holds that statutes cannot lower the standard set by court rules of procedure. (Epstein *v.* State, 128 N. F. 353, Ind. 1920, and note in *Minn. Law Rev.,* 5: 73, Dec., 1920.)

[13] Legislative power cannot be delegated even by the legislature itself, but the Constitution gives considerable power to Congress over the determination of executive and judicial competence. *Infra,* sec. 60. But see Goodnow, *op. cit.,* p. 41.

of Congress to declare war. On the other hand for the treaty power to provide that in defined circumstances the United States would declare war, would not invade the power of Congress but would merely limit its discretion in the future exercise of this power. In certain circumstances the practical effect might be the same, but the legal difference would nevertheless exist. It appears that constitutional law merely guarantees to each organ continued possession of its delegated powers. The degree of discretion which the organ may actually enjoy in exercising these powers depends largely upon constitutional understandings.

55. *Prohibition upon Exercise of Uncharacteristic Power by Any Department.*

Each department is prohibited from "exercising powers (not inherent or expressly delegated) which from their essential nature do not fall within its division of governmental functions." [14] Thus Congress cannot exercise such judicial powers as punishing for contempt unless necessary for performing its legislative functions,[15] nor such executive powers as directing the detailed movement of troops[16] or appointing officers.[17] The courts cannot exercise such executive powers as the giving of advisory opinions[18] or the making of decisions which are reviewable by executive or legislative officers.[19] The theory has been most difficult to apply as a restriction upon the executive because methods closely approaching a judicial and a legislative character often seem essential to the performance of executive duties. Though the theory that the legis-

---

[14] Willoughby, *op. cit.*, p. 1263.

[15] Kilbourn *v.* Thompson, 103 U. S. 168. Nor can Congress exercise judicial power by deciding specific cases involving private rights, Willoughby, *op. cit.*, p. 1264.

[16] *Ex parte* Milligan, 4 Wall. 2, Willoughby, *op. cit.*, p. 1207.

[17] Constitution, II, sec. 2. Congress, however, has the inherent power to appoint subordinate officers necessary for the conduct of its internal business, Goodnow, *op. cit.*, p. 38.

[18] See Thayer, Cases of Const. Law, 1: 175, and Willoughby, *op. cit.*, p. 13.

[19] Hayburn's Case, 2 Dall. 409; Gordon *v.* U. S., 2 Wall. 561; Willoughby, *op. cit.*, p. 1275.

lature cannot delegate its power exists, the courts actually give the force of law to executive orders and regulations issued under authority of statute.[20] This is justified by the theory that the ordinances are not legislation but merely the application of a policy determined by Congress in the delegating act. So also executive boards and commissions are permitted to proceed as courts and give decisions of a definitive character in certain types of cases.[21] The almost complete control over the organization and jurisdiction of federal courts given by the Constitution to Congress[22] makes any attempt by the courts to prevent the vesting of judicial functions in administrative bodies virtually impossible.[23]

A. *Effect on the Power to Meet International Responsibilities.*

56. *The Government as a Whole Competent to Meet Responsibilities.*

The doctrine of separation of powers does not impose any limitation upon the power of the United States to meet its international responsibilities. International law and treaty provisions have very seldom directed the instrumentality through which responsibilities shall be met. The responsibility rests on the nation and it can ordinarily determine its own instrumentality for performance. Consequently if any organ of the government has power to meet a particular responsibility, or to provide for meeting it, we may be sure the government as a whole has the power. Treaties have occasionally required that responsibilities be met through a particular instrumentality, as that certain controversies be submitted to an international tribunal, or that the *compromis* of arbitrations be made by the President with advice and consent of the Senate.[24] Such reference to domestic organs has usually

---

[20] Field *v.* Clark, 143 U. S. 649; Goodnow, *op. cit.,* pp. 42, 85.

[21] U. S. *v.* Ju Toy, 198 U. S. 253; Willoughby, *op. cit.,* p. 1278, *et seq.*

[22] Constitution, I, sec. 8, cl. 9; III, sec. 1, sec. 2, cl. 2, seems to give Congress complete control over the courts except the original jurisdiction of the Supreme Court. *Ex Parte* McCardle, 7 Wall. 506.

[23] Willoughby, *op. cit.,* p. 1277.

[24] See pecuniary claims convention with Latin American States, 1910, Charles, Treaties, 345; arbitration treaty with Great Britain, 1908, Art. V, Malloy, Treaties, p. 814. For other treaty provisions referring to specific organs see Wright, *Columbia Law Rev.,* 20: 123-4.

been declaratory of the Constitution, and has been inserted out of excess of caution to give notice to the foreign government of constitutional steps which must be taken, or by insistence of one department of the government to prevent anticipated usurpations by another. If, however, a treaty required that certain acts be performed by a particular organ, which, under the theory of separation of powers, could not exercise such a power, that clause of the treaty could not be executed by the United States. Such a treaty clause, however, would be unconstitutional from the start. The question would relate, therefore, to the power to make treaties rather than to the power to meet international responsibilities.[25]

57. *Power of President and Courts to Meet International Responsibilities.*

Although the doctrine of separation of powers does not legally limit the power of the government to meet its responsibilities, it often throws practical difficulties in the way of prompt action. Congress is by nature slow moving but often under the constitutional distribution of powers it alone has power to meet certain international responsibilities. Were the President and the courts vested with adequate authority to act, delay in the meeting of responsibilities might often be avoided. The President and courts cannot, under the doctrine which prohibits the delegation of legislative power, be vested with such exclusive congressional powers as that to appropriate money and to declare war. Thus a prompt meeting of responsibilities requiring such acts depends upon congressional observance of the constitutional understanding which enjoins all departments to exercise such powers as they have in order promptly to meet international responsibilities.[26]

Often, however, it is within the power of Congress to vest the President and courts by general law with adequate power to meet responsibilities, and a mass of legislation with this purpose has grown up dealing especially with the enforcement of neutrality, the protection of diplomatic officers, the protection of foreign securities, the suppression of piracy, the extradition of criminals,

---

[25] *Supra*, secs. 45, 46.
[26] *Infra*, sec. 258.

and the enforcement of many treaties such as that for supressing the slave trade and for the protection of migratory birds. No general law has as yet been passed giving the President and courts adequate power to protect the rights of resident aliens guaranteed by international law and treaty, though Congress, undoubtedly, has power to pass such laws.[27]

B. Effect on the Power to Make International Agreements.
58. Limitations upon the Government as a Whole.

In considering limitations derived from the separation of powers, upon the power of the national government to make international agreements, we need consider only the limitations upon the full treaty-making power. Whatever independent power the President may enjoy in making international agreements is *a fortiori* subject to the same limitations.[27a] These limitations exist by virtue of the constitutional prerogatives of Congress, of the courts and of the President.

59. Limitations Derived from Powers of Congress.

"The treaty making power," said Calhoun, "is limited by such provisions of the Constitution as direct certain acts to be done in a particular way, and which prohibit the contrary, of which a striking example is to be found in that which declares that 'no money shall be drawn from the Treasury but in consequence of appropriations to be made by law.'"[28]

Undoubtedly, the treaty power is prohibited from depriving organs of the government of rights, privileges or powers inherent or delegated by the Constitution, or from giving them powers not appropriate to their nature. There does not appear to have ever been a treaty attempting to deprive Congress of a delegated power or to confer upon it power of a non-legislative nature. It is believed that a treaty declaring that war should automatically exist in certain circumstances would be an unconstitutional deprivation of Congress's power to declare war,[29] and that a treaty giving

---

[27] *Infra*, sec. 120.

[27a] For an additional limitation upon the President's agreement-making power see appendix.

[28] Works, 1: 203; Moore, Digest, 5: 166.

[29] See Taft, address before League to Enforce Peace, May 26, 1916, Enforced Peace, p. 64, and Hughes address, May 28, 1917, *Proc. Acad. Pol. Sci.*, vol. 7, No. 2, p. 14, quoted in *Am. Jl. Int. Law*, 12: 75–76.

Congress power to appoint an officer of the United States, as for instance a representative in an international body, would be an unconstitutional delegation to Congress of power not of a legislative character.[30]

Jefferson stated among "exceptions" from the treaty-making power: "those subjects of legislation in which it gave a participation to the House of Representatives." He noticed, however, that this exception "would leave very little matter for the treaty power to work on."[31] Practice does not sustain Jefferson's contention. Most treaties have dealt with subjects within the delegated powers of Congress and have been held valid.[32] Congress has questioned the validity of treaties requiring an appropriation, notably the Jay treaty of 1794[33] and the Alaska Purchase treaty of 1867.[34] The Senate refused consent to a commercial treaty with the German states in 1844 because of "want of constitutional competency."[35] President Jefferson himself seriously questioned the constitutionality of the Louisiana annexation treaty,[36] and authorities have ques-

---

[30] The exclusive mode of making appointments described in the Constitution, II, sec. 2, does not include appointments by Congress. See also Goodnow, *op. cit.,* p. 39; Willoughby, *op. cit.,* p. 1180.

[31] Jefferson, Manual of Parl. Prac., sec. 52, printed in Senate rules, 1913; H. of R. Rules, 1914; and Moore, Digest, 5: 162.

[32] Crandall, *op. cit.,* p. 182; Wright, *Am. Jl. Int. Law,* 12: 93. "The principle of interpretation on which the doubt is suggested appears to be radically unsound and to belong in the category of notions which tend to bring constitutional law into disrepute. That the United States cannot internationally agree to forego the exercise of any power which the Constitution has conferred on Congress, or other department of government, is a supposition contradicted by every exercise of the treaty-making power since the government came into existence. When we reflect upon the number and extent of the powers conferred upon the national government, and upon their distribution and the methods prescribed for their exercise, it is obvious that the attempt to act upon such a supposition would exclude the United States from any part in the progress of the world through the amelioration of law and practice by international action." Moore, Principles of American Diplomacy, 1918, p. 65.

[33] Wharton, Digest, 2: 19; Moore, Digest, 5: 224; Crandall, *op. cit.,* p. 165; Wright, *Am. Jl. Int. Law,* 12: 66.

[34] Moore, Digest, 5: 226–228; Crandall, *op. cit.,* p. 175.

[35] Crandall, *op. cit.,* pp. 189–190; Wright, *Am. Jl. Int. Law,* 12: 68.

[36] Crandall, *op. cit.,* p. 172; Moore, Digest, 5: 225; Wright, *Am. Jl. Int. Law,* 12: 69; Adams, History of U. S., 2: 83.

tioned the constitutionality of treaties making certain acts crimes,[37] treaties of guarantee which might require war for fulfillment,[38] and treaties forbidding privateering.[39] But treaties on all these subjects and in fact most other subjects within the delegated powers of Congress have been made, regularly acted upon and applied by the courts without question of constitutionality.

> "If this be the true view of the treaty-making power," said Calhoun with reference to the Senate rejection of the German treaty in 1844, "it may be truly said that its exercise has been one continual series of habitual and uninterrupted infringements of the Constitution. From the beginning and throughout the whole existence of the Federal Government it has been exercised constantly on commerce, navigation, and other delegated powers." [40]

Treaties of this kind often require action by Congress for execution and the degree of discretion Congress may exercise in executing them is determined by constitutional understandings, but the treaty is undoubtedly valid. It does not deprive Congress of power but only of its full discretion in the exercise of power.

60. *The Delegation of Legislative Power.*

As an implication from the doctrine of separation of powers it is recognized that legislative power cannot be delegated.[41] The Constitution gives to Congress and to the treaty-making power considerable authority to designate or even create organs for the exercise of judicial and executive power[42] and such provision is

---

[37] For objection of Secretary of State Marcy to treaties making privateering a crime see Moore, Digest, 2: 978; 5: 169; Wright, *Am. Jl. Int. Law*, 12: 79–80; Crandall, *op. cit.*, p. 242.

[38] For objection of W. J. Bryan and others see Wright, *Am. Jl. Int. Law*, 12: 73.

[39] Black, Constitutional Law, 1910, p. 274; Moore, Principles of American Diplomacy, p. 64.

[40] Moore, Digest, 5: 164; Willoughby, *op. cit.*, p. 491; Wright, *Am. Jl. Int. Law*, 12: 68.

[41] Field *v.* Clark, 143 U. S. 649; Willoughby, *op. cit.*, pp. 1317–1332.

[42] Congress has power to create inferior federal courts (Constitution, I, sec. 8, cl. 9; III, sec. 1), to regulate their jurisdiction and the appellate jurisdiction of the Supreme Court (III, sec. 2, cl. 2), to create "offices" (II, sec. 2, cl. 2), and to create and regulate a military and naval establishment (I, sec. 8, cl. 12–16). See also McCulloch *v.* Md., 4 Wheat. 316, holding

not considered incompatible with the theory of separation of powers, but no organs other than those specifically empowered thereto by the Constitution can be authorized to exercise legislative power.

"The Legislative," said John Locke, "neither must nor can transfer the power of making laws to anybody else, or place it anywhere but where the people have."[43]

However, this does not mean that all powers which the Legislature might exercise are incapable of delegation. It is well established that Congress can delegate to the President or other authority power to decide when[44] and where[45] the conditions exist which are to bring its enacted policy into operation, and the method[46] by which such a policy is to be administered. The legislative power, which cannot be delegated, is not confined to the making of permanent laws but includes such political powers of Congress as appropriating money and declaring war.[47] Furthermore, " legislative power " is not confined to the powers of Congress but includes political powers given by the Constitution to other organs. Thus the treaty-making power exercises legislative power which cannot be delegated since its acts, by Article VI, constitute "the supreme law of the land" and this, notwithstanding the apparent contradiction in the statement of Article I, section 1, that "*All* Legislative power herein granted shall be vested in a Congress of the United States."[48]

---

that Congress may create other instrumentalities, necessary and proper for carrying out constitutional powers. The treaty power may provide for courts. *In re* Ross, 140 U. S. 453; The Königin Luise, 184 Fed. 170 (1910); Wright, *Am. Jl. Int. Law,* 12: 70. See also *infra,* secs. 225, 226.

[43] Treatise on Civil Government, Works, vol. 5, sec. 142, quoted Cooley, Constitutional Limitations, 6th ed., p. 137.

[44] Martin *v.* Mott, 12 Wheat. 19; Field *v.* Clark, 143 U. S. 649 (1892).

[45] Dalby *v.* Wolf, 14 Iowa 228 (1862). Legislative power may be delegated to local bodies, State *v.* Noyes, 30 N. H. 279.

[46] Morrill *v.* Jones, 106 U. S. 466; *Ex Parte* Killock, 165 U. S. 526.

[47] The phraseology of the clauses conferring these powers indicates that they cannot be delegated. Constitution, I, sec. 8, cl. 2; sec. 9, cl. 7.

[48] The principle that legislative power cannot be delegated has always been assumed to be applicable to the treaty power. See Senate For. Rel.

SEPARATION OF POWERS.

Thus "legislative power" includes the power to make general laws and political decisions in whatever organ vested by the Constitution and does not include the executive power of carrying out policies and enforcing decisions, nor the judicial power of deciding questions of fact and applying law to particular cases.

61. *Congressional Delegation of Power to Make International Agreements.*

Although Congress has no power to make treaties, it has power to make laws on many subjects which may be appropriate for international agreement. Within this field it has delegated power to the President[49] to make international agreements in pursuance of a policy outlined by Legislation and such delegation has been sustained by the courts. Thus by an act of 1872[50] Congress provided that "for the purpose of making better postal arrangements with foreign countries," the postmaster-general, acting under the advice of the President, might "negotiate and conclude postal treaties." The United States has become a party to the Universal Postal Union Convention under this authority.[51] Similar provision for the conclusion of patent, copyright and trademark agreements have been made.[52]

Committee. Rept. 62d Cong., 1st sess., S. Doc. 98, p. 6, and remarks of Senator Walsh, Mont., *Cong. Rec.*, 58: 8609, Nov. 8, 1919, quoted in *Am. Jl. Int. Law*, 12: 91, and *Col. Law Rev.*, 20: 133.

[49] A possible encroachment upon the Senate's prerogative in treaty-making is considered *infra*, secs. 159, 162. See also note in appendix.

[50] U. S. Rev. Stat., sec. 398, Compiled Stat., sec. 587, founded on Act of 1792, see Crandall, *op. cit.*, p. 131.

[51] Moore, Digest, 5: 870.

[52] Patents Act, March 3, 1903, 32 Stat. 1225, Rev. Stat., sec. 4887. Copyrights Acts, March 3, 1891, 26 Stat. 1110, Moore, Digest, 2: 45, and March 4, 1909, sec. 8, 35 Stat. 1077, Comp. Stat., sec. 9220, Crandall, *op. cit.*, p. 127. Trademarks Act, March 3, 1881, 21 Stat. 502; Feb. 20, 1905, 33 Stat. 724, as amended in 1906 and 1909, Comp. Stat., sec. 9485. In the Trademark Cases (100 U. S. 82, 99) the Supreme Court held Congress incompetent to pass and enforce general trademarks laws but implied that such laws if confined to interstate and foreign commerce or to the protection of treaty rights would be valid. In most cases trademark agreements have been by treaty (See Secretary of State Hay to the Secretary of the Interior, Nov. 4, 1898, Moore, Digest, 2: 37), but the statute provided for the registration of trademarks used in interstate or foreign commerce by persons residing in foreign countries which, "by treaty, convention or law, applies

Under the McKinley Tariff Act of 1890 authority was given the President to suspend by proclamation the free entry of specified articles from countries which did not give reciprocity. Ten reciprocity agreements were negotiated by the President through exchange of notes which were made effective by proclamation and remained so until repeal of the McKinley Act in 1894.[53] In Field v. Clark[54] the Supreme Court held this provision of the McKinley Act valid since by it Congress had not delegated legislative power but merely power to carry out the policy outlined by Congress in the Act. The Dingley Tariff of 1897 and the Payne-Aldrich Tariff of 1909 contained similar provisions for reciprocity which have been carried out by a number of agreements.[55] Similar provision for reciprocity with Canada made in an act of 1911 has never been carried out because of the unwillingness of Canada to act.[56] We may conclude that power to make agreements in pursuance of enacted legislative policy is not "legislative power" and Congress may authorize the President to deal in this manner with subjects within its competence.

62. *Treaty Delegations of Power to National Organs.*

Treaties have on occasion delegated power to both national and international organs. These provisions have often been attacked on the ground that "legislative power" has been unconstitutionally delegated. The Cuban treaty of 1903, Article VII, authorized the

---

such privileges to citizens of the United States" (sec. 3, Comp. Stat., sec. 9489). Apparently the President might independently recognize the extension of laws to American citizens by foreign nations, entitling their citizens to the privileges of the act, but in fact, such recognition seems always to have been by treaty, except with reference to reciprocal protection in consular courts in China and Morocco. See Crandall, *op. cit.*, p. 130; Willoughby, *op. cit.*, p. 477.

[53] U. S. Tariff Commission, Reciprocity and Commercial Treaties, 1919, pp. 27, 153; Crandall, *op. cit.*, p. 122; Willoughby, *op. cit.*, pp. 478. See also Gresham, Secretary of State, to Mr. Mendonça, Brazilian Minister, Oct. 26, 1894, Moore, Digest, 5: 359-362.

[54] Field v. Clark, 143 U. S. 649 (1892).

[55] U. S. Tariff Commission, *op. cit.*, pp. 29, 32, 205, 271; Crandall, *op. cit.*, p. 123; Fish, Am. Diplomacy, p. 471.

[56] Act July 26, 1911, 37 Stat. 4, Comp. Stat., sec. 5326; Crandall, *op. cit.*, p. 125; U. S. Tariff Commission, *op. cit.*, pp. 36-38, 371.

SEPARATION OF POWERS. 107

President to acquire naval bases in Cuba and in accord therewith President Roosevelt acquired Guantanamo by executive agreement.[57] Here the President was clearly carrying out the policy laid down by the treaty and the case was clearly within the precedents of congressional delegation of power to make international agreements.

One of the proposed Senate reservations to the treaty of Versailles provided for denunciation of the League of Nations Covenant on two years, notice by "concurrent resolution" of Congress.[58] The only constitutional authorities for terminating treaties are Congress by an act signed by the President or passed over his veto, the treaty-making power and possibly the President alone.[59] Clearly the termination of a law, such as a treaty, is an exercise of legislative power and cannot be delegated to any authority other than those specified for that purpose by the Constitution.[60] It was contended by the President and in the Senate, the writer

---

[57] The provision of the treaty was also contained in an act of Congress of March 2, 1901 (the Platt Amendment), and in the Cuban Constitution. An agreement to make the lease was signed February 16, 1903, and the lease itself was signed July 2, 1903, while the treaty, although signed May 22, 1903, was not proclaimed until July 2, 1904. Thus the lease was in reality authorized by the act of Congress rather than by the treaty. See Malloy, Treaties, pp. 358-363. For other examples see Crandall, *op. cit.*, p. 117.

[58] Lodge Reservation No. 1, in form voted on by Senate, Nov. 19, 1919, and March 19, 1920. For text of Lodge Reservations see Cong. Rec., Nov. 19, 1919, 58: 9289; March 19, 1919, 59: 4915; The League of Nations, World Peace Foundation, Boston, III, No. 4, pp. 166, 182, and note, *Col. Law Rev.*, 20: 156.

[59] Jefferson, Manual, sec. 52, Senate Rules, 1913, p. 150; House Rules, 1914, sec. 592; Hinds, Precedents, 5: 6270; President Hayes, Message, March, 1879, Richardson, Messages, 7: 519; Sen. Rept., No. 97, 34th Cong., 1st Sess.; Taft, Our Chief Magistrate, p. 117; Willoughby, *op. cit.*, p. 518; Crandall, *op. cit.*, pp. 401-462; Wright, *Col. Law Rev.*, 20: 129. See also *infra*, secs. 181-187.

[60] The Constitution provides that "Every Order, Resolution, or Vote to which the Concurrence of the Senate and House of Representatives may be necessary (except on a question of Adjournment) shall be presented to the President of the United States; and before the same shall take Effect, shall be approved by him, or being disapproved by him, shall be repassed by two thirds of the Senate and House of Representatives, according to the Rules and Limitations prescribed in the case of a Bill."

believes correctly, that delegation of this power to a mere majority of the two houses of Congress without the President's approval would be an unconstitutional delegation of legislative power.[61]

An extended controversy has arisen over the delegation of power to the President by general arbitration treaties, to make the *compromis* or instrument submitting specific cases to arbitration. The I Hague Convention of 1899, as also that of 1907, provided a panel of arbitrators, a method for selecting a court and a procedure for arbitrating cases. By Article 16, the parties including the United States recognized arbitration " as the most efficacious and at the same time the most equitable method of deciding controversies which have not been settled by diplomatic methods." Under these provisions, in 1903, President Roosevelt submitted the Pious Fund claim against Mexico to the Hague Tribunal, without consulting the Senate.[62] Opinion has differed as to whether the Hague Convention delegated this power. Simeon E. Baldwin has said:[63]

"The Hague Convention when ratified by the Senate, became thus a standing warrant, or, so to speak, a power of attorney, from the United States to the President, to submit such international controversies as he might think fit to the ultimate decision of the International Court of Arbitration."

Ex-Secretary of State Foster, however, took a contrary view:[64]

"I apprehend that should our government decide to refer any dispute with a foreign government to the Hague Tribunal, President Roosevelt, or whoever should succeed him, would enter into a convention with the foreign government, very carefully setting forth the question to be arbitrated, and submit that convention to the Senate for its advice and consent. If I read the Constitution of the United States and the Hague Convention aright, such would be the only course permissible by those instruments."

[61] "A statute or a treaty might end upon the occurrence of a fortuitous event or upon the determination of a certain fact or of a certain condition by a certain officer, he having no discretion on the subject at all; but when it becomes a question of the exercise of his judgment or his discretion about whether the law should remain in force or whether it should be repealed, considering the good of the country, that would be an unlawful delegation of legislative power." Senator Walsh, Mont., Cong. Rec., Nov. 8, 1919, 58: 8609. "I doubt whether the President can be deprived of his veto power under the Constitution even with his own consent." President Wilson, letter to Senator Hitchcock, Jan. 26, 1920.

[62] Willoughby, *op. cit.*, p. 475.
[63] *Yale Review*, 9: 415, quoted, Willoughby, *op. cit.*, p. 476.
[64] *Yale Law Jl.*, 11: 76, quoted Willoughby, *loc. cit.*

SEPARATION OF POWERS.

It may be observed that since the President has power under the Constitution to settle claims of the United States *against* foreign countries[65] he unquestionably had power to submit the Pious Fund claim to arbitration aside from the Hague Convention or from the arbitration provision of the Mexican treaty of 1848 in force in 1903.[66] Thus claims against Venezuela were submitted to the Hague Tribunal in 1903 and 1909 by executive protocols.[67] The North Atlantic Fisheries arbitration with Great Britain, the remaining Hague Case to which the United States has been a party, was, however, submitted by a treaty,[68] though in this case treaty submission had been expressly required by the general arbitration treaty with Great Britain of 1908,[69] and the United States had made express reservation to the Hague Convention of 1907 requiring that submission to the Hague Court be by "general or special treaties of arbitration."[70]

The same question was raised with reference to the proposed Hay arbitration treaties of 1905, providing for arbitration of "differences" of a "legal nature" which do not affect the "vital interests, the independence or the honor of the two contracting states and do not concern the interests of third parties." These treaties required conclusion of a "special agreement" defining the matter in dispute, the powers of the arbitrators and the procedure. The Senate was willing to consent only if the word "treaty" was substituted for "agreement" and President Roosevelt refused to submit the treaties thus amended thinking that a general arbitration treaty was valueless if each specific submission required conclusion of a "special treaty."[71] In 1908, however, Secretary Root con-

---

[65] *Infra*, sec. 171.
[66] Art. 21, Malloy, Treaties, p. 1117.
[67] *Ibid.*, pp. 1870, 1889.
[68] *Ibid.*, p. 835.
[69] Art. II, *Ibid.*, p. 814.
[70] *Ibid.*, p. 2247. See also Scott, ed., Reports of the Hague Conferences, pp. xxvii, 903.
[71] Willoughby, *op. cit.*, pp. 473–475; Taft, The United States and Peace, 1914, p. 95; Sutherland, *op. cit.*, p. 129.

110   THE CONTROL OF AMERICAN FOREIGN RELATIONS.

cluded many treaties substantially of the form of the Hay treaties with the Senate amendment.[72]

Aside from the question of policy, it seems that the Hay treaties in their original form would not amount to an unconstitutional delegation of legislative power.[73] They merely authorize the President to carry out the policy of arbitrating certain classes of disputes laid down by the general treaty and are well within the decision of Field *v.* Clark.[74]

63. *Treaty Delegation of Power to International Organs.*

Where treaties have delegated power to international bodies, constitutional questions have often been raised. The courts have sustained treaties submitting claims, boundary questions, etc., to international arbitration courts and have held that the decision of such a court is of the same legal weight in the United States as the treaty itself. Thus after the Bering Sea Arbitration Tribunal had held that American jurisdiction in Bering Sea terminated at the three mile limit, the United States Circuit Court of Appeals refused to apply the acts of Congress for protecting the seal herds, to vessels engaged in sealing beyond that limit.[75]

Where, however, treaties have provided for an international commission or court which shall decide whether or not a particular dispute is of a justiciable character as defined by the general treaty, doubt has been expressed in the Senate. The proposed international Prize Court Convention of 1907 with its attached protocol of 1910 provided that claims against the United States for defined types of prize decisions might be brought in the international Prize Court by private individuals, and the court would itself decide whether the case was within the described classes *i.e.*, whether it had jurisdiction. This treaty and protocol, although never operative, were consented to by the Senate in 1911.[76]

---

[72] As example see British treaty, Malloy, Treaties, p. 814.

[73] Crandall, *op. cit.*, p. 120; Willoughby, *op. cit.*, p. 475; Taft, The United States and Peace, p. 95; Moore, *Pol. Sci. Quarterly,* 20: 403.

[74] Field *v.* Clark, 143 U. S. 649 (1892).

[75] U. S. *v.* La Ninfa, 75 Fed. 513.

[76] Charles, Treaties, p. 262. A constitutional objection of a different kind connected with this convention is considered, *infra,* sec. 64. The Hague Convention of 1907 provided in article 53 that the Permanent Court might

SEPARATION OF POWERS. 111

In 1911 President Taft negotiated arbitration treaties with Great Britain and France providing for the arbitration of defined classes of cases and for decision by an international joint high commission upon the question of whether a specific dispute was within these classes.[77] The Senate Foreign Relations Committee reported adversely on the latter provision:[78]

> "This recommendation is made because there can be no question that, through the machinery of the joint commission, as provided in Articles II and III and with the last clause of Article III included, the Senate is deprived of its constituent power to pass upon all questions involved in any treaty submitted to it in accordance with the Constitution. The committee believes that it would be a violation of the Constitution of the United States to confer upon an outside commission, powers which, under the Constitution, devolve upon the Senate. . . . To vest in an outside commission the power to say finally what the treaty means by its very general and indefinite language is to vest in that commission the power to make for us an entirely different treaty from that which we supposed ourselves to be making."

The delegation of power here objected to was of the same sort as that to which exception had been taken in the Hay treaties of 1905. In the one case, however, delegation was to the President, in the other to an international commission.[79] Neither case

---

arrange the *compromis* on application of *one* party where the dispute is "covered by a general treaty of arbitration concluded or renewed after the present convention has come into force," specifying subjects for compulsory arbitration; and where the dispute arises from contract debts due by one power to the nationals of another. (Malloy, Treaties, p. 2238.) The Senate consented to ratification of the treaty with a reservation to this article asserting that the United States "excludes from the competence of the permanent court the power to frame the '*compromis*' required by general or special treaties of arbitration concluded or hereafter to be concluded by the United States, and further expressly declares that the '*compromis*' required by any treaty of arbitration to which the United States may be a party shall be settled only by agreement between the contracting parties, unless such treaty shall expressly provide otherwise." (*Ibid.*, p. 2248, and Scott, ed., Reports of the Hague Conferences, introduction, p. xxvii.)

[77] These treaties though never ratified are printed in Charles, Treaties, pp. 380-389.

[78] 62d Cong., 1st sess., S. Doc. 98, p. 6; *Cong. Rec.*, 47: 3935.

[79] It may be noticed that the Taft treaties accepted the point upon which the Senate had insisted in 1905 and required that the "*compromis*" submitting each case be a treaty consented to by the Senate, even after the Joint High Commission had given its decision. See next note.

seems to involve a delegation of legislative power, but rather of judicial power, to interpret the treaty. The minority report of the Senate Committee signed by Senators Root and Cullom pointed out that the majority view could "not be maintained except on the theory that all general treaties of arbitration" involve a like unconstitutional delegation of power, the only difference being that the treaties under consideration submitted "certain described classes" of cases to arbitration, instead of particular cases. The decision of the joint high commission on what questions are justiciable "is not delegating to a commission power to say what shall be arbitrated; it is merely empowering the commission to find whether the particular case is one that the United States have said shall be arbitrated."[80] President Taft, Senator Sutherland, J. B. Moore, and other constitutional authorities have endorsed this opinion.[81]

A logical carrying out of the majority theory would seem to deny any power to conclude treaties in good faith, for all treaties require interpretation, and to say that the interpretations must always be according to the will of the existing treaty-making power of the United States, however that may differ from the intent of the original negotiators, is virtually to substitute political expediency for treaty obligation. Good faith would seem to require that the true intent of the instrument govern its application through its entire life, and it is hard to see where a more impartial determination of what this intent was could be obtained than in an international tribunal. The common law doctrine that no one should be judge in his own case would seem as applicable to international as to private relations.[82]

[80] *Ibid.*, p. 9. This report was signed by Senators Root and Cullom. In a special minority report, Senator Burton pointed out that even after decision by the joint high commission the "*compromis*" would go to the Senate. "In such case, as in every other case, it would be within the power of the Senate to refuse its advice and consent to the special agreement, but it would be contrary to its treaty obligation." *Ibid.*, p. 12. See also Wright, *Am. Jl. Int. Law*, 12: 93, *Col. Law Rev.*, 20: 133.

[81] Taft, The United States and Peace, p. 113; Our Chief Magistrate, p. 107; Sutherland, *op. cit.*, p. 132; Moore, *Independent*, Aug. 8, 1911.

[82] See *infra*, sec. 139.

SEPARATION OF POWERS.

This particular question has not been raised in connection with the League of Nations Covenant because, according to Article XIII, disputes can be submitted to arbitration only by consent of the parties and in the United States this consent would be indicated by the treaty-making power in concluding the instrument of submission.[83] Senator Knox and others have, however, in effect asserted that the powers conferred upon the Council and Assembly of the League of Nations are in part legislative, and hence in so far the treaty would be unconstitutional.[84] It is believed that this criticism overlooks three important aspects of the Covenant. (1) "Decision at any meeting of the Assembly or of the Council (except where otherwise expressly provided) shall require the agreement of *all the members of the* League represented at the meeting,"[85] thus the United States would not be delegating legislative power any more than it has in participating in international conferences such as the Hague, Algeciras or Versailles Conferences. It will be noticed that it is not the agreement of the American representative which is required but of the "member of the League," that is, of the United States itself, and as has been noticed the United States cannot be bound by any agreement unless the proper constitutional organ has acted.[86] Thus if the decision was of a character which could only be made by the treaty-making power, the United States would not be bound until the Senate had consented. Apparently the only decisions, aside from questions of procedure,[87] which by express exception might be made without consent of the United States, are to admit new members (Art. I)

---

[83] The scheme drafted by Mr. Root and others for the international court authorized by Article XIV of the Covenant would, however, raise the issue, since Article XXXIV provides: "In the event of a dispute as to whether a certain case is within any of the categories above mentioned, the matter shall be settled by the decision of the court." *Am. Jl. Int. Law,* Supp. 14: 379 (Oct., 1920). This was modified by the Assembly of the League of Nations in December, 1920, *Ibid.,* 15: 264.

[84] Address in Senate, March 1, 1919.

[85] Art. V. The United States is by the terms of the Covenant represented in both the Council and the Assembly.

[86] *Supra,* sec. 24.

[87] These may be settled by a majority vote (Art. V). Amendments to the Covenant, though requiring ratification by only a majority of the members represented in the Assembly, require ratification by all the members

which requires two-thirds of the Assembly but which is clearly not an exercise of legislative power, and to make a report in a dispute likely to lead to a rupture, to which the United States is a party. (Art. XV.)[88] This will be discussed presently.

(2) The other consideration which seems to have been overlooked by critics of the Covenant is that no legislative or binding political power has been conferred upon the Council or Assembly. The powers of these bodies are limited to the giving of " advice " or the making of " proposals," " recommendations " or " reports," which even if unanimous are of binding effect in only three cases.[89] These three cases are: (*a*) The limits of armament once agreed upon by members "shall not be exceeded without the concurrence of the Council." (Art. VIII, sec. 4.) (*b*) If a country has voluntarily accepted a mandate, and has neglected to fully define "the degree of authority, control or administration" which it is to exercise, the Council may "explicitly define" these powers in each case. (Art. XXII, sec. 8.) (*c*) A dispute likely to lead to a rupture must be submitted to the Council or Assembly and if no solution is reached the Council or Assembly make a report.

"If a report by the Council is unanimously agreed to by the members thereof, other than the representatives of one or more of the parties to the dispute, the members of the League agree that they will not go to war with any party to the dispute which complies with the recommendations of the report." (Art. XV, sec. 6.)

represented in the Council, thus always including the United States (Art. 26).

[88] See Lowell, *The Covenanter*, N. Y., 1919, p. 81, and British Official Commentary, printed in Pollock, The League of Nations, London, 1920, p. 208.

[89] Lowell, *The Covenanter*, pp. 40, 80. Some doubt exists as to whether the "advice" which the Council may give as to the method of carrying out the guarantees of Article X is obligatory. Lowell (*Ibid.*, p. 40) and Pollock (*op. cit.*, p. 128) believe not, while the Official Swiss Commentary holds that for members that have assented to the "advice," if unanimous, it is obligatory. (League of Nations, World Peace Foundation, III, No. 3, p. 125.) So far as the "advice" extends merely to an interpretation of the meaning of the treaty, we are inclined to agree with the latter opinion (*supra*, sec. 35), which appears to be consonant with the interpretation of similar terms in article XVI by the Second Assembly of the League (see Report of International Blockade Committee, Second Assembly Document No. 28, part II, and resolutions adopted October 4, 1921, Official Journal, Special Supp. No. 6, p. 25).

SEPARATION OF POWERS.

If the dispute is submitted to the Assembly it has the same effect "if concurred in by the Representatives of those Members of the League represented on the Council and by a majority of the other Members of the League, exclusive in each case of the Representatives of the parties to the dispute." (Art. XV, sec. 10.)

Although binding decisions may be given in the first two cases by unanimous action of the Council, the power exercised would not be "legislative" but merely a carrying out of the policy already agreed upon in the treaties providing for disarmament or acceptance of the mandatory. Decision on such a question clearly may be delegated.[90] In the third case which relates to the settlement of political controversies which the parties have not agreed to submit to arbitration, it will be observed that the decision even if unanimous with exception of the parties to the dispute is not strictly binding. If the United States were a party to the dispute it would not be legally bound to follow the report, even if all other members of the Council or Assembly had signed it. Doubtless, however, there would be a practical compulsion, in view of the fact that it could get no members of the League as allies in case it went to war with the other party to the dispute.[91]

(3) A third consideration which should be noticed is that the most discussed provisions of the Covenant such as Articles X, XII, and XVI do not delegate power at all. They are guarantees which leave to the members of the League discretion in deciding upon the method for carrying them out in concrete cases.[92] Of course the United States would have to follow constitutional provisions in doing so.[93] It does not appear that there is any unconstitutional delegation of legislative power in the League of Nations Covenant.

64. *Limitations Derived from Powers of the Judiciary.*

The constitutionality of a treaty seems never to have been questioned on the ground that it was itself an exercise of

---

[90] *Supra,* sec. 60.
[91] See British Commentary, Pollock, *op. cit.,* p. 212; Swiss Commentary, *op. cit.,* p. 137.
[92] Lowell, *The Covenanter,* p. 37.
[93] W. H. Taft, *The Covenanter,* p. 60 *et seq.* See also Wright, *Am. Jl. Int. Law,* 12: 75, and *supra,* sec. 59.

116   THE CONTROL OF AMERICAN FOREIGN RELATIONS.

judicial power though treaties or arbitrations based upon them have interpreted statutes and international law and the courts have followed such decisions.[94] Nor is there any encroachment upon the judicial power when treaties vest judicial powers in bodies other than the supreme and inferior courts of the United States. Consular courts abroad and international courts founded on treaty do not exercise "the judicial power of the United States" in the meaning of Article III of the Constitution[95] and foreign consular courts in the United States for the trial of seamen of vessels of the consul's nationality have been held of "ministerial" rather than judicial character, though the grounds for this distinction is not apparent.[96]

A treaty depriving courts of any inherent right, privilege or power would, undoubtedly, be void,[97] though a treaty may exempt certain persons from the judicial power of subpoena[98] and need not provide security of tenure and compensation for the judges

---

[94] U. S. v. La Ninfa, 75 Fed. 513; Comegys v. Vasse, 1 Pet. 193 (1828); Meade v. U. S., 9 Wall. 691; Wright, *Am. Jl. Int. Law*, 12: 85, and *supra*, note 75.

[95] "The treaty-making power vested in our government extends to all proper subjects of negotiation with foreign governments. It can, equally with any of the former or present governments of Europe, make treaties providing for the exercise of judicial authority in other countries by its officers appointed to reside therein. . . . The Constitution can have no operation in another country. When, therefore, the representatives or officers of our government are permitted to exercise authority of any kind in another country, it must be on such conditions as the two countries may agree, the laws of neither one being obligatory upon the other." *In re* Ross, 140 U. S. 453 (1890). Nor is the "Judicial power of the United States" exercised by congressional courts in the territories (Am. Ins. Co. v. Canter, 1 Pet. 511); nor by presidential courts organized in territory under military occupation (Neeley v. Henkel, 180 U. S. 109) or in annexed territory under military government. (Cross v. Harrison, 16 How. 164; Magoon, Reports, pp. 16, 30.) Such presidential courts may exercise local jurisdiction but may not be given an admiralty and prize jurisdiction. (Jecker v. Montgomery, 13 How. 498.)

[96] Cushing, Att. Gen., 8 Op. 390, 1857. See also the Königin Luise, 184 Fed. 170 (1910), and Wright, *Am. Jl. Int. Law*, 12: 71.

[97] *Infra*, sec. 53.

[98] Dillon's case, *supra*, sec. 46.

SEPARATION OF POWERS. 117

in consular and other courts it establishes, as they do not exercise the "judicial power of the United States." [99]

Treaties cannot vest courts exercising "the judicial power of the United States" with non-judicial functions.[100] Thus doubt has been expressed whether treaties could provide for appeal from federal courts to an international tribunal, since with such a review by an authority not exercising "the judicial power of the United States" the original hearing by the federal court would be rendered non-judicial in character. Such an international tribunal could not be endowed by Congress with the "judicial power of the United States" since its judges could not be assured the security of tenure and compensation required of courts exercising that power and the Supreme Court has expressly held that courts established by Congress in the territories and courts established abroad or in the United States by treaty do not exercise that power.[101] In the case of Gordon v. United States the Supreme Court refused to hear appeals from the Court of Claims which would subsequently be reviewable by the Secretary of the Treasury, saying:[102]

"The Supreme Court's jurisdiction and powers and duties being defined in the organic law of the government, and being all strictly judicial, Congress cannot require or authorize the court to exercise any other jurisdiction or power, or perform any other duty. . . . The award of execution is a part, and an essential part, of every judgment passed by a court exercising judicial power. It is no judgment in the legal sense of the term, without it. Without such an award judgment would be inoperative and nugatory, leaving the aggrieved party without a remedy. . . . Such is not the judicial power confided to this court, in the exercise of its appellate jurisdiction; yet it is the whole power that the court is allowed to exercise under this act of Congress."

The XII Hague Convention of 1907 proposed an International Prize Court with appellate jurisdiction in prize cases. Doubts as to its constitutionality were felt by Secretary Root, on the grounds of this case, and he instructed the American delegation to the London Naval Conference (designed to codify the law for this court) to

[99] *Supra,* note 95.
[100] *Supra,* sec. 55.
[101] *Supra,* note 95.
[102] Gordon v. U. S., 117 U. S. 697.

propose a supplementary protocol, whereby, instead of subjecting decisions of the United States courts to appeal and possible reversal in the International Prize Court, a direct claim might be brought there against the United States "in the form of an action in damages for the injury caused by the capture."[103] This suggestion was adopted by the Naval Conference in a final protocol[104] and was ultimately incorporated in a protocol signed by all signatories of the original Prize Court Convention.[105]

"The (American) delegation remarked that for certain states the functioning of the International Prize Court is not compatible with that of the Constitution. The decision of national courts cannot be annulled by foreign decisions in certain countries, such as the United States of America. Recourse to the Prize Court might have that effect of annulling a decision of the Supreme Court of the United States of America, a result incompatible with their Constitution."[106]

The option permitted by the protocol would eliminate this possibility. It seems probable that the difficulty might have been equally met by domestic legislation providing special courts for the original hearing of Prize Cases.

"Congress," said the Supreme Court in the Gordon Case, "may undoubtedly establish tribunals with special powers to examine testimony and decide, in the first instance, upon the validity and justice of any claim for money against the United States, subject to the supervision and control of Congress, or a head of any of the executive departments."[107]

The establishment of such special tribunals not exercising the judicial power of the United States would, however, be a cumbersome process if applied merely to prize courts and would become impracticable if appeal to an international tribunal were provided in all cases involving international law or treaty.

---

[103] U. S. For. Rel., 1909, p. 303.

[104] *Ibid.*, p. 318; Report of U. S. delegates, *Ibid.*, p. 305, and President Taft's message, Dec. 6, 1910, *Ibid.*, 1910, p. viii.

[105] Charles, Treaties, p. 263. Neither the Protocol nor the original convention has been ratified though ratification was advised by the Senate, Feb. 15, 1911.

[106] Proceedings, London Naval Conference, British Par. Pap. Misc. No. 5 (1909), p. 222. See American statement, *Ibid.*, p. 216.

[107] Gordon *v.* U. S., 117 U. S. 697.

SEPARATION OF POWERS.

65. *Limitations Derived from Powers of the President.*

A treaty may delegate ministerial powers within the United States but it may not deprive the President of rights, privileges, or powers inherent or expressly granted by the Constitution. Some of the proposed Senate reservations to the Treaty of Versailles seemed to be unconstitutional as in certain circumstances they would deprive the President of his veto,[108] of his power to direct the movement of troops,[109] of his power to conduct foreign negotiations in person or through agents[110] and of his power to make interim appointments.[111]

---

[108] "Notice of withdrawal by the United States (from the League of Nations) may be given by concurrent resolution of the Congress of the United States," *i.e.*, by a resolution not submitted to the President. Lodge Reservations, No. 1. See Wright, *Col. Law Rev.*, 20: 128, and *supra*, sec. 62.

[109] "Congress . . . under the Constitution, has the sole power to declare war or authorize the employment of the military or naval forces of the United States." Lodge Reservations, No. 2. "The President is made Commander-in-Chief of the army and navy by the Constitution, evidently for the purpose of enabling him to defend the country against invasion, to suppress insurrection, and to take care that the laws be faithfully executed. If Congress were to attempt to prevent his use of the army for any of these purposes, the action would be void." Taft, Our Chief Magistrate, pp. 128–129. See also Wright, *Col. Law Rev.*, 20: 134–136.

[110] "Until such participation and appointment have been so provided for (*i.e.*, by act of Congress) and the powers and duties of such representatives have been defined by law, no person shall represent the United States under either said League of Nations or the treaty of peace with Germany or be authorized to *perform any act for or on behalf of the United States thereunder.*" Lodge Reservation No. 7. This was somewhat modified in the reservations as voted on March 19, 1920. With reference to the independent powers of the President, the Senate Foreign Relations Committee reported in 1894: "Many precedents could be noted to show that such power has been exercised by the President on various occasions without dissent on the part of Congress. These precedents also show that the Senate of the United States, though in session, need not be consulted as to the appointment of such agents." (*Cong. Rec.*, 2d Sess., p. 127, quoted Corwin, *op. cit.*, p. 64.) See also Wright, *Col. Law Rev.*, 20: 136–137.

[111] "No citizen of the United States shall be selected or appointed as a member of said commissions, committees, tribunals, courts, councils or conferences except with the approval of the Senate of the U. S." Lodge Reservation No. 7 but eliminated in revision voted on March 19, 1920. This conflicts with the constitutional provision: "The President shall have

The manner in which the power to make treaties must be exercised in the United States does not affect the power of the national government as a whole to make international agreements. The distribution of power in making treaties between the President and the Senate will be considered in a later chapter.[112] Suffice it to say here, that controversy has arisen over the power of the President to negotiate treaties by agents to whose appointment the Senate has not consented, to make executive agreements without Senate consent, and to ignore directions of Congress in negotiation and treaty making.

C. Effect on Power to Make National Decisions.

66. Alleged Encroachments.

The doctrine of separation of powers does not limit the power of the United States to make national decisions on international questions. It does, however, limit the power of particular organs to make such decisions. The details of this distribution of power will be considered in a later chapter.[113] A few of the controversies which have arisen may be suggested here.

Congressional resolutions recognizing foreign states or governments, expressing national sentiment or policy, directing the President in foreign policy, or ordering the detailed movement of troops, have been alleged to encroach upon the President's exclusive power in these matters.

Congressional delegations of power to the President to decide when the conditions, previsioned by statutes, actually exist, and upon such decision to put legislative policies into effect by proclamation have been questioned.

Presidential proclamations of neutrality and war, and confiscation orders in time of war, have been questioned as encroachments upon the powers of Congress.

Finally, judicial decisions on political questions have been alleged to encroach upon the powers of the President and Congress.

---

power to fill up all vacancies that may happen during the recess of the Senate, by granting commissions which shall expire at the end of their next session." II, sec. 2, cl. 3. See Wright, *Col. Law Rev.*, 20: 138.

[112] *Infra*, chap. XIV.
[113] *Infra*, chap. XV.

CHAPTER VIII.

Conclusion on Constitutional Limitations.

67. *Traditional Statements of Limitations upon the Treaty Power.*

As we have seen, limitations upon the power of national organs are of three kinds, in defense of the rights and privileges of individuals, the rights and privileges of the states, and the rights, privileges and powers of the organs of the national government. The observance of these limitations is considered essential to the preservation respectively of individual liberty, the autonomy of the states, and the separation of powers.

These three types of limitations are expressed in the classic statement of Justice Field in reference to the treaty power:[1]

"The treaty power, as expressed in the Constitution, is in terms unlimited except by those restraints which are found in that instrument against the action of the government or of its departments, and those arising from the nature of the government and of that of the States. It would not be contended that it extends so far as to authorize what the Constitution forbids, or a change in the character of the government or in that of one of the States, or a cession of any portion of the territory of the latter, without its consent. Fort Leavenworth Railroad Co. v. Lowe, 114 U. S. 525, 541. But with these exceptions, it is not perceived that there is any limit to the questions which can be adjusted touching any matter which is properly the subject of negotiation with a foreign country. Ware v. Hylton, 3 Dall. 199; Chirac v. Chirac, 2 Wheat. 259; Hauenstein v. Lynham, 100 U. S. 483; 8 Opinions Attys. Gen. 417; People v. Gerke, 5 California 381."

Jefferson and Calhoun each attempted to define the limits of the treaty power in well-known statements. Calhoun wrote:[2]

"It (the treaty-making power) is ... limited by all the provisions of the Constitution which inhibit certain acts from being done by the government, or any of its departments; of which description there are many. It is also limited by such provisions of the Constitution as direct certain acts to

---

[1] Geofroy v. Riggs, 133 U. S. 258, 267 (1890).
[2] Calhoun, Discourse on Constitutional Government of U. S., Works, I: 203; Moore, Digest, 5: 166.

be done in a particular way, and which prohibit the contrary, of which a striking example is to be found in that which declares that no money shall be drawn from the Treasury but in consequence of appropriations to be made by law. This not only imposes an important restriction on the power, but gives to Congress as the law-making power, and to the House of Representatives as a portion of Congress, *the right to withhold appropriations;* and thereby, an important control over the treaty-making power, whenever money is required to carry a treaty into effect; which is usually the case, especially in reference to those of much importance. There still remains another, and more important limitation, but of a more general and indefinite character. It can enter into no stipulation calculated to change the character of the government; or to do that which can only be done by the constitution-making power; or which is inconsistent with the nature and structure of the government."

This seems to follow the recognized view. It should be noticed, however, that while, under constitutional law (though not under international law), Congress has the right to withhold appropriations, yet by constitutional understandings[3] it ought not to do so. Thus though a treaty could not vest the power to make appropriations in any organ other than Congress, yet, the fact that a treaty requires an appropriation does not impeach the validity of a treaty, as Calhoun himself clearly stated while Secretary of State:[4]

"The treaty-making power has, indeed, been regarded to be so comprehensive as to embrace, with few exceptions, all questions that can possibly arise between us and other nations, and which can only be adjusted by their mutual consent, whether the subject matter be comprised among the delegated or the reserved powers. So far, indeed, is it from being true, as the report supposed, that the mere fact of a power being delegated to Congress excludes it from being the subject of treaty stipulations; that even its exclusive delegation, if we may judge from the habitual practice of the government, does not—of which the power of appropriating money affords a striking example. It is expressly and exclusively delegated to Congress, and yet scarcely a treaty has been made of any importance which does not stipulate for the payment of money. No objection has ever been made on this account. The only question ever raised in reference to it is, whether Congress has not unlimited discretion to grant or withhold the appropriation."

[3] *Infra,* sec. 256.
[4] Mr. Calhoun, Sec. of State, to Mr. Wheaton, Minister to Prussia, June 28, 1844, Moore, Digest, 5: 164. See also *infra,* sec. 59.

CONSTITUTIONAL LIMITATIONS.

Jefferson wrote in his Manual of Parliamentary Practice:[5]

"To what subjects this power extends, has not been defined in detail by the Constitution, nor are we entirely agreed among ourselves. (1) It is admitted that it must concern the foreign nation, party to the contract, or it would be a mere nullity, res inter alios acta. (2) By the general power to make treaties, the Constitution must have intended to comprehend only those objects which are usually regulated by treaty and cannot be otherwise regulated. (3) It must have meant to except out of these the rights reserved to the states; for surely the President and Senate cannot do by treaty what the whole government is interdicted from doing in any way. (4) And also to except those subjects of legislation in which it gave a participation to the House of Representatives. This last exception is denied by some, on the ground that it would leave very little matter for the treaty power to work on. The less the better, say others."

This statement is both erroneous and incomplete, it seems, therefore, unfortunate that it should be reprinted in both Senate and House manuals without explanatory comment.[6] It does not state all of the limitations which actually exist and the last two limitations stated do not exist. The last is effectively refuted by the statement quoted from Calhoun. The third is thus dealt with by Attorney General Griggs:[7]

"The regulation of fisheries in navigable waters within the territorial limits of the several States is, in the absence of a treaty, a subject of State rather than of Federal jurisdiction; but the government of the United States has power to enter into treaty stipulations on the subject, e.g., with Great Britain, for the regulation of the fisheries in the waters of the United States and Canada along the international boundary; and the fact that a treaty provision would annul and supersede a particular State law on the subject would be no objection to the validity of the treaty."

The limitation referred to last by Justice Field and first and second by Jefferson applies to the exercise of all powers in the field of foreign relations. They must be *bona fide* directed toward the conduct of international relations. Thus a purported declaration of war, really designed to excuse an invasion of the residual powers of the states, would doubtless be void; though it might be difficult to discover a court with sufficient temerity to declare it so, if con-

---
[5] Art. 52, Moore, Digest, 5: 162.
[6] Senate, Manual, 1913, p. 149; Rules of H. of R., 1914, sec. 587, p. 252.
[7] Griggs, Att. Gen., 22 Op. 214 (1898), Moore, Digest, 5: 161-162. See also *supra*, sec. 50.

stitutional government had so lapsed in vigilance as to present the opportunity. Such acts can only be prevented by operation of the political checks upon government.[8]

68. *Most Limitations Unimportant in Practice.*

Although in theory constitutional limitations apply to the organs of government in the conduct of foreign relations, as well as domestic affairs, yet in practice it is discovered that many limitations, especially those for the protection of individual and states' rights, are applicable only within American territory and hence do not limit the exterritorial action of national organs.[9] Furthermore, even when limitations are legally applicable, their enforcement is apt to belong to the political departments of government because of the disinclination of the courts to pass on "political questions."[10] Obviously the political departments are more likely to err on the side of an efficient exercise of national power than on the side of an excessive regard for constitutional limitations. Finally, even when such cases do come before the courts, they show an unquestionable tendency to interpret limitations less rigorously where foreign affairs are involved.[11] "In the exercise of its international and military power," says Freund, "the state is freed from many of the restraints under which it must conduct the peaceful government of its own citizens."[12] Though this can hardly be accepted in constitutional theory, except as explained above, undoubtedly, it is true in fact,[13] and for reasons thus explained by Hamilton:[14]

"As the duties of superintending the national defense and of securing the public peace against foreign or domestic violence involve a provision for casualties and dangers to which no possible limits can be assigned, the power

---

[8] Willoughby, *op. cit.*, p. 504; Corwin, National Supremacy, pp. 302–308.

[9] *In re* Ross, 140 U. S. 453.

[10] Foster *v.* Neilson, 2 Pet. 253; The Prize Case, 2 Black 635; Texas *v.* White, 7 Wall. 700, *Infra,* sec. 107.

[11] Dillon's case, 7 Sawyer 561, Fed. Cas. No. 3914 (1854); Moore, Digest, 5: 79; *Supra,* sec. 46.

[12] Freund, The Police Power, Chicago, 1904, p. 4.

[13] Note the long leash given to the military power during the Civil War as compared with the law as subsequently stated in *Ex Parte* Milligan, 4 Wall. 2; Rhodes, History of U. S., 4: 248 *et seq.*

[14] The Federalist, No. 31, Ford ed., p. 194.

of making that provision ought to know no other bounds than the exigencies of the nation and the resources of the community."

69. *Important Limitations from Separation of Powers.*

In fact the only important legal limitation upon the foreign relations power seems to be that, resulting from the doctrine of separation of powers, that all acts must be performed by the organ designated for that purpose by the Constitution. With a proper application of the understandings of the Constitution this limitation does not interfere with an adequate meeting of international responsibilities and carrying out of national policies except in one case. This is where the achievement of these ends requires that powers be vested in an international body created by treaty. As we have seen there is no difficulty in vesting such a body with authority to decide on questions of fact and law since the treaty power, or the treaty power supplemented by congressional legislation have been held fully competent to create agencies for these purposes.[15] A difficulty might arise, in case such a body were given appellate jurisdiction over the Supreme Court but this could be eliminated either by treaty provision for starting original action in the international tribunal or, in certain cases, by congressional provision for special tribunals within the United States, not exercising the judicial power of the United States, for the original hearing, from which appeal might be taken to the international court.[16]

A delegation of political power, that is legislative or treaty-making power, to such a body would be unconstitutional, but this never seems to have been contemplated. Bodies such as the Assembly and Council of the League of Nations, in which all binding political decisions require the assent of the American representative, would not violate this principle, since the American representative would presumably be instructed to withhold his consent or give merely tentative consent in any matter within the exclusive competence of Congress or the treaty-making power until those organs had acted.[17]

---

[15] *Supra,* sec. 60, note 42; *infra,* secs. 225–227.
[16] *Supra,* sec. 64.
[17] *Supra,* sec. 63.

A too rigid application of the doctrine of separation of powers will inevitably produce friction between the departments and impair the ability of the government rapidly and efficiently to meet international responsibilities and to decide upon and carry out national policies. / This difficulty may be greatly reduced through the regular observance by each organ of certain constitutional understandings, directing the method by which discretionary power ought to be exercised. Thus before making a decision each independent organ ought to consider the views of other independent organs whose cooperation will be necessary in order to carry out such decision; and after a decision has been made by any organ acting within its constitutional powers, all other independent organs ought to consider themselves bound to so exercise their powers as to give that decision full effect. The development of and adhesion to these understandings is most essential if foreign relations are to be carried on effectively by a government guaranteeing the separation of powers by its fundamental law.[13]

---

[18] *Infra,* sec. 249.

PART IV.

The Power to Conduct Foreign Relations under the Constitution.

CHAPTER IX.

The Position of the Foreign Relations Power in the Constitutional System.

A. *Source of National Powers.*

70. *Distribution of Powers Between States and National Government.*

The Constitution establishes a federal government, certain powers being expressly or impliedly delegated to the national government, the rest, unless prohibited to the states, being reserved to the states respectively or to the people. Now the control of foreign affairs has been very largely vested in the national government. Its organs are given power to send and receive diplomatic officers, to make treaties, to grant letters of marque and reprisal, to declare and conduct war, to assume jurisdiction in cases involving foreign diplomatic officers, foreign states or the interpretation of treaties, to pass laws relating to foreign commerce, naturalization, piracies and offences against the law of nations and any other laws that may be necessary and proper for carrying any of these powers into execution.

On the other hand, the states are expressly forbidden to enter into any treaty, alliance, or confederation or, unless Congress consent, into any agreement or compact with a foreign power; to grant letters of marque and reprisal or without the consent of Congress to engage in war unless invaded or in imminent danger thereof; to lay tonnage, import or export duties, except for executing their inspection laws. The only powers connected with foreign relations which the states seem competent to exercise without congressional consent relate to the meeting of international responsibilities. The states have power to provide aliens within their borders the protection and to assure them the other rights, guaranteed by international law and treaty, and state judges are expressly enjoined to observe treaties as the supreme law of the land, anything in the state constitution or laws to the contrary notwithstanding. Full power to enforce treaties and international law within the state could doubtless be conferred upon national officers and courts by act of Congress under the necessary and proper clause, but the legislation at present in force is not complete and state authorities alone must be relied on to meet certain international responsibilities.

71. *Theory of Sovereign Powers in National Government.*

In view of the almost complete prohibition of the states from the control of foreign relations, it has been argued that the national government must necessarily have all powers in this field enjoyed by sovereign nations. Thus said Justice Field in the Chinese Exclusion Cases:[1]

"While under our Constitution and form of government the great mass of local matters is controlled by local authorities, the United States, in their relation to foreign countries and their subjects or citizens, are one nation, invested with powers which belong to independent nations, the exercise of which can be invoked for the maintenance of its absolute independence and security throughout its entire territory."

Justice Gray repeated the theory in Fong Yue Ting *v.* United States:[2]

"The United States are a sovereign and independent nation, and are invested by the Constitution with the entire control of international relations, and with all the powers of government necessary to maintain that control and to make it effective."

Aside from the power to exclude aliens, the court has derived the power to acquire territory from this theory,[3] but in other cases the latter power has been implied from the power to make treaties, and to declare war.[4]

---

[1] Chinese Exclusion Cases, 130 U. S. 581.
[2] Fong Yue Ting *v.* U. S., 149 U. S. 698.
[3] Jones *v.* U. S., 137 U. S. 202, and discussion by Willoughby, *op. cit.*, p. 340. See also cases cited, *Ibid.*, pp. 454-455.
[4] American Insurance Co. *v.* Canter, 1 Pet. 511; Flemming *v.* Page, 9 How. 603; Willoughby, *op. cit.*, p. 339. The power to admit new states to the Union has also been suggested as a ground for annexation, though such an interpretation of the clause (Constitution, IV, sec. 3, cl. 1) was not

THE FOREIGN RELATIONS POWER. 131

The general theory of national powers derived from sovereignty has not been approved by commentators[5] or by the weight of judicial decisions. Thus in Kansas v. Colorado Justice Brewer emphatically repudiated the "doctrine of sovereign and inherent powers."[6]

"But," he said, "the proposition that there are legislative powers affecting the nation as a whole which belong to, although not expressed in the grant of powers, is in direct conflict with the doctrine that this is a government of enumerated powers. That this is such a government clearly appears from the Constitution, independently of the amendments, for otherwise there would be an instrument granting certain specified things made operative to grant other and distinct things. This natural construction of the original body of the Constitution is made absolutely certain by the Tenth Amendment."

Chief Justice Taney had earlier insisted that no argument could be drawn "from the nature of sovereignty, or the necessities of government for self-defense in time of tumult and danger."[7]

72. *Theory of National Sovereignty in Foreign Relations.*

But though the general theory of sovereign powers, which would vest in the national government all powers not expressly prohibited, cannot be maintained, more support can be cited for the theory if confined to the control of foreign relations. Thus Willoughby says:

"From these express grants of power to the General Government, and prohibitions of treaty powers to the States, the intention of the framers

---

intended by the drafter of the Constitution. See letter of Gouverneur Morris to Livingston, 1803, Life and Writings (Sparks), 3: 192, quoted in Willoughby, *op. cit.*, p. 328.

[5] Willoughby, *op. cit.*, p. 69, who, however, approves a limited application of the theory in respect to foreign relations, *Ibid.*, p. 45. "It cannot, therefore, be maintained that, merely because the United States is classed as a 'sovereign nation,' the government or any part of it can therefore perform a sovereign act beyond the scope of the purposes for which it was created, for although the nation is sovereign the Government is not. Complete sovereignty resides in the people as a whole, and not in any or all of the public officers." D. J. Hill, Present Problems of Foreign Policy, N. Y., 1919, p. 155.

[6] Kansas v. Colorado, 206 U. S. 46.

[7] *Ex Parte* Merryman, Taney's reports, p. 246; Thayer, Cases on Const. Law, 2: 2361, 2368.

132   THE CONTROL OF AMERICAN FOREIGN RELATIONS.

of the Constitution to invest the Federal Government with the exclusive control of foreign affairs is readily deducible.

"The control of international relations vested in the General Government is not only exclusive but all-comprehensive. That is to say, the authority of the United States in its dealings with foreign powers includes not only those powers which the Constitution specifically grants it, but *all those powers which States in general possess with regard* to matters of international concern.

"This appeal, however, to the fact of 'national sovereignty' as a source of federal power is not a valid one outside of the international field. It cannot properly be resorted to when recognition of an international obligation on the part of the United States is not involved, and when, therefore, the matter is purely one relating to the reserved powers of the States or to the private rights of the individuals. To permit the doctrine to apply within these fields would at once render the Federal Government one of unlimited powers."[8]

The writer is unable to accept this doctrine. The fact that powers relating to the control of foreign relations are expressly enumerated by the Constitution, which enumeration would be rendered superfluous by the theory, the fact that the states actually exercise some powers which directly affect foreign relations, such as the protection of domiciled aliens, the fact that certain constitutional limitations such as those contained in the bill of rights are generally acknowledged to limit the scope of treaty-making and other activities in the control of foreign relations seem to indicate that the national foreign relations power is neither implied from sovereignty, nor exclusive, nor all-comprehensive, though it undoubtedly, very nearly enjoys the two latter characteristics. The writer is not aware of any judicial decision which requires the theory for support, and he considers that certain judicial dicta, unquestionably supporting it, are overborne by the repeated assertions of the Supreme Court that the national government is a government of delegated power. Consequently in the field of foreign relations as in other fields he assumes that all national powers must be founded upon express or implied delegation by the Constitution.

73. *Theory of Resultant Powers.*

However, powers may be implied as a "resultant" of a group

---

[8] Willoughby, *op. cit.*, pp. 451, 454. See also *Ibid.*, p. 65.

of express powers—it is not necessary that implied powers be traced always to a single express delegation.

"It is to be observed," said Chief Justice Marshall, "that it is not indispensable to the existence of every power claimed for the Federal Government that it can be found specified in the words of the Constitution, or clearly and directly traceable to some one of the specified powers. Its existence may be deduced fairly from more than one of the substantive powers expressly defined, or from them all combined. It is allowable to group together any number of them and to infer from them all that the power claimed has been conferred." [9]

Thus the power to recognize foreign states and governments may be implied from the powers of receiving and commissioning diplomatic officers; [10] the power to exclude and expel aliens may be implied from the powers of regulating foreign commerce, naturalizing aliens and declaring war; [11] the power to annex and govern territory may be implied from the power of making treaties, declaring war, and admitting new states to the Union.[12] We assume,

---

[9] Cohens *v.* Va., 6 Wheat. 264; U. S. *v.* Gettysburg Electric Ry. Co., 160 U. S. 668, 681–683 (1896). See Willoughby, *op. cit.,* p. 66, and Legal Tender Cases, 12 Wall. 457, quoted *ibid.,* p. 65.

[10] Corwin, The President's Control of Foreign Relations, p. 71.

[11] Although in the Chinese Exclusion Cases (130 U. S. 581, 1889) and Fong Yue Ting *v.* U. S. (149 U. S. 698, 1893) certain expressions of the court support the contention that the power of exclusion and expulsion are derived from national sovereignty in foreign affairs, yet it is to be noted that in both of these cases the court carefully enumerated the specific grants of power of which these so-called sovereign powers are the resultant. The argument in the Chinese Exclusion Cases, that the power to make war for defense implies a power to take lesser defensive measure, and that the occasion for and methods of such defense is a political question not subject to judicial determination, may also be noticed. "It matters not in what form such aggression and encroachment come, whether from the foreign nation acting in its national character or from vast hordes of its people crowding in upon us. The government, possessing the powers which are to be exercised for protection and security, is clothed with authority to determine the occasion on which the powers shall be called forth; and its determination, so far as the subjects affected are concerned, is necessarily conclusive upon all its departments and officers." Thus when the court spoke of "sovereign powers" it had in mind powers *resultant* from a group of express or implied powers, and not powers deduced from an abstract theory of sovereignty.

[12] The case of Jones *v.* U. S. (137 U. S. 202), which is cited by Willoughby as not only practically upholding the right of the United States to acquire territory by discovery and occupation, but applying the principle that 'the

therefore, that the foreign relations power in common with all other national powers, exists only as far as (1) expressly delegated by the Constitution, (2) implied from expressly delegated powers, or (3) implied as a "resultant" from a group of express or implied powers.[13]

B. Essential Nature of the Foreign Relations Power.
74. *Controversy as to Nature of Foreign Relations Power.*

Since the beginning of the government under the Constitution there has been a controversy as to the essential nature of the for-

---

United States may exercise a power not enumerated in the Constitution, provided it be an international power generally possessed by sovereign states" (*op. cit.*, p. 341), really turned on the principle of "political question." "Who is the sovereign, *de jure* or *de facto,* of a territory is not a judicial, but a political, question, the determination of which by the legislative and executive departments of any government conclusively binds the judges, as well as all other officers, citizens, and subjects of that government. This principle has always been upheld by this court, and has been affirmed under a great variety of circumstances." Apparently the President's power to recognize acquisitions of territory by the United States, through the operation of international law, flows from his constitutional position as the representative organ of the government. It is to be noted that he has recognized such acquisitions aside from congressional legislation. (Moore Digest, 1 : 555.) Thus such acquisitions are made by operation of international law. Recognition thereof is a political function of the President, and the courts are bound by such decision. The act of Congress (Act of Aug. 18, 1856, Rev. Stat., secs. 5570–5578) involved in this case defines the circumstances under which and the procedure by which American citizens, discovering Guano Islands, can benefit by the rule of international law and the rights and degree of protection to which they are entitled, thus falling under the power to govern territory. Constitution, art. IV, sec. 3, par. 2. (See Moore, Digest, 1 : 556 *et seq.*)

[13] Unquestionably the enumerated powers relating to foreign affairs, either by implication or combination, will permit Congress to pass practically any laws properly within that field. Consequently in practice this theory of congressional power differs little from the theory asserting that congressional powers can be deduced from national sovereignty in foreign affairs. J. B. Moore in Proc. Am. Phil. Soc., Minutes, 60: xvi, quoting Taney, C. J., in Holmes vs. Jennison, 14, Pet. 540; "all the powers which relate to our foreign intercourse are confided to the general government." The difficulty of the sovereignty theory, however, lies in the fact that a recognition of congressional sovereignty in foreign affairs would seem to exempt Congress from constitutional limitations arising from individual rights, states' rights and the separation of powers in this field. "Sovereignty" is not only plenitude of power, but also absence of limitation. See *supra,* note 5.

eign relations power. One school has contended that such powers are essentially executive and hence all delegations of power to Congress in this field must be strictly construed while delegations of power to the President may be liberally construed. Some have gone even farther and in view of the constitutional statement that "The Executive power shall be vested in a President of the United States of America" have contended that all foreign relations powers not otherwise expressly delegated are by this general grant of executive power vested in the President. Another school has taken the reverse view, supporting a liberal legislative power and a narrow construction of executive powers.

75. *Foreign Relations Power not Essentially Judicial.*

The courts have been perfectly clear that these powers are not of an essential judicial nature, and consequently have considered themselves incompetent to decide them. They have usually called them "political questions" and have accepted the decisions of the political branches of the government without question.[14] However, the political branches of the government include both the legislative and executive branches, consequently judicial opinions give us little assistance in our effort to determine whether these powers are essentially legislative or essentially executive.

76. *Theory of Essentially Executive Nature. Early Opinion.*

Supporters of the essentially executive character of foreign relations powers notice that writers with whom the members of the federal convention were familiar such as Locke, Montesquieu, De Lolme and Blackstone appeared to classify the control of foreign relations as executive. In European countries, especially in Great Britain, the Chief Executive conducted foreign relations. Furthermore, they say, the debates in the federal convention tended in this direction. The treaty-making power, vested in Congress under the Confederation, was first given to the Senate by the Convention, but finally the President was added and in the ultimate draft the subject is concluded in the section dealing with Executive power, indicating that the Convention had become convinced of its executive char-

---

[14] *Infra*, sec. 107.

acter. Washington's recognition of the new French republic by reception of Citizen Genet upon his own responsibility set a precedent which has since been followed. His proclamation of neutrality, when many thought the French alliance treaty required war, was loudly denounced by the Jeffersonian Republicans, but the precedent has been invariably followed since when occasion has arisen for proclaiming neutrality. This first neutrality proclamation occasioned a lively pamphlet debate between Hamilton and Madison under the names of "Pacificus" and "Helvidius," and Hamilton, who supported the executive character of the proclamation, won, if future practice is to be the judge.[15]

"It deserves to be remarked," he wrote, "that as the participation of the Senate in the making of treaties, and the power of the legislature to declare war, are exceptions out of the general 'executive power' vested in the President, they are to be construed strictly, and ought to be extended no further than is essential to their execution. While, therefore, the legislature can alone declare war, can alone actually transfer the nation from a state of peace to a state of hostility, it belongs to the 'executive power' to do whatever else the law of nations, cooperating with the treaties, of the country enjoins in the intercourse of the United States with foreign powers."

77. Essentially Executive Nature. Practice.

Advocates of this theory notice that in practice the President alone has recognized foreign governments and states and proclaimed neutrality. He has initiated all foreign negotiations and has held himself free to ignore congressional resolutions or acts on the subject. He has even authorized foreign military expeditions on his own authority and has initiated all wars. He has on his own responsibility executed treaties of extradition, guarantee, and intervention. He has made executive agreements terminating hostilities, outlining terms of peace, annexing territory and providing for administration in foreign territory, and he has denounced treaties.

78. Essentially Executive Nature. Recent Opinion.

A debate on the extent of executive prerogative in foreign relations was indulged in by Senators in 1906 on the occasion of President Roosevelt's negotiation of the Algeciras convention through

---

[15] Hamilton, Works (Federal ed., Lodge), 4: 443.

personal agents, whose appointments had not been consented to by the Senate. Senator Spooner of Wisconsin supported the President.[16]

"From the foundation of the Government it has been conceded in practice and in theory that the Constitution vests the power of negotiation and the various phases—and they are multifarious—of the conduct of our foreign relations exclusively in the President. And, Mr. President, he does not exercise that constitutional power, nor can he be made to do it, under the tutelage or guardianship of the Senate or of the House or of the Senate and House combined. . . .

"Mr. President, I do not stop at this moment to cite authorities in support of the proposition, that so far as the conduct of our foreign relations is concerned, excluding only the Senate's participation in the making of treaties, the President has the absolute and uncontrolled and uncontrollable authority. . . .

"We as the Senate, a part of the treaty-making power, have no more right under the Constitution to invade the prerogative of the President to negotiate treaties, and that is not all—the conduct of our foreign relations is not limited to the negotiation of treaties—we have no more right under the Constitution to invade that prerogative than he has to invade the prerogative of legislation. . . .

"I do not know whether it will be any 'light' to the Senator from South Carolina, but in Mr. Jefferson's opinion on the Powers of the Senate, a very celebrated document, which he gave at the request of the President, this language was used: 'The transaction of business with foreign nations is *executive altogether.* It belongs, then, to the head of that department, except as to such portions of it as are especially submitted to the Senate. *Exceptions are to be construed strictly.*'"

79. *Theory of Essentially Legislative Nature. Early Opinion.*

However, supporters of the essentially legislative character of the foreign relations power are not without ammunition. Whatever

---

[16] Cong. Rec., Jan. 23, Feb. 6, 1906, 40: 1417-1421, 2125-2148; Reinsch, Readings in Am. Fed. Govt., 81-124; Corwin, *op. cit.*, pp. 170, 172, 176, 203. Senator Beveridge remarked during this debate: "Does not the Senator (Bacon) think that in the natural division of the powers of the Government into legislative, executive, and judicial the treaty-making power has always been considered an executive function, and therefore, if the Constitution had been silent upon the subject of treaties, it would have been completely under the President's control, under that provision of the Constitution which confides in the President executive power, and that the section concerning treaties is merely a limitation upon that universal power?" *Ibid.*, p. 184. "All duties in connection with foreign relations not otherwise specified fall within the sphere of the executive." Sen. Doc. No. 56, 54th Cong., 2d sess. See also *infra*, sec. 92.

may have been the opinion of theoretic writers and the practice of European nations, the fact is undoubted that the first American Government vested all foreign relations powers in Congress and the Constitutional Convention started from the assumption that these powers were legislative. The particular powers in the field which they delegated to the President in part or in full may have been in view of particular expediencies. But the most important foreign relations powers were left largely legislative. The power to declare war, to define piracies and offenses against the law of nations and to regulate foreign commerce are left with Congress and the power to make treaties and to appoint ambassadors, public ministers and consuls requires the consent of the Senate.

Furthermore, whatever Jefferson may have said or done at other times, certainly he denounced Hamilton's theory of the essentially executive nature of the foreign relations power in 1793 and urged Madison to "take up your pen, select the most striking heresies, and cut him to pieces in face of the public."[17] Madison actually entered the lists and wrote, under the name of "Helvidius":[18]

"In the general distribution of powers, we find that of declaring war expressly vested in the Congress, where every other legislative power is declared to be vested; and without any other qualifications than what is common to every other legislative act. The constitutional idea of this power would seem then clearly to be, that it is of a legislative and not an executive nature. . . .

"There are sufficient indications that the power of treaties is regarded by the Constitution as materially different from mere executive power, and as having more affinity to the legislative that to the executive character.

"One circumstance indicating this is the constitutional regulation under which the Senate give their consent in the case of treaties. In all other cases the consent of the body is expressed by a majority of voices. In this particular case, a concurrence of two-thirds at least is made necessary, as a substitute or compensation for the other branch of the legislature, which, on certain occasions, could not be conveniently a party to the transaction.

"But the conclusive circumstance is, that treaties, when formed according to the constitutional mode, are confessedly to have the force and operation of *laws,* and are to be a rule for the courts in controversies between man and man, as much as any *other laws.* They are even emphatically declared by the Constitution to be 'the supreme law of the land.'

[17] Jefferson, Writings, P. L. Ford, ed., 6: 338.
[18] Madison, Writings, Hunt, ed., 6: 147–150.

"So far the argument from the Constitution is precisely in opposition to the doctrine. As little will be gained in its favour from a comparison of the two powers with those particularly vested in the President alone. . . .

"Thus it appears that by whatever standard we try this doctrine, it must be condemned as no less vicious in theory than it would be dangerous in practice. It is countenanced neither by the writers on law; nor by the nature of the powers themselves; nor by any general arrangements, or particular expressions, or plausible analogies, to be found in the Constitution.

"Whence then can the writer have borrowed it?

"There is but one answer to this question.

"The power of making treaties and the power of declaring war are royal prerogatives in the *British government,* and are accordingly treated as *executive prerogatives* by British *commentators.*"

80. *Essentially Legislative Nature. Practice.*

In practice it can be shown that Congress has occasionally passed resolutions advising or directing the opening of negotiations with a view to the conclusion or modification of treaties and the President has usually followed this advice. Congress has also passed resolutions directing the termination of treaties and the use of force abroad aside from the exercise of its express powers of declaring war, defining piracies and offenses against the law of nations and regulating foreign commerce. The Senate, moreover, has, throughout American history, exercised its power to reject treaties, or consent to their ratification with amendments or reservations.

81. *Essentially Legislative Nature. Recent Opinion.*

In the Senatorial Debate of 1906 referred to, Senator Bacon of Georgia supported the legislative nature of the foreign relations power:[19]

"Mr. Beveridge (Indiana). I will ask this question: If the Constitution had said nothing about the treaty-making power, where would the treaty-making power have been lodged?

"Mr. Bacon. I have received that question from the Senator several times. I have said that I did not agree with him that it would be with the Executive.

"Mr. Beveridge. Where would it be?

"Mr. Bacon. I think, undoubtedly, in the legislative branch of the Government, for reasons which I will give.

"Mr. Beveridge. That is the whole question.

---

[19] *Supra,* note 16.

140 THE CONTROL OF AMERICAN FOREIGN RELATIONS.

"Mr. Bacon. Here is where the sovereignty of the Government was intended to be in almost its totality—in the legislative branch of the Government, and the vast array of powers in the first article of the Constitution proves it; and, further than that, the Constitution of the United States was intended to take the place of and to supersede the Articles of Confederation, under which articles the power to make treaties did lodge in Congress alone; and it was not to be presumed when the Constitution was formed in the absence of some special and particular designation, that it was the intention to confer it upon the Executive. The presumption would be the other way."

82. *Theory of a Fourth Department Different from Either Executive or Legislative.*

Although on the whole those favoring the executive prerogative have the better of the argument, especially in the light of practice in such matters as recognition and treaty negotiation, yet there does not seem warrant for a full acceptance of the view stated by Senator Spooner. We are inclined to reject both views in their extreme forms and to accept that of the Federalist which held the foreign relations power to be neither legislative nor executive but a fourth department of government.[20]

However, to sustain this distinction we must recognize the ambiguity of the term "executive power." Writers on administrative law have recognized the two distinct functions frequently vested in the chief executive, designated respectively as "political" and "administrative" functions.[21] The political functions exhausted the early conception of "executive power" and corresponded very closely to what we call the foreign relations power. During the nineteenth century, however, the administrative functions of the chief executive or the functions of executing the law and directing the national civil services have increased in importance and now it is to these that writers and courts usually refer when they speak of "executive power." Thus though foreign relations power is almost synonymous with executive power according to the earlier usage, under present usage the two are distinct.

This is especially true in the United States. Here the political functions of the executive are largely in the field of foreign rela-

---

[20] *Infra*, sec. 85.
[21] Goodnow, Principles of the Administrative Law of the U. S., p. 66; Willoughby, *op. cit.*, p. 1156.

tions.[22] Though the President has been gaining an increasing political influence in domestic affairs through the veto, the patronage, and his extra-constitutional position as head of his political party, yet, lacking the powers of initiating legislation, personally forcing it through the legislature, and if necessary proroguing or dissolving that body, commonly exercised by European executives, he has not assumed the dominating position in domestic policy found there. His legal powers have been in the main confined to executing the law and directing the national civil service.

In foreign affairs, on the other hand, the President's political powers are as great as those of the executive in most European countries, but for their exercise he usually requires the advice and consent of the Senate. Thus, these powers have tended to be dissociated from the ordinary executive powers exercised independently by the President but within the limits of detailed statutes.

83. *A Fourth Department. Opinion of Theoretical Writers.*

A careful examination of the views of Locke and Montesquieu will indicate that they regarded the control of foreign relations as a distinct department of government. Locke used the term "federative" to designate this department and distinguished it from both the "executive" and "legislative" departments.[23]

> "But because the laws, that are at once, and in a short time made, have a constant and lasting force, and need a perpetual execution or an attendance thereunto; therefore, it is necessary there should be a power always in being which should see to the execution of the laws that are made, and remain in force. And thus the legislative and executive power come often to be separated.
>
> "There is another power in every commonwealth. . . . Though in a commonwealth the members of it are distinct persons still in reference to one another, and as such are governed by the laws of the society; yet in reference to the rest of mankind, they make one body. . . . Hence it is that the con-

---

[22] The only ones which are not are the veto power given by Art. I, sec. 7, par. 3, and those in Art. II, sec. 3. "He shall from time to time give to the Congress information of the State of the Union, and recommend to their Consideration such Measures as he shall judge necessary and expedient; he may, on extraordinary occasions, convene both Houses, or either of them, and in Case of Disagreement between them, with respect to the Time of Adjournment, he may adjourn them to such time as he shall think proper."

[23] Treatise of Civil Government, secs. 144-148, Works, ed. 1801, 5: 425-6.

troversies that happen between any man of the society with those that are out of it are managed by the public, and an injury done to a member of their body engages the whole in the reparation of it. This, therefore, contains the power of war and peace, leagues and alliances, and all the transactions, with all persons and communities without the commonwealth; and may be called federative, if anyone pleases. So the thing be understood, I am indifferent as to the name.

"These two powers, executive and federative, though they be really distinct in themselves, yet one comprehending the execution of the municipal laws of the society within itself, upon all that are parts of it; the other the management of the security and interest of the public without, with all those that it may receive benefit or damage from; yet they are always almost united. And though this federative power in the well- or ill-management of it be of great moment to the commonwealth, yet it is much less capable to be directed by antecedent standing, positive laws, than the executive; and so must necessarily be left to the prudence and wisdom of those whose hands it is in, to be managed for the public good: for the laws that concern subjects one amongst another, being to direct their actions, may well enough precede them. But what is to be done in reference to foreigners, depending much upon their actions, and the variation of designs, and interests, must be left in great part to the prudence of those who have this power committed to them to be managed by the best of their skill, for the advantage of the commonwealth.

"Though, as I said, the executive and federative power of every community be really distinct in themselves, yet they are hardly to be separated and placed at the same time in the hands of distinct persons; for both of them requiring the force of the society for their exercise, it is almost impracticable to place the force of the commonwealth in distinct, and not subordinate hands; or that the executive and federative power should be placed in persons that might act separately, whereby the force of the public would be under different commands: which would be apt some time or other to cause disorder and ruin."

Montesquieu's triple division was the same:[24]

"In every government," he says, "there are three sorts of power: the legislative; the executive, in respect to things dependent on the law of nations; and the **executive in regard to things that depend on the civil law**. By virtue of the first, the prince or magistrate enacts temporary or perpetual laws, and amends, or abrogates those that have been already enacted. By the second, he makes peace or war, sends or receives embassies, establishes the public security, and provides against invasion. By the third, he punishes criminals, or determines the disputes that arise between individuals. The latter we shall call the judiciary power, and the other simply the executive power of the state."

[24] L'Esprit des Lois, lxi, c. 6, Philadelphia, 1802, 1: 181. Note Madison's paraphrase of this in the Federal Convention, *infra*, note 34.

Both of these writers grouped judicial and "executive" powers in one department which Locke designated "executive" and Montesquieu "judicial." Each considered the conduct of foreign relations a distinct department of government, which Locke called "federative" and Montesquieu, "executive." Confusion results from the different meaning given to the term "executive" by the two men, but in substance their classifications were precisely the same. This classification of departments was also that which they actually observed in the British government of the time.

84. *A Fourth Department. British and Colonial Precedents.*

In the 18th century the prerogative of the British Crown in Council concerned largely war, foreign relations, colonies, appointments and removals, the summoning, proroguing and dissolution of Parliament. The Crown administered the finances and the commercial regulations but it did so under authority delegated by Parliament, which levied all taxes, made all appropriations, and passed general laws for defining commercial policy. With the exception of taxation, however, domestic administration was almost entirely conducted by the courts and the justices of the peace.[25]

---

[25] The English Government has been undergoing continuous functional differentiation throughout its history. Locke and Montesquieu caught the process at a particular time and crystallized it in the theory of separation of powers. In the period of the Norman and Angevin kings the functions of government were: (1) *Military,* controlled by the king under restrictions of feudal and customary law, and naval, exercised at first through the Cinque ports with their Warden, and later delegated to the Lord High Admiral; (2) *Financial,* in which the Crown was gradually forced to rely on parliamentary grants, merely retaining control of the administrative machinery for collecting and disbursing, exercised through the Justiciar later supplanted by the Treasurer and through the Exchequer with its chancellor; (3) *Judicial,* in which the Crown delegated authority to the central courts of Common Pleas, King's Bench and Exchequer, which, though appointed by the Crown, tended to acquire an independence from its control. A certain residuum of judicial power, however, remained on the one hand in the House of Lords and on the other in the Crown, who exercised it through the Lord Chancellor and the Privy Council.

As time went on, relations of a peaceful kind with foreign nations were established and the making of treaties and sending and receiving of diplomatic officers were added to the military functions of the Crown. These

144   THE CONTROL OF AMERICAN FOREIGN RELATIONS.

Not until the late eighteenth and nineteenth centuries did the great ministries for domestic administration develop,[26] and not until this time did the responsibility of the Cabinet to Parliament become established.[27] Even during the 19th and 20th centuries, the prerogative in foreign relations has been exercised by the Crown in Council quite independently both of party politics and of parliamentary responsibility.[28] The distinction has continued to exist between the foreign relations power exercised rather independently by the Crown in Council and the executive power exercised by the Crown under powers delegated by Parliament and through ministers responsible to that body.

The executive power as known to the constitutional fathers in the colonial governor was similar to that of the British Crown in

---

were conducted by the Secretary of State. Parliament soon began to insist that, in exchange for its grants of money, the King should reform abuses, first requested by petition, but tending to assume the form of definite bills. Thus in addition to taxation, Parliament acquired the function of legislation. As population increased and the problems of local administration became more complex, the courts, and especially the Justices of the Peace, added to their judicial functions much of an administrative character. Thus by the time of the Revolution of 1688 the functions of government were distributed among three fairly distinct departments. The Crown controlled military, naval and foreign affairs, the administration of finances and power of appointment. Parliament controlled the raising and appropriation of revenue and the enactment of general laws. The Courts and Justices of the Peace administered criminal and civil laws and performed practically all functions of domestic administration, except finance. This division of power was described by John Locke, taken from him by Montesquieu and Blackstone and from them by the American Constitutional Fathers. (See Medley, English Constitutional History, 2d ed., pp. 112, 231, 367, 392.)

[26] Before 1782 the important ministerial offices were Lord Chancellor, Lord High Admiral in Commission, Secretary at War, two Secretaries of State, one each for northern and southern Europe, Lord Treasurer in Commission, Chancellor of the Exchequer and Board of Trade. None of these really concerned domestic administration except finances. The Secretary of State for Home Affairs was created in 1782; Board of Works and Public Buildings, 1851; Committee on Education, later a Board of Education, in 1856; Local Government Board, 1871; Board of Agriculture and Fisheries, 1889. (Medley, *op. cit.*, p. 112 *et seq.*)

[27] "The first definite recognition of this corporate responsibility (of the cabinet) may be said to date from 1782." (Medley, *op. cit.*, p. 109.)

[28] See Low, The Governance of England, N. Y., 1915, p. 301; Ponsonby, Democracy and Diplomacy, London, 1915, p. 45 *et seq.*

the 18th century with the very important exception of the foreign relations power. The colonial governor exercised merely such powers as summoning and dissolving the legislature and appointing and removing officers.

"Administrative matters," says Goodnow, "outside of those directly connected with the military powers of the governor had not been attended to by the central colonial government but, in accordance with English principles of local government, by various officers in the local districts of the state who were regarded as local in character and who often at the same time discharged judicial functions." [29]

This was also true of the succeeding state governors. Since all powers of the national government under the Continental Congress and Articles of Confederation were vested in Congress no conception of the scope of executive or legislative power could be gained from this experience, though the need of a more efficient control of foreign relations was strongly felt and was one leading motive toward the formation of the Constitution.[30]

85. *A Fourth Department. Opinion of Constitutional Fathers.*

When the presidency was first considered in the federal convention it was undoubtedly conceived as analogous to the colonial and state governors who exercised at that time neither foreign relations powers nor administrative powers but merely political powers in domestic affairs.[31]

The Senate was thought of as the repository of power in foreign relations.[32] As discussion advanced, however, the analogy of the Presidency to the British Crown was pressed upon the convention by such men as Hamilton and Gouverneur Morris,[33] while Madison referred to Montesquieu's conception of "executive power" as a definition of the President's powers.[34] The view of these men

---

[29] Goodnow, *op. cit.*, p. 71.
[30] Farrand, *op. cit.*, 1: 426, 513.
[31] James Wilson, Farrand, *op. cit.*, 1: 65, 153.
[32] *Ibid.*, 1: 426.
[33] Hamilton, Farrand, 1: 288; G. Morris, *Ibid.*, 1: 513; 2: 104; Mercer, *Ibid.*, 1: 297; Sherman, *Ibid.*, 1: 97.
[34] "A dependence of the Executive on the Legislature would render it the executor as well as the maker of laws; and according to the observation of Montesquieu, tyrannical laws may be made that they may be executed in

which vested the President with political powers regarding foreign relations was, in the main, accepted, but to curb possible autocratic exercises of power by the President, the Senate was given a veto on treaties, while the power to declare war was left with Congress. The powers finally delegated to the President, and included in Article II of the Constitution as finally drafted by Gouverneur Morris, are mostly in the diplomatic fields.

The powers of domestic administration which we now regard as the essential executive powers were not within the power of either the colonial governor or the British monarch in the eighteenth century and it was not intended that they should be within the President's discretionary control. The fathers intended that these powers should be exercised by officers largely under the detailed control of Congress and in the early acts organizing departments of government this plan was carried out.

> "In the United States," says Willoughby, "it was undoubtedly intended that the President should be little more than a political chief; that is to say, one whose functions should in the main consist in the performance of those political duties which are not subject to judicial control. It is quite clear that it was intended that he should not, except as to these political matters, be the administrative head of the government, with general power of directing and controlling the acts of subordinate administrative agents." [35]

Later, through the use of the implied or perhaps inherent power of the President to remove officers, and by a wide interpretation of the clause requiring the President "to take care that the laws be faithfully executed," originally indicating supervision rather than direction, the administrative powers of the President increased. At the same time the term "executive power" changed in meaning

---

a tyrannical manner. There was an analogy between the Executive and Judiciary departments in several respects. The latter executed the laws in certain cases as the former did in others. The former expounded and applied them for certain purposes as the latter did for others. The difference beween them seemed to consist chiefly in two circumstances—1. The collective interest and security were much more in the power belonging to the Executive than to the Judiciary department. 2. In the administration of the former much greater latitude is left to opinion and discretion than in the administration of the latter." Madison, Farrand, *op. cit.*, 2: 34.

[35] Willoughby, *op. cit.*, p. 1156. See also Goodnow, *op. cit.*, p. 78.

and although it still included the notion of political functions, its primary association was with the new administrative functions.

Thus when the constitutional convention gave "executive power" to the President, the foreign relations power was the essential element in the grant, but they carefully protected this power from abuse by provisions for senatorial or congressional veto. This power ought to be distinguished from the power of the President as head of the administration which he exercises independently within the limits of congressional legislation and which by present usage forms the essential element in "executive power."

Whether consideration is given to the works of theoretical writers known to the fathers, the precedents of England, the colonies or the Confederation, or the discussion of the Federal convention itself, we may conclude that The Federalist expressed the opinion of the constitutional convention as to the nature of the foreign relations power, so far as they had an opinion on that subject, when with prevision of the later significance of the term "executive power" it classified the treaty power as a fourth department of government;[36]

"The essence of the legislative authority is to enact laws, or, in other words, to prescribe rules for the regulation of the society; while the execution of the laws and the employment of the common strength, either for this purpose or for the common defense, seem to comprise all the functions of the executive magistrate. The power of making treaties is plainly neither the one nor the other. It relates neither to the execution of the subsisting laws nor to the enactment of new ones, and still less to an exertion of the common strength. Its objects are contracts with foreign nations, which have the force of law, but derive it from the obligations of good faith. They are not rules prescribed by sovereign to the subject, but agreements between sovereign and sovereign. The power in question seems, therefore, to form a distinct department, and to belong, properly, neither to the legislative nor to the executive. The qualities elsewhere detailed as indispensable in the management of foreign negotiations point out the Executive as the most fit agent in those transactions; while the vast importance of the trust, and the operation of treaties as laws, plead strongly for the participation of the whole or a portion of the legislative body in the office of making them."

---

[36] The Federalist, No. 75 (Hamilton), Ford ed., p. 500. Hamilton later shifted to a defense of the wholly executive nature of the foreign relations power. *Supra,* sec. 76.

86. *A Fourth Department. Functional Classification.*

Functionally it would seem that the foreign relations power, which both frames and carries out foreign policies, both contracts and meets international responsibilities, is essentially different from either the legislative power, which frames domestic laws and policies, or the executive power which administers domestic laws and policies. According to the terminology of Professors Goodnow [37] and other writers on administrative law the conduct of foreign relations involves both "politics" and "administration" in external affairs and is distinct from either "politics" or "administration" in internal affairs.

87. *A Fourth Department. Practice.*

In practice the control of foreign relations has differed from the control of either legislation or domestic administration. While the President has suggested legislation in messages to Congress he has not as a rule taken a position of active leadership in the formulation of domestic policy. The initiative has been with the committees of Congress and the President's discretion has been closely limited by law enforceable in the courts. It is true the President controls administrative officials through his removal power. He instructs officials as to the method of executing the laws under authority given him by Congress and sometimes he even supplements legislation by instructions or regulations of a general character not specifically authorized.[38] But he must always act within the confines of an ever-increasing mass of congressional legislation. Congress has described the powers of officials and the methods of administration in considerable detail and the President, or rather his subordinates, are forced by the courts to observe such legislation. As legislation of this character increases in mass and detail, and as the practices and methods of permanent services become fixed by tradition as well as law, the President's discretion as head of the administration becomes reduced. His functions in this capacity tend to assume a purely supervisory and ministerial character.

---

[37] Goodnow, *op. cit.,* p. 666, and Willoughby, *op. cit.,* p. 1156.
[38] Goodnow, *op. cit.,* pp. 47, 75.

In foreign relations, however, the President exercises discretion, both as to the means and as to the ends of policy. He exercises a discretion, very little limited by directory laws, in the method of carrying out foreign policy. He has moved the navy and the marines at will all over the world. He has exercised a broad discretion in issuing both standing regulations and instructions and special instructions for the diplomatic, consular, military and naval services. Though Congress has legislated on broad lines for the conduct of these services it has descended to much less detail than in the case of services operative in the territory of the United States. In the foreign affairs the President, also, has a constitutional discretion as the representative organ and as commander-in-chief which cannot be taken away by Congress and because of the exterritorial character of most of his action, his subordinates are not generally subject to judicial control.

But more than this he has initiated foreign policies, even those leading to treaties and those leading to war, and has generally actively pushed these policies when the cooperation of other organs of government is necessary for their carrying out. Though Congress may by resolution suggest policies its resolutions are not mandatory and the President has on occasion ignored them. Ultimately, however, his power is limited by the possibility of a veto upon matured policies, by the Senate in the case of treaties, by Congress in the case of war. This contrast between the domestic and foreign powers of the President is thus emphasized by Rawle: [39]

"On a full view of the powers and duties of the President, the reader will probably perceive that they are of more importance in respect to foreign relations than the internal administration of government.

"At home, his path though dignified, is narrow. In the tranquility which we have hitherto in time of peace enjoyed, little more has been requisite, in either his legislative or executive functions than regularly to pursue the plain mandates of laws, and the certain text of the constitution. . . .

"But it is in respect to external relations; to transactions with foreign nations, and the events arising from them, that the President has an arduous task. Here he must chiefly act on his own independent judgment."

88. *The Foreign Relations Department. Conclusion.*

In foreign affairs, therefore, the controlling force is the reverse

---

[39] Rawle, A View of the Constitution, Philadelphia, 1825, pp. 182–183.

of that in domestic legislation. The initiation and development of details is with the President, checked only by the veto of the Senate or Congress upon completed proposals. In domestic legislation on the other hand, the initiative and drafting of details is with Congress, checked by the President's limited veto upon completed bills. In practice it seems possible to distinguish four great departments of government, not only according to their functions, but also according to their organization and methods. The legislative power is vested in Congress with a limited presidential veto. The foreign relations power is vested in the President with an absolute senatorial or congressional veto. The executive power is vested in the President acting independently within the limits of detailed congressional legislation defining the power and procedure of administrative officials. The judicial power is vested in the courts acting independently within the narrowly defined limits of procedure and jurisdiction defined by the common law and congressional legislation.

CHAPTER X.

The Power to Meet International Responsibilities.

89. *The Law of International Responsibility.*

The principles determining the responsibility of states under international law have not been fully formulated and such formulation has proved difficult because of the divergencies of practice which have sometimes resulted from differences in national power. Borchard has given the best survey of the subject and the following statement is based largely on his work.[1]

1. *Acts of Government Organs.*

The state is responsible for tortious acts committed by executive, diplomatic, naval, military, and superior administrative officers of the central government or local subdivisions unless plainly outside of their functions and promptly disavowed. For such acts by inferior administrative officers, the state is responsible only if there is evidence either express, by authorization of a superior officer or of the law, or tacit, by the failure to afford redress or to punish the offending officer, that it sanctioned the act.[2] Judicial errors are not in themselves torts, though the courts may involve the international responsibility of the state if they fail to apply international law or deny justice.[3]

The state is also responsible for the authorization of acts violative of international law, or treaty, or unreasonably discriminatory, by constitutional provision, legislative act, executive or administrative decree, or judicial decision of central or local *de jure*

---

[1] Borchard, Diplomatic Protection of Citizens Abroad, p. 177 *et seq.* See also Hall, International Law (Higgins), pp. 226–232; Oppenheim, Int. Law, 1: sec. 148 *et seq.* For definition of "responsibility" see *infra*, sec. 141.

[2] Borchard, *op. cit.*, pp. 189–192.

[3] *Ibid.*, p. 195.

authority.[4] The promulgation of such constitutional provision, statute, ordinance or decision, if sufficiently concrete to raise a presumption that international law will be violated, is a ground for immediate protest. Other states are not obliged to await the actual commission of an act in violation of their rights.[5]

2. *Acts or Omissions of Individuals within State Jurisdiction.*

The state is responsible for the nonfulfillment of contractual obligations made by private individuals or by public officers, *ultra vires,* and for tortious acts committed in its jurisdiction by private individuals, inferior officers or any officers acting without authority, only in case its courts "deny justice" or executive and administrative officers fail to exert "due diligence" in the maintenance of order and enforcement of international law and treaty.[6] The definition of "denial of justice" involving an investigation of the adequacy of municipal law remedies and the degree of their observance in the particular case and of "due diligence," involving the establishment of criteria applicable to mob violence, insurrection, war and neutrality, has proved the most difficult branch of the subject of responsibility. In other cases of responsibility the government itself is at fault and the responsibility of the state is direct and immediate. In the present case the original fault is not by the government, and the state is responsible indirectly or vicariously and only after municipal law remedies have been exhausted.[7]

3. *Non-fulfillment of Obligation.*

The state is responsible for the non-fufillment of contractual obligations made by any legislative, executive or administrative organ acting within legal authority derived from a *de jure* govern-

---

[4] *Ibid.,* p. 181.

[5] See Ambassador Bryce to Secretary of State Knox, February 27, 1913, Diplomatic History of the Panama Canal, 65th Cong., 2d sess., Sen. Doc., No. 474, p. 101, *supra,* sec. 15.

[6] Borchard, *op. cit.,* pp. 183, 213, 283. As to two meanings of expression "denial of justice," see *ibid.,* p. 335.

[7] *Ibid.,* p. 180. See also Hall, *op. cit.,* p. 226. Oppenheim, *loc. cit.,* originated the expression "vicarious responsibility" in this connection.

INTERNATIONAL RESPONSIBILITIES.

ment or generally recognized *de facto* government of the state as a whole, and for the non-performance of acts required by international law. Contractual obligations made under authority of political subdivisions of the state or under authority of local *de facto* governments, or *de facto* governments which never attain general recognition, do not involve an international responsibility unless the state received a benefit therefrom.[8] The question of whether force may be used to compel the payment of public contract debts (involved in the Drago Doctrine and II Hague Conventions 1907) relates to the remedy and not to the legal responsibility.[9]

The state is responsible for the reparation which treaty or international law may impose, in case of failure to meet any of the foregoing responsibilities.

90. *State Power to Meet International Responsibilities.*

Extensive powers for the employment of military force, the raising and appropriation of money, the administration of justice and criminal law, and the organization and administration of public services are given to the national government by the Constitution. Are these powers sufficient to meet all present and possible international responsibilities? The states originally had full power to meet international responsibilities except as restricted by their own constitutions and they retain that power except as expressly or impliedly limited by the Federal Constitution. The delegation of power to the national government does not of itself deprive states of concurrent power, unless the power is by nature exclusive.[10] The express prohibition of treaty-making and of agreement-making without consent of congress prevents them from extraditing criminals without express authorization by congress or treaty. Justice Taney held in 1839 that extradition belonged "exclusively to the Federal Government" and the action of Governor Jennison of Vermont in issuing a warrant for the arrest of one Holmes charged with murder in Canada was "repugnant to the Constitution of the United States."[11]

---

[8] Borchard, *op. cit.*, p. 184.
[9] *Ibid.*, pp. 286, 308.
[10] Cooley *v.* Board of Port Wardens, 13 How. 294.
[11] Holmes *v.* Jennison, 14 Pet. 540, 579 (1840); Moore, Digest, 4: 242.

However, the states still have power to meet many international responsibilities involving action within their own borders. Thus the jurisdiction of state courts usually extends to many cases involving the enforcement of treaty provisions such as those according civil rights, rights of property and inheritance to resident aliens, and in such cases, under the Federal Constitution they are obliged to apply the treaty as the supreme law of the land. State courts usually also have jurisdiction under common law to give justice to aliens in civil cases and to punish many offenses against the law of nations such as libels and conspiracies against foreign governments. The state executive ordinarily has power to employ the militia to preserve order and accord aliens within the state's territory the protection required by international law and treaty and state legislatures generally have power to pass acts for the punishment of offenses against international law.[12]

91. *National Power to Meet International Responsibilities.*

Does the national government have power to take over the entire burden from the states? Authorities say yes, and have rested on three theories. The argument drawn from the assumed enjoyment by the national government of sovereign powers with respect to matters transcending state limits has been discussed and found wanting.[13] Repudiating this argument, Willoughby says:[14]

" Starting from the premise that in all that pertains to international relations the United States appears as a single sovereign nation, and that upon it rests the constitutional duty of meeting *all international responsibilities,* the Supreme Court has deduced corresponding federal *powers."*

This argument seems equally untenable. It commits the fallacy of deducing powers from responsibilities which Professor Willoughby himself denounced later in the same book.[15] The supreme court has not relied on such an argument but on specific delegations of power by the Constitution;[16]

---

[12] *Infra,* secs. 98, 110, 136.
[13] *Supra,* sec. 71.
[14] Willoughby, *op. cit.,* p. 64. See also *ibid.,* p. 451.
[15] See *infra,* sec. 93.
[16] U. S. *v.* Arjona, 120 U. S. 479, 483; Moore, Digest, 2: 430.

"As all official intercourse between a State and foreign nation is prevented by the Constitution and exclusive authority for that purpose given to the United States, the National Government is responsible to foreign nations for all violations by the United States of their international obligations, and for this reason Congress is expressly authorized to define and punish ... offenses against the law of nations."

In addition to the clause here referred to, the "necessary and proper" clause accords the national government powers adequate to meet all international responsibilities, derived from valid acts or commitments made by national organs.[17]

92. *Theory of Inherent Executive Power to Meet International Responsibilities*

How is the power to meet international responsibilities distributed among the departments of the national government?

Hamilton, Roosevelt and others have considered the President empowered to take measures for meeting all responsibilities by the first clause of Article II which vests him with "the executive power of the United States."

"It would not consist with the rules of sound construction, to consider this enumeration of particular authorities" (in Article II), wrote Hamilton in the Pacificus Paper, "as derogating from the more comprehensive grant in the general clause, further than as it may be coupled with express restrictions or limitations; as in regard to the cooperation of the Senate in the appointment of officers, and making of treaties; which are plainly qualifications of the general executive powers of appointing officers and making treaties. The difficulty of a complete enumeration of all the cases of executive authority would naturally dictate the use of general terms, and would render it improbable that specification of certain particulars was designed as a substitute for those terms, when antecedently used. The different mode of expression employed in the Constitution, in regard to the two powers, the legislative and the executive, serves to confirm this inference. In the article which gives the legislative powers of the government the expressions are, 'All legislative powers herein granted shall be vested in a Congress of the United States.' In that which grants the executive power, the expressions are, 'The executive *power* shall be vested in a President of the United States.' This enumeration ought, therefore, to be considered as intended merely to specify the principal articles implied in the definition of executive power; leaving the rest to flow from the general grant of that power, interpreted in conformity with other parts of the Constitution, and with the principles of free govern-

---

[17] *Infra*, sec. 95.

ment. The general doctrine of the Constitution then is, that the executive power of the nation is vested in the President, subject only to the exceptions and qualifications which are expressed in the instrument." [18]

President Roosevelt affirmed belief in the same doctrine over a century later in his autobiography: [19]

"I declined to adopt the view that what was imperatively necessary for the Nation could not be done by the President unless he could find some specific authorization to do it. My belief was that it was not only his right but his duty to do anything that the needs of the Nation demanded unless such action was forbidden by the Constitution or by the laws. Under this interpretation of executive power I did and caused to be done many things not previously done by the President and the heads of departments. I did not usurp power, but I did greatly broaden the use of executive power. In other words, I acted for the public welfare, I acted for the common well-being of all our people, whenever and in whatever manner was necessary, unless prevented by direct constitutional or legislative prohibition."

As an illustration of the exercise of power "not explicitly given me by the Constitution" he cites the making and carrying out of the executive agreement with San Domingo whereby he took over the administration of her customs houses.[20]

This view of executive authority has not been supported by writers of a more legalistic temperament:

"The general grant of executive power to the President," says Goodnow, "meant little except that the President was to be the authority in the government that was to exercise the powers afterwards enumerated as his." [21]

"The true view of the Executive functions is," says President Taft, ' as I conceive it, that the President can exercise no power which cannot be fairly and reasonably traced to some specific grant of power or justly implied and included within such express grant as proper and necessary to its exercise. Such specific grant must be either in the Federal Constitution or in an act of Congress passed in pursuance thereof. There is no undefined residuum of power which he can exercise because it seems to him to be of public interest, and there is nothing in the Neagle case and its definition of a law of the United States, or in other precedents, warranting such an inference."

---

[18] Hamilton, in document quoted *supra*, sec. 78.
[19] Roosevelt, Autobiography, pp. 388–389.
[20] *Op. cit.*, pp. 551–552.
[21] Goodnow, *op. cit.*, p. 73.

Later President Taft attacks the Roosevelt doctrine on practical grounds:

> "My judgment is that the view of Mr. Garfield and Mr. Roosevelt ascribing an undefined residuum of power to the President is an unsafe doctrine and that it might lead under emergencies to results of an arbitrary character, doing irremediable injustice to private right. The mainspring of such a view is that the Executive is charged with responsibility for the welfare of all people in a general way, that he is to play the part of a Universal Providence and set all things right and that anything that in his judgment will help the people, he ought to do, unless he is expressly forbidden not to do it. The wide field of action that this would give to the Executive one can hardly limit." [22]

93. *President's Duty to Execute the Laws.*

The responsibility of the President to "take care that the laws be faithfully executed" was held in the Neagle case[23] to confer power upon the President to authorize an individual to employ force for the protection of a federal justice. Here again we seem to find power derived from responsibility. If this doctrine were carried out and as the court said in this case, the term "laws" includes not only acts of congress and treaties but also "the rights, duties and obligations growing out of . . . international relations," a most inadmissible result would be reached. The President would be found to have power to declare war, pay out money, reduce the military establishment and perform all other acts necessary to meet international responsibilities. We must agree with Willoughby[24] that the doctrine of the Neagle case is "justified only in exceptional circumstances" and "the obligation to take care that the laws of the United States are faithfully executed, is an obligation but confers in itself no powers. It is an obligation which is to be fulfilled by the exercise of those powers which the Constitution and Congress have seen fit to confer." The constitutional requirement in question means that the President shall exercise his power as commander-in-chief to

---

[22] Taft, *op. cit.*, pp. 140, 144. See also Senatorial debate of 1831, quoted Corwin, *op. cit.*, p. 59.
[23] *In re* Neagle, 135 U. S. 1.
[24] Willoughby, *op. cit.*, pp. 1155. But see Goodnow, *op. cit.*, pp. 47, 75, and Hamilton, quoted Corwin, *op. cit.*, p. 15.

move the forces, his power as head of the civil administration to direct and instruct diplomatic, consular and other officers within the scope of their powers as fixed by congress, his power to negotiate treaties, his power to receive diplomatic officers and his other powers given specifically by the Constitution or by congress in the manner most appropriate to execute the laws, including international law and treaties. It does not mean that he can supply means not provided by law or take measure not within the scope of his delegated powers, however appropriate they might be for the meeting of international responsibilities. Within his recognized powers, however, assuming the existence of the military, naval and civil organizations as provided by congress, the President has power to meet many international responsibilities without the aid of congress.

94. *Power of Courts to Meet International Responsibilities.*

The federal courts are obliged by the Constitution to apply treaties as the supreme law of the land and have held that they must apply international law in appropriate cases, though subsequent express statutes will prevail in either case.[25] This, however, is an obligation and not a power. The view taken by the courts in a few early cases that from these duties they could derive jurisdiction to enforce international law even by criminal punishments has not prevailed.[26] The extension of federal judicial power by Article III of the Constitution:

"to all cases, in law and Equity, arising under this Constitution, the Laws of the United States, and Treaties made, or which shall be made under their Authority;—to all Cases of admiralty and maritime jurisdiction; to controversies to which the United States shall be a party; and to controversies . . . between a State or the Citizens thereof, and Foreign states, Citizens or Subjects"

seems to give an opportunity for a full cooperation of the federal courts in meeting international responsibilities. This jurisdiction, however, with exception of the original jurisdiction of the Supreme Court which includes cases affecting diplomatic officers and consuls,

---

[25] *Infra*, secs. 106–108.
[26] *Infra*, sec. 129.

is subject to regulation by congress. Thus in fact, aside from the recourses offered diplomatic officers and consuls to the Supreme Court, the federal courts can aid in the meeting of international responsibilities only in so far as congress has specifically conferred jurisdiction upon them. Their jurisdiction has in fact been extended to most of the cases described in the Constitution and their application of international law and treaties, in prize cases, cases affecting foreign sovereigns, diplomatic, military and naval officers, cases affecting domiciled aliens, sojourning foreign vessels and others is an effective means of meeting many international responsibilities. Congress has defined a considerable number of crimes at international law, such as piracy, offenses against neutrality, offenses against foreign ministers and offenses against foreign currency, which are made punishable by the federal courts.[27]

95. *Power of Congress to Meet International Responsibilities.*

Aside from the exercise of specific powers, such as the appropriation of money, the regulation of commerce, provision for the punishment of piracies and offenses against the law of nations, declaration of war, grant of letters of marque and reprisal, making of rules concerning capture, maintenance and regulation of an army and navy, Congress can " make all laws which shall be necessary and proper for carrying into execution . . . all . . . powers vested by this Constitution in the Government of the United States or in any department or officer thereof." This clause unquestionably confers power upon Congress sufficient to meet every possible international responsibility. Accepting the doctrine of the Supreme Court that the exercise of sovereignty may be limited only by its own consent,[28] it follows that every international responsibility must have originated in a constitutional exercise of power by some organ of the national government, either through positive action or tacit recognition. Thus responsibilities founded on treaty originate in a

---

[27] *Infra,* secs. 113–118.
[28] The Schooner Exchange *v.* McFaddon, 7 Cranch 116, quoted with approval in the Chinese Exclusion Cases, 130 U. S. 581 (1889). See also *infra,* sec. 138.

valid act of the treaty power, responsibilities founded on arbitral decisions originate either in a valid act of the treaty power or of the President, responsibilities founded on general international law originate in the tacit acceptance of that law by the terms of the Constitution[29] and by the President in continuing membership in the family of nations, as evidenced through the continued exchange of diplomatic officers.[30] In providing for carrying these powers into execution, therefore, Congress would be providing for meeting the international responsibilities they created. Thus if the President or the Courts are unable properly to meet any international responsibility it is not from a defect in the Constitution, but from failure of Congress fully to exercise its powers under the "necessary and proper" clause. Congress has in fact enacted many laws whose purpose is the enforcement of international law and treaty.[31] It has never failed to make an appropriation when called for by treaty and has often made appropriations to satisfy claims based on international law as determined by diplomatic correspondence or arbitration.[32]

96. *Power to Meet International Responsibilities by Treaty.*

An international responsibility may occasionally require conclusion of a treaty. Suffice it to say that the President, acting with advice and consent of two-thirds of the senate, is authorized to make treaties on all subjects suitable for international agreement.[33]

---

[29] Willoughby, *op. cit.*, p. 1018, and *Am. Jl. Int. Law*, 2: 357.
[30] Maine, Int. Law, pp. 37–38, quoted in Moore, Digest, 1: 7.
[31] *Infra*, secs. 112–118.
[32] *Infra*, sec. 149.
[33] *Infra*, sec. 173.

CHAPTER XI.

The Power to Meet International Responsibilities Through the Observance of International Law.

97. *Conditions Favoring the Observance of International Law.*

The responsibility of the nation for acts of government organs imposes a duty upon every organ to abstain from action in violation of international law or treaty. This responsibility will be met if every independent organ of government is careful to exercise its discretionary power in accordance with this duty, consequently there can be no question of the *power* of the government to meet this responsibility. Is it probable that independent organs *will* recognize international law, rather than national policy, as a proper guide in the exercise of their powers? No organ is in fact wholly independent. The government is a complex organization, the action of each organ being to a certain extent influenced by that of others. We may, therefore, investigate the conditions which tend to assure the observance of international law and treaty by the various organs of government in the present state of public law.

98. *Observance of International Law by the States.*

A state constitution or legislative provision in violation of customary international law is valid unless in conflict with a Federal constitutional provision or an act of Congress as would usually be the case. However, it appeared in 1842 that the criminal laws of New York made no exception in favor of persons entitled to immunity under international law and the United States had no means of relieving Alexander McLeod from the operation of those laws, although the Secretary of State admitted the responsibility to do so under international law. Congress has power to pass legislation assuring respect for international law by the states and such legislation was passed soon after this incident.[1] If a state law disregards a treaty

---

[1] Act of Aug. 29, 1842, Rev. Stat., sec. 753. See Moore, Digest, 2: 24–30.

it is void. The courts both federal and state are obliged to apply treaties "anything in the Constitution or Laws of any State to the Contrary notwithstanding."[2] Thus state confiscation acts were held void as in violation of the treaty of peace with Great Britain of 1783 and many other state statutes discriminating against aliens have been similarly invalidated.[3]

99. *Observance of International Law by the Constitution.*

If the Constitution proves in any respect in violation of international law there is no recourse except to the amending process, but in view of the generality of its provisions, a conflict, incapable of reconciliation by interpretation, is not likely to occur. The courts have held that they must interpret the Constitution in accord with international law if possible and thus have protected the immunities of diplomatic officers against the constitutional clause guaranteeing the accused a right "to have compulsory process for obtaining witnesses in his favor."[4] The 18th amendment has been held to permit the customary exemption from search of the baggage of diplomatic officers.

100. *Observance of International Law by Congress.*

The observance of international law and treaty by Congress depends upon the discretion of that body. An act of Congress if constitutional is valid within the United States even though in direct violation of international law or treaty as was illustrated by the Chinese exclusion act of 1888.

"It must be conceded," said the Supreme Court, "that the act of 1888 is in contravention of express stipulations of the treaty of 1868 and of the supplemental treaty of 1880, but it is not on that account invalid or to be

---

[2] U. S. Constitution, Art. VI, sec. 2.

[3] Ware *v.* Hylton, 3 Dall. 199. On this case see Crandall, *op. cit.*, pp. 154–160. H. St. George Tucker, Limitations of the Treaty Making Power, Boston, 1915, has been led by what J. B. Moore calls an "apprehensive" interpretation of the Constitution (*Pol. Sci. Quar.*, 32: 320) to take a novel view of this case. Crandall, *loc. cit.*, effectively deals with this interpretation. See also *infra*, sec. 50.

[4] See cases of Dubois and Comancho, Moore, Digest, 4: 643–645; Wright, *Am. Jl. Int. Law*, 11: 5; and *supra*, sec. 45.

OBSERVANCE OF INTERNATIONAL LAW. 163

restricted in its enforcement. . . . The question whether our government was justified in disregarding its engagements with another nation is not one for the determination of the courts. . . . The court is not the censor of the morals of the other departments of the Government." [5]

In spite of the protests of China, the act remained in effect. The same was true of the act of Congress exempting American vessels from tolls in the use of the Panama Canal. Great Britain considered the act in disregard of the Hay-Pauncefote treaty but it remained effective until repealed by Congress itself, at the solicitation of President Wilson whose judgment "very fully considered and maturely formed" found it "in plain contravention of the treaty." [6]

Congress has sometimes made express exception from the operation of statutes out of deference to international law. Thus, the various acts describing rules of navigation "shall not be construed as applying to ships of war or to government ships." [7] The selective draft act of 1917 as amended August 31, 1918, exempted foreign consular and diplomatic officers from registration and resident aliens except declarants of co-belligerent nationality from service.[8] The Supreme Court is given only such jurisdiction of cases against foreign diplomatic officers "as a court of law can have consistently with the law of nations." [9] An act of 1790 expressly exempts resident "public ministers," their "domestics and domestic servants" and their "goods and chattels" from all legal process,[10] and an act of 1888 excepts "the ownership of legations, or the ownership of residences by representatives of foreign governments or attachés, thereof" from the general law prohibiting alien landholding in the District of Columbia.[11] Frequently Congress has shown respect for treaties by excepting persons entitled to treaty privileges from the operation of statutes or by making the operation of the statute de-

---

[5] Chinese Exclusion Cases, 130 U. S. 581 (1889).
[6] Message, March 5, 1914, *Cong. Rec.*, 51: 4313.
[7] Act Aug. 1, 1912, sec. 5, 37 Stat. 242, Comp. Stat., sec. 7994.
[8] Acts July 9, 1918, and Aug. 31, 1918, amending act May 18, 1917, secs. 4, 5, Comp. Stat., sec. 2044b, e.
[9] Rev. Stat., 687, Judicial Code of 1911, sec. 233, 36 Stat., 1156, Comp. Stat., sec. 1210.
[10] Rev. Stat., 4063, Comp. Stat., 7611.
[11] Act March 9, 1888, 25 Stat. 45, Comp. Stat., sec. 3501.

pendent upon denunciation of the treaty according to its own terms. Thus certain provisions of the La Follette seaman's act were to remain in abeyance until conflicting treaties should be properly terminated[12] and acts of Congress for the restoration of captured prizes,[13] for the imposition of discriminatory tariffs or import prohibitions[14] and for levying tonnage duties[15] and for prohibiting alien landholding in the territories and the District of Columbia[16] were not to apply in conflict with existing treaties.

101. *Checks upon Congressional Disregard of International Law.*

Although disregard of international law and treaty by Congress is prevented primarily by that body's own sense of international responsibility, the Constitution does provide certain checks against such disregard. The treaty-making power may conclude a treaty or provide for an arbitration either of which would supersede an earlier act of Congress. Thus the act of Congress of 1889 as judicially interpreted extended American jurisdiction in Behring Sea, one hundred Italian miles from shore, in disregard of the principle of international law limiting maritime jurisdiction to the marine league. This act was held to be superseded by the arbitration based on a treaty with Great Britain of 1892.[17]

The President's veto has proved a check upon congressional disregard of international responsibilities. Since the President feels the pressure of foreign nations he is likely to be more sensitive to violations of international law than the houses of Congress. Thus President Hayes vetoed the first Chinese exclusion bill as in violation of the Burlingame treaty of 1868. After explaining some con-

---

[12] Act March 4, 1915, 38 Stat. 1184, secs. 16, 17; Comp. Stat., sec. 8382a, b.

[13] Rev. Stat., sec. 4652; Comp. Stat., sec. 8426.

[14] Underwood tariff, Oct. 3, 1913, sec. IV, j, sub. secs. 1, 2, 7; 38 Stat. 195, 196; Comp. Stat., 5305, 5306, 5311. According to sec. IV, b, 38 Stat. 192, the Cuban reciprocity treaty of 1902 was unaffected by the tariff.

[15] Rev. Stat., sec. 4227; Comp. Stat., sec. 7820.

[16] Act March 3, 1887, 24 Stat. 476, March 2, 1897, 29 Stat. 618, Comp. Stat., secs. 3490, 3498.

[17] La Ninfa, 75 Fed. 513, 1896.

stitutional objections to the act he referred to the "more general considerations of interest and duty which sacredly guard the faith of the nation, in whatever form of obligation it may have been given," and concluded "in asking the renewed attention of Congress to this bill, I am persuaded that their action will maintain the public duty and the public honor." [18] President Arthur vetoed the second Chinese exclusion bill for similar reasons.[19] The President may also use his powers of persuasion upon Congress to cause the repeal of an act in disregard of international law or treaty as did President Wilson with success in the Panama Canal tolls controversy.[20]

The courts are bound by acts of Congress, but said Chief Justice Marshall, "an act of Congress ought never to be construed to violate the law of nations if any other possible construction remains." [21] With this principle Marshall construed the broad jurisdiction over offenses at sea conferred by various acts of Congress as confined to American vessels or vessels within American jurisdiction as defined by international law.[22] It seems that the court neglected an opportunity to apply this principle in the Behring Sea cases of 1887, a neglect which may have been partly responsible for the expensive and futile arbitration later entered into.[23] In the case of American Banana Co. v. United Fruit Co., however, the supreme court applied the principle by interpreting the Sherman Anti-Trust Act, though general in terms, as applying only within the jurisdiction of the United States as defined by international law.[24]

---

[18] Richardson, *op. cit.*, 7: 519–520.
[19] Message, April 4, 1882, *ibid.*, 8: 112.
[20] *Supra*, note 6.
[21] Murray v. The Charming Betsey, 2 Cranch 64, 118, 1804.
[22] U. S. v. Palmer, 3 Wheat. 610, 1818; U. S. v. Pirates, U. S. v. Klintock, U. S. v. Holmes, 5 Wheat. 144, 152, 184, 200, 412, 1820.
[23] *Infra*, sec. 107.
[24] "All legislation is prima facie territorial, words having universal scope, such as every contract in restraint of trade, . . . will be taken as a matter of course to mean only every one subject to such legislation, not all that the legislator may subsequently be able to catch." American Banana Co. v. United Fruit Co., 219 U. S. 347, 1909. See also Sandberg v. McDonald, 248 U. S. 185, *Am. Jl. Int. Law*, 13: 339.

102. *Observance of International Law by the Treaty-making Power.*

The President and Senate ought not to make treaties in disregard of the rights of third states under international law or earlier treaties and have not often done so. Frequently treaties have expressly excepted the rights of third states under existing treaties or general international law. Thus the Hague Conventions on war and neutrality by their own terms "do not apply except between contracting powers and then only if all the belligerents are parties to the Convention."[25] American arbitration treaties have usually excepted from the scope of obligatory arbitration cases "concerning the interests of third parties" and Article 25 of the Jay treaty with Great Britain of 1794 expressly provided that "nothing in this treaty contained shall ... be construed or operate contrary to former and existing public treaties with other sovereigns or states." If there is a conflict, however, the later treaty is valid as municipal law until superseded by another treaty or an act of Congress.[26]

But, as in the case of acts of Congress, courts attempt to construe treaties in accord with the rights of third states. Thus they gave a very narrow construction to the special privileges in American ports given to French privateers and war vessels by the treaty of 1778, out of respect for the British right to demand from a neutral state impartiality in regulating the use of its ports.[27]

103. *Observance of International Law by the President.*

The President might recognize a state or government or an acquisition of territory in disregard of international law, or proclaim neutrality in desregard of a treaty of alliance or wrongfully intervene in a foreign state, and his act would be followed by the courts.[28] There is no guarantee that the President will exercise his discretionary powers in accord with international law and treaty,

---

[25] See also League of Nations Covenant, Art. 20.

[26] Bolcher *v.* Darrell, Fed. Cas. 1607, 1795; The Phoebe Ann, 3 Dall. 319. See also Wright, Conflicts between International Law and Treaties, *Am. Jl. Int. Law,* 11: 566 *et seq.* (July, 1917).

[27] The Phoebe Ann, *supra.* Wright, *op. cit.,* pp. 574–5; Moore, Digest, 5: 591–598.

[28] *Infra,* sec. 107.

except his own sense of international responsibility and a fear of a possible impeachment.[29] Congress has passed laws defining and limiting the purposes for which the army, navy and militia may be used, but the validity of such legislation, except as applied to the militia, has been questioned.[30]

104. *Observance of International Law by Military and Civil Services.*

Usually, however, the President is obliged to act through services which are subject to control by acts of Congress and judicial processes. Congress has provided for the organization of the diplomatic, consular, naval, military and administrative services but has not generally attempted to regulate their conduct in detail. A few statutory regulations are designed to assure observance of international law by public officers of which may be mentioned that forbidding ministers to give information relating to the affairs of the foreign state to which they are accredited except to the Department of State,[31] that forbidding administrative officers from serving process on resident diplomatic officers and others entitled to immunity under international law,[32] that forbidding the injury or destruction of prizes or maltreatment of those on board by naval forces,[33] and that requiring the restoration of recaptured prizes originally the property of neutral individuals on the principle of reciprocity.[34]

These services are regulated in detail by executive regulations and instructions, which, though issued by and subject to alteration by the President, in fact furnish a fairly permanent law for their guidance. These regulations have usually enjoined a strict ob-

---

[29] Impeachment lies for moral and political offenses as well as crimes in the legal sense. Willoughby, *op. cit.*, p. 1124. See also Corwin, John Marshall and the Constitution, p. 78.

[30] *Infra*, sec. 125.

[31] Act Aug. 18, 1850, Rev. Stat., sec. 1751.

[32] Rev. Stat., sec. 4063, Comp. Stat., sec. 7611.

[33] Articles for Government of the Navy, Rev. Stat., sec. 1624, Arts. 6, 11, 12. See also Rev. Stat., sec. 4617, Comp. Stat., sec. 8397, and Wright, Enforcement of International Law through Municipal Law, pp. 183 *et seq*.

[34] Rev. Stat., sec. 4652, Comp. Stat., sec. 8426.

168   THE CONTROL OF AMERICAN FOREIGN RELATIONS.

servance of international law and treaty. The "Diplomatic Instructions," "Consular Regulations," "Rules of Naval Warfare" and "Rules of Land Warfare," each a volume officially issued from time to time, are largely codifications of international law and treaty provisions.[35] The permanent army regulations forbid armed forces passing into foreign territory without license, and army officers are required to observe proper formalities in dealing with the representatives of foreign governments.[36] The permanent navy regulations require naval commanders "scrupulously to respect the territorial authority of foreign civilized nations in amity with the United States," to observe local regulations on entering foreign jurisdiction, to exchange the proper salutes when meeting foreign public vessels, to refuse asylum to criminals, slaves and political refugees while in foreign ports, to observe strict neutrality in wars to which the United States is not a party, and "when the United States is at war, the Commander-in-Chief shall require all under his command to observe the rules of humane warfare and the principles of international law."[37] Treasury regulations have required customs officials to respect the immunities of diplomatic officers.[38]

The diplomatic and consular regulations are enforced by the President's disciplinary control and power of removal and by statutory provisions for bonding and criminal liability enforced by the courts.[39] Military and naval regulations and instructions are enforced by courts martial whose jurisdiction, however, is largely confined to the statutory articles of war, and by military commissions.[40]

---

[35] See Wright, *op. cit.*, p. 68.

[36] Army Regulations, 1913, secs. 398, 407, 889, ch. 3; Digest of Opinions of Judge Ad. Gen., 1912, Howland ed., pp. 90, 106.

[37] Navy Regulations, 1913, secs. 1502, 1633-35, 1645-47. Naval commanders are allowed some discretion under these regulations. See note at head of Chap. 15, Navy Reg., 1913, p. 159, r. For case in which Navy regulations were enforced against a commander see Moore, Digest, 1: 240-241. See Wright, *op. cit.*, 68, 126, 177, 213.

[38] Moore, Digest, 4: 676.

[39] Wright, *op. cit.*, p. 69.

[40] Navy, see Rev. Stat., sec. 1624, Arts. 22, 24, 26, 38, and Wright, *op. cit.*, p. 68, 177. Army, see Rev. Stat. secs. 1342-1343, Lieber's Instructions, Gen. Ord. 100, 1863, art. 13; Digest of Opinions of Judge Ad. Gen. 1912, p. 1067; Wright, *op. cit.*, p. 210.

The federal courts, in exercising prize jurisdiction, exercise a considerable control over the navy in time of war. They not only return captured vessels and cargoes not liable to condemnation under international law,[41] but decree damages against naval officers for illegal captures.[42] They exercise a similar jurisdiction over captured vessels in time of peace, and may thus prevent illegal seizures upon the high seas or in foreign territorial waters by vessels of the navy or revenue cutter service.[43] In such cases, however, the courts sometimes refuse relief on the ground that the question is political.[44] Although the courts exercise less control of the army than of the navy in time of war, yet they may give relief in case military action violates property rights protected by international law. Thus in Mitchell v. Harmony[45] the court applied international law to determine the right of military officers to confiscate enemy property in the occupied territory of Mexico and in Brown v. the United States[46] the court refused to confiscate enemy property in American territory holding that international law regarded such confiscation with disfavor and the court could not permit it unless authorized by an express act of Congress. In other cases the courts have held that the President's power in conducting war is limited by international law and any action he may authorize contrary to that law is void. Congress alone can authorize military methods conflicting with international law and as we have seen the courts will not presume such a conflict.[47]

---

[41] The Nereide, 9 Cranch 388; The Paquette Habana, 175 U. S. 677.

[42] Little v. Barreme, 2 Cranch 170.

[43] La Jeune Eugenie, 2 Mason 409, 1822; Rose v. Himeley, 4 Cranch 241; Hudson v. Guestier, 6 Cranch 281, 1810; The Marianna Flora, 11 Wheat. 1, 1826; The Antelope, 10 Wheat. 66, 122, 1825; La Ninfa, 75 Fed. 513, 1896.

[44] Ship Richmond v. U. S., 9 Cranch 102, 104, 1815; Davisson v. Sealskins, 2 Paine 324; Moore, Digest, 2: 364-365, and *supra*, sec. 107.

[45] Mitchell v. Harmony, 13 How. 115.

[46] Brown v. U. S., 8 Cranch 110. See also McVeigh v. U. S., 11 Wall. 259, 1870, in which the court relaxed the rule which permits an alien enemy no status in court and permitted him to defend, and Wright, *Am. Jl. Int. Law*, 11: 19.

[47] Mitchell v. Harmony, 13 How. 115; Miller v. U. S., 11 Wall. 268; Fleming v. Page, 9 How. 603; Willoughby, *op. cit.*, p. 1196, says: "With respect to the persons and property of the enemy, however, he (the military

105. *Observance of International Law by the Courts.*

Judicial action may give grounds for international complaint in case justice is denied to aliens by the courts in civil or criminal trials and in case international law or treaty are not applied in cases affecting aliens or foreign governments.[48] The guarantees of "due process of law" to all persons in the United States by the Vth and XIVth amendments are applicable respectively against the national and state governments, and in both federal and state courts. Together with other more specific constitutional guarantees relating especially to criminal trials, they seem to assure aliens a procedure and an absence of unreasonable discrimination in the law applied, sufficient to prevent a "denial of justice" as understood in international law.

However, the alien may feel greater confidence in federal than in state courts because of the decreased chance of local prejudice. Under present statutes he is entitled to bring action against citizens in civil cases in the federal district court if over $3,000 is in controversy or if "for tort, only in violation of the laws of nations or of a treaty of the United States."[49] Ambassadors and consuls of foreign governments are entitled to bring suits originally in the Supreme Court, though they may also sue in the state courts. They may be sued, however, only in the federal courts, and diplomatic officers only in the Supreme Court and then only so far as the law of nations permits.[50]

---

commander) is subject only to the limitations which the laws of war, as determined by international usage, supply, and for violations of these he is responsible only to the military tribunals." But on page 1212 he says: "Indeed, the President, in the exercise simply of his authority as commander-in-chief of the army and navy, may, unless prohibited by congressional statute, commit or authorize acts not warranted by commonly received principles of international law." Sutherland, however (*op. cit.,* p. 77), says: "The usages and laws of war alone, and not the Constitution of the United States, fix the limits" of the President's authority in conducting military operations. See also British case of the Zamora, L. R. 1916, 2 A. C. 77, holding an order in council contrary to international law void; Wright, *Am. Jl. Int. Law,* 11: 2, and *supra,* sec. 47.

[48] Borchard, *op. cit.,* p. 335.
[49] Judicial code of 1911, sec. 24, pars. 1, 17, 36 Stat. 1091, 1093.
[50] *Ibid.,* sec. 24, par. 18, sec. 233; sec. 256, par. 8.

Any alien not resident in the state may have an action brought against him in a state court, removed to a federal district court if it is of a type which might have originated in that court. If "from prejudice or local influence he will not be able to obtain justice" in the state court, he may have any suit removed.[51] Any alien may also have the case removed:

> "In any civil suit or criminal prosecution commenced in any State court for any cause whatsoever," if he "is denied or can not enforce in the judicial tribunals of the State, or in the part of the State where such suit or prosecution is pending, any right secured to him by any law providing for the equal civil rights . . . of all persons within the jurisdiction of the United States." [52]

Finally, any person who can show a federal court under habeas corpus that he is entitled to immunity under international law or treaty may be released from the state court.[53]

106. *Courts Apply International Law and Treaties as Part of the Law of the Land.*

The courts regard international law as part of the law of the land and apply it in suitable cases.

> "International law," said Justice Gray, "is a part of our law, and must be ascertained and administered by the courts of justice of appropriate jurisdiction, as often as questions of right depending upon it are duly presented for their determination. For this purpose, where there is no treaty, and no controlling executive or legislative act or judicial decision, resort must be had to the customs and usages of civilized nations; and, as evidence of these, to the works of jurists and commentators, who, by years of labor, research, and experience, have made themselves peculiarly well acquainted with the subjects of which they treat. Such words are resorted to by judicial tribunals, not for the speculations of their authors concerning what the law ought to be, but for trustworthy evidence of what the law really is." [54]

This principle has been applied in admiralty and prize cases;[55] in cases involving the immunities of sovereigns, diplomatic officers,

---

[51] *Ibid.*, sec. 28.
[52] *Ibid.*, sec. 31.
[53] *Supra*, note 1.
[54] The Paquette Habana, 175 U. S. 677. See also Willoughby, *op cit.*, 1014–1018.
[55] *Ibid.*, and also The Nereide, 9 Cranch 388.

172   THE CONTROL OF AMERICAN FOREIGN RELATIONS.

public vessels, military persons, consuls, etc.;[56] in cases involving the limits of jurisdiction, especially in boundary rivers, bays, etc.;[57] in cases involving the status of aliens and especially alien enemies;[58] in cases involving the rights of persons in newly acquired territory;[59] and in cases involving the privileges and responsibilities of neutrality, war and insurgency.[60] Under the terms of Article VI of the Constitution treaties are the supreme law of the land and after proclamation are applicable by all courts, state and federal.

107. *This Principle not Applicable to Political Questions.*

The principle, however, that courts apply international law and treaty in appropriate cases is subject to certain modifications. Thus if the controversy involves "a political question" the courts hold that they must follow the decision of the political organs, irrespective of international law and treaty.[61] But no definite line has ever been drawn between principles of international law and treaty provisions which are of a political character and those which are of a legal character. In such matters as the annexation or cession of territory,[62] the recognition of insurgency,[63] belligerency,[64] new governments,[65] new states,[66] the termination of treaties,[67]

[56] The Exchange *v.* McFaddon, 7 Cranch 116; Underhill *v.* Hernandez, 168 U. S. 250.

[57] The Appollon, 9 Wheat. 362.

[58] McVeigh *v.* U. S., 11 Wall. 259, 1870; Watts *v.* Unione Austriaca de Navigazione, 248 U. S. 9 (1918).

[59] U. S. *v.* Percheman, 7 Pet. 51; Villas *v.* City of Manila, 220 U. S. 345, 1911.

[60] The Santissima Trinidad, 7 Wheat. 283; The Three Friends, 166 U. S. 1; The Appam, 37 Sup. Ct. 337.

[61] Crandall, *op. cit.*, 364–370; Willoughby, *op. cit.*, 999–1011; Moore, Digest, 1: 245, 744.

[62] Jones *v.* U. S., 137 U. S. 202, 212–213, 1890; Williams *v.* Suffolk Insurance Co., 13 Pet. 415; Foster *v.* Neilson, 2 Pet. 253; *In re* Cooper, 138 U. S. 404; U. S. *v.* Reynes, 9 How. 127.

[63] The Three Friends, 116 U. S. 1, 63, 1897; Kennett *v.* Chambers, 14 How. 38.

[64] U. S. *v.* Palmer, 3 Wheat. 610; The Divina Pastora, 4 Wheat. 52; The Santissima Trinidad, 7 Wheat. 283; The Prize Cases, 2 Black 635.

[65] The Sapphire, 11 Wall. 164, 1870, Oetjen *v.* Central Leather Co., 246 U. S. 297, 1917, Ricaud *v.* American Metal Co., 246 U. S. 304, 1917. The recognition of a particular person as diplomatic representative of a foreign government is also a political question, *Ex parte* Baiz, 135 U. S. 403.

and of war,[68] the courts ordinarily follow the decisions of the political organs. Sometimes, however, no definite decision has been given by those organs. In such cases, the courts, holding that they "have no more right to decline the jurisdiction which is given than to usurp that which is not given,"[69] have investigated facts and international law giving a decision thereon, always attempting, but sometimes without complete success, to avoid decision on questions of policy. Thus the Supreme Court decided upon the status of Pine Island near Cuba and upon the status of Cuban insurgents in 1896 on the basis of international law, generally known facts and various rather indefinite statements in executive proclamations and correspondence.[70] Very often international law is utilized by the courts to buttress opinions founded primarily on decisions by the political organs of government. Thus the Supreme Court not only held that the United States had taken possession of the island of Navassa by executive proclamation under an act of Congress but that under international law it was entitled to do so on the principle of discovery and occupation.[71] Where international questions, even if of political significance, are susceptible of exact determination by application of international law the courts do not hesitate to settle them. Prize cases are of this kind, so also are cases involving the immunities of sovereigns, diplomatic officers and public vessels.[72]

[66] The Nereide, 9 Cranch 388, 1815; Cherokee Nation *v.* Georgia, 5 Pet. 1; Neeley *v.* Henkel, 180 U. S. 109, 1901.

[67] Doe *v.* Braden, 16 How. 635; Terlinden *v.* Ames, 184 U. S. 270; Willoughby, *op. cit.*, 1007, *infra*, sec. 182.

[68] The Protector, 12 Wall. 700, 1871.

[69] *In re* Cooper, 143 U. S. 472, 502–505, 1892; Moore, Digest, 1: 744, *infra*, sec. 247.

[70] Pearcy *v.* Stranahan, 205 U. S. 257 (1907); The Three Friends, 166 U. S. 1.

[71] Jones *v.* U. S., 137 U. S. 202, 212. The British court of Queens Bench (Mighell *v.* Sultan of Johore, 1894, 1 Q. B. 149, 158), however, thought the opinion of the appropriate political department incapable of examination and questioned the course pursued by Sir Robert Phillimore in the Charkieh (L. R. 4 A. and E., 59, 1873), in examining the history of Egypt since A. D. 638 to determine its status. See A. D. McNair, Judicial Recognition of States and Governments, British Year Book of International Law, 2: 57, 66.

[72] *Supra*, sec. 106.

It seems that far from encroaching upon powers of the political departments of government the courts have if anything been over-cautious. It would seem that a decision founded squarely upon international law might well have been given in the first Behring Sea cases, and had such been done the United States might have avoided the expense of a protracted litigation and arbitration where from the first there was no reasonable legal defense. An act of 1868[73] had forbidden the killing of "otter, mink, marten, or fur-seal, or other fur-bearing animal, within the limits of Alaska territory, or in the waters thereof." The Treasury Department in enforcing this provision acted upon a claim asserted by Russia in 1821 to a jurisdiction beyond the three-mile limit in Behring Sea,[74] but when the question of definition came before Congress a bill definitely approving the extended jurisdiction was not passed, the act of 1889 merely asserting that the earlier statute should "include and apply to all the dominions of the United States in the waters of Behring Sea," thus leaving open the question of the extent of these waters.[75] The district court in Alaska, however, affirmed by the Supreme Court, held that the political departments had decided for the wider jurisdiction and that Canadian vessels captured while seal fishing sixty miles from shore were liable.[76] It would seem that under the circumstances, the courts might well have held the statutes to imply an invitation for judicial decision based on international law. After the arbitration of 1893 had declared unequivocally for the three-mile limit, the Circuit Court of Appeals held that the act of 1889 must be interpreted accordingly.[77]

108. *This Principle not Applicable to Cases Covered by Written Law.*

Apart from political questions courts are bound by plain terms of the Constitution, by treaties, by acts of Congress, and by executive

---

[73] Act June 17, 1868, Rev. Stat., sec. 1856.

[74] Moore, Int. Arb., p. 769.

[75] Act March 2, 1889, 25 Stat. 1099; Moore, Int. Arb., p. 765.

[76] U. S. *v.* La Ninfa, 49 Fed. 575, 1891; *In re* Cooper, 143 U. S. 472, 502-505.

[77] U. S. *v.* La Ninfa, 75 Fed. 513. As a result of the arbitration the United States paid Great Britain $473,151.26 as indemnity for the seizures. See Moore, Digest, 1: 890-929, and Int. Arb., pp. 765-960.

OBSERVANCE OF INTERNATIONAL LAW.

orders under authority thereof, in spite of principles of international law and earlier treaties. They, however, attempt to interpret such documents in accord with international law, frequently with success,[78] and they refuse to apply state constitutions and statutes in conflict with treaty.[79]

In general the courts do apply international law and treaty, and because of the opportunity for a careful consideration of the sources and reason of that law which their deliberate methods afford, they assure the application of international law in cases not covered by written law. Through their powers of nullifying state laws in conflict with treaty and of interpreting acts of Congress and of the President, they minimize the probability of disregard by other organs of the government.

---

[78] Murray *v.* The Charming Betsey, 2 Cranch 64, and see Wright, Conflicts of International Law with National Laws and Ordinances, *Am. Jl. Int. Law,* 11: 1 *et seq.* (Jan., 1917).

[79] Ware *v.* Hylton, 3 Dall. 199, and *supra,* note 3.

CHAPTER XII.

THE POWER TO MEET INTERNATIONAL RESPONSIBILITIES THROUGH THE ENFORCEMENT OF INTERNATIONAL LAW.

109. *"Due Diligence."*

The responsibility of the nation for acts or omissions of individuals within its jurisdiction requires all organs of government to use "due diligence" to preserve order and to prevent violations of international law and treaty by persons within its jurisdiction. While the responsibility discussed in the preceding chapter relates only to the conduct of public officials and hence will be met if officials consistently observe the limitations prescribed for them by international law and treaties in exercising their powers, this responsibility relates primarily to the conduct of private individuals. The conduct of public officials is, however, indirectly involved, inasmuch as the nation will be responsible if they neglect proper measures to compel individuals within their jurisdiction to observe these limitations. The government is supposed to enforce law and maintain order with reasonable efficiency within its jurisdiction and is responsible for failure to do so. A lack of "due diligence" is the expression used to describe the degree of negligence which justifies a claim founded on failure to meet this responsibility.

While it is the judicial and executive organs of government which operate directly on individuals, often these organs must be authorized to act by legislation or treaty. Consequently any of the departments may be obliged to exercise their powers if this responsibility is to be met. The decision of the Geneva Arbitration Tribunal in the Alabama Claims case made this point clear. "The Government of Her Britannic Majesty," said the court, "cannot justify itself for a failure in due diligence on pleas of insufficiency of the legal means of action which it possesses."[1]

---

[1] Malloy, Treaties, p. 719.

Defining due diligence the Tribunal said:[2]

"The due diligence referred to in the first and third of the said rules (of Article V of the Treaty of Washington) ought to be exercised by a neutral government in exact proportion to the risks to which either of the belligerents may be exposed from a failure to fulfill the obligations of neutrality on their part."

The XIII Hague Convention of 1907 in Articles 8 and 25 practically repeated the first and third rules of the treaty of Washington but substituted the phrase "means at its disposal" for "due diligence." The drafting committee of the Hague Convention merely noted that "The expression due diligence, which has become celebrated by its obscurity, since its solemn interpretation, has been omitted."[3] Apparently no essential difference in meaning was intended. "Means at its disposal" do not mean merely those provided by existing legislation but those which the legislature ought to provide. In spite of the committee's disparaging remark, the term "due diligence" has continued in usage.[4]

110. *Enforcement by the States.*

The states retain full power of criminal legislation except as expressly or impliedly limited by the federal Constitution. Before the Constitution the states' powers in this regard were almost exclusive and Congress urged them to provide for the punishment of offenses against the law of nations. In 1784 the court of oyer and terminer of Philadelphia found one DeLongchamps guilty of "a crime against the whole world" for committing an assault upon the Secretary of the French legation.[5] The court declared the person of a public minister and his "comites" or household "sacred and inviolable." "Whoever," said the court, "offers any violence to him not only affronts the sovereign he represents but also hurts the common safety and well-being of nations." The court found difficulty in awarding sentence and finally concluded "the defendant cannot be imprisoned until his most Christian Majesty

---
[2] *Ibid.,* p. 718; Moore, Int. Arb., p 4082.
[3] Scott, ed., Reports of Hague Conferences, p. 845.
[4] Borchard, *op. cit.,* p. 278.
[5] Res Publica *v.* DeLongchamps, 1 Dall. III; Moore, Digest, 4: 622.

shall declare that the reparation is satisfactory." Apparently a *de facto* incarceration without formal sentence of imprisonment, which if given at all would have to be "certain and definite," seemed the only way of satisfying the dilemma arising from the court's theory that it was not only administering Pennsylvania law but also international law and that in this case the latter left determination of the sentence to the offended king of France. This theory, derived from the claim by France of a right herself to punish offenders against her diplomatic representatives abroad, and supported by a similar claim of the Czar in the case of his Ambassador in London in 1708, is now obsolete.

Since adoption of the Constitution, the enforcement of international law has been largely undertaken by the national government and, where undertaken, the jurisdiction of federal courts has been made exclusive.[6] This does not mean, however, that states are prohibited from making acts, violative of international law or treaty, offenses against their own sovereignty.[7] The grant of powers of criminal legislation to the National government by the Constitution or even the exercise of such powers by Congress does not in itself divest the states of power to punish similar offenses. States may cooperate with the United States in enforcing international law and treaty within their own boundaries so far as such action does not interfere with national action. They cannot, however, perform acts for this purpose, which will be effective outside their borders. Thus state authorities cannot extradite persons to foreign governments on the basis of national treaties,[8] unless expressly authorized thereto by the treaty.[9]

A few offenses against international law and treaty are still untouched by national laws, and the states must be relied on. Thus Secretary Bayard, after noting that national law did not punish "treason and sedition against foreign sovereigns," said:[10]

---

[6] Judicial Code of 1911, sec. 256, pars. 1–4, 8.
[7] Fox *v.* Ohio, 5 How. 416 (1847).
[8] Holmes *v.* Jennison, 14 Pet. 540, 579 (1840); U. S. *v.* Rauscher, 119 U. S. 407, 414; Moore, Digest, 4: 240 *et seq.*
[9] See Mexican treaty, 1899, art. 19; Moore, Digest, 4: 244.
[10] Moore, Digest, 2: 432.

"I may add, however, that if any persons in the State of Pennsylvania take measures to perpetrate a crime in a foreign land, such an attempt, coupled with preparations to effectuate it, though not cognizable in the federal courts, is cognizable in the courts of the state of Pennsylvania."

Other powers of enforcement, still exclusively in state hands, notably that of protecting resident aliens, will be considered later.[11]

111. *Enforcement under the National Constitution.*

The National Constitution confers certain independent powers upon the executive and judicial branches for the enforcement of international law and treaties, but these powers are insufficient. The Constitution has, however, given Congress authority to provide adequate means of enforcement, especially in the power " to define and punish piracies and felonies committed on the high seas and offenses against the law of nations" and in the power " to make all laws which shall be necessary and proper for carrying into execution the foregoing powers and all other powers vested by the Constitution in the Government of the United States or in any department or officer thereof," thus including the treaty power.[12]

A. Enforcement by Legislative Action.

112. *Congressional Resolutions before the Constitution.*

Even before the adoption of the Constitution Congress realized the necessity for legislation to prevent violations of international law. It resolved on May 22, 1779, that the United States would cause the " law of nations to be most strictly observed," and on November 23, 1781, recommended that state legislatures provide for the punishment of offenses relating to violation of safe conducts, breaches of neutrality, assaults upon public ministers, infractions of treaties, and " the preceding being only those offenses against the law of nations which are most obvious, and public faith and safety requiring that punishment should be coextensive with all crimes, Resolved, that it be further recommended to the several states to

---

[11] *Supra,* sec. 120.
[12] U. S. Constitution, art. 1, sec. 8, cl. 10, 18.

erect tribunals in each state, or vest ones already existing with power to decide on offenses against the law of nations not contained in the foregoing enumeration." [13]

113. *Offenses against Persons Protected by International Law.*

By an act of September 24, 1789, the first Congress under the Constitution gave district courts jurisdiction of suits brought by aliens for torts "in violation of the law of nations or of a treaty of the United States," and the Supreme Court was given exclusive jurisdiction of suits against public ministers "as a court of law can have consistently with the law of nations." These provisions remain unchanged in the present judicial code of 1911.[14] An act of April 30, 1790, still in effect, prescribes criminal penalties for assaulting or serving out process against public ministers or their "domestics or domestic servants . . . in violation of the law of nations." [15]

An act of August 29, 1842, passed after the McLeod case had shown the inability of the national government to release persons entitled to immunity under international law from state jurisdiction, gives federal courts jurisdiction to release on habeas corpus, persons claiming any right under treaty or a right "the validity and effect of which depends upon the law of nations." [16]

114. *Offenses Committed on the High Seas.*

The crimes act of April 30, 1790, provided for the punishment of various crimes committed on the high seas but the courts interpreted this act in accord with international law, as confined to crimes committed by American citizens or in American vessels in all cases except piracy.[17] The act was amended in 1819 so as to punish all persons guilty of "piracy as defined by the law of na-

---

[13] Journ. Cong., 5: 161, 232; 7: 181, Ford ed., 14: 635, 914; 21: 1137.

[14] 1 Stat. 76, secs. 9, 13; Rev. Stat., sec. 563, cls. 16, 687; Jud. Code of 1911, 36 Stat. 1087, sec. 24, cls. 17, 233.

[15] 1 Stat. 117, secs. 25, 28; Rev. Stat., secs. 4062, 4064.

[16] 5 Stat. 539; Rev. Stat. 753.

[17] U. S. *v.* Palmer, 3 Wheat. 610; U. S. *v.* Klintock, 5 Wheat. 144, 152; Moore, Digest, 2: 956.

ENFORCEMENT OF INTERNATIONAL LAW. 181

tions."[18] These laws are embodied in the present criminal code of 1910.[19]

In the Scotia and other cases the court has recognized the international navigation regulations as obligatory.[20]

"Undoubtedly," said Justice Strong, "no single nation can change the law of the Sea. That law is of universal obligation, and no statute of one or two nations can create obligations for the world. Like all the laws of nations, it rests upon the common consent of civilized communities. It is of force, not because it was prescribed by a superior power, but because it has been generally accepted as a rule of conduct."

These rules were adopted by Congress in an act of 1864. With modifications agreed upon in a conference of 1889, Congress again adopted them by an act of August 19, 1890, subject to the action of other powers. After protracted negotiations the rules were finally put into operation July 1, 1897. The act of Congress has provided penalties against masters, pilots, and vessels in case of violation.[21]

115. *Offenses against Neutrality.*

The first neutrality act was passed June 5, 1794, after it had been discovered that the President and courts lacked power effectively to enforce neutrality with their independent powers. The act as amended in 1797 and 1818 is still in effect, and is included in the criminal code of 1910.[22] Further amendments were made in 1915 and 1917.[23]

These laws provide for punishment of American citizens accepting commissions while the United States is neutral, and for punish-

---

[18] U. S. *v.* Smith, 5 Wheat. 153.
[19] Criminal Code of 1910, sec. 290 *et seq.*
[20] The Scotia, 14 Wall. 170, 1871. But see The Lottawanna, 21 Wall. 558, Willoughby, *op. cit.,* pp. 1015–1017.
[21] Act Sept. 4, 1890, secs. 1, 2, 26 Stat. 423; Comp. Stat., secs. 7979, 7980; June 7, 1897, secs. 3, 4, 30 Stat. 103; Comp. Stat. 7907, 7908; Moore, Digest, 2: 474.
[22] Criminal Code of 1910, secs. 9–18. See also Fenwick, The Neutrality Laws of the United States, Washington, 1913, and Wright, The Enforcement of International Law Through Municipal Law in the United States, 1915, pp. 114 *et seq.*
[23] Act March 4, 1915, 38 Stat. 1226; May 7, 1917, June 15, 1917, secs. 1–10, 40 Stat. 221–223; Comp. Stat., secs. 10, 182.

ment of any one recruiting for foreign belligerents in American territory. Persons with unneutral intent fitting out and arming or augmenting the forces of vessels, or setting on foot military or naval expeditions or enterprises in American territory are also liable, as are persons taking out of the United States a vessel built or converted as a war vessel with knowledge that it is likely to reach the hands of a belligerent or aiding interned belligerent persons to escape.

The acts give the President power to expel vessels from waters in which "by the law of nations" they ought not to remain, and to detain or prevent the departure of vessels "which by the law of nations or the treaties of the United States" are not entitled to depart. The President is authorized to use the land and naval forces "as he may deem necessary to carry out the purposes" of the neutrality laws. The acts provide for withholding the clearance from vessels suspected of using the territory "in violation of the laws, treaties or obligations of the United States under the law of nations," for bonding armed merchant vessels using American ports and for detention by customs officials of suspected vessels not bonded. They give district courts jurisdiction to restore prizes illegally taken in American waters, to decide proceedings for the forfeiture of vessels violating neutrality and for enforcing the criminal provisions of the act. It has been held that the law applies not only to acts in behalf of belligerents but also to acts in behalf of insurgents, though not to acts in behalf of recognized governments operating against insurgents.[24]

116. *Offenses against Foreign Governments.*

An act of May 16, 1884, provided punishment for forging or counterfeiting foreign securities and the act was held to be within the power of Congress to punish offenses against the law of nations, though it contained no specific statement that the offense was of that character.[25] The counterfeiting of foreign coins has been made punishable by various acts since 1877.[26]

---

[24] The Three Friends, 166 U. S. 1 (1897); U. S. *v.* Trumbull, 48 Fed. 99 (1891); Ex parte Toscano, 208 Fed. 938 (1913).
[25] Criminal Code of 1910, secs. 156–162; U. S. *v.* Arjona, 120 U. S. 479.
[26] *Ibid.*, secs. 162–173.

By the act of August 11, 1848, superseded by the act of June 22, 1860, the American Minister, in countries permitting extraterritorial jurisdiction by treaty, is authorized to try resident American citizens for felonies or insurrection against the government of such states.[27] An act of April 22, 1898, amended on March 14, 1912, provided for the embargo of arms and munitions to American countries proclaimed by the President to be in a "condition of domestic violence" and for criminal punishment of persons violating such embargo.[28] As has been noticed the neutrality laws have been utilized to prevent the giving of aid to insurgents against friendly governments.[29]

By the espionage act of June 15, 1917, conspiracy to destroy specific property in foreign territory is made punishable, as is having in possession property for use in aid of foreign governments "as a means of violating any of the . . . obligations of the United States under any treaty or the law of nations."[30]

117. *Offenses Relating to International Boundaries.*

There appears to be a special responsibility to prevent acts near a frontier likely to injure the adjacent state, such as interference with running water, bounding or flowing into it, or the toleration of marauders, conspirators, or insurgents with designs on adjacent territory.[31] By an act of 1902 Congress recommended an international commission to consider the use of Canadian boundary waters and by act of 1906, provided that such waters should only be diverted on permits issued by the Secretary of War and that persons violating this provision should be subject to criminal punishment.[32] By a treaty with Great Britain of 1909 (Art. VII), similar requirements are made and their supervision put in charge of an international joint commission. A convention of 1889 with Mexico sev-

---

[27] Rev. Stat., secs. 4090, 4102; Comp. Stat. 7040, 7647; Moore, Digest, 1: 613–616.
[28] 30 Stat. 739; 37 Stat. 630; Comp. Stat. 7677–7678.
[29] *Supra*, note 24.
[30] 40 Stat. 226, sec. 5; 230, sec. 22.
[31] Moore, Digest, 2: 481.
[32] 32 Stat. 373; 34 Stat. 627; Comp. Stat., secs. 9984, 9989, a–c.

eral times renewed, provided a commission for adjusting Rio Grande boundary difficulties and a convention of 1906 provided for the distribution of Rio Grande water for irrigation purposes.[33]

Several protocols have been made for the suppression of marauders on the Mexican border and legislation providing for the embargo of arms to American countries in a condition of domestic violence was passed with particular reference to Mexico.[34] Doubtless under treaties and general laws, as well as the special acts referred to, the President has adequate power to meet responsibilities connected with international boundaries.

118. *Offenses against Treaties.*

A number of acts have been passed for preventing the violation of treaties by private individuals. An act of 1847 provided for the punishment of aliens committing piracy as defined by treaty.[35] Various acts passed since 1808 for the punishment of slave traders seem to give adequate authority to prevent violation of the international Slave Trade Convention. Acts passed in 1828, 1842 and 1862 and on other occasions were designed to enforce particular conventions for suppressing the slave trade and trade in liquor and arms with natives.[36]

An act of August 12, 1848, amended on June 22, 1860, and June 6, 1900, provides for the extradition of persons as required by treaties.[37] An act of March 2, 1829, amended in 1855, provided for the return of deserting seamen as required by treaty on application of foreign consuls.[38] This act, however, terminated upon denunciation of the treaties as required by the La Follette Seaman's Act of March 4, 1915.[39] An act of April 14, 1792, superseded by acts of August 8, 1846, and June 11, 1864, gives United States district Courts and United States commissioners power to enforce the awards,

---

[33] Moore, Digest, 2: 434–445.
[34] *Supra*, note 28, and Malloy, Treaties, etc., p. 1144 *et seq.*
[35] 9 Stat. 175; Rev. Stat. 5374; Criminal Code of 1910, sec. 305.
[36] 4 Stat. 276; 5 Stat. 623; Crandall, *op. cit.*, p. 239.
[37] 9 Stat. 302; 12 Stat. 83; Rev. Stat., secs. 5270–5279; 31 Stat. 656.
[38] 4 Stat. 359; 10 Stat. 614; Rev. Stat., sec. 280; Crandall, *op. cit.*, p. 233.
[39] 38 Stat. 1184, sec. 17; Comp. Stat., sec. 8382b; 10129.

arbitrations or decrees of foreign consuls exercising jurisdiction in the United States as authorized by treaties.[40]

Among other acts of Congress imposing criminal penalties for infraction of treaties by individuals may be mentioned an act of February 22, 1888, for enforcing the International Cable Convention of 1885; an act of January 5, 1905, amended in 1910 in pursuance of the Red Cross Conventions of 1864 (Arts. 27–28) and 1906, and the X Hague Convention of 1907 (Art. 29) applying them to naval warfare, providing punishment for use of the Red Cross symbol in advertising or in other unauthorized manner; an act of August 1, 1912, providing punishment for masters of vessels failing to give reasonable assistance in case of maritime accident as required by the general convention on salvage of 1910; an act of August 24, 1912, providing punishment for persons taking seal in the North Pacific in violation of the Behring Sea sealing convention of 1911; an act of August 13, 1912, for enforcing the international radio convention of that year by providing punishment for persons using radio without license and for operators wilfully interfering with radio communication or otherwise violating the convention, and an act of July 3, 1918, providing for enforcement of the migratory bird treaty with Great Britain of that year.[41]

In view of the abundance of congressional legislation giving effect to treaties and the apparently plain terms of the "necessary and proper" clause of the Constitution there would seem no room for questioning the power of Congress to pass such legislation. The power has, however, been questioned when treaties have called for legislation on subjects not otherwise within congressional power. The Supreme Court has answered with no uncertain voice. Said Justice Harlan in 1900:[42]

"The power of Congress to make all laws necessary and proper for carrying into execution as well the powers enumerated in Section 8 of Article

---

[40] 13 Stat. 12; Rev. Stat., sec. 728; Jud. Code of 1911, 36 Stat. 1163, sec. 27; Comp. Stat., sec. 1248; Crandall, *op. cit.*, p. 234.

[41] 40 Stat., c. 128; Comp. Stat., sec. 8837 a–c. Congress has not sufficiently legislated for the enforcement of all existing treaties, for example see *infra,* note 67.

[42] Neeley *v.* Henkel, 180 U. S. 109.

I of the Constitution, as all others vested in the Government of the United States, or in any department or officers thereof, includes the power to enact such legislation as is appropriate to give efficacy to any stipulations which it is competent for the President, by and with the advice and consent of the Senate, to insert in a treaty with a foreign power."

In the trademark cases, the Supreme Court held Congress incompetent to legislate on that subject, but, said Justice Miller:[43]

"In what we have here said we wish to be understood as leaving untouched the whole question of the treaty-making power over trademarks and of the duty of Congress to pass any laws necessary to carry treaties into effect."

Finally in Missouri v. Holland the Supreme Court sustained the migratory bird treaty with Great Britain and the act of Congress to enforce it, although a similar act not based on treaty had shortly before been held unconstitutional.[44]

"If the treaty is valid," said Justice Holmes, "there can be no dispute about the validity of the statute under Article 1, sec. 8, as a necessary and proper means to execute the powers of the government."

It is clear that by the multiplication of treaties the power of Congress may be extended into fields of criminal jurisdiction, heretofore entirely within state control.

119. *General Empowering Statutes.*

Most of the acts of Congress referred to confer power upon the President or other executive authority to take preventive measures and to use the military forces, but in addition general acts as early as 1792 have conferred on the President power to call forth the militia or use the army and navy "to execute the laws of the union, suppress insurrection and repel invasion."[45]

120. *Sufficiency of Existing Legislation to Protect Resident Aliens.*

It appears that Congress has enacted legislation to prevent: (1) offenses against diplomatic officers and other persons especially pro-

---

[43] Trade Mark Cases, 100 U. S. 82 (1879).
[44] Missouri v. Holland, 252 U. S. 416 (1920).
[45] Acts May 2, 1792, Feb. 28, 1795, March 3, 1807, Jan. 21, 1903 (Dick Act), and subsequent amendments, 1 Stat. 264, 424; 2 Stat. 443; 32 Stat. 776, sec. 4; 35 Stat. 400; 38 Stat. 284. See also *supra*, sec. 125.

tected by international law; (2) offenses committed on the high seas, especially piracy and violations of the international rules of navigation; (3) offenses against neutrality; (4) offenses against the sovereignty or territory of foreign nations, especially the counterfeiting of their securities, conspiracy to destroy property within their territory, and insurrection against them; (5) offenses relating to international boundaries and (6) offenses against treaties, especially those suppressing international nuisances such as the slave trade, aiding the administration of justice as by extradition, protecting international resources such as fur seal and migratory birds, protecting international services such as the Red Cross, Submarine Cables, Radio Communication, etc.

This legislation does not appear fully adequate to meet all international responsibilities arising from the acts of individuals, the most notable lacuna being in the protection of resident aliens. Presidents Harrison, McKinley, Roosevelt and Taft each urged legislation authorizing criminal prosecution in the federal courts of persons violating the rights of aliens under treaties or international law and adequate executive authority to take preventive measures, but in view of the inroad such legislation would make upon the police jurisdiction of the states it has not been passed.[46] On several occasions the United States has been obliged to pay indemnities because of its inability under existing laws to exercise "due diligence" in this respect.[47] The power of Congress to pass such legislation, at least for the protection of the rights of aliens guaranteed by treaty, cannot be questioned,[48] and it would seem that an offense against the rights of aliens under general international law would be an "offense against the law of nations" and so within the power of Congress.

121. *Sufficiency of Existing Legislation for Punishing Offenses Against Foreign Governments.*

Offenses against the sovereignty and territory of foreign states are not fully covered by national law. Libels upon foreign states

---

[46] Moore, Digest, 6: 820 *et seq.*
[47] *Ibid.*
[48] Baldwin *v.* Franks, 120 U. S. 678; Corwin, National Supremacy, p. 286 *et seq.;* Taft, The United States and Peace, 40 *et seq., supra,* sec. 49.

or sovereigns, conspiracy to promote insurrection or revolution in foreign states, or to assassinate the ruler of a foreign state do not appear to be punishable by national laws though they have been made the subject of international discussion and are indictable offenses in many countries. Some of these acts are punishable in state courts.[49]

It is not clear, however, just how far a nation is bound to suppress such acts in its territory. Field lays down in his International Code that:[50]

"One who uses his asylum for prompting hostilities against a foreign country may be proceeded against under the law of the nation of his asylum, or may be surrendered to the nation aggrieved."

It does not appear, however, that American law recognizes an international responsibility either itself to punish such offenses or to aid the foreign government in punishing them.[51] As has been noticed very few offenses against foreign states are punishable in the federal courts. The counterfeiting of foreign securities is the most important exception. The statutes relating to insurrection and conspiracy to destroy property abroad have been enacted for national defense rather than for the enforcement of international law. The same is true of the acts of Congress providing for the exclusion and deportation of alien anarchists and for the punishment of persons acting while the United States is at war so as "to bring the form of government of the United States into contempt, scorn, contumely and disrepute." Such alien, sedition, and espionage acts are for the protection of the United States rather than for the suppression of anarchy or sedition as an international crime.[52] President Roosevelt in 1901 urged that "anarchy be declared an offense against the law of nations through treaties among all civi-

---

[49] Moore, Digest, 2: 430.
[50] Field, Int. Code, sec. 207, p. 86.
[51] Moore, Digest, 2: 430.
[52] Alien Act, June 25, 1798 (for two years), 1 Stat. 570; Exclusion of seditious aliens, act Feb. 5, 1917, and expulsion of such aliens, act Oct. 16, 1918. Sedition act, July 14, 1798 (for two years), 1 Stat. 596; June 15, 1917, Title I, sec. 3, amended May 16, 1918, sec. 1 (for war period), 40 Stat. 353; Comp. Stat., sec. 10211i. See Abrams v. U. S., 250 U. S. 616 (1919).

lized powers." This result has not been achieved, though a number of American extradition treaties, concluded thereafter, expressly exclude attempts against the life of the Head of a State from the category of political offenses.[53]

122. *Sufficiency of Existing Legislation in Aid of Foreign Criminal Justice.*

Nor has the United States held that there is any international duty to aid foreign criminal justice. Although Congress has provided, in pursuance of a generally recognized duty of comity, for the execution by Federal courts of letters rogatory from foreign states requesting the taking of testimony in " suits for the recovery of money or property," it has made no provision for the taking of testimony in criminal cases.[54] The states also have generally refused to compel testimony for foreign criminal trials.[55]

"The taking of testimony," said the Attorney-General of Pennsylvania, "by deposition for criminal cases is unknown to our system of jurisprudence, and section 9 of Article I of the Declaration of Rights in our Constitution provides that in all criminal prosecutions the accused hath the right to meet the witnesses face to face. I am, therefore, of the opinion that the courts of this Commonwealth are not competent to receive these letters rogatory and to enforce the testimony of this witness by deposition or answers to interrogatories, to be used in the criminal cause."

The same distinction has been recognized in reference to the execution of foreign judgments. In civil cases, the rule of reciprocity has been established by international comity, thus the federal courts carry out the judgments of foreign courts which will reciprocate.[56] But not so with criminal judgments. The United States has never itself enforced a criminal judgment of a foreign state nor has it as a general practice turned over fugitives, accused or convicted of crimes in foreign courts, except on the express stipulation of treaty.[57] The only exception to the rule appears to

---

[53] Moore, Digest, 2: 434. See Treaties, Brazil, 1897, ratified 1903; Denmark, 1902; Guatemala, 1903; Spain, 1904; Protocol, 1907; Cuba, 1904.
[54] Moore, Digest, 2: 110.
[55] *Ibid.*, 2: 112.
[56] Hilton *v.* Guyot, 159 U. S. 113 (1895); Moore, Digest, 2: 217–224.
[57] Moore, Digest, 2: 110; 4: 245 *et seq.*

be the case of Arguelles, who was extradited to Spain by President Lincoln in 1864, although no treaty required such action.[58] The position of the United States has been that "both by the law and practice of nations, without a treaty stipulation, one government is not under any obligation to surrender a fugitive from justice to another government for trial,"[59] and that "the President has no power 'to make the delivery' unless under treaty or act of Congress."[60] Congress has passed acts in pursuance of treaties of extradition, but the opinion has been expressed that Congress might authorize extradition without treaty.[61] Since such a law, with the above stated theory, could not be justified as the "punishment of an offense against the law of nations" it is difficult to see where the power of Congress would come from.

It has been held that the federal Constitution prohibits extradition under state authority unless such procedure is expressly stipulated in treaty or act of Congress. This is due to the express prohibition of the states from treaty-making or agreement-making without the consent of Congress.[62]

B. Enforcement by Action of the Treaty Power.

123. *Treaties as a Basis for Executive and Judicial Action.*

Treaties are the supreme law of the land and it might seem that they would in themselves furnish sufficient authority for executive or judicial enforcement of the obligations they impose. This is doubtless true of executive action. Courts have held that troops may be interned and persons extradited by executive authority on the basis of treaty alone.[63] It has been held, however, that courts

---

[58] *Ibid.*, 4: 249.

[59] Mr. Buchanan, Sec. of State, to Mr. Wise, Sept. 27, 1845, Moore, Digest, 4: 246.

[60] Wirt, Att. Gen., 1 Op. 509, 521; Terlinden *v.* Ames, 184 U. S. 270, 289 (1902); Moore, Digest, 4: 248, 253.

[61] Willoughby, *op. cit.*, p. 479.

[62] *Supra*, sec. 90.

[63] *Ex parte* Toscano, 208 Fed. 938; U. S. *v.* Robbins, Fed. Cas. No. 16175; *In re* Metzger, 5 How. 176, 188; Crandall, *op. cit.*, 230 *et seq.*

cannot exercise criminal jurisdiction or compel the extradition of fugitives unless Congress has passed enabling legislation.[64]

124. *Treaties as a Basis for Congressional Action.*

Treaty provisions requiring positive enforcement within American jurisdiction have been of three kinds. Sometimes they state definite acts which the government must prevent. Thus the V Hague Convention of 1907 says, "a neutral power must not allow any of the acts referred to in articles 2 to 4 to occur on its territory."[65] Sometimes treaties state the degree of diligence which the government must exercise to achieve a given result leaving it discretion in determining the method to be used. Thus article III of the Chinese treaty of 1880 affirmed by article IV of the treaty of 1894 requires the United States to "exert all its powers to devise measures for the protection (of resident Chinese) and to secure to them the same rights, privileges, immunities and exemptions as may be enjoyed by the citizens or subjects of the most favored nation and to which they are entitled by treaty."[66] Finally, treaties sometimes merely require that the government endeavor to have legislation passed. Thus by article 27 of the Geneva convention of 1906:[67]

"The signatory powers whose legislation may not now be adequate engage to take or recommend to their legislatures such measures as may be necessary to prevent the use, by private persons or by societies other than those upon which this convention confers the right thereto, of the emblem or name of the Red Cross or Geneva Cross, particularly for commercial purposes by means of trademarks or commercial labels. The prohibition of the use of the emblem or name in question shall take effect from the time set in each act of legislation, and at the latest five years after this convention goes into effect. After such going into effect, it shall be unlawful to use a trademark or commercial label contrary to such prohibition."

---

[64] The Estrella, 4 Wheat. 298; The British Prisoners, 1 Wood. and Min. 66 (1845).

[65] See also Submarine Cable Convention, 1884, art. II.

[66] See also XIII Hague Convention, 1907, secs. 8, 25.

[67] See also African Slave Trade Convention, 1890, art. xii, and Treaty of Peace with Great Britain, 1783, art. V. President Cleveland recommended legislation prohibiting the sale of arms in central Africa as required by the former, in his message of December 4, 1893, but Congress has not acted. (Moore, Digest, 2: 471.)

192 THE CONTROL OF AMERICAN FOREIGN RELATIONS.

This has been the usual form in general international conventions.

Although the obligation of Congress to act is doubtless greater under treaties of the first form than the last, it would appear that the difference is wholly one of degree. Under any of the three forms, the United States will be responsible if it fails to exert the diligence required by the treaty, and in none of them is criminal prosecution possible in the United States without enabling legislation.

C. Enforcement by the President.

125. Independent Powers of the President.

Although Congress has passed general laws giving the President power to use the military and naval forces and the militia to enforce the laws, suppress insurrection and repel invasion, and many special laws giving him power to use the forces for particular purposes, the President has always taken the view that these laws except as applied to the militia were unnecessary, and that as commander-in-chief and as chief executive, he has independent power to employ the army and navy and direct the civil administration in order to execute the laws and treaties of the United States. President Fillmore in response to a resolution of inquiry called attention to the different position occupied by the President with reference to the militia, which may only be called out as Congress shall provide, and to the army and navy of which the President is permanent commander-in-chief. As to the latter, he said:[68]

"Probably no legislation of Congress could add to or diminish the power thus given, but by increasing or diminishing, or abolishing altogether the army and navy."

By an act of June 18, 1878, Congress made it unlawful and a penal offense:[69]

"to employ any part of the Army of the United States as a posse comitatus or otherwise, for the purpose of executing the laws, except in such cases and under such circumstances as such employment of said force may be expressly authorized by the Constitution or by act of Congress."

[68] Richardson, Messages, 5: 105; Finley-Sanderson, The Executive, p. 214; *supra*, sec. 119.

[69] 20 Stat. 152, sec. 15; Comp. Stat., sec. 1902; Finley-Sanderson, *op. cit.*, p. 270.

ENFORCEMENT OF INTERNATIONAL LAW. 193

This, however, does not affect President Fillmore's theory since he claimed no power to use the army other than as "expressly authorized by the Constitution." The court held in Martin *v.* Mott[70] that the President could determine when the exigency existed for calling forth the militia as specified by Congress, and no power could review his action. It seems equally certain that he can determine when a proper constitutional occasion for using the army has occurred and is not limited by congressional expressions in this regard. Certainly the opinions of the Supreme Court in the Debs and Neagle cases support this theory.[71] However, the issue is largely theoretic because the delegations of authority actually made by Congress seem sufficiently broad to cover all probable exigencies.

126. *President's Use of Military Forces.*

In practice the President has used the military forces in American territory to enforce international law and treaty on many occasions. He has thus used them to enforce the protocols with Mexico requiring suppression of marauding Indians and others near the border; to preserve order in case of mob violence as in the Chicago strikes of 1894 giving rise to the Debs case, and to suppress nuisances on the high seas or in neighboring territory. The suppression of pirates in Amelia Island in 1817, of Indians in Florida by Jackson in 1819, and the pursuit of Villa in Mexico by General Pershing in 1916 are illustrations of action of the latter kind.[72] The most important executive use of military forces in American territory is of course that by President Lincoln on the outbreak of the Civil War. The militia were called out April 15, 1861, under authority of general laws and the army and navy employed before Congress had given express authorization.[73] We may conclude that

---

[70] Martin *v.* Mott, 12 Wheat. 19.

[71] *In re* Neagle, 135 U. S. 1; *In re* Debs, 158 U. S. 564. See also *Infra*, sec. 222.

[72] Moore, Digest, 2: 418–425, 435–446; 402–408; *Am. Year Book*, 1916, p. 79 *et seq.* For President's use of force to meet responsibilities outside of the territory see *infra*, sec. 151, and for his power to use force in general, *infra*, secs. 221–224.

[73] Blockade was proclaimed April 19, 1861. The first act of Congress

the President is endowed with sufficient power to employ the armed forces, whenever he believes it necessary in order to enforce any constitutional provision, treaty or act of Congress, or to suppress mob violence or insurrection likely to obstruct national services.

127. *President's Direction of Administrative Action.*

Although the position of the President as chief executive does not carry with it power to create agencies for enforcing international law and treaties (though such a suggestion is contained in the Neagle case), it has been held to confer a power of directing administrative action of the agencies actually existing through instructions, practically enforceable by the removal power.[74]

Thus the President has been able to accord special police protection to diplomatic officers and other foreigners entitled to protection when necessary.[75] He has ordered the extradition of fugitives when required by treaty and the courts have sustained the action. Thus President John Adams extradited one Jonathan Robbins under the Jay treaty and was eloquently sustained in this action by Marshall, then in Congress. "The treaty," he said, "stipulating that a murderer shall be delivered up to justice, is as obligatory as an act of Congress making the same declaration." The President's power was sustained in the case of the British Prisoners in 1845 and in the Metzger case in 1847.[76] But in the latter case before the fugitive was delivered, the New York supreme court intervened and released the prisoner on *habeas corpus,* on the theory that the treaty was not executable without congressional legislation.[77] This resulted in the act of 1848 providing for extradition.[78]

---

recognizing that war existed was on July 13, 1861. Willoughby, *op. cit.,* pp. 88, 1209.

[74] *Infra,* secs. 227, 230.

[75] Moore, Digest, 4: 622 *et seq.*

[76] U. S. *v.* Robbins, Fed. Cas. No. 16175; The British Prisoners, 1 Wood. and Minn. 66; *In re* Metzger, 5 How. 176; Taft, Our Chief Magistrate, p. 87; Crandall, *op. cit.,* p. 231.

[77] *In re* Metzger, 1 Barb. 248 (N. Y., 1847).

[78] 9 Stat. 302; Rev. Stat., secs. 5270–5279.

A similar view was expressed by Justice Catron in 1852[79] but in 1893 the supreme court through Justice Gray sustained the early position of Adams and Marshall.[80]

> "The surrender, pursuant to treaty stipulations, of persons residing or found in this country, and charged with crime in another, may be made by the executive authority of the President alone, when no provision has been made by treaty or by statute for an examination of the case by a judge or magistrate. Such was the case of Jonathon Robbins, under article 27 of the treaty with Great Britain of 1794, in which the President's power in this regard was demonstrated in the masterly and conclusive argument of John Marshall in the House of Representatives."

However, as statutes now make full provision for extradition, the question of the President's independent power is of merely speculative interest. The President has authorized the extradition of a fugitive in the absence of treaty in only one case, that of Arguelles extradited to Spain by President Lincoln in 1864, and the majority of authorities hold that he here acted in excess of power. Willoughby believes that Congress might authorize presidential extradition in the absence of treaty, but since international law does not require such extradition it is hard to locate the source of such a power of Congress.[81]

It was held by Justice Story that the President did not have power to authorize the carrying out of awards of foreign consuls based on treaty in the absence of congressional legislation.[82] It would seem that by analogy to the case of extradition of fugitives, the President might authorize the return of deserting seamen on the basis of treaty provisions but no case involving the point seems to have arisen and legislation was early provided. It has been stated by Attorney General Cushing that there is no authority to return deserting seamen in the absence of treaty. As has been noted the statutes and treaties on this subject were both terminated by the La Follette Seaman's Act of 1915.[83]

---

[79] *In re* Kaine, 14 How. 103, 111 (1852).
[80] Fong Yue Ting *v.* U. S., 149 U. S. 698, 714 (1893).
[81] *Supra,* sec. 122.
[82] Moore, Digest, 2: 298; 5: 223.
[83] Cushing, Att. Gen., 6 Op. 148, 209; Moore, Digest, 4: 417-424; **Crandall**, *op. cit.*, p. 233; *supra*, sec. 118.

On August 4, 1793, Hamilton issued instructions to customs officials for the enforcement of neutrality and in the World War instructions for the supervision and censorship of radio stations, the detention of vessels suspected of carrying arms to belligerent warships and of submarines intended for sale to belligerents were based on independent executive authority.[84] Subsequent statutes have authorized most of these instructions.[85] In the case of *Ex parte Toscano*[86] the Federal District Court held that insurgent Mexican troops entering the territory and interned according to provisions of the Vth Hague Convention, under executive authority, were entitled to no relief under constitutional guarantees. "Due process of law" had been given them through executive compliance with the treaty, which was itself "supreme law of the land." It appears that the President has considerable independent power to authorize military and administrative action when necessary to enforce treaties or statutes, but in view of the wide powers expressly conferred upon him by acts of Congress it is now seldom necessary for him to go outside of such express delegations.

D. Enforcement by the Courts.

128. *Early Assumptions of Common Law Criminal Jurisdiction by Federal Courts.*

In his first neutrality proclamation of April 22, 1793, President Washington stated that he had:[87]

"given instructions to those officers to whom it belongs to cause prosecutions to be instituted against all persons who shall within the cognizance of the courts of the United States violate the law of nations with respect to the powers at war or any of them."

On the basis of this proclamation prosecution was brought against Gideon Henfield for aiding in fitting out and serving on a vessel

---

[84] Am. State Pap., For. Rel. 1: 140; Moore, Digest, 7: 891; Richardson, Messages, 10: 86; Naval War College, International Law Topics, 1916, pp. 110, 115; *Am. Jl. Int. Law,* 9: 177; Wright, The Enforcement of International Law, p. 122.

[85] *Supra,* sec. 115.

[86] *Ex parte* Toscano, 208 Fed. 938 (1913).

[87] 11 Stat. 753; Richardson, Messages, 1: 157.

for the use of France then at war with Great Britain. The United States circuit court of Pennsylvania, composed of Justices Wilson, Iredell and Peters, asked the Grand Jury to return an indictment against him for an offense against the law of nations. Although the Grand Jury refused to indict, the opinion of the court was clear that federal courts had jurisdiction to punish such offenses even though no express statute defined the offense or conferred the jurisdiction. Justice Jay expressed a similar opinion in another charge to the Grand Jury and Attorney General Randolph asserted it in an official opinion.[88]

Jurisdiction of crimes defined only by international law was also asserted in the case of United States *v.* Ravara (1793) in which the Genoese consul was indicted for sending threatening letters to the British minister.[89] This act was considered in violation of the diplomatic protection guaranteed to foreign ministers and hence a breach of the law of nations. Although the accused was found guilty, he was ultimately released on giving up his exequatur. In this case, however, international law was appealed to merely for a definition of the crime, since the circuit court had been given jurisdiction of cases against Consuls by act of Congress.[90]

129. *Federal Courts Have No Common Law Jurisdiction.*

Soon after, however, in United States *v.* Worrall (1798), the criminal jurisdiction of the federal courts was said to rest on statute alone and this opinion was repeated in the Supreme Court in *Ex parte* Bollman (1807) and United States *v.* Hudson (1812).[91] Four years later the question was raised in a slightly different form in United States *v.* Coolidge (1816). In the circuit court Justice Story had sustained an indictment for the forcible rescue by two

---

[88] *In re* Henfield, Fed. Cas. No. 6360, and *ibid.*, p. 1116; Am. State Pap., For. Rel., 1: 151.

[89] U. S. *v.* Ravara, 2 Dall. 297; Fed. Cas. No. 6122; Moore, Digest, 5: 65.

[90] *Infra*, note 93.

[91] U. S. *v.* Worrall, 2 Dall. 384; *Ex parte* Bollman, 4 Cranch 75; U. S. *v.* Hudson, 7 Cranch 32; Willoughby, *op. cit.*, p. 1031; J. B. Moore, Four Phases of American Diplomacy, 1912, p. 64; Wharton, Criminal Law, 1, sec. 254.

American privateers of a prize on its way to Salem under a prize master, although no such crime was specifically defined by statute. Reasoning from the 11th section of the judiciary act which gave federal circuit courts "exclusive cognizance of crimes cognizable under authority of the United States," he said:

> "The jurisdiction is not as has sometimes been supposed in argument over all crimes and offenses especially created and defined by statute. It is of all crimes and offenses 'cognizable under the authority of the United States,' that is, of all crimes and offenses to which, by the Constitution of the United States, the judicial power extends. The jurisdiction could not, therefore, have been given in more broad and comprehensive terms."

Story's opinion, however, was not supported by his brother justice on circuit and on certification to the supreme court he was overruled.[92] However, though federal courts cannot assume jurisdiction either under common law or under such broad grants as that here in question or it may be added under treaty, they may exercise criminal jurisdiction over offenses not specified by statute where jurisdiction has been expressly given them by act of Congress. Thus they may have jurisdiction because of the nature of the parties, in which case federal courts apply the criminal law of the state in which they sit.[93]

130. *Federal Courts Have No Criminal Jurisdiction from Treaties Alone.*

The federal courts have refused to exercise jurisdiction over crimes defined by treaty until Congress has acted. They have followed the same opinion with reference to extradition. In the case of the British Prisoners,[94] although asserting that where extradi-

---

[92] U. S. *v.* Coolidge, Fed. Cas. 14857, and *ibid.*, 1 Wheat. 415 (1816). Rawle supports Story's opinion with elaborate argument in A View of the Constitution, 1825, pp. 250–265.

[93] U. S. *v.* Ravara, 2 Dall. 297, Fed. Cas. No. 6122; Moore, 5: 65; Tenn. *v.* Davis, 100 U. S. 257; Duponceau, *op. cit.*, p. 34; Willoughby, *op. cit.*, p. 1020. In the case of an indictment against the Russian consul Kosloff in 1815 the Pennsylvania court refused jurisdiction (Comm. *v.* Kosloff, 5 Serg. and Rawle 545), and no action was begun in the federal courts, although by statute they then had exclusive jurisdiction in cases against consuls. Duponceau, *op. cit.*, p. 36; Moore, Digest 5: 66.

[94] The British Prisoners, 1 Wood. and M. 66.

tion is required by "the supreme law of a treaty, the executive need not wait . . . for acts of Congress to direct such duties to be done and how," Justice Woodbury said for the circuit court:

"If a treaty stipulated for some act to be done, entirely judicial . . . it could hardly be done without the aid or preliminary direction of some act of Congress prescribing the court to do it and the form."

At present the law is clear. The jurisdiction of federal courts, with exception of the original jurisdiction of the Supreme Court defined by the Constitution itself, is confined to that which Congress has expressly conferred and the only offenses cognizable are those defined by acts of Congress, or, in case jurisdiction exists because of the nature of the parties, those defined by the law of the state in which the court is sitting. It may be noted that extraterritorial courts, authorized by treaty and established by act of Congress, have been given jurisdiction over offenses committed by American citizens within the country wherein the court exercises authority, if the offense is one defined by act of Congress or by common law as supplemented by regulations issued by the American minister in that country.[95]

131. *Statutory Criminal Jurisdiction of Federal Courts.*

However, as has been noted, a considerable number of offenses against international law have been defined by Congress and the federal courts have been given cognizance of them. The statutes relating to the protection of diplomatic officers, to piracies and offenses on the high seas, to offenses against foreign governments or territory and to most offenses against treaties are always operative. Those punishing offenses against neutrality, however, are operative only during the existence of foreign hostilities, the recognition of which belongs to the President. The President has usually issued a formal neutrality proclamation calling attention to the neutrality laws,[96] but the courts have held that the neutrality laws may

---

[95] Rev. Stat., sec. 4086; Moore, Digest, 2: 631.

[96] Printed in Richardson, Messages, see index, "Neutrality," and Wright, Enforcement of Int. Law, p. 115. For those of World War see Naval War College, Int. Law Doc., 1916, p. 82.

be applied against insurgents who have in fact been recognized as such by the political departments of the government even if no such formal proclamation has issued: [97]

"The distinction," said the Supreme Court, "between recognition of belligerency and recognition of a condition of political revolt, between recognition of the existence of war in a material sense and of war in a legal sense, is sharply illustrated by the case before us. For here the political department has not recognized the existence of a *de facto* belligerent power engaged in hostility with Spain, but has recognized the existence of insurrectionary warfare prevailing before, at the time and since this forfeiture is alleged to have been incurred."

132. *Admiralty Jurisdiction of Federal Courts.*

Although criminal jurisdiction must be given very specifically, by act of Congress, this is not true of admiralty jurisdiction. In order to enforce neutrality the courts have assumed jurisdiction to restore prizes in cases not covered by statute, and even before passage of the first neutrality act,[98] under the general grant of admiralty jurisdiction.

"In the absence of every act of Congress in relation to this matter, the court would feel no difficulty in pronouncing the conduct here complained of an abuse of the neutrality of the United States, and although in such cases the offender could not be punished, the former owner would, nevertheless, be entitled to restitution."

So said the Supreme Court in 1819.[99] Almost one hundred years later the same view was expressed by the Supreme Court in the case of the Appam: [100]

"The violation of American neutrality is the basis of jurisdiction, and the admiralty courts may order restitution for a violation of such neutrality. In each case the jurisdiction and order rests upon the authority of the courts of the United States to make restitution to private owners for violations of neutrality where offending vessels are within our jurisdiction, thus vindicating our rights and obligations as a neutral people."

The federal courts also assume jurisdiction to enforce the general maritime law through admiralty actions in rem, even when no

---

[97] The Three Friends, 166 U. S. (1897).
[98] Glass *v.* The Betsey, 3 Dall. 6; Talbot *v.* Jensen, 3 Dall. 133.
[99] The Estrella, 4 Wheat. 298, 311.
[100] The Appam, 243 U. S. 124, 156 (1916).

statute specifically governs the case. Thus in the case of the Belgenland, the Supreme Court sustained the jurisdiction upon the libel of a Belgian steamer for running into and sinking a Norwegian barque in mid ocean.[101]

"Although the courts will use a discretion about assuming jurisdiction of controversies between foreigners in cases arising beyond the territorial jurisdiction of the country to which the courts belong, yet where such controversies are *communis juris,* that is, where they arise under the common law of nations, special grounds should appear to induce the courts to deny its aid to a foreign suitor when it has jurisdiction of the ship or party charged. The existence of jurisdiction in all such cases is beyond dispute; the only question will be, whether it is expedient to exercise it."

Although federal courts, under the general grant of admiralty jurisdiction, may take cognizance of all cases against vessels alleged to have violated international law, and decree confiscation, restoration, salvage, or damages, this does not extend to criminal jurisdiction against persons.[102] As with offenses committed on land, so offenses at sea are only cognizable when specifically defined by statute. The court has held, however, that the phrase "piracy as defined by the law of nations," is sufficiently explicit to give jurisdiction over this offense.[103]

133. *Civil Jurisdiction of Federal Courts in Cases Affecting Aliens.*
Due diligence in the enforcement of international law requires that justice be assured to aliens in their claims against private individuals arising within the jurisdiction whether resting on contract or tort. This does not mean that aliens are exempt from the law of the land with reference to such claims. It does mean, however, that (1) the law shall not be unreasonably discriminatory against them, (2) that courts exist and proceed in a manner to give them reasonable assurance of an impartial application of the law, and (3) that they are accorded opportunity to invoke the aid of the courts in settlement of their controversies.[104] The constitutional guarantees

---

[101] The Belgenland, 114 U. S. 355.
[102] The Estrella, 4 Wheat. 298, 311.
[103] U. S. *v.* Smith, 5 Wheat. 153 (1820).
[104] Borchard, *op. cit.,* pp. 330, 335; Moore, Digest, 6: 267, 280.

of due process of law to all " persons " within the jurisdiction, aliens as well as citizens, as judicially interpreted and enforced against both state legislatures and Congress, seem to insure against unreasonably discriminatory laws.[105] These guarantees as well as the constitutional provisions designed to assure the independence of the courts, such as those giving security of tenure and compensation, together with the respectable traditions of common law judicial procedure, tend also to give confidence in a fair procedure.[106]

By permitting aliens to bring their suits against individuals before such courts, the United States will generally be exerting due diligence and no international claim can be made, whatever the decision of the court, unless the subject matter is controlled by international law. The state courts usually have common law jurisdiction and are open to both aliens and foreign states in all cases not made exclusive in federal courts,[107] but under constitutional and statutory provisions, the federal courts are also available in most cases.

"The judicial power (of the United States) shall extend to all cases in law and equity arising under this Constitution, the laws of the United States, and treaties made, or which shall be made, under their authority;—to all cases of ambassadors, other public ministers and consuls;—to all cases of admiralty and maritime jurisdiction;—to controversies . . . between a state or the citizens thereof, and foreign states, citizens or subjects. In all cases affecting ambassadors, other public ministers and consuls . . . the Supreme Court shall have original jurisdiction. In all other cases before mentioned the Supreme Court shall have appellate jurisdiction, both as to law and fact, with such exceptions, and under such regulations as the Congress shall make."[108]

Except for the original jurisdiction of the Supreme Court the federal courts may only exercise this judicial power as expressly given by act of Congress.[109] Under present statutes ambassadors, public ministers and consuls may bring any suit originally in the Supreme Court though they may also sue in the state courts.[110] Foreign states and

---

[105] U. S. Const. Am. V, XIV.
[106] *Ibid.*, Art. III, sec. 1.
[107] Mexico *v.* Arrangoiz, 11 How. Prac. 1 (N. Y., 1855); Scott, Cases on Int. Law, p. 170.
[108] U. S. Const., Art. III, sec. 2.
[109] *Ex parte* McCardle, 7 Wall. 506; Willoughby, *op. cit.*, p. 976.
[110] Judicial Code of 1911, sec. 233, 36 Stat. 1156.

aliens may bring suits against a citizen in the federal district court if over $3,000 is in controversy or if "for a tort only, in violation of the law of nations or of a treaty of the United States."[111] They may also bring suits against citizens under many special types of law, whatever the matter in controversy, such as suits within the admiralty and maritime jurisdiction, suits under the copyright, patent, trademark, commercial, bankruptcy, immigration laws, etc.[112] Also all suits in which a deprivation of constitutional right is claimed.[113] Even if they begin action in a state court, appeal lies from the highest state court to the Supreme Court of the United States if a right under the Constitution, an act of Congress, a treaty or any authority under the United States is claimed.[114] The courts are not ordinarily open to civil suits by one alien against another,[115] though in admiralty actions in rem arising under the general maritime law on the high seas, where the two aliens are of different nationality, such cases will usually be heard.[116] Cases against aliens may in many cases be removed to federal courts by the defendant if they are not brought there originally.[117]

134. Conclusion.

The enforcing of international law and treaty in the territory of the United States requires executive and judicial action. The President must utilize the military and administrative forces to preserve order and prevent violations of international law and treaty. The criminal courts must punish offenders against international law and treaty, and the civil courts must be prepared to afford relief to aliens with just claims against individuals. Under the American constitutional system the President has power to direct existing military and civil administrations, to enforce the laws and treaties and pre-

---

[111] *Ibid.*, sec. 24, pars. 1, 17.
[112] *Ibid*, sec. 24, pars. 3, 7, 8, 19, 22.
[113] *Ibid.*, sec. 24, pars. 12-14.
[114] *Ibid.*, sec. 237, as amended Dec. 23, 1914, 38 Stat. 790, and Sept. 6, 1916, 39 Stat. 726.
[115] Montalet *v.* Murray, 4 Cranch 46.
[116] The Belgenland, 114 U. S. 355.
[117] *Ibid.*, secs. 28, 31; *supra*, sec. 105.

vent obstructions of national services. However, the tendency has been to confine this action to circumstances in which it is authorized by specific legislation.

The state courts are bound to apply treaties and are open to civil suits by aliens but federal courts are dependent on statute for jurisdiction. The broad grants of jurisdiction in admiralty matters, suits involving treaties, and the civil rights of aliens, give the federal courts an opportunity to afford relief in civil matters, but for enforcing criminal penalties for violations of international law or treaty, they must be endowed with specific power. Congress must legislate or the United States may find itself without the means necessary for exercising due diligence in enforcing international law and treaties within its territory.

CHAPTER XIII.

THE POWER TO MEET INTERNATIONAL RESPONSIBILITIES THROUGH PERFORMANCE OF NATIONAL OBLIGATIONS.

135. *Nature of this Responsibility.*

The responsibility of the nation for the non-fulfillment of its obligations requires, not only that each organ of the government employ its powers to the fullest extent to perform all acts, which are specifically required by treaty, agreement, contract, or the operation of international law, but also that organs exist with powers sufficient to assure a full performance. For acts of government organs, the responsibility of the nation is met if all organs confine their exercises of power within the limits of international law and treaty. For acts or omissions of individuals, the responsibility of the nation is met if all organs employ "due diligence" to enforce order and the observance of international law and treaty by persons within their jurisdiction. The present responsibility can be met only if organs exist competent and willing to execute specific obligations.

136. *Performance of Obligations by the States.*

The states cannot perform national obligations. They cannot themselves contract treaty or political obligations with foreign nations. They may enter into contract with foreign individuals, or nations, as by sale of bonds or other securities,[1] but a failure to pay these would not involve a national responsibility so long as the foreign bondholder has as favorable an opportunity to collect as the domestic.[2] Some of the states have established courts of claims in which they may be sued, though the general principle of the non-suability of sovereigns applies to them.[3] While under the XIth amendment states cannot be sued by foreign individuals in the fed-

---

[1] *Infra*, sec. 157.
[2] *Supra*, sec. 89, pars. 2, 3.
[3] Willoughby, *op. cit.*, p. 1105; Wright, Enforcement of Int. Law, p. 103.

eral courts, there seems to be no constitutional bar to such a suit by foreign states. National statutes, however, have not provided for such a jurisdiction and commentators doubt whether it could be exercised.[4]

In case of mob violence in the states we have seen that the national government is responsible for a lack of due diligence, and this irrespective of remedies, such as action against counties or municipalities, which the state law may give.[5] "The Italian Government," wrote Baron Fava, Italian Ambassador, in reference to the lynching of three Italians in Erwin, Mississippi, in 1901, and in response to the American suggestion that Mississippi was responsible, "will not cease to denounce the systematic impunity enjoyed by crime, and to hold the federal government responsible therefor."[6]

A. The Nature of National Obligations.

137. Obligations Founded on International Agreement.

National obligations may arise either (1) from express agreement or (2) from the operation of general international law.

Agreement of the nation may be evidenced by contracts with individuals, by executive or military agreements, or by conventions or treaties. Any of these instruments if made by competent authority will bind the nation. Contracts or executive agreements usually require the performance of definite acts such as the payment of money, the movement of troops, the conclusion of a treaty, but conventions and treaties often state general principles of law for the guidance of individuals as well as specific obligations to be performed by public authorities. During the nineteenth century treaties have

---

[4] Willoughby, *op. cit.*, p. 1060. In Cherokee Nation *v.* Georgia (5 Pet. 1, 1831) jurisdiction was refused on the ground that the Cherokees were not a foreign nation, thus implying that if they had been jurisdiction would have existed. The only case between a state and an undoubted foreign nation is that of Cuba *v.* N. Car. (242 U. S. 665, 1917), but no opinion was given because of dismissal on motion of the plaintiff. See Scott, Judicial Settlement of Controversies between States of the American Union, 1919, pp. 105-106.

[5] *Supra*, sec. 89, pars. 2, sec. 120.

[6] Moore, Digest, 6: 849.

tended to be regulative, rather than political in character. Their predominant character has changed from that of political contracts to codes of law or administrative regulations providing for international administration in a smaller or wider circle.[7]

A similar distinction has been recognized by American courts, in classifying certain treaty provisions as "self-executing." Practically this distinction depends upon whether or not the courts and the executive are able to enforce the provision without enabling legislation. Fundamentally it depends upon whether the obligation is imposed on private individuals or on public authorities.

"A treaty," said Chief Justice Marshall, "is in its nature a contract between two nations, not a legislative act. . . . In the United States a different principle is established. Our Constitution declares a treaty to be the law of the land. It is, consequently, to be regarded in courts of justice as equivalent to an act of the legislature, *whenever it operates of itself*, without the aid of any legislative provision. But when the terms of the stipulation import a contract, when either of the parties engages to perform a particular act, the treaty addresses itself to the political, not the judicial, department; and the legislature must execute the contract before it can become a rule for the courts."[8]

Treaty provisions which define the rights and obligations of private individuals and lay down general principles for the guidance of military, naval or administrative officials in relation thereto are usually considered self-executing. Thus treaty provisions assuring aliens equal civil rights with citizens, defining the limits of national jurisdiction, and prescribing rules of prize, war and neutrality, have been so considered.[9] However, many treaty provisions are difficult to classify. Thus a treaty regulating the taking of seal in a defined area of Behring Sea and specifically enjoining the governments concerned to enforce the regulation imposes a primary obligation upon individuals and might seem self-executing. But it also imposes

---

[7] Wright, *Am. Jl. Int. Law*, 13: 243, 245.
[8] Foster *v.* Neilson, 2 Pet. 253, 314 (1829). See also *infra*, sec. 256.
[9] Hauenstein *v.* Lynham, 100 U. S. 483; La Ninfa, 75 Fed. 513; The Phoebe Ann, 3 Dall. 319; *Ex parte* Toscano, 208 Fed. 938. There has been a question in the United States whether treaties regulating commerce and tariffs are of this kind. See *infra*, sec. 154.

a responsibility upon the government to prevent infractions and punish violators. Extradition treaties are of similar character. They affect primarily the individual fugitive from justice by withdrawing his right of asylum, but they also specifically require the government, to whose territory he has fled, to surrender him. In view of the constitutional principle that federal courts can only punish crimes defined by statute,[10] such treaties are not self-executing in the United States, except in so far as executive action is sufficient to carry them out.[11] They ordinarily require legislation to be effectively executed. In spite of this fact, the obligation of such treaties rests primarily upon individuals and the responsibility of the government is measured by the standard of "due diligence," whether or not the treaty specifies the steps which are to be taken in prevention and punishment.[12] Thus such treaty provisions have been considered in the preceding chapter.

On the other hand certain treaty obligations are addressed solely to public authorities, of which may be mentioned those requiring the payment of money, the cession of territory, the guarantee of territory or independence, the conclusion of subsequent treaties on described subjects, the participation in international organizations, the collection and supplying of information, and direction of postal, telegraphic or other services, the construction of buildings, bridges, lighthouses, etc. It is with the power to perform such obligations that we are here concerned.

138. *Obligations Founded on General International Law.*

Although all international law is said to rest ultimately upon the agreement of states,[13] in fact this agreement is assumed of principles established by long practice and custom or the concurrence of authoritative writers.[14] International law imposes few if in fact

---

[10] *Supra*, sec. 129.
[11] *Supra*, secs. 125–127.
[12] *Supra*, sec. 124.
[13] The Exchange *v.* McFaddon, 7 Cranch 116.
[14] The Paquette Habana, 175 U. S. 677. See for sources of international law, Draft Code for an International Court, Art. 35, *Am. Jl. Int. Law*, Supp., 14: 379, Oct. 1920, and Wright, *Minn. Law Rev.*, 5: 436.

any obligations requiring specific performance. It requires that states preserve order in their territory and exercise especial vigilance in such matters as the protection of diplomatic officers, the preservation of neutrality, the suppression of nuisances such as piracy. But here the state's responsibility is indirect. The law of neutrality requires that neutral states intern troops and vessels illegally in their jurisdiction and restore prizes illegally captured or brought within their jurisdiction, but these requirements are designed primarily as means for the enforcement of law against individuals in the neutral state's jurisdiction. Certain ceremonial observances such as exchanging salutes by public vessels, though customary, are really matters of courtesy rather than law. Doubtless good citizenship in the family of nations requires that states exchange diplomatic officers and cooperate in matters of world service; that they aid each other in the suppression of crime and administration of justice; that they attempt to prevent war by offering mediation and suggesting arbitration; but except as provided in treaty, international law does not require such acts.[15]

However, in case international law or treaty is violated, international law imposes the obligation of reparation. This may take the form of payment of money, cession of territory, the making of formal amends such as apology or salute of flag. Sometimes a demand has been made for the trial or delivery of a criminal in reparation, but it has been generally held that international law does not require such reparation.[16] It is with the power to meet "claims" or demands for reparation and to perform specific obligations of contract, agreement and treaty that we are at present concerned.

139. *The Determination of Obligations.*

The precise determination of national obligations, by the application of the principles and rules of international law and treaty to concrete facts, has always proved a difficult problem. It is a recognized common law principle that no one should be judge in his own

---

[15] Hall, International Law (Higgins), pp. 56-60.
[16] Wright, Enforcement of Int. Law, pp. 94-100, *supra,* sec. 110.

case, and there has been judicial opinion in England to the effect that even an act of Parliament infringing this principle would be in so far void.[17] The same principle is recognized in the federal system of the United States and a jurisdiction is established to try cases between the states of the union.[18] So also in international law it has been recognized on occasion that treaties should be interpreted not by each party according to its own opinion,[19] but by judicial process,[20] arbitration,[21] or agreement of the parties.[22]

However, there is another common law principle, that the state cannot be sued without its own consent. This principle is founded not only on the historical tradition that "the king can do no wrong" and on legal precedents, but also on practical grounds.[23]

"A sovereign," said Justice Holmes for the Supreme Court, "is exempt from suit not because of any formal conception or obsolete theory, but on the logical and practical ground that there can be no legal right as against the authority that makes the law on which the right depends."

This consideration has led Hobbes, John Austin and others to conclude, starting from the premise that the state is the only source of law, that the state cannot be subject to law and consequently international law and treaties impose only moral obligations.[24] Cer-

---

[17] Dr. Bonham's Case, 8 Co. Rep. 107a, 114a (1600); Day v. Savadge, Hob. 85, 87 (1610); City of London v. Wood, 12 Mod. 669, 687 (1701); Thayer, Cases on Const. Law, 47 et seq.; Hobbes, Leviathan, chap. 15, Everyman ed., p. 81.

[18] U. S. Const., Art. III, sec. 2.

[19] "Neither of the parties who have an interest in the contract or treaty may interpret it after his own mind." Vattel, Le Droit des Gens, 1: 2, c. 17, sec. 265. See also Wright, *Minn. Law Rev.*, 4: 29.

[20] Wilson v. Wall, 73 U. S. 83, 84 (1867); Moore, Digest, 5: 208; Crandall, op. cit., p. 364.

[21] I Hague Conventions, 1907, arts. 38, 82; Treaties concluded by United States with Great Britain and other countries, 1908, art. 1, Malloy, Treaties, 814; League of Nations Covenant, art. 13.

[22] Crandall, op. cit., pp. 225, 387; Dalloz, Juris. Gen., Supt., t. 17 (1896), s. v. Traité Int. No. 14; Wright, *Am. Jl. Int. Law*, 12: 92.

[23] Kawananako v. Polyblank, 205 U. S. 349, 353 (1907).

[24] Hobbes, Leviathan, chap. 26, 2; Austin, Lectures on Jurisprudence, 5th ed., London, 1911, 1: 263, 278; Gray, Nature and Sources of the Law, 1909, pp. 77-81; Holland, Jurisprudence, 11th ed., pp. 53, 365.

tainly an attempt to apply the two common law principles referred to leads to an apparent contradiction. By the first the state must submit to suit, by the second it cannot be sued.

140. *Justiciable and Non-justiciable Questions.*

In practice a partial reconciliation of the two principles has been reached through the consent of states to be sued or to submit to the decision of an international authority in certain types of cases. The distinction has been made between *justiciable* and *non-justiciable* questions. States have admitted that questions of the former type ought to be settled by impartial external authority and have actually so settled them, while in the latter type of questions, they have tenaciously maintained the doctrine that the state cannot be sued and each has acted as judge in its own case.[25]

This distinction does not aid us to determine what questions are actually justiciable nor does the similar distinction often made between legal and moral obligations. It is doubtless true, as President Wilson and Vattel before him pointed out, that when the element of judgment exists, the decision belongs to the conscience of the party alone, the obligation is moral, and hence the question is non-justiciable.[26] But this does not tell us in what cases the element of judgment exists. Nor do we get farther along by the definition of non-justiciable questions, attempted in many general arbitrations, as questions involving "national honor, vital interests and independence."[27] These general terms can be made as broad or limited as the inclination of the parties suggests in any particular case.

Attempts to define non-justiciable questions have proved unsuccessful, but this does not mean that the distinction is worthless. The truth is that with the theory of national sovereignty, all national obligations, whether founded on treaty or general international law, are presumed to be moral obligations and hence non-justiciable.[28]

---

[25] Crandall, *op. cit.*, p. 358.
[26] President Wilson, Statement to Senate For. Rel. Committee, Aug. 19, 1919, Hearings, 66th Cong., 1st sess., Sen. Doc. No. 106, p. 515; Vattel, Le Droit des Gens, Introduction, sec. 17.
[27] See Treaty U. S.-Great Britain, 1908, art. 1, Malloy, Treaties, p. 814.
[28] See *Infra*, sec. 142.

But states have in the past consented to submit certain controversies to legal decision and by classifying these controversies we can discover what types of dispute have actually been considered justiciable. We can thus by induction arrive at a definition of justiciable questions and regard all others as non-justiciable. Such a definition of justiciable questions has been attempted in Article XIII of the League of Nations Covenant:

"Disputes as to the interpretation of a treaty, as to any question of international law, as to the existence of any fact which if established would constitute a breach of any international obligation, or as to the extent and nature of the reparation to be made for any such breach, are declared to be among those which are generally suitable for submission to arbitration." [28a]

141. *The Obligation of Treaties and International Law.*

Treaties are presumably made to be kept. "It is an essential principle of the law of nations," asserted the London protocol of 1871, "that no power can liberate itself from the engagements of a treaty, nor modify the stipulations thereof, unless with the consent of the contracting powers by means of an amicable arrangement." [29] The same principle was emphasized by the scrap of paper incident of 1914 and implies that treaties should be interpreted by impartial authority.

Clearly if international law deserves the name, its obligations must be of a legal character and controversies relating to them must be justiciable.[30] Most text-writers recognize the distinction between obligations of international law and requirements of international courtesy and comity.[31] In the latter, an element of judgment is reserved, the obligation is "imperfect" or moral, and controversies relating to them are non-justiciable, but not so with the former. In practice this distinction necessarily exists, because by definition,[32] international law consists only of those rules and principles for the infraction of which nations have been accustomed to make formal international claim or protest, and hence for the settle-

---

[28a] Also in State of Permanent Court of International Justice, art. 36.

[29] Satow, Diplomatic Practice, 2: 131; Hall, *op. cit.*, p. 365; Wright, *Minn. Law Rev.*, 5: 441–443, *supra*, sec. 33.

[30] See J. B. Moore, *Am. Pol. Sci. Rev.*, 9: 4–6.

[31] Hall, *op. cit.*, pp. 14, 56.

[32] *Supra*, sec. 9.

PERFORMANCE OF NATIONAL OBLIGATIONS. 213

ment of which they are not content to rely on the conscience of other states.

But though treaties and international law both impose obligations of a theoretically legal character, yet their interpretation is generally a question for determination by national organs *in first instance.* According to our classification, international law and treaty impose responsibilities which may require (1) mere observance by public organs, (2) enforcement against individuals within the jurisdiction or (3) the performance of specific acts by public organs. Now primary decision upon the existence of and means of meeting responsibilities of the first two types belongs to national organs. No international controversy can occur until a failure to meet the responsibility or at least definite authorization of a violation is alleged.[33] It is, therefore, only responsibilities of the third type, now under consideration, which can raise a question for international discussion, and such a question may be raised by a claim for (1) specific performance or (2) reparation. These are the two types of *obligations* imposed by international law.[34] They imply "a tie; whereby one (state) is bound to perform some act for the benefit of another"[35] and are thus to be distinguished from *responsibilities*, almost synonymous with liabilities, which imply a situation in which

---

[33] Friendly controversies merely to ascertain rights, resulting in decisions of the nature of declaratory judgments would be an exception. Boundary controversies are sometimes of this character, though usually they are occasioned by incidents alleged to constitute an encroachment.

[34] These two obligations bear a certain resemblance to the two obligations known in Roman law as *obligationes ex contractu* and *ex delicto* and in common law as contracts and torts. There is, however, a difference. The distinction between contracts and torts depends upon whether or not the obligation is founded on special agreement or on general law; whereas the distinction we here make depends upon whether or not the obligation can be carried out or merely compensated for. In fact, however, practically the only international obligations which can furnish grounds for a demand for specific carrying out are founded on special agreements. But on the other hand, obligations which may furnish grounds for a claim for compensation may be founded upon either general law or special agreement. See Salmond, Jurisprudence, pp. 558–559.

[35] Holland, Jurisprudence, p. 241.

214 THE CONTROL OF AMERICAN FOREIGN RELATIONS.

one state may suffer if it acts, permits action, or fails to act so as to injure others.[36]

142. *Practice in Submitting Disputes to Arbitration.*

Although under the League of Nations Covenant, apparently any question involving either of these obligations should be considered justiciable, it appears that in the past states have been very reluctant to consider disputes relating to the performance of political acts, even when required by treaty, as fully justiciable. They have been unwilling to be controlled by any authority other than their own consciences in questions involving sovereignty, such as the method by which guarantees are to be fulfilled or laws enforced within their own territory. Thus Lord Derby said of the Luxemburg neutralization guarantee: "We are bound in honor—you cannot put a legal construction upon it—to see in concert with others that these arrangements are maintained."[37] And President Wilson said of the guarantee in Article X of the League of Nations Covenant:[38]

---

[36] "Liability or responsibility is the bond of necessity that exists between the wrongdoer and the remedy of the wrong." (Salmond, Jurisprudence, sec. 126.) In the terminology which has developed from discussion of Professor Hohfeld's article on Fundamental Legal Conceptions (*Yale L. J.*, 23: 16), we say that B is under an *obligation* (or duty) when the services of organized society can be enlisted against him by A and correlatively that A has a *right*. On the other hand, B is under a *liability* (or responsibility) when organized society permits A to act against him and correlatively A has a *power*. (See addresses at meeting of Association of American Law Schools in Chicago, Dec. 29, 1920, especially that by Kocourek, *Am. Law School Rev.*, 4: 615.)

Rights and obligations imply a society organized to the extent of providing agencies for authoritatively judging justiciable controversies between its members. There are no true rights or obligations where each man is judge of the merits of his own case. (*Supra*, sec. 139.) Powers and liabilities, however, may exist in a society organized only to the extent of refusing to permit self help in certain cases. There are no true powers or liabilities where each man is judge of the limits of his own competence. Moral rights and duties may exist in a society not organized at all. (*Supra*, sec. 140) The family of nations has passed from the last to the second stage and is slowly advancing to the first. (*Infra*, sec. 142; Wright, *Col. Law Rev.*, 20: 147–148.)

[37] Hansard, Debates, 3d Ser., 187: 1922; Hall, *op. cit.*, p. 355.

[38] Statement to Senate For. Rel. Committee, Aug. 19, 1919, 66th Cong., 1st sess., Sen. Doc. 106, p. 502.

PERFORMANCE OF NATIONAL OBLIGATIONS. 215

"It is a moral, not a legal, obligation, and leaves our Congress absolutely free to put its own interpretation upon it in all cases that call for action. It is binding in conscience only, not in law."

The North Atlantic Fisheries arbitration court seemed to sanction the same view when it refused to hold that Great Britain was bound to gain American assent to fishery regulations within those territorial waters in which the United States claimed a treaty servitude: [39]

"The right to regulate the liberties conferred by the treaty of 1817 is an attribute of sovereignty, and as such must be held to reside in the territorial sovereign unless the contrary be provided."

In practice claims for reparation have been the type most frequently submitted to arbitration, though cases involving the limits of jurisdiction such as boundaries, public vessels, etc., have occasionally been so settled.

B. *Power to Interpret National Obligations.*

143. *By National Political Organs: Congress.*

The agencies competent to interpret and apply international law and treaty, and thereby to decide upon the existence of national obligations, may be classified as (1) national political organs, (2) international political organs, (3) national judicial organs and (4) international judicial or quasi-judicial organs.

Political questions according to the courts are beyond their competence and must be left to the political departments. Thus they have held that it belongs to the political departments to decide whether or not a treaty has been terminated and until such decision is given the courts will continue to apply it as municipal law.[40] The principle has been, that the organ with power to fulfill an alleged political obligation is competent to decide whether the obligation really exists.

"Where the construction of a treaty is a matter of national policy," wrote Secretary of State Bayard, "the authoritative construction is that of the

---

[39] Wilson, The Hague Arbitration Cases, Boston, 1915, p. 154.
[40] *Infra*, sec. 182.

political branch of the government. It is the function of the Executive or of Congress, as the case may be." [41]

So Congress has asserted that it alone can interpret responsibilities claimed to oblige an appropriation of money, a declaration of war or other act exclusively within its control. As has been pointed out, if the President as the representative organ should interpret such a responsibility, his interpretation would bind the United States under international law,[42] but in recognition of the constitutional principle he has not usually done so. Thus Secretary of State Bayard refused to authorize an unconditional signature of a declaration interpreting the Submarine Cable Convention of 1884: [43]

" It is to be observed," he wrote, "in this connection that the treaty in question is not self-executing, and that it requires appropriate legislation to give it effect. If, under these circumstances, the Executive should now assume to interpret the force and effect of the convention, we might hereafter have the spectacle, when Congress acted, of an Executive interpretation of one purport and a different congressional interpretation, and this in a matter not of Executive cognizance."

144. *By National Political Organs: The Senate.*

The Senate, in consenting to the ratification of treaties, has decided upon the action necessary to meet responsibilities created by preliminaries of peace, protocols and other agreements requiring the negotiation of subsequent treaties. So the Senate assumed the right to decide whether or not ratification of the Treaty of Versailles was required in fulfillment of the responsibilities undertaken by the President's exchange of notes with the Allied powers of November 5, 1918, and the armistice with Germany of November 11.[44] So also the Senate has asserted its right to decide whether a particular controversy is within the scope of a general arbitration treaty, and has therefore insisted upon a voice in the

---

[41] Mr. Bayard, Sec. of State, to Mr. McLane, Min. to France, Nov. 24, 1888, Moore, Digest, 5: 209. See Martin *v.* Mott, 12 Wheat. 19, *infra*, sec. 223, note 97.

[42] *Supra*, secs. 34, 38.

[43] Note cited, *supra*, note 41.

[44] *Supra*, sec. 30, note 53.

conclusion of the *compromis* submitting a particular case to arbitration. The latter claim has not been admitted by Presidents or supported by the better authorities, who have held that the power to apply a general treaty to particular cases is not a political question and may be delegated.[45] With reference to general and permanent interpretations of treaties or agreements, however, the President has admitted the Senate's claim.

"Had the protocol varied the treaty, as amended by the Senate of the United States," wrote President Polk in reference to a protocol explaining the treaty of Guadaloupe Hidalgo with Mexico, "it would have no binding effect."[46]

Apparently the presumption that the President speaks for the nation would generally be superseded in such a case by the duty of foreign nations to acquaint themselves with the authority in the United States competent to make international agreements, and the United States would not be bound by such general interpretation unless the foreign nation had reason to suppose it had been consented to by the proper authorities.[47]

145. *By National Political Organs: The President.*

Where power to fulfill responsibilities is vested in the President, he may decide what action is necessary. Thus Presidents have often decided when the circumstances contemplated by treaties or agreements of guarantee and protection, such as those with Colombia (1846), Mexico (1882–1894), Cuba (1903) and Hayti (1916), exist, and on their own responsibility have moved troops or war vessels.[48] In his message of December 7, 1903, President Roosevelt explained at length his interpretation of the treaty of 1846 with Colombia. By Article 35 of this treaty the United States had "guaranteed, positively and efficaciously to New Granada, (Colombia) . . . the perfect neutrality of the . . . Isthmus, with the view that the free transit from the one to the

---
[45] *Supra*, sec. 62.
[46] Moore, Digest, 5: 208; see also *supra*, secs. 27, 28, 38, and *infra*, sec. 177.
[47] *Supra*, sec. 24.
[48] Taft, Our Chief Magistrate, pp. 85–87.

other sea may not be interrupted or embarrassed in any future time while this treaty exists; and, in consequence, the United States also guarantee, in the same manner, the rights of sovereignty and property which New Granada has and possesses over the said territory." In fulfillment of this guarantee President Roosevelt had ordered the war vessel Nashville to Colon, with instructions: [49]

"In the interests of peace make every effort to prevent Government troops at Colon from proceeding to Panama. The transit of the Isthmus must be kept open and order maintained."

With this action, the insurrection soon ended in success, and President Roosevelt promptly recognized the New Republic of Panama. In the message he called attention to previous occasions from 1856 to 1902, in which the United States had been obliged to exercise a "police power" in connection with this guarantee and the President had ordered sailors and marines to land and to patrol the Isthmus.[50]

146. *By International Political Organs.*

A political interpretation of national obligations is not necessarily unilateral. Undoubtedly agreement is a more satisfactory method of reaching a decision and has been judicially approved. Thus said Justice Story for the Supreme Court: [51]

"The parties who formed this treaty, and they alone, have a right to annex the form of a passport. It is a high act of sovereignty, as high as the formation of any other stipulation of a treaty. It is matter of negotiation between the governments. The treaty does not leave it to the discretion of either party to annex the form of the passport; it requires it to be the joint act of both."

"The interpretation of a treaty in case of difficulty," said the French Court of Cassation, "can result only from a reciprocal agreement of the two governments." [52]

---

[49] Richardson, Messages, 10: 566.
[50] *Ibid.*, 10: 664.
[51] The Amiable Isabella, 6 Wheat. 1, 71–73 (1821).
[52] Dalloz, Juris, Gen., Supt., t. 17 (1896), s. v. Traité, Int., No. 14.

PERFORMANCE OF NATIONAL OBLIGATIONS. 219

An interpretation by political agreement would ordinarily require negotiation through the Department of State, acting either through the Secretary of State at Washington or through a diplomatic officer in the foreign capital. All claims must be presented to the Department of State, not to the President direct or to Congress.[53] If claims of American citizens upon foreign governments, they must be presented in proper form and with ample evidence, but the department reserves full discretion to refuse to press them.[54] If claims from foreign citizens or governments against the United States, they must be presented officially as from the government of the claimant's state. The Department of State will not consider claims from foreign individuals, only from recognized governments.[55]

However, the department is free to accept an offer of mediation by a foreign government, or to submit the controversy to a council of conciliation, commission of inquiry or other body set up to discover facts and agree on recommendations.[56] Such recommendations are not binding upon the political organs of the government but are often accepted. Under the Bryan Peace treaties concluded with twenty states in 1914 and 1915, controversies not otherwise settled must be submitted to a joint commission before force is resorted to. Similar provision is made in the League of Nations Covenant (Article XV).[57]

The controversy may be settled by the conclusion of a treaty which is of course binding on the United States. Many claims have been thus settled. The claims of the United States on account of spoliations by French vessels before 1800 and the claims of France for reparation on account of the alleged non-fulfillment of the alliance treaty of 1778 were balanced off by the treaty of 1801. Claims against France were liquidated by a

---

[53] Borchard, *op. cit.*, pp. 355, 653; Moore, Digest, 4: 687, 781; *supra*, sec. 12, note 22.
[54] Moore, Digest, 6: 609 *et seq.*
[55] *Ibid.*, 6: 607–609; 4: 694.
[56] *Ibid.*, 6: 1012 *et seq.*; Borchard, *op. cit.*, p. 366 *et seq.*
[57] Canadian Boundary controversies must be submitted to a commission by art. viii of the treaty of 1911, Charles, Treaties, p. 42.

treaty concluded in 1831. Treaties of peace usually liquidate prewar claims. This was true of the treaties of Guadaloupe Hidalgo and Paris. By article VII of the latter:

> "The United States and Spain mutually relinquish all claims for indemnity, national and individual, of every kind, of either Government, or of its citizens or subjects, against the other Government, that may have arisen since the beginning of the late insurrection in Cuba and prior to the exchange of ratifications of the present treaty, including all claims for indemnity for the cost of the war."

Often such a treaty liquidation will involve an obligation of the Government to compensate its own citizens.[58] This was true of the provision just stated, which was followed by the statement that:

> "The United States will adjudicate and settle the claims of its citizens against Spain relinquished in this article."

Boundary questions have often been settled by treaty, as was the Maine Boundary by the Webster-Ashburton treaty of 1842 and the Oregon boundary by a treaty of 1846.

The power to settle claims against the government by agreement has sometimes been delegated to officers other than the Secretary of State. Thus an act of March 2, 1919, provided:[59]

> "The Secretary of War, through such agency as he may designate or establish, is empowered, upon such terms as he or it may determine to be in the interest of the United States, to make equitable and fair adjustments and agreements, upon the termination or in settlement or readjustment of agreements or arrangements entered into with any foreign government or governments or national thereof, prior to November twelfth, nineteen hundred and eighteen, for the furnishing to the American Expeditionary Forces or otherwise for war purposes of supplies, materials, facilities, services, or the use of property, etc."

147. *By National Courts.*

The interpretation and application to concrete circumstances of international law and treaty is not in essence a political or legislative act and undoubtedly the political organs may delegate power to make such interpretation to other organs. This power is essen-

---

[58] Borchard, *op. cit.*, p. 379; Moore, Digest, 6: 1025.
[59] 40 Stat., c. 94, sec. 3, Comp. Stat., 3115, 14/15c.

tially judicial in character and has often been delegated to the courts.

Certain claims virtually against the government may be decided by prize courts. Such courts may decree restitution of captured vessels, compensation if the vessel has been requisitioned or destroyed, or damages if the capture has been illegal. Damages are in theory awarded against the officer making the capture, but in fact such awards are usually paid by the government.[60] Federal District Courts have been given exclusive jurisdiction in prize matters with appeal to the Supreme Court.[61] They are free to apply international law and treaty and hold it their duty to do so except as expressly modified by act of Congress.[62] Both neutral and enemy persons are entitled to present claims in such courts.[63] It has been held that prize courts may be constituted by Congress alone. Courts set up under authority of the President in occupied territory cannot exercise prize jurisdiction.[64]

Congress has also established a Court of Claims from which appeal may be taken to the Supreme Court. Its jurisdiction extends to claims presented by aliens whose governments will reciprocate, not founded on tort, or treaty.[65] The decisions of this court or of the Supreme Court, if appeal is taken, are considered final and Congress always appropriates therefor.[66] The Court of Claims may also consider any claim presented to it by Congress and make a report thereon, which however is not binding.[67] Under the Tucker Act of 1887 and subsequent amendments the Federal District Courts

[60] Moore, Digest, 7: 593-597.

[61] Judicial Code of 1911, sec. 24, par. 3; sec. 250, par. 2.

[62] The Nereide, 9 Cranch 388; The Paquette Habana, 175 U. S. 677, *supra*, sec. 106.

[63] The claimant in the Paquette Habana, *supra*, was an enemy subject. See British case, The Mowe, L. J. (1915), p. 57, *Am. Jl. Int. Law*, 9: 547.

[64] Jecker v. Montgomery, 13 How. 498.

[65] Judicial Code of 1911, secs. 136, 145, 153, 155; 36 Stat. 1135, Willoughby, *op. cit.*, p. 982.

[66] U. S. v. New York, 160 U. S. 615; *In re* Sanborn, 148 U. S. 226; Willoughby, p. 1275.

[67] Judicial Code of 1911, sec. 151.

enjoy concurrent jurisdiction with the Court of Claims in claims not exceeding $10,000.[68]

Congress has often set up special courts or commissions to settle claims of individuals. Of this character may be mentioned commissions to liquidate the claims settled by the treaty with Spain of 1819, claims settled by the Alabama Arbitration of 1871, and claims settled by the Spanish treaty of 1898. Sometimes special jurisdiction is conferred to settle particular claims. So the Court of Claims was given jurisdiction to settle the French Spoliation claims, the courts were given jurisdiction to settle various specified types of claims arising out of the Civil War, and by an act of 1850 the federal courts were given jurisdiction to settle the claim of one Repentigny to a tract of land in Michigan founded on an ancient French grant. The act expressly provided in this case that the decision should be based on "(1) the law of nations, (2) the laws of the country from which the title was derived, (3) the principles of justice, and (4) the stipulations of treaties."[69]

148. *By International Courts.*

National courts are bound by national law if expressed in unmistakable form, and may not be free to apply international law and treaty. All international claims, whether decided upon by national courts or not, if not satisfactorily settled, may be presented to the President through the Department of State.[70] As we have seen they may then be settled by political negotiation and agreement or submission to a political body such as a council of conciliation. However, the department may submit them to arbitration or an international court and under the provisions of certain treaties it is bound to so submit certain types of controversies. By a treaty with various American states adopted at the Fourth International American Congress in 1910:[71]

"The High Contracting Parties agree to submit to arbitration all claims for pecuniary loss or damage which may be presented by their respective citizens and which cannot be amicably adjusted through diplomatic channels,

---

[68] *Ibid.*, sec. 24, par. 20.
[69] U. S. *v.* Repentigny, 5 Wall. 211 (1866).
[70] *Supra*, sec. 12.
[71] Charles, Treaties, etc., p. 346.

when said claims are of sufficient importance to warrant the expense of arbitration."

"The decision shall be rendered in accordance with the principles of international law."

By the II Hague Convention of 1907 armed force cannot be used for the recovery of contract debts between governments unless an offer of arbitration has been refused, and by a large number of treaties concluded in 1908 for five years, most of which have since been renewed, the United States has agreed to submit to arbitration " Differences which may arise of a legal nature or relating to the interpretation of treaties existing between the two contracting parties and which it may not have been possible to settle by diplomacy" and which "do not affect the vital interests, the independence, or the honor of the two Contracting States, and do not concern the interests of third parties." [72] The League of Nations Covenant (Art. XIII) recommends the submission of specified types of cases to arbitration or to the proposed International Court of Justice but does not require it.

In making such submissions, if no general treaty exists, a special treaty to which the Senate has consented is necessary for the submission to arbitration of national claims or claims by foreign states or individuals against the United States.[73] Claims of American citizens against foreign states may be submitted on the basis of a *compromis* under authority of the President or Secretary of State, since it is within the discretion of these officials to decide whether such claims shall be pressed at all.[74] Even if an arbitration of such claims results successfully for the United States the government may withhold the money from the individual claimant if it discovers fraud. Thus claimants in the L'Abra and Wyle claims against Mexico were unable to compel the Secretary of State by mandamus to turn over to them the money paid by Mexico to the United States as a result of the arbitration.[75] The United States govern-

---

[72] Malloy, Treaties, p. 814.

[73] Foster, *Yale L. J.*, 11: 77; Moore, Digest 5: 211.

[74] J. B. Moore, *Pol. Sci. Quar.*, 20: 403; Willoughby, *op. cit.*, p. 475; Moore, Digest, 5: 211.

[75] L'Abra Silver Mining Co. *v.* U. S., 175 U. S. 423 (1899); Foster, The Practice of Diplomacy, 374–377.

ment had discovered fraud after the arbitration and ultimately returned the money to Mexico. Where a general arbitration treaty exists, the better authorities hold that the President may submit claims falling within it on his own authority, unless the general treaty requires otherwise. The Senate however has taken a different view.[76]

Arbitration awards are considered final and obligatory and have practically always been met by the United States.[77] In the few cases where they have not, the United States has contended that the arbitration court exceeded or abused its powers.[78] Unless such exception is taken at once by the political organs, the courts hold arbitration awards authorized by treaty the supreme law of the land.[79]

Although often recommended, no international court of justice was established until 1921. The International Prize Court to be set up by the XII Hague Convention of 1907 never came into being. Such a court, authorized by Article XIV of the League of Nations Covenant, was established by action of the Second Assembly of the League, September, 1921, on the basis of a code prepared by a commission of jurists in 1920 and approved with modifications by the council and by the First Assembly and ratified at that time by 29 members of the League.[80] An international court of claims before

---

[76] Willoughby, *op. cit.*, p. 475, *supra*, sec. 62, *infra*, sec. 163. The Anglo-American claims treaty of 1910, differing from those of 1853 and 1871, requires that each schedule of claims under the treaty be approved by the Senate as a special treaty (Charles, Treaties, p. 50, and Sir Cecil Hurst in British Year Book of International Law, 2: 193).

[77] I Hague Conventions, 1907, pp. 81–83.

[78] Moore, Digest, 7: 59–62; Darby, International Tribunals, 1904, p. 785, No. 46.

[79] Comegys *v.* Vasse, 1 Pet. 193, 212; La Ninfa, 75 Fed. 513 (1896); Moore, Digest, 7: 55.

[80] For draft plan of organization by Root *et al.* see *Am. Jl. Int. Law*, Supp., 14: 371 (Oct., 1920), and for code as adopted see A League of Nations, 4: 281 *et seq.* 13 additional states had signed but not ratified the code in September 1921 and 13 states had accepted the clause providing for compulsory jurisdiction, *ibid.*, 278, 291.

PERFORMANCE OF NATIONAL OBLIGATIONS. 225

which private individuals might bring cases against governments has also been suggested. With reference to such a court Borchard says:[81]

"The divorce of pecuniary claims from political considerations a union, which now not only results in inexact justice, but often gross injustice, and the submission of such claims to the determination of an independent tribunal, must make a universal appeal to man's sentiment for justice."

C. Power to Perform National Obligations.

149. *Appropriations.*

A decision having been made as to what action is required in order to meet the obligation, it becomes the duty of organs empowered thereto by the Constitution to perform those acts.

Under the power to raise taxes for the general welfare, Congress undoubtedly has power to make appropriations for this purpose. Where Congress itself has decided that the obligation is due it will of course make the appropriation. Where a decision by a national court acting within its jurisdiction or an international arbitration court has been given, appropriations have been made as a matter of course. Where the Department of State has admitted the validity of a claim Congress has generally made the appropriation. Thus on January 30, 1896, Secretary of State Olney, after discussion with the Italian Ambassador with reference to the lynching of three Italian citizens in Colorado, reported to the President:

"The facts are without dispute and no comment or argument can add to the force of their appeal to the generous consideration of Congress."[82]

President Cleveland said in his message to Congress of February 3, 1896:[83]

"Without discussing the question of the liability of the United States for these results, either by reason of treaty obligations or under the general rules of international law, I venture to urge upon the Congress the propriety of making from the public Treasury prompt and reasonable pecuniary provision for those injured and for the families of those who were killed."

---

[81] Borchard, *op. cit.*, p. 864. See also pp. 328, 373, 443.
[82] U. S. For. Rel., 1895, 2: 938; Moore, Digest, 6: 842.
[83] Richardson, Messages, 9: 664; Moore, Digest, 6: 843.

226   THE CONTROL OF AMERICAN FOREIGN RELATIONS.

By an act of June 30, 1896, Congress provided: [84]

"To the Italian Government for full indemnity to the heirs of three of its subjects who were riotously killed, and to two others who were injured in the State of Colorado by residents of that State, ten thousand dollars."

Where appropriation has been required for the execution of treaties, Congress has never failed to act[85] but has asserted a right to exercise discretion. Thus a house resolution of 1796 relating to the Jay treaty states:[86]

"When a treaty stipulates regulations on any of the subjects submitted by the Constitution to the power of Congress, it must depend for its execution as to such stipulations on a law or laws to be passed by Congress; and it is the constitutional right and duty of the House of Representatives in all such cases to deliberate on the expediency or inexpediency of carrying such treaty into effect and to determine and act thereon as in their judgment may be most conducive to the public good."

This attitude though virtually repeated on several later occasions has not been generally approved outside of the House of Representatives and undoubtedly a moral obligation to make the appropriation exists.[87]

150. *Cession of Territory.*

Treaties or arbitration awards may require a cession of territory. Such provisions affecting small tracts of territory in boundary settlements have been considered self-executing.[88] The

---

[84] Moore, Digest, 6: 843. In later appropriation acts for similar claims Congress paid "out of humane considerations and without reference to the question of liability, therefor," *ibid.*, 6: 845, 849. See also report of Senator Lodge, 1901, *ibid.*, 6: 852.

[85] Appropriation acts for this purpose are listed, Crandall, *op. cit.*, p. 179.

[86] Annals, 4th Cong., 1st sess., p. 771. The resolution was affirmed without debate in 1871. *Cong. Globe,* 42d Cong., 1st sess., p. 835; Wharton, 2: 19; Moore, Digest, 5: 224; Crandall, 165 *et seq.;* Wright, *Am. Jl. Int. Law,* 12: 66. See also Gallatin to Everett, Jan., 1835, Moore, Digest, 5: 232.

[87] Crandall, *op. cit.*, p. 177; Willoughby, *op. cit.*, p. 483; Dana's Wheaton, sec. 543; Wharton, Digest, 2: 67–68; *supra,* sec. 59; *infra,* sec. 256.

[88] The Webster-Ashburton treaty adjusting the Maine Boundary was considered self-executing with respect to territory claimed by Maine, but given

same view would probably be taken of a large cession if conditions were such that it could be considered constitutional.[89]

151. *Guarantees and Use of Military Force.*

Treaties of guarantee, or requiring the employment of force in policing or other operations have usually been carried out by the President. Thus on many occasions the President has dispatched troops to Panama in maintenance of the guarantee in the Colombia treaty of 1846 and Presidents have also dispatched troops to Cuba, Hayti and China in pursuance of treaties and protocols requiring protection.[90] Congressional legislation has often provided expressly for the use of force in pursuance of treaty. Article 8 of the Webster-Ashburton treaty of 1842 required that the contracting powers keep naval forces of specified size off the coast of Africa for the suppression of the slave trade. Congress passed an act authorizing the President to dispatch vessels for this purpose, and the President so acted.[91]

If a guarantee treaty requires a declaration of war, Congress alone can carry it out, although its discretion ought to be confined to consideration of whether the contemplated circumstances exist and whether war is the most effective means of carrying out the guarantee.[92]

152. *Conclusion of Subsequent Treaties.*

Protocols and preliminaries of peace may require the conclusion

---

to Canada by the treaty. Little *v.* Watson, 32 Maine 214, 224 (1850); Crandall, *op. cit.*, p. 223. The Supreme Court of the United States has recognized boundary settlements between states of the Union. Va. *v.* Tenn., 148 U. S. 503. See also La Ninfa, 75 Fed. 513, in which the arbitration award fixing jurisdictional limits in Behring Sea was held self-executing.

[89] Willoughby, *op. cit.*, p. 512; Crandall, *op. cit.*, p. 220 *et seq.; supra,* sec. 50.

[90] *Supra,* secs. 126, 145; *infra,* secs. 221–224.

[91] Moore, Digest, 2: 939. See also *ibid.*, 2: 941; Rev. Stat., sec. 5557; Criminal Code of 1910, sec. 260, 35 Stat., 1140, Comp. Stat., secs. 10, 433. In reference to Slave trade treaty of 1862, see Moore, Digest, 2: 946. In reference to General act of Brussels for suppression of the slave trade, *ibid.*, 2: 949.

[92] *Supra,* sec. 37, *infra,* sec. 211. See also Wright, *Am. Jl. Int. Law,* 12: 72–79.

of definitive treaties along prescribed lines. Such provisions can only be carried out by the treaty power. A protocol calling for conclusion of a treaty for arbitration of the Behring Sea controversy was carried out by a treaty in 1891. Spain objected to the definitive treaty of peace as insisted upon by the United States in 1898 on the ground that it was in violation of the preliminaries of peace in some respects. Treaties often require the conclusion of subsequent treaties. This has been true of many general arbitration treaties specifically requiring special treaties submitting cases within the scope of the general treaty. The League of Nations Covenant contemplates treaties on many subjects in which international cooperation is urged. In such cases the treaty power may act within the discretion allowed it by the general treaty.[93]

153. *Participation in International Organization.*

Treaties requiring the appointment of officers for participating in international organizations, such as the permanent Court of Arbitration and Bureau established by the I Hague Convention of 1899, and 1907, and for putting administrative regulations into effect such as the Behring Sea seal fisheries treaty, the international radio treaty, etc., can be carried out by the President, though Congress has often passed acts expressly authorizing participation in such organizations and enforcement of such regulations.[94] If permanent offices with a fixed salary are required, an act of Congress would be essential for the execution of such provisions.[95]

154. *Commerce and Revenue Laws.*

Treaties requiring a modification of the tariff system might seem self-executing and have been held so in dicta by the courts.[96] On at least one occasion a foreign state has been given reduced rates

---

[93] *Supra*, sec. 144.

[94] The President is authorized to use naval vessels to enforce the Submarine cable treaty of 1885, by act of Feb. 27, 1888, 25 Stat. 41, Comp. Stat., sec. 10087. He is authorized to enforce the Behring Sea Seal fisheries treaty of 1911 by act of Aug. 24, 1912, 37 Stat. 499, Comp. Stat., sec. 8838. For acts authorizing participation in various international organizations, see *infra*, sec. 242.

[95] *Infra*, sec. 242.

[96] Bartram *v.* Robertson, 122 U. S. 116; Whitney *v.* Robertson, 124 U. S. 190; Willoughby, *op. cit.,* p. 492.

on the basis of treaty without congressional authorization.[97] Congress, however, has insisted that such treaties are not self-executing but require express congressional action for execution. This practice has generally been acquiesced in by the other organs of government.[98]

155. *Formal Amends in Reparation.*

Satisfactory reparation may sometimes require acts other than the payment of money or cession of territory. Formal amends such as the firing of salutes or sending of apologies may be authorized by the President.[99] Sometimes states have demanded that individuals be criminally punished or turned over to them for punishment by way of reparation. Thus, aside from indemnity, Italy demanded as reparation for the New Orleans lynching of 1891: "The official assurance by the Federal government that the guilty parties should be brought to trial."[100] In his next message to Congress President Harrison asked for legislation giving federal courts jurisdiction in such cases but without success. Doubtless such legislation is expedient for meeting the international responsibility of enforcing international law and treaty within the jurisdiction but it cannot be said that this particular form of reparation is required.[101] The release of prisoners held in custody in violation of international law is however a form of reparation which may be demanded. Such a reparation was demanded by Great Britain in the McLeod case in 1842.[102] At present legislation provides for release in such cases on habeas corpus to the federal courts.[103]

---

[97] Switzerland on application of Most-favored-nation clause of treaty of 1850, in 1899. Moore, Digest, 5: 283–284. See also report of Ambassador Bryce to British Government, Jan. 31, 1912. Parl. Pap., Misc., No. 5 (1912), No. 23, quoted in Ponsonby, Democracy and Diplomacy, p. 154.
[98] Crandall, *op. cit.*, pp. 195–200; Wright, *Am. Jl. Int. Law*, 12: 68.
[99] Moore, Digest, 6: 1034–1037.
[100] *Ibid.*, 6: 838.
[101] *Supra*, sec. 138.
[102] Moore, Digest, 2: 24–30.
[103] Rev. Stat., sec. 753; Comp. Stat., sec. 1281.

CHAPTER XIV.

THE POWER TO MAKE INTERNATIONAL AGREEMENTS.

156. *Power of the States to Make Agreements with Consent of Congress.*

The courts have never pointed out the exact distinction between "Treaties, Alliances, and Confederations," which the states cannot make at all and "compacts and agreements," which they can make with the consent of Congress,[1] though Professor Hall has suggested that the latter refers to "trifling and temporary arrangements between States and foreign powers without substantial political and economic effect."[2] In 1842, Chief Justice Taney held, in an evenly divided court, that the extradition of a criminal, by the governor of Vermont to Canada, would be an "agreement" with Canada, which the state could not make without consent of Congress. The term, "agreement," he thought must be construed so as "to prohibit (without consent of Congress) every agreement, written or verbal, formal or informal, positive or implied, by the natural understanding of the parties."[3] Taney's view was endorsed by the full court forty-four years later in United States *v.* Rauscher.[4]

There do not appear to have been any "agreements or compacts" made with consent of Congress, by states of the Union with foreign states, though following the "Aroostook War," in 1839, on authority of the Secretary of State, the Governor of Maine, and the Lieutenant-Governor of New Brunswick concurred in a *modus vivendi,* pending settlement of the boundary controversy,[5] and the consent of Maine and of Massachusetts was gained by the National Government during negotiation of the Webster-

---
[1] U. S. Const., Art. I, sec. 10, cl. 1, 3.
[2] *Proc. Acad. of Pol. Sci.,* 7: 555.
[3] Holmes *v.* Jennison, 14 Pet. 540.
[4] U. S. *v.* Rauscher, 119 U. S. 407.
[5] Crandall, *op. cit.,* p. 144.

Ashburton treaty of 1842, which finally settled the boundary.[6] "Agreements or compacts" with other states of the Union have often been made by states with the consent of Congress[7] and there is no doubt but that the same power applies to foreign states as was, in fact, admitted by Chief Justice Taney in the case referred to.

157. *Power of the States to Make Agreements Independently.*

Although dicta in the Rauscher case asserted that "There is no necessity for the States to enter upon the relations with foreign nations which are necessarily implied in the extradition of fugitives," and that "at this time of day, and after the repeated examinations which have been made by this court, into the powers of the Federal Government, to deal with all such international questions exclusively," such a state power cannot be admitted, yet it appears that there may be a small field within which states can agree with foreign nations even without consent of Congress. Such a field exists in relations between the states of the Union.

"There are many matters," said the Supreme Court, "upon which different States may agree, that can, in no respect, concern the United States. If, for example, Virginia should come into possession and ownership of a small parcel of land in New York, which the latter State might desire to acquire as a site for a public building, it would hardly be deemed essential for the latter state to obtain the consent of Congress before it could make a valid agreement with Virginia for the purchase of the land. If Massachusetts, in forwarding its exhibits to the World's Fair at Chicago, should desire to transport them a part of the distance over the Erie Canal, it would hardly be deemed essential for that State to obtain the consent of Congress before it could contract with New York for the transportation of the exhibits through the State in that way. If the bordering line of the two States should cross some malarious and disease producing district, there could be no possible reason, on any conceivable grounds, to obtain the consent of Congress for the bordering States to agree to unite in removing the cause of the disease. So, in the case of threatened invasion of cholera, plague or other causes of sickness and death, it would be the height of absurdity to hold that the threatened States could not unite in providing means to prevent and repel the invasion of the pestilence without obtaining the consent of Congress, which might not be in session.

---

[6] *Infra*, sec. 50.
[7] Green *v.* Biddle, 8 Wheat. 1; Crandall, *op. cit.*, p. 145; Willoughby, *op. cit.*, p. 235.

"If, then, the terms 'compact' or 'agreement' in the Constitution do not apply to every possible compact or agreement between one State and another, for the validity of which the consent of Congress must be obtained, to what compacts or agreements does the Constitution apply? Looking at the clause in which the terms 'compact' or 'agreement' appear, it is evident that the prohibition is directed to the formation of any combination tending to the increase of political power in the States, which may encroach upon or interfere with the just supremacy of the United States."[8]

As the constitutional clause seems to place agreements with foreign states in exactly the same class as agreements with other states of the Union, it would seem that states might agree with foreign nations for the purchase of land, for the transit of exhibits, for the removal of sources of disease, or, as in the case cited, for the exact demarkation of a boundary, without congressional consent.[9] Such agreements would have to be entirely devoid of political significance, and Congress would doubtless be the ultimate judge on that point. Acquiescence by Congress in such a compact would be considered tacit consent, as was explained in the case just quoted, but if Congress subsequently denied the validity of a compact, thereby indicating its belief that the compact was one to which its consent was necessary, the courts would undoubtedly follow its interpretation of a "political question" and hold such compact void. Contracts of a purely business character between a state and a foreign government, such as are involved in the sale of state bonds to a foreign government, do not require the consent of Congress any

---

[8] Va. v. Tenn., 148 U. S. 503; Willoughby, *loc. cit.*

[9] The Supreme Court said in Fort Leavenworth R. R. v. Lowe (114 U. S. 541): "It is undoubtedly true that the State, whether represented by her legislature, or through a convention specially called for that purpose, is incompetent to cede her political jurisdiction and legislative authority over any part of her territory to a foreign country, without the concurrence of the General Government," though according to this opinion she may cede it to the general government itself. Willoughby (*op. cit.*, 508, note 23) suggests a possible exception "with reference to such an unimportant matter as the administration of fishing upon boundary waters." Barnett (*Yale L. J.*, 13, 23, 27) suggests that there may "properly be an autonomy in local external affairs, at least as to the States bordering on Canada or Mexico, just as there is a local autonomy in matters purely domestic." Butler, however, doubts it. (*Op. cit.*, I, sec. 123.) See Mathews, The States and Foreign Relations, *Mich. L. R.*, 19: 692.

more than do such contracts between states of the union.[10] Agreements and contracts of the kind here referred to do not involve a national responsibility.[11]

158. *Power of the National Government to Make Agreements.*

Thus with limited exceptions, the power to make agreements is vested exclusively in the national government, and apparently the Constitution vests it in two authorities, the President acting alone, and the President acting with advice and consent of two-thirds of the Senate. President Washington pointed out in his message on the Jay treaty that the House of Representatives had no part in treaty-making.[12] The House has several times asserted, by resolution, its power to exercise a free discretion as to the execution of treaties requiring an appropriation or other legislation. This has never extended to a claim to participation in treaty-making, and with its more limited interpretation has never been accepted by other branches of the government.[13]

159. *Congress cannot Make International Agreements.*

It is true that Congress has sometimes passed legislation which by its terms is to go into effect as to any foreign nation, upon proclamation by the President, that such nation offers a specified reciprocity, but such arangements are not agreements, since either party is entitled to discontinue them at its own discretion.[14] Sometimes Congress has delegated authority to the President to make agreements with foreign nations upon subjects within its powers, but here, also, the arrangement seems to be terminable at discretion of Congress and is, in fact, an agreement made by the President.[15] Congressional resolutions may suggest the making of a treaty on a specified subject, or the modification by negotiation of an

---

[10] S. Dak. *v.* N. Car., 192 U. S. 286 (1904).
[11] *Supra,* sec. 136.
[12] Richardson, Messages, 1: 195.
[13] *Supra,* sec. 149, note 82.
[14] Field *v.* Clark, 143 U. S. 649; Taft, Our Chief Magistrate, p. 111.
[15] *Supra,* sec. 61; Moore, Digest, 5: 362.

existing treaty, but such resolutions may be ignored by the President.[16]

160. *The Courts cannot Make International Agreements.*

The courts, also, are devoid of treaty-making power:[17]

"This court," said Justice Story, "does not possess any treaty-making power. That power belongs, by the Constitution, to another department of the government; and to alter, amend, or add to any treaty, by inserting any clause, whether small or great, important or trivial, would be on our part an usurpation of power, and not an exercise of judicial functions."

Courts must construe and interpret treaties in applying them to cases, but such constructions cannot apply to political question or supply omissions.[18]

A. *The Power to Make Executive Agreements.*

161. *The Obligation of Executive Agreements.*

The President with advice and consent of two-thirds of the Senate may make any agreement whatever, on a subject suitable for international negotiation and not violative of constitutional limitations. This treaty-making power is not limited by the President's independent power of making agreements, but the latter power unquestionably exists. With respect to such Presidential agreements, the questions arise: (1) What subject matter may they cover?

---

[16] *Infra,* sec. 203. Congress has undertaken regulation of Indian affairs formerly vested in the treaty-making power. "During the first eighty years of government under the Constitution, agreements with the Indian Tribes were made exclusively by the President and the Senate, in the exercise of the treaty-making power. The passage of the act of 1871 was strongly opposed by certain members of the House as well as of the Senate, on the ground that it involved an infringement of the treaty-making power vested in the President and the latter body. It was admitted that if the President should undertake to make a treaty with the Indians, Congress could not interfere with his so-doing, by and with the advice and consent of the Senate, but it was, on the other hand, maintained that Congress had the power to declare whether the tribes were independent nations for the purposes of treaty-making, and to render its declaration effective by refusing to recognize any subsequent treaties with them; and this view prevailed. (See especially, *Cong. Globe,* 41st Cong., 3d Sess., 1870–1871, part 1, pp. 763–765; part 3, pp. 1821–1825.)" Moore, Digest, 5: 220.

[17] The Amiable Isabella, 6 Wheat. 1, 71–73.

[18] *Ibid.,* and *supra,* sec. 107.

(2) What sort of an obligation do they impose? No general answer can be given to the latter question. An executive agreement may impose an absolute obligation as would be true of the executive settlement of a claim by an American citizen against a foreign government. After the President has agreed to a settlement, the claim becomes *res adjudicata* and if against the American citizen, cannot be raised by a subsequent administration against the foreign government. If injustice has been done the American citizen, it is a moral duty of the United States itself to compensate him.[19] On the other hand, an executive agreement may impose an obligation strictly binding only the President, who makes it, as would be true of an exchange of notes over foreign policy, such as the Root-Takahira agreement, or the Lansing-Ishii agreement.

In general, the President can bind only himself and his successors in office by executive agreements, but in certain cases, executive agreements may impose a strong moral obligation upon the treaty-making power and Congress, and they may even be cognizable in the courts. The form of the obligation does not affect its obligatory character. Executive agreements may be by exchange of notes, protocols, cartels, *modi vivendi*, etc., but in any case the obligation depends upon the subject matter.[20]

162. *Administrative Agreements under Authority of Act of Congress.*

To discover the subjects on which the President may make international agreements, we must examine his constitutional powers. For this purpose we may distinguish his powers as (1) head of the administration, (2) as commander-in-chief, (3) as the representative organ in international relations. The President is Chief Executive and head of the Federal administration with power to direct and remove officials and the duty to "take care that the laws be faithfully executed." But the exercise of these powers, and the meeting of this responsibility is dependent upon the laws which Congress may pass, organizing the administration and defin-

---

[19] Meade *v.* U. S., 9 Wall. 691; Borchard, *op. cit.*, p. 379; Comegys *v.* Vasse, 1 Pet. 193, 212.

[20] See also *infra*, sec. 166.

ing the powers and responsibilities of office. In this capacity, therefore, the President may only make international agreements, under authority expressly delegated to him by Congress, or the treaty power, or agreements of a nature which he can carry out within the scope of existing legislation. Congress has often delegated power to the President to make agreements within the scope of a policy defined by statute, on such subjects as postal service, patents, trademarks, copyrights and commerce.[21] Such agreements appear to be dependent for their effectiveness upon the authorizing legislation, and are terminable, both nationally and internationally, at the discretion of Congress.

"It cannot be supposed," wrote Secretary of State Gresham, "that it was intended, by the simple exchange of notes on January 31, 1891, to bind our governments, as by a treaty, to certain duties or remissions of duty on the specified articles, beyond the time when the Congress of the United States might, in the exercise of its constitutional powers, repeal the legislation under which the arrangement was concluded." [22]

While in effect, however, they are binding on the courts,[23] and the President, through his control of the administration, can usually see that they are observed.

163. *Administrative Agreements under Authority of Treaty.*

The administrative powers of the President permit him to carry out treaties, which are the supreme law of the land, so far as Congress has supplied him with the necessary administrative machinery and supplies. International agreements for this purpose, and under express authority of treaty, have been made with reference to the definite marking and mapping of boundaries.[24] Under authority of the treaty with Cuba (1903), as well as of congressional legislation, President Roosevelt acquired a lease at Guantanamo, Cuba, for a naval base.[25] The first Hague Convention of 1899 apparently gave the President power to conclude *compromis* for submitting cases to arbitration, but the Senate has since

---

[21] *Supra,* sec. 61; Taft, *op. cit.,* p. 135.
[22] Moore, Digest, 5: 362.
[23] Field *v.* Clark, 143 U. S. 649.
[24] Crandall, *op. cit.,* pp. 117–118.
[25] *Ibid.,* p. 139.

INTERNATIONAL AGREEMENTS. 237

refused to consent to treaties delegating this power to the President.[26]

164. *Independent Administrative Agreements.*

The President, as head of the administration, may also make international agreements, without express authority of statute or treaty, though it would seem that such agreements should not go beyond his own powers of execution. In 1850, however, President Fillmore authorized an agreement, whereby Great Britain ceded Horseshoe Reef, near the outlet of Lake Erie, on condition that the United States erect a lighthouse thereon, and refrain from fortifying it. The execution of this agreement required congressional appropriation and permanent abstention of Congress from authorizing fortification of this island. It would seem properly a subject for treaty, rather than executive agreement, but Congress had already made the necessary appropriation in 1849. This was reenacted in 1854.[27]

In 1864, President Lincoln agreed to extradite Arguelles to Spain, though no treaty required such action. It has generally been held since, that he exceeded his powers in thus making an agreement for extradition, yet on September 23, 1913, the President entered into an agreement with Great Britain for extradition between the Philippine Islands or Guam and British North Borneo, of fugitives for offenses specified in existing treaties.[28]

165. *Recent Practice.*

Perhaps the most remarkable example of such agreements is that made by President Roosevelt in 1905 for administering the customs houses of San Domingo: [29]

"The Constitution," writes President Roosevelt in his Autobiography, "did not explicitly give me power to bring about the necessary agreement with Santo Domingo. But the Constitution did not forbid my doing what I did. I put the agreement into effect, and I continued its execution for two

---

[26] Willoughby, *op. cit.*, p. 473; Crandall, *op. cit.*, pp. 119-120, *supra*, sec. 62.

[27] Malloy, treaties, etc., p. 663, 9 Stat. 380, 627; 10 Stat. 343.

[28] Crandall, *op. cit.*, p. 117; Corwin, The President's Control of Foreign Relations, p. 125.

[29] Roosevelt, Autobiography, pp. 551-552.

years before the Senate acted; and I would have continued it until the end of my term, if necessary, without any action by Congress. But it was far preferable that there should be action by Congress, so that we might be proceeding under a treaty which was the law of the land, and not merely by a direction of the Chief Executive, which would lapse when that particular Executive left office. I, therefore, did my best to get the Senate to ratify what I had done. There was a good deal of difficulty about it. Enough Republicans were absent to prevent the securing of a two-thirds vote for the treaty, and the Senate adjourned without any action at all, and with the feeling of entire self-satisfaction at having left the country in the position of assuming a responsibility and then failing to fulfill it. Apparently the Senators in question felt that in some way they had upheld their dignity. All that they had really done was to shirk their duty. Somebody had to do that duty, so accordingly I did it. I went ahead and administered the proposed treaty anyhow, considering it as a simple agreement on the part of the Executive which would be converted into a treaty whenever the Senate acted. After a couple of years, the Senate did act, having previously made some utterly unimportant changes, which I ratified and persuaded Santo Domingo to ratify."

This statement indicates that agreements of considerable political importance may be made by the President and that they cannot be prevented by the Senate, when the President controls the necessary means of execution. It is to be noted, however, that in President Roosevelt's opinion, they are binding only on the President that makes them. The latter limitation often does not apply in practice, though presumably the foreign government would have no ground for objection if a subsequent President discontinued such an executive agreement. President Taft describes the executive agreement made by him as Secretary of War, under authority of President Roosevelt, for defining the relative jurisdictions of the United States and Panama in the cities of Colon and Panama at either end of the Canal.[30]

" The plan contained a great many different provisions. I had no power to make a treaty with Panama, but I did have, with the authority of the President, the right to make rules equivalent to law in the Zone. I therefore issued an order directing the carrying out of the plan agreed upon in so far as it was necessary to carry it out on our side of the line, on conditions that, and as long as, the regulations to be made by Panama were enforced by that government. This was approved by Secretary Hay, and the President, and has constituted down until the present day, I believe, the basis upon which the two governments are carried on in this close proximity.

---

[30] Taft, *op. cit.*, p. 112.

It was attacked vigorously in the Senate as a usurpation of the treaty-making power of the Senate and I was summoned before a committee in the Senate to justify what had been done. There was a great deal of eloquence over this usurpation of the Senate's prerogative by Mr. Morgan and other Senators, but the modus vivendi continued as the practical agreement between the nations for certainly more than seven years, and my impression is that it is still in force in most of its provisions."

A similar agreement with Panama was made in October, 1914, for enforcing the neutrality of the Canal during the European war.[31]

166. The Validity of Administrative Agreements.

Other *modi vivendi* made by the President have related to fisheries and boundary lines, pending permanent settlement by treaty or arbitration.[32] With reference to a *modus vivendi* made in 1859 for joint occupation of the Island of San Juan, pending decision of the Fuca sound boundary question, the court said:[33]

"The power to make and enforce such a temporary convention respecting its own territory is a necessary incident to every national government, and adheres where the executive power is vested. Such conventions are not treaties within the meaning of the Constitution, and, as treaties supreme law of the land, conclusive on the courts, but they are provisional arrangements, rendered necessary by national differences involving the faith of the nation and entitled to the respect of the courts. They are not a casting of the national will into the firm and permanent condition of law, and yet in some sort they are for the occasion an expression of the will of the people through their political organ, touching the matters affected; and to avoid unhappy collision between the political and judicial branches of the government, both which are in theory inseparably all one, such an expression to a reasonable limit should be followed by the courts and not opposed, though extending to the temporary restraint or modification of the operation of existing statutes. Just as here, we think, this particular convention respecting San Juan should be allowed to modify for the time being the operation of the organic act of this Territory (Washington) so far forth as to exclude to the extent demanded by the political branch of the government of the United States, in the interest of peace, all territorial interference for the government of that island."

In this case the court had refused to take jurisdiction of a murder committed on the island. Thus the island claimed by the United States, and justly so according to the final arbitration, was removed

---

[31] Naval War College, Int. Law. Docs., 1916, p. 94.
[32] Crandall, *op. cit.*, p. 113.
[33] Watts *v.* U. S., 1 Wash. Terr. 288, 294 (1870); Crandall, *op. cit.*, p. 107.

from the jurisdiction of the territory by executive agreement. Although in theory only temporary, in fact the arbitration was not held until 1871 and the joint occupation continued until 1873, a period of fourteen years.[34] Even longer, however, was the operation of the North Atlantic fisheries *modus vivendi* of 1885, which practically continued until the arbitration of 1909.

After considering such agreements as these, Professor Corwin gives his "final verdict" that "the President's prerogative in the making of international compacts of a temporary nature and not demanding enforcement by the courts, is one that is likely to become larger before it begins to shrink." [35]

167. *The Power to Make Military Agreements.*

As Commander-in-Chief, the President undoubtedly has power to make Cartels for exchange of prisoners of war, suspensions of arms, capitulations and armistices with the enemy. Such agreements may be made by commanding officers in the field if of a local and temporary effect such as a suspension of arms, but if of a general effect such as an armistice, they must be by authority of the Commander-in-Chief.[36] Thus, President Lincoln was justified in repudiating the armistice made by General Sherman with General Johnston in 1865 on the ground that a general armistice was within the President's power alone and General Sherman had exceeded his powers.[37] The same is usually true of licenses to trade. The President was expressly authorized by act of Congress in 1861 to license trade with the enemy. The court held that the power was his alone and condemned a vessel running the blockade to New Orleans with a license from the Collector of Customs in New Orleans authorized by General Banks and approved by Rear Admiral Farragut.[38]

---

[34] Moore, Int. Arbitrations, p. 222.

[35] Corwin, *op. cit.*, p. 112.

[36] Lieber's Instructions, Gen. Ord. 100, 1863, Arts. 135, 140; Halleck, Int. Law, 4th ed. (Baker), 2: 346-347.

[37] *Ibid.*, 2: 356, *supra*, sec. 26.

[38] The Sea Lion, 5 Wall. 630 (1866); Moore, Digest, 7: 255.

168. *Armistices and Preliminaries of Peace.*

But if it is difficult to draw the line separating the power of the President and that of field officers and admirals, it is equally difficult to draw the line between the power of the President as Commander-in-Chief and the treaty-making power. An armistice ending hostilities necessarily contains certain preliminaries of peace. This was true of the preliminaries of peace with Spain of August 12, 1898, and the preliminaries of peace and armistice with Germany of November 5 and 11, 1918. In each, the general conditions of peace were outlined, and in each the defeated enemy alleged that the conditions on which it had agreed to end hostilities were not carried out in the definitive treaty.[39] But though a defeated enemy may have little recourse in such circumstances, a more difficult question is raised, with reference to the obligation of the Senate to consent to the ratification of a treaty in accord with the terms of the armistice. Can the President by ratification of an armistice, containing political terms of peace, oblige the full treaty-power to ratify the same terms in the final treaty? This issue was raised with reference to Article X of the League of Nations Covenant, which though included in the President's XIVth point, and formally agreed to by the allies and Germany in the exchange of notes of November 5, 1918, on the basis of which the armistice of November 11 was made, was rejected by the Senate when it appeared in the final treaty.[40] Clearly an armistice ought not to affect the political terms of peace beyond the minimum necessary to bring hostilities to an end. Within this minimum, however, the President, as Commander-in-Chief, is competent to conclude armistices, and his agreement ought to be observed by the Senate in consenting to the definitive peace treaty. In the protocol of 1901 ending the Boxer uprising in China, the President not only agreed to a termination of military operations, but also to the indemnity which China should pay and other conditions, such as razing forts, and improving watercourses in which she would cooperate.[41]

---

[39] On the obligation of armistices see Moore, 7: 336, *supra,* sec. 30, note 54.
[40] *Supra,* sec. 30; Wright, *Minn. Law Rev.,* 4: 35.
[41] Crandall, *op. cit.,* p. 104, *infra,* sec. 251.

169. *Validity of Military Agreements.*

The President's power as Commander-in-Chief permits him to conclude agreements in time of peace as well as war. So President Monroe agreed to a delimitation of armaments on the Great Lakes in 1817, which, however, he submitted a year later to the Senate, where it received ratification as a treaty. A series of agreements were made with Mexico between 1882 and 1896 for the mutual pursuit of border Indians and the President has often authorized the transit of foreign troops across the territory, a power thus justified by the Supreme Court:[42]

"While no act of Congress authorizes the executive department to permit the introduction of foreign troops, the power to give such permission without legislative assent was probably assumed to exist from the authority of the President as Commander-in-Chief of the military and naval forces of the United States."

In a dissenting opinion in this case, Justice Gray thought that foreign troops could be admitted only by express consent of the nation which "must rest upon express treaty or statute." "It is not necessary," he added, "to consider the full extent of the power of the President in such matters." In spite of this dissent the power has been exercised by the President on many occasions and is cognizable in the courts because it brings into operation the accepted principle of international law, that armed troops and public vessels of foreign powers, within the territory by permission, are exempt from jurisdiction.[43] An anology may be made between the power of the President as Commander-in-Chief to permit the entry of foreign military forces, and his power as the representative organ to receive foreign diplomatic officers. In both cases, the President's act entitles the foreign agency to exemption from jurisdiction.[44]

Most military agreements have been temporary in duration and of a character to be fulfilled by the President in the exercise of his independent power as Commander-in-Chief. The power of admitting troops may, however, require cooperation of the courts and

---

[42] Tucker *v.* Alexandroff, 183 U. S. 424, 435.
[43] The Exchange *v.* McFaddon, 7 Cranch 116, 139.
[44] *In re* Baiz, 135 U. S. 403.

the power to make armistices and preliminaries of peace may require cooperation of the treaty power. An agreement of permanent character, and limiting Congress as well as the President ought, doubtless, to be by treaty, as was ultimately decided of the Great Lakes disarmament agreement of 1817.

170. *Power to Make Diplomatic Agreements.*

Because of his power to "receive ambassadors and other public ministers" and to negotiate treaties, the President is the representative organ of the government and the sole organ of foreign communication. As such he has certain powers of agreement making. Thus agreements, usually by exchange of notes, defining executive policy have often been concluded. The Hay open door policy of 1899-1900, the Root-Takahira and Lansing-Ishii agreements of 1908 and 1917, defining American policy in the Far East, and the Gentlemen's agreement of 1907, relating to Japanese immigration, are of this character. Such agreements are in strictness binding only on the President under whose authority they are made, but if not repudiated would be presumed to have been accepted by a succeeding President. Thus Secretary Lansing in publishing the Lansing-Ishii agreement stated that it was a reaffirmation of the "open door" policy.[45]

Of similar character are agreements to conclude treaties. We have referred to preliminaries of peace made under the President's power as Commander-in-Chief. From his power as representative organ, the President has agreed to negotiate treaties on specified subjects. Thus an agreement preliminary to the treaty submitting the Behring Sea case to arbitration and agreements for negotiating canal treaties with Costa Rica and Nicaragua have been made.[46] Such agreements merely require that treaty negotiations be attempted. They would seem to impose no obligation upon the Senate to accept the treaty or at most an extremely attenuated obligation.

---

[45] League of Nations (World Peace Foundation, Boston), I, No. 8, p. 459.

[46] Crandall, *op. cit.*, p. 111.

171. *Diplomatic Agreements Settling Controversies.*

The most frequent types of agreement made under the President's representative powers are those settling international controversies. Unless authorized by express treaty or act of Congress this power is confined to the settlement of claims by American citizens against foreign governments. Such settlement of individual claims may be made either by direct negotiation, or by submission of the case to a conciliation commission or to arbitration. J. B. Moore states that thirty-one cases have been settled directly by formal executive agreement, and twenty-seven by arbitration based on executive agreement. In nineteen such cases formal treaties have been made for submitting the case to arbitration.[47]

The settlement of foreign claims against the United States or of national claims involving territory, maritime jurisdiction, belligerent and neutral rights, etc., has generally been by treaty, or by arbitration authorized by treaty.[48] In a few cases of foreign pecuniary claims, the President through the Secretary of State has agreed to urge upon Congress the justice of the claim, but he has never assumed to bind the United States to pay such a claim without a treaty.[49] Should he do so, doubtless the foreign government would be entitled to hold the United States bound, since in reference to the meeting of international responsibilities, the representative organ speaks for the nation under international law.[50]

"In two instances claims of foreigners against the United States were submitted to arbitral tribunals by executive agreement, but in both instances it was expressly provided that any awards that might be made should be a claim, not against the United States, but solely against the estates of certain American citizens, whose estates were to be adjusted before the same arbitral tribunal." [51]

---

[47] Moore, *Pol. Sci. Quar.*, 20: 414.
[48] Foster, *Yale Law Jl.*, 11: 77 (Dec., 1901); Moore, Digest, 5: 211; Willoughby, *op. cit.*, p. 469.
[49] See attitude of the Executive in Chinese and Italian Lynching cases, 1890-1901, Moore, Digest, 6: 834, 842.
[50] *Supra*, sec. 34.
[51] C. C. Hyde, "Agreements of the United States other than Treaties," Greenbag, 17: 233, cited Willoughby, *op. cit.*, p. 469.

172. *Validity of Diplomatic Agreements.*

The President may and must interpret treaties and international law in applying their rules and principles for the settlement of claims of American citizens but he has no power to make general interpretations of treaty, or of international law. In fact, however, his decisions establish precedents, which his successors will find it difficult to avoid. Thus the agreement of President McKinley to accept the last three principles of the Declaration of Paris, during the Spanish war, would doubtless go far toward establishing these principles as international law obligatory upon the United States in future wars.[52] The President has no authority to agree to general interpretations or reservations to treaties. Such documents are not valid unless consented to by the Senate.[53] But the precedents established by presidential interpretation in particular cases may amount to an authoritative interpretation. Thus the Spanish Treaty Claims Commission felt justified in applying Article VII of the treaty with Spain of 1795, which forbade the "embargo or detention" of "vessels or effects" of subjects or citizens of the other contracting power, to detention of goods on land. The negotiators of the treaty appear to have intended application only to property at sea. No question was raised for over seventy years, after which the American Secretary of State consistently maintained the broad interpretation.[54]

"Whether or not," said the court, "the clause was originally intended to embrace real estate and personal property on land as well as vessels and their cargoes, the same has been so construed by the United States and this construction has been concurred in by Spain; and therefore the commission will adhere to such construction in making its decisions."

"There is," says President Taft, "much practical framing of our foreign policies in the executive conduct of our foreign relations."[55]

---

[52] Proclamations and Decrees during the war with Spain, p. 77.

[53] *Supra*, secs. 27, 28.

[54] General Principles adopted April 28, 1903, No. 10, Special Report, Wm. E. Fuller, Washington, 1907, p. 23; Crandall, *op. cit.*, p. 384. Executive interpretation of the Alaska Purchase treaty was followed by the court in determining the extent of jurisdiction in Behring Sea prior to the arbitration, and in general the court follows executive interpretation of political questions (*supra*, sec. 107).

[55] Taft, *op. cit.*, p. 113; *supra*, sec. 38.

Though in theory the President's independent power is confined to making agreements of temporary effect, confined to particular cases or binding the Executive alone, yet in practice and by the operation of precedents he may, by such agreements, bind other departments and through interpretations of treaties and international law bind the state as a whole.

B. *The Power to Make Treaties.*

173. *The Subject Matter of Treaties.*

The framers of the American Constitution did not anticipate or desire the conclusion of many treaties.[56] For this reason they made the process of treaty conclusion difficult, requiring that the President act only with the advice and consent of two-thirds of the Senators present,[57] some even wishing to require adhesion of the House of Representatives[58] or two-thirds majority of the entire Senate.[59] This hope, however, has scarcely been realized. With a total of 595 treaties from its foundation to August, 1914, the United States

---

[56] In the Federal Convention, Gouverneur Morris "was not solicitous to multiply and facilitate treaties," and Madison "observed that it had been too easy in the present Congress to make treaties, although nine States were required for that purpose." Farrand, Records of the Federal Convention, 2: 393, 548. See also Jefferson, Manual of Congressional Practice, sec. 52, and letter to Madison, March 23, 1815, Moore, Int. Law Digest, 5: 162, 310.

[57] Under the Articles of Confederation, the treaty-making power was vested in nine States in Congress (Art. IX), and in some of the early drafts of the Constitution it was vested in Congress (Farrand, 2: 143), later in the Senate (*ibid.*, 2: 169, 183), and the President was finally added on the argument that treaty-making was properly an executive function (*ibid.*, 2: 297), and that a national agency was necessary as an offset to the special State interest of the Senate. (*Ibid.*, 2: 392.)

[58] Pennsylvania especially desired this. G. Morris, of that State, wanted to add "but no treaty shall be binding on the United States which is not ratified by a law" (Farrand, 2: 297, 392). Later, Wilson, of Pennsylvania, proposed to add "and House of Representatives," saying that "as treaties are to have the operation of laws they ought to have the sanction of laws also." On vote, Pennsylvania alone supported the motion. (*Ibid.*, 2: 538.) This is the vote referred to by Washington in his celebrated message on the Jay Treaty where he refused to recognize the claim of the House of Representatives to participate in treaty-making. (*Ibid.*, 3: 371; Annals of Congress, 4th Cong., 1st Sess., p. 761, Richardson, Messages, 1: 195.)

[59] Farrand, 2: 549.

has averaged more than four a year, and for the twentieth century, fifteen a year, or a treaty ratified every three weeks.[60] And this, in spite of the frequent differences between the President and the Senate often resulting in the failure to ratify.[61]

These treaties have been on a very wide variety of subjects. The United States has ratified treaties *politically* organizing international society. Such have been alliances, as that with France in 1778; guarantees of territory or neutrality as in the French treaty of 1778 (Art. XI), the treaty with New Granada or Colombia of 1846 (Art. XXXV), with Panama in 1903 (Art. I), and with Haiti in 1916 (Art. XIV); limitations of the power to declare war by requiring delay as in the twenty Bryan treaties of 1914 or by limiting the objects for which force may be used as in the II Hague Convention of 1907; and limitations of armament as in the Great Lakes agreement of 1817. The United States has also ratified many treaties *administratively* organizing international society, such as postal, telegraphic, cable, radio, sanitary, slave trade, fishery, migratory bird and other conventions. It has become a party to treaties *legally* organizing international society through the definition of principles of international law as in the Geneva and Hague Conventions, through the establishment of international courts and arbitration tribunals and through the agreement to submit certain types of cases to arbitration. Finally there have been treaties of annexation and boundary, treaties settling claims, treaties of commerce and navigation, consular and extradition conventions, and conventions defining the rights of aliens.[62]

No treaty has ever been declared unconstitutional.[63] By practice, by the terms in which the power is granted in the Constitution,

---

[60] By 25-year periods, treaties have been concluded as follows: 1778–1799, 21; 1800–1824, 20; 1825–1849, 63; 1850–1874, 141; 1875–1899, 142; 1900–1914, 208. This is in accord with the official enumeration of treaties (excluding Indian treaties), begun by the Department of State on January 29, 1908, with Treaty Series, No. 489. (See Check-list of U. S. Public Documents, 1911, p. 978.) Including the protocols and *modi vivendi* printed in Malloy and Charles' Collections, the total for the period would be 633.

[61] *Infra*, sec. 177.

[62] See Foster, Practice of Diplomacy, pp. 243–244.

[63] Corwin, National Supremacy, p. 5; Anderson, *Am. Jl. Int. Law*, 1: 647; Willoughby, *op. cit.*, p. 493, *supra*, sec. 46.

and by direct statement of the supreme court,[64] we may be certain that the power extends to "any matter which is properly the subject of negotiations with a foreign country," limited only by express or implied constitutional prohibitions the effect of which is in the main confined to the means through which the purposes of the treaty may be attained.[65]

174. *The Initiation of Treaties.*

Treaties may of course be initiated or suggested by a foreign power, but if by the United States, the initiative has ordinarily been taken by the President. Congress has sometimes suggested negotiations by joint or concurrent resolutions originating in the House of Representatives as well as the Senate. Thus resolutions of 1890, 1897, and 1910 suggested the negotiation of arbitration treaties and acts of 1916 and 1921, negotiations for general disarmament. A resolution of 1904 suggested the negotiation of a treaty for protecting the Behring Sea seals and one of 1909 the protection of American citizens in Russia. In most of these cases, negotiations were attempted, not always with success (at least once, success was frustrated by the Senate veto), but says Crandall:[66]

"Although it is not to be doubted that the President will always give careful consideration to the views of Congress, deliberately expressed as to instituting negotiations, he cannot be compelled to exercise a power entrusted to him under the Constitution by a resolution of either house or of both houses of Congress."

The reason was pointed out in a report of the Senate foreign relations committee in 1815:

"Since the President conducts correspondence with foreign nations, he would be more competent to determine when, how and upon what subjects negotiations could be urged with the greatest prospect of success."[67]

---

[64] Geofroy *v.* Riggs, 133 U. S. 258 (1890); Wright, The Constitutionality of Treaties, *Am. Jl. Int. Law*, 13: 262.

[65] *Supra*, secs. 67–69.

[66] Crandall, *op. cit.*, p. 74.

[67] Compilation of Reports of the Senate Committee on Foreign Relations, Sen. Doc., No. 231, 56th Cong., 2d Sess., 8; 22; Crandall, *op. cit.*, p. 75; Hayden, *op. cit.*, p. 206, *infra*, sec. 203.

175. *The Appointment of Negotiators.*

Before 1815, special missions, appointed by the President with advice and consent of the Senate, were sent to conclude the most important treaties, although a number of less important missions, such as that of John Paul Jones to Algeria in 1792, were commissioned by the President alone. Since 1815 "treaties have, with few exceptions, been negotiated through the Secretary of State, the regular diplomatic representatives and consular officers, or special agents, empowered and commissioned to negotiate the treaty by the President without special confirmation for this purpose by the Senate." [68] Commissioners to the Panama Congress of 1826, to negotiate the treaty of Washington with Great Britain in 1871, and to negotiate with China in 1880 appear to be the only special missions consented to by the Senate since the war of 1812. Possibly the difficulty which President Madison encountered in getting the Senate to consent to the appointments of commissioners for concluding the treaty of Ghent ending that war, accounts in part for this fact. Over four hundred commissioners and agents have been authorized to negotiate by the President alone, including the important missions ending the Mexican, Spanish and World Wars, and the missions representing the United States at the two Hague, the Algeciras, the Versailles and the limitation of armament conferences. The Senate objected to this practice of negotiating through presidential agents in the case of the Korean treaty of 1882, but in 1888 and in 1893 the Senate Foreign Relations Committee recognized the legitimacy of the practice.[69]

"The President of the United States," said Senator Sherman, Chairman of the Committee in 1888, "has the power to propose treaties subject to ratification by the Senate, and he may use such agencies as he chooses to employ, except that he cannot take any money from the treasury to pay these agents without an appropriation by law. He can use such instruments as he pleases."

176. *The Negotiation and Signature of Treaties.*

Negotiation and signature have usually been under authority of the President alone. He has usually prepared the instructions and

---

[68] Crandall, *op. cit.*, p. 76.
[69] Cong. Rec., Aug. 7, 1888, p. 7285. See also *infra, secs.* 239, 240.

250 THE CONTROL OF AMERICAN FOREIGN RELATIONS.

full powers of the negotiators. Not since the first few years of the Republic have these been submitted to the Senate. In about eighteen instances the advice of the Senate has been sought by the President prior to signature of the treaty and almost half of these cases occurred in the administration of Washington, prior to the negotiation of the Jay treaty (1794) which established the precedent of Presidential independence in negotiation.[70] Only once was advice sought by the President in person and on that occasion, a few months after the Constitution went into operation, President Washington's experiences were such that an eye witness described his departure from the Senate chamber as "with sullen dignity" and "a disconsolate air."[71] On the few occasions since this experience when Senate advice has been sought before signature, it has been by message responded to by Senate resolution. Thus in 1830 President Jackson sought the advice of the Senate on an Indian treaty prior to signature, but in doing so apologized "for departing from a long and for many years an unbroken usage in similar cases," which departure he thought justified by distinctive considerations applicable to Indian treaties. In only ten later cases has such prior advice been sought, though informal conferences with individual senators or with the Senate Foreign Relations Committee have been more frequent.[72]

"The fact," said Senator Bacon in 1906, "that he (Washington) conferred personally with the Senate as to the propriety of making treaties before attempting to negotiate them, shows what he understood to be the intention of the Convention—that the Senate should be not simply the body to say yes or no to the President when he proposed a treaty, but that the Senate should be the advisor of the President whether he should attempt to negotiate a treaty. What possible doubt can there be under such circumstances as to what was his understanding of the purpose and intention of those who framed the Constitution? And what possible doubt can there be that his understanding was correct? . . . It is true that that practice

---

[70] Hayden, *op. cit.*, p. 80.

[71] Maclay, Sketches of Debates in the First Senate of the United States, G. W. Harris, ed., p. 125. See also Crandall, *op. cit.*, 67–68; Hayden, *op. cit.*, 18–27, and *infra,* sec. 260.

[72] Senate debate, Feb. 6, 1906, cited *supra*, sec. 76, note 16. See also Richardson, Messages, 2: 478. See also Senator Lodge, *Scribners,* 31: 33, Sen. Doc. 104, 57th Cong., 1st Sess.; and Crandall, *op. cit.*, pp. 68–72, 75.

has been abandoned, so far as concerns the President coming in person to sit in a chair on the right of the presiding officer to confer with members of the Senate, as our rules still provide he shall do should he come here personally, showing we recognize the propriety of his coming and his right to come.[73] But nevertheless during my official term it has been the practice of Presidents and Secretaries of State to confer with Senators as to the propriety of negotiating or attempting to negotiate a treaty.

"I know in my own experience that it was the frequent practice of Secretary Hay, not simply after a proposed treaty had been negotiated, but before he had ever conferred with the representatives of the foreign power, to seek to have conferences with Senators to know what they thought of such and such a proposition; and if the subject-matter was a proper matter for negotiation, what Senators thought as to certain provisions; and he advised with them as to what provisions should be incorporated.

"I recollect two treaties in particular. One is the general arbitration treaty. I do not know whether he conferred with all Senators, but I think he did. I think he conferred with every Senator in this Chamber, either in writing or in person, as to the general arbitration treaty. He certainly conferred with me."

Such informal conferences clearly lack legal significance. They do not bind the Senate in any way.[74] The practice, however, indicates the development of an important constitutional understanding.[75]

On some occasions, notably for concluding the Treaty of Paris ending the Spanish war, Senators have been appointed as commissioners to negotiate, a practice deplored by Senator Hoar on the grounds that it prevents an independent consideration of the treaty by the Senate.[76]

Signature of treaties has, since very early times, been under the authority of the President alone. On several occasions the American negotiators have appended reservations to their signatures of multilateral treaties such as the Hague Conventions.[77]

---

[73] But see opinion of Senator Lodge, *infra*, sec. 266, note 35.

[74] See Senator Spooner's suggestion following Senator Bacon's remarks, and Corwin, *op. cit.*, p. 188, footnote.

[75] *Infra*, sec. 266, par. 4.

[76] *Cong. Rec.*, 57th Cong., 2d Sess., p. 2695; Senator Hoar, Autobiography, 2: 50; Crandall, *op. cit.*, p. 78; Corwin, *op. cit.*, p. 66. Senators Lodge and Underwood were appointed delegates to the conference on limitation of armament, 1921.

[77] Crandall, *op. cit.*, pp. 76, 93; Scott, ed., Reports of the Hague Conferences, Introduction, pp. xxv *et seq.*; A. D. White, Autobiography, 2: 339–341.

177. Consent to the Ratification of Treaties.

The need of Senate consent to treaties is absolute, consequently the Senate may reject a treaty altogether, though, according to Jay, such action would be improper if it had consented to the full powers and instructions of the negotiators and these instructions had been faithfully observed.[78] But with the present practice of presidential negotiation and signature, this limitation is unimportant. Of about 650 signed treaties the Senate has refused consent to ratification of about twenty.[79] Among the more important treaties thus vetoed may be mentioned commercial and reciprocity treaties with Switzerland, 1835; with the German Zollverein, 1844; with Great Britain for Canada in settlement of the fisheries question, 1888; and the Kasson reciprocity treaties of 1899; annexation treaties with Texas, 1844; Hawaii, 1855; San Domingo, 1869; and Denmark for the Virgin Islands, 1868; arbitration and claims treaties including the Johnson-Clarendon treaty for settlement of the Alabama claims, 1868; and the Olney-Pauncefote general arbitration treaty with Great Britain, 1897; canal treaties with Colombia, 1869 and 1870; the Knox financial administration treaties with Nicaragua and Honduras, 1911; and the Treaty of Versailles, 1920. It is to be noticed that in most of these cases, the end sought was eventually achieved, though in the cases of annexation of Hawaii and the Virgin Islands, and settlement of the Canadian fisheries question, not until many years later. This practice appears to conflict with the assertion of John Quincy Adams as Secretary of State, that the King of Spain was under an absolute obligation to ratify the Florida purchase treaty of 1819 on failure of which the United States would be entitled " to compel the performance of the engagement as far as compulsion can accomplish it."[80] Other Secretaries of State have

---

[78] Crandall, *op. cit.*, p. 79, *supra*, sec. 25.

[79] Crandall, *op. cit.*, p. 82; Moore, Digest, 3: 26; Latané, U. S. and Latin America, N. Y., 1920, p. 283; Jones, Caribbean Interests of the U. S., N. Y., 1916, pp. 170, 179. For resolution rejecting Treaty of Versailles, see Cong. Rec., March 19, 1920, 59: 4916. For summary of Senate Proceedings on this treaty see League of Nations (World Peace Foundation), vol. 3, No. 4. For Proceedings in cases of treaties rejected by the Senate see 66th Cong., 1st Sess., Sen. Doc. No. 26, pp. 80 *et seq.*

[80] Moore, Digest, 5: 189-190.

explained, however, that the United States is under no similar obligation to ratify negotiated treaties, because the other party is presumed to understand the lack of identity between the negotiating and ratifying authorities under our Constitution, even when the right of reservation has not, as it has in most cases, been expressly reserved in the full powers of the negotiators.[81]

The Senate's right to qualify its consent to ratification by reservations, amendments and interpretations was established through a reservation to the Jay treaty of 1794,[82] has been exercised in about seventy cases,[83] and has been judicially recognized.[84]

"In this country a treaty is something more than a contract, for the Federal Constitution declares it to be the law of the land. If so, before it can become a law, the Senate, in whom rests the authority to ratify or approve it, must agree to it. But the Senate are not required to adopt or reject it as a whole, but may modify or amend it."

A refusal of the Senate either to reject or consent to ratification is of questionable propriety. Senator Sumner of Massachusetts, as Chairman of the Senate Foreign Relations Committee, succeeded in keeping the treaty for cession of the Virgin Islands by Denmark, submitted to it on December 3, 1867, pigeon-holed for over two years, when it was finally rejected.[85]

The Senate may suggest interpretations or pass resolutions not qualifying its consent to a treaty, as it did in the case of the Treaty of Paris ending the Spanish war. A majority of the Senate passed a resolution favoring the ultimate independence of the Philippines but the court held that such resolutions are legally of no effect.

---

[81] *Supra*, sec. 26; Moore, Digest, 5: 200; Crandall, *op. cit.*, p. 94.

[82] Hayden, *op. cit.*, p. 75.

[83] Senator Lodge, *loc. cit., supra*, note 67; Crandall, *op. cit.*, pp. 79–81; Treaty Reservations by Foreign Powers and the United States, Sen. Doc. 72, 67th Cong., 1st Sess., 1921; David Hunter Miller, Reservations to Treaties, N. Y., 1919; Q. Wright, Amendments and Reservations to the Treaty, Minn. L. R., 4: 14.

[84] Haver *v.* Yaker, 9 Wall. 32. See also Brown, J., in Fourteen Diamond Rings *v.* U. S., 183 U. S. 176 (1901); Willoughby, *op. cit.*, p. 462.

[85] Moore, Digest, 1: 610. The French guarantee treaty, signed at the same time as the treaty of Versailles, appears to have been reposing in the archives of the Senate Foreign Relations Committee since its submission to the Senate by President Wilson in 1919.

"The meaning of the treaty," said the Supreme Court, "cannot be controlled by subsequent explanations of some of those who may have voted to ratify it." [86]

178. The Ratification of Treaties.

The final act of ratification belongs to the President.[87] He may refuse to submit a treaty to the Senate altogether as he has done in nine instances; he may submit it with recommendations for amendment as he has done in eleven cases; he may withdraw it from the Senate before that body has voted on it, illustrated by ten cases; and he may refuse to ratify a treaty consented to by the Senate with or without reservations as he has done in fifteen cases.[88] Thus Presidents Roosevelt and Taft each abandoned arbitration treaties when it appeared that the Senate was prepared to insist upon essential alterations.[89] As he is the best judge of the advisability of initiating negotiations on a given subject, so he is the best judge of the probability of a foreign nation accepting reservations or amendments. Foreign nations sometimes regard it as a discourtesy to have modifications of a negotiated treaty presented to them as an ultimatum, without their having had an opportunity to discuss them.[90] It is therefore often advisable for the President to abandon a treaty which he thinks will probably be unacceptable to the other signatory.

179. The Exchange of Ratifications.

The exchange of ratifications is performed under authority of the President and makes the treaty internationally binding.[91] The other party to the treaty may refuse to accept Senate amendments

---

[86] Fourteen Diamond Rings v. U. S., 183 U. S. 176. See also N. Y. Indians v. U. S., 170 U. S. 1 (1898); Moore, Digest, 5: 210; Crandall, op. cit., p. 88; supra, sec. 27.

[87] Shepherd v. Insurance Co., 40 Fed. 341, 347; Willoughby, op. cit., p. 466; Crandall, op. cit., pp. 81, 94, 97; Taft, op. cit., p. 106; Black. Constitutional Law, p. 124; Foster, op. cit., p. 274; Senator Spooner of Wis., debate referred to supra, sec. 76, note 16; Moore, Digest, 5: 202.

[88] Crandall, op. cit., pp. 95, 99.

[89] Ibid., p. 98; Taft, op. cit., p. 106; Charles, Treaties, etc., p. 380.

[90] Willoughby, op. cit., p. 464, and supra, sec. 26.

[91] Crandall, op. cit., p. 93, and supra, sec. 29.

or reservations in which case the treaty fails. Thus Great Britain rejected, after Senate alteration, a boundary settlement treaty in 1803, a slave trade convention in 1824 and the first Hay-Pauncefote Canal treaty in 1900.[92] During exchange of ratifications, however, no new interpretations or reservations should be made. The President's representatives exchanged explanations to the Mexican peace treaty of 1848 and Clayton-Bulwer canal treaty with Great Britain of 1850 on exchange of ratifications, but, not having been submitted to the Senate, these explanations were of doubtful validity. Napoleon reserved on the treaty of 1801, at exchange of ratifications, but President Jefferson promptly resubmitted the treaty to the Senate which consented to the new reservation. This has been the usual practice.[93]

180. *The Proclamation of Treaties.*

After ratifications have been exchanged, the treaty must be proclaimed to have validity as the law of the land and this act is in the power of the President alone.[94] As an international obligation the treaty is binding from exchange of ratifications and such obligation is held to date back to the time of signature.[95] As a law binding individuals, however, the rule is different:[96]

"As the individual citizen, on whose rights of property it operates, has no means of knowing anything of it while before the Senate, it would be wrong in principle to hold him bound by it, as the law of the land, until it was ratified and proclaimed. And to construe the law, so as to make the ratification of the treaty relate back to its signing, thereby divesting a title already vested, would be manifestly unjust, and cannot be sanctioned."

Thus a secret treaty might be internationally binding in the United States but it could not be the supreme law of the land. We must, therefore, regard proclamation as the first step in the execution of a treaty rather than the last step in its making. A treaty which is not self-executing may require legislation in addition to procla-

---

[92] Moore, Digest, 5: 199–200; Hayden, *op. cit.,* p. 145; *supra,* sec. 26.
[93] Crandall, *op. cit.,* pp. 85–92; and *supra,* sec. 27.
[94] Crandall, *op. cit.,* pp. 94–95; Moore, Digest, 5: 210.
[95] Haver *v.* Yaker, 9 Wall. 32, *supra,* secs. 15, 29.
[96] *Ibid.* See also Rev. Stat., sec. 210; Comp. Stat., sec. 308, and *supra,* sec. 15, note 14.

mation to be executable. The power to perform such acts has been considered elsewhere.[97]

C. The Power to Terminate Treaties.

181. *Change in Conditions.*

Certain provisions of treaty may be terminated by war. The courts have power, in controversies coming before them, to distinguish, on the basis of international law, those provisions of treaty thus affected, from those which are unaffected or merely suspended during the war, in case the political organs of the government have made no decision.[98] In controversies with foreign governments, the President may recognize these distinctions. Certain provisions may become obsolete by a change of material conditions, through operation of the implied clause "rebus sic stantibus." It belongs to the President as the representative organ to decide when treaty provisions are thus terminated.[99]

182. *Violation of Treaty by One Party.*

Treaties may become voidable by reason of violation by the other party and question has been raised whether the power to declare such a treaty void rests with Congress or the treaty-making power.[100] Justice Iredell thought the power belonged to Congress[101] and on July 7, 1798, Congress held that it had the power when it declared that:[102]

"Whereas the treaties concluded between the United States and France have been repeatedly violated on the part of the French government; and the just claims of the United States for reparation of the injuries so committed have been refused, and their attempts to negotiate an amicable adjustment of all complaints between the two nations have been repelled with indignity, etc.," therefore, "Be it enacted . . . That the United States are of right freed and exonerated from the stipulations of the treaties and of the

---

[97] *Supra*, chap. x and sec. 137.
[98] Society for the Propagation of the Gospel *v.* New Haven, 8 Wheat. 464, 494 (1823), Moore, Digest, 5: 372–386.
[99] Moore, Digest, 3: 190; 5: 335–341; *supra*, sec. 107, note 63.
[100] Mr. Madison to Mr. Pendleton, Jan. 2, 1791, *ibid.*, 5: 321.
[101] Ware *v.* Hylton, 3 Dall. 199, 261 (1796). *Infra*, sec. 187.
[102] 1 Stat., 578; Moore, Digest, 5: 356; Richardson, Messages, 7: 518.

INTERNATIONAL AGREEMENTS. 257

consular convention, heretofore concluded between the United States and France; and that the same shall not henceforth be regarded as legally obligatory on the Government or citizens of the United States."

This appears to be the only case of the kind. The courts have repeatedly held that until the political departments have acted they are bound to apply voidable treaties.[103]

"If the attitude of Italy was, as contended, a violation of the obligation of the treaty, which in international law would have justified the United States in denouncing the treaty as no longer obligatory, it did not automatically have that effect. If the United States elected not to declare its abrogation, or come to a rupture, the treaty would remain in force. It was only voidable, not void; and if the United States should prefer, it might waive any breach which in its judgment had occurred and conform to its own obligations as if there had been no such breach. 1 Kent's Comm., p. 175."

183. *Conclusion of New Treaty.*

Treaties may be terminated by negotiation of a new treaty by the same parties, for which the treaty power alone is competent. Thus in vetoing the Chinese exclusion act of 1879 President Hayes wrote:[104]

"The bill before me does not enjoin upon the President the abrogation of the entire Burlingame treaty, much less of the principal treaty of which it is the supplement. As the power of modifying an existing treaty, whether by adding or striking out provisions, is a part of the treaty-making power under the Constitution, its exercise is not competent for Congress, nor would the assent of China to this partial abrogation of the treaty make the action of Congress in thus procuring an amendment of a treaty a competent exercise of authority under the Constitution."

Provisions of an earlier treaty will of course be superseded by conflicting provisions of a later treaty between the same parties,[105] but in order to terminate the earlier treaty as a whole the intention so to do must be clearly expressed, as was indicated by the controversy over effect of the proposed Hay-Pauncefote canal treaty of 1900

---

[103] Charlton *v.* Kelly, 229 U. S. 447; Ware *v.* Hylton, 3 Dall. 199, 261 (1796); *In re* Thomas, 12 Blatch 370; Terlinden *v.* Ames, 184 U. S. 270, 288 (1902); Doe *v.* Braden, 16 How. 638; Jones *v.* Walker, 2 Paine 688; Moore, Digest, 5: 320; Willoughby, *op. cit.,* p. 1007, *supra,* sec. 107, note 63.
[104] Richardson, Messages, 7: 519.
[105] Cushing, Att. Gen., 6 Op. 291; Wright, *Am. Jl. Int. Law,* 11: 576; Moore, Digest, 5: 363-4.

and the actual treaty of 1901 upon the Clayton-Bulwer treaty of 1850.[106]

184. *Denunciation by Congress.*

Finally a treaty may be terminated by denunciation, according to its own terms. A period of six months' to a year's notice is usually required. There has been question whether notice should be given by Congress, by the treaty-making power or by the President, and examples can be found of each practice. Congress has frequently passed resolutions of denunciation as it did of the British treaties of 1827 in 1846; of 1854 in 1866; and of 1871 in 1885 as to certain articles. The President has usually carried out such resolutions, but in 1865, even though he had signed a congressional resolution which "adopted" and "ratified" his notice for terminating the Great Lakes disarmament agreement of 1817, President Lincoln withdrew the notice and the treaty continued effective.[107] President Hayes doubted the competence of Congress to direct the President to negotiate modifications of an existing treaty and pointed out that unless a treaty expressly provided for partial denunciation such a step would be impossible.[108]

"As the other high contracting party has entered into no treaty obligations except such as include the part denounced, the denunciation by one party of the part necessarily liberates the other party from the whole treaty."

President Wilson, however, conducted negotiations for modification of all treaty provisions in conflict with the La Follette Seaman's Act of March 1915 as directed by Section 16 of that Act. He, however, refused to act under the like direction of Article 34 of the Jones Merchant Marine Act of June 5, 1920. It would seem, therefore, that the President is the final authority to denounce a treaty,

---

[106] Moore, Digest, 3: 212 *et seq.* Sir Edward Grey, British Sec. of State for Foreign Affairs, to British Ambassador Bryce, Nov. 14, 1912, Diplomatic History of the Panama Canal, 63d Cong., 2d Sess., Sen. Doc. 474, pp. 85–86.

[107] Fifty-sixth Cong., 1st Sess., House Doc., No. 471, pp. 32–34; Crandall, *op. cit.*, p. 462.

[108] Richardson, Messages, 7: 519.

and while he may not be able to give notice without consent of Congress or other authority, he cannot be compelled to act by Congress. This would be in accord with the general practice of presidential independence in conducting foreign relations.[109]

185. *Denunciation by the Treaty-Making Power.*

The Senate has contended that consent of the House of Representatives to the denunciation of a treaty is not necessary and the Danish treaty of 1826 was denounced by the President with consent of the Senate alone. This method was questioned by Senator Sumner on the ground that it was the repeal of a law to which Congress must assent, but was sustained by the Foreign Relations Committee:[110]

> "As to this convention, and all others of like character, the committee are clear in the opinion that it is competent for the President and Senate, acting together, to terminate it in the manner prescribed by the 11th article (of the treaty) without the aid or intervention of legislation by Congress, and that when so terminated it is at an end to every extent, both as a contract between the governments and as a law of the land."

186. *Denunciation by the President.*

Finally there have been several examples of denunciation by the President alone. President Taft tells of his denunciation of the Russian treaty of 1832 in 1911. The issue had arisen over Russian persecution of American Jews:[111]

> "The resolution of the House of Representatives was drawn in language which would have given offense to Russia, as doubtless its framers intended to do. With the responsibility of maintaining as friendly relations as possible with all the world, it seemed to me that if the treaty had to be abrogated, it ought to be done as politely as possible, with the hope of negotiating a new treaty less subject to dispute, and giving more satisfactory results. With the knowledge that the resolution was sure to pass the Senate, I took the step of annulling the treaty myself and giving a year's notice to Russia of the annulment in proper and courteous expressions, on the ground that we had differed so radically as to its construction and the treaty was so old that it would be wiser to make a new treaty more

---

[109] See *infra,* secs. 174, 202, 203.

[110] Thirty-fourth Cong., 1st Sess., Senate Report, No. 97, reprinted in *Cong. Rec.,* Nov. 8, 1919, 58: 8605. See also Message of Pres. Pierce, Dec. 3, 1855, Richardson, Messages, 3: 334; Crandall, *op. cit.,* p. 459.

[111] Taft, *op. cit.,* pp. 116–117.

definite and satisfactory. I sent notice of this annulment at once to the Senate, and in this way succeeded in having the Senate substitute a resolution approving my action for the resolution which came over from the House. The House was thus induced to approve my action and the incident was closed for the time."

The Swiss treaty of 1850 appears to have been denounced by the President alone in 1899.[112] Willoughby approves this method of denunciation, but thinks "in important cases the President would undoubtedly seek senatorial approval before taking action."[113] Although the power may seem sustainable by analogy to the President's power of removal without consent of the Senate, admitted since the first Congress, even when the appointment requires such consent, yet it has seldom been practised and has been often doubted.[114] It would appear that the final act of sending notice is at the President's discretion and when he gives notice the treaty is terminated under international law but he ought not to act without consent either of Congress or of the Senate, except in extraordinary circumstances.

187. *Legislative Abrogation.*

A treaty may be abrogated as "the law of the land" by resolution of Congress or by the passage of conflicting legislation. It is somewhat difficult to locate the constitutional power for such legislation when terminating treaties on subjects not within the legislative competence of Congress. Rawle considers it "an incident to the right of declaring war." At any rate it has been sustained in many cases.[115]

"It must be conceded," said the Supreme Court in the Chinese Exclusion Case, "that the act of 1888 is in contravention of express stipulations of the treaty of 1868 and of the supplemental treaty of 1880, but it is not on that account invalid or to be restricted in its enforcement. The treaties were of no greater obligation than the act of Congress. By the Constitution, laws made in pursuance thereof and treaties made under the authority of

---

[112] Crandall, *op. cit.,* pp. 116–117.

[113] Willoughby, *op. cit.,* p. 518.

[114] See remarks of Senator Walsh, of Mont., *Cong. Rec.,* Nov. 8, 1919, 58: 8608–8609.

[115] The Chinese Exclusion Case, 130 U. S. 581; The Cherokee Tobacco Case, 11 Wall. 616; The Head Money Cases, 112 U. S. 580; Moore, Digest, 5: 356–370. Rawle, A View of the Constitution, 1825, p. 61.

INTERNATIONAL AGREEMENTS. 261

the United States are both declared to be the supreme law of the land, and no paramount authority is given to one over the other. . . . It can be deemed only the equivalent of a legislative act, to be repealed or modified at the pleasure of Congress. In either case the last expression of the sovereign will must control. . . . The question whether our government was justified in disregarding its engagements with another nation is not one for the determination of the courts. . . . The court is not the censor of the morals of the other departments of the Government."

However, as the court noticed, such legislation does not affect the international obligation of the treaty. President Arthur in vetoing the Chinese exclusion bill of 1882 said: [116]

"A nation is justified in repudiating its treaty obligations only when they are in conflict with great paramount interests. Even then all possible reasonable means for modifying or changing these obligations by mutual agreement should be exhausted before resorting to the supreme right of refusal to comply with them."

President Hayes's veto of a similar bill in 1879 though based partly on constitutional grounds referred to "the more general considerations of interest and duty which sacredly guard the faith of the nation, in whatever form of obligation it may have been given." [117] To make "a scrap of paper" of a treaty by legislation will at once give basis for international demands. Thus France refused to recognize the legitimacy of American abrogation of her treaties in 1798 and compensation was made by sacrifice of the spoliation claims by the treaty of 1800.[118] China has consistently protested against the disregard of her treaties by various exclusion acts.[119]

188. *Conclusion.*

We conclude that the power of making international agreements is largely vested in the President. The states' power in this respect is practically nil. Though the Senate has an absolute veto on treaties, and Congress may suggest the opening of negotiations, may authorize executive agreements and may refuse to execute treaties, yet the real initiative, the negotiation and the final decision to ratify

---

[116] Richardson, Messages, 8: 112.

[117] *Ibid.,* 7: 520. See also Message of Pres. Harrison, Dec., 1890, in referring to violation of Hawaiian Reciprocity Treaty by the tariff act, Richardson, 9: 110; Moore, Digest, 5: 368, and *supra,* sec. 101.

[118] Moore, Digest, 5: 357, 609–612.

[119] See references to U. S. Foreign Relations, Moore, Digest, 4: 198, 202.

are all at the discretion of the President. Furthermore, many agreements of a temporary or purely executive or military character may be made by him without consulting the Senate at all.

While executive agreements usually terminate with the passing from office of the President under whose authority they were negotiated, or the repeal of the statute on which they were founded, this would not be true of agreements transferring a lease or other title to territory for a term of years or permanently. Treaties may be terminated as municipal law by legislative abrogation or judicial recognition of their obsolescence under principles of international law, but the international obligation may be ended only by operation of international law recognized by the President, by legislative denunciation of a voidable treaty, or by denunciation under the terms of the treaty itself by the President acting ordinarily with consent of the Senate or Congress.

CHAPTER XV.

The Power to Make Political Decisions in Foreign Affairs, Recognition, Annexation, Citizenship and the Determination of Policy.

189. *Distinction Between Domestic and Foreign Affairs.*

The meeting of international responsibilities and the making of international agreements do not include all matters which have to do with the conduct of foreign relations. Many decisions which may be made by nations without the consent of other states and practically without limitation by international law and treaty, affect foreign nations very closely. The recognition of foreign states and governments, the declaration of war and the proclamation of neutrality are examples which at once spring to the mind. This field is, however, difficult accurately to define. There is hardly a law passed by even a state legislature which may not affect a resident alien and so under conceivable circumstances become a subject of international discussion. Such matters, however, as the regulation of foreign commerce, the control of immigration, the raising of armies, the development of a navy and the building of fortifications within its territory, are of very direct interest to foreign nations. Yet, except so far as regulated by treaties, they are considered domestic questions.

Arbitration treaties have often excepted questions affecting national " independence " from compulsory submission and the League of Nations Covenant (Art. XV) recognizes that disputes between nations may " arise out of a matter which by international law is solely within the domestic jurisdiction " of one party, and in such disputes the Council of the League is incompetent to make a recommendation. The United States Supreme Court has similarly recognized certain questions undoubtedly interesting to foreign nations as within the " independence " of the nation.[1]

---

[1] The Chinese Exclusion Case, 130 U. S. 581 (1889).

264   THE CONTROL OF AMERICAN FOREIGN RELATIONS.

"That the government of the United States, through the action of the legislative department, can exclude aliens from its territory is a proposition which we do not think open to controversy. Jurisdiction over its own territory to that extent is an incident of every independent nation. It is a part of its independence."

Writers on international law have usually drawn the line between foreign affairs and domestic affairs according to the line of territorial jurisdiction.[2]

"It being a necessary result of independence that the will of the state shall be exclusive over its territory, it also asserts authority as a general rule over all persons and things, and decides what acts shall or shall not be done within its dominion. It consequently exercises jurisdiction there, not only with respect to the members of its own community and their property, but with respect to foreign persons and property."

Although in practice states are internationally responsible for many events which occur or acts which take effect entirely within their borders,[3] yet territorial autonomy is generally recognized by international law and we will confine attention to those political decisions directly affecting matters beyond national boundaries.

190. *State Power to Make Political Decisions in Foreign Affairs.*

The states have been deprived of almost all power to make political decisions in foreign affairs. Their war power is confined to the maintenance of a militia for domestic use or to ward off an actual or imminent invasion.

"No state," says the Constitution, "shall grant letters of marque and reprisal, . . . or without the consent of Congress keep troops or ships of war in time of peace or engage in war unless actually invaded or in such imminent danger as will not admit of delay."[4]

They have no powers dependent upon war and treaty-making such as that of annexing territory, nor upon diplomatic and representative powers such as those of recognizing new states and governments,

---

[2] Hall, Int. Law, p. 49.
[3] *Supra,* sec. 89.
[4] U. S. Const., Art. I, sec. 10, cl. 3.

though state legislatures have sometimes passed resolutions recommending national action in these matters.[5]

In political matters even indirectly affecting foreign relations the states are excluded. They cannot lay export or import duties except to enforce inspection laws; they cannot lay tonnage duties; regulate immigration or foreign commerce except necessary local regulations upon which Congress has not acted, nor naturalize aliens.[6] The intention of the Constitution is undoubtedly to render the states incompetent to make political decisions which affect foreign nations in more than the most remote degree, yet state laws have occasionally given rise to international controversy, especially where discrimination against resident aliens is alleged. The San Francisco ordinance of 1906 segregating Japanese school children and the California laws of 1913 and 1920 forbidding landholding to certain classes of aliens are in point.[7]

"Even a state of the Union," said a Senate report of 1897, "although having admittedly no power whatever in foreign relations, may take action uncontrollable by the Federal Government, and which, if not properly a *casus belli*, might nevertheless as a practical matter afford to some foreign nation the excuse of a declaration of war. We may instance the action which might have been taken by the State of Wyoming in relation to the Chinese massacres, or by the State of Louisiana in relation to the Italian lynchings, or by the State of New York in its recent controversy with German insurance companies with relation to the treatment of its own insurance companies by Germany." [8]

191. *National Power to Make Political Decisions in Foreign Affairs.*

The national government is given by the Constitution political powers, not only directly affecting foreign relations, such as the war power, the treaty-making power, and the power to send and receive diplomatic officers; but also most powers which might indirectly

---

[5] In 1897 Nebraska adopted a resolution extending to Cuba their sympathy. Sen. Doc. 82, 54th Cong., 2d sess. For state resolutions favoring recognition of Ireland, Armenia, Jewish State, the League of Nations, etc., see Cong. Rec., 57: 3866; 58: 43, 48–51, 54, 6859; 59: 7510.

[6] U. S. Const., art. 1, sec. 10, cl. 3. The Passenger Cases, 7 How. 283; Cooley v. Port Wardens, 12 How. 299; Chirac v. Chirac, 2 Wheat. 259.

[7] *Supra*, sec. 15, note 10; sec. 50, note 83.

[8] Sen. Doc. No. 56, 54th Cong., 2d sess., p. 5.

affect them, such as the powers to regulate foreign commerce, to levy customs duties, and to naturalize aliens. So extensive are these powers that the court has construed them as together conferring upon the national government all the powers in foreign relations enjoyed by other sovereign nations.[9]

"The United States are a sovereign and independent nation, and are vested by the Constitution with the entire control of international relations, and with all the powers of government necessary to maintain that control and make it effective."

How are these powers distributed among the departments of government?

"It is clear all through the Constitution, and has never been disputed, that the intention was to distribute the powers of the Government between its three branches, subject to such checks as the veto of the President or advice and consent of the Senate; and not to place any given power in two or all three branches of the Government concurrently.

"The existence of the same power for the same purposes in both the legislative and executive branches of the Government might lead to most unfortunate results. For instance, if the legislative and executive branches both possessed the power of recognizing the independence of a foreign nation, and one branch should declare it independent while the other denied its independence, then, since they are coordinate, how could the problem be solved by the judicial branch?

"The distinction must be borne in mind between the existence of a constitutional power and the existence of an ability to effect certain results. For instance, Congress alone has the power to declare war. The Executive, however, can do many acts which would constitute a *casus belli*, and thus indirectly result in war; but this does not imply in the Executive a concurrent power to declare war, and the war which would result would be one declared by a foreign power. It is possible even that the judiciary, by declaring some act of Congress at an inopportune moment to be unconstitutional or otherwise incapable of execution according to its intent, or by some decision in a prize cause or otherwise, could give rise to a war with a foreign power, yet no one would claim that the judiciary had the power to declare war."[10]

Though the constitutional fathers doubtless had the purpose ascribed to them in this Senate report, yet it is by no means true that they succeeded in keeping the powers of the various departments from overlapping in the field of foreign affairs. An illustration is

---

[9] Fong Yue Ting *v.* U. S., 149 U. S. 698 (1893). *Supra,* secs. 71–73.
[10] Sen. Doc. No. 56 (cited *supra,* note 7), p. 4.

furnished by the power to regulate the landing of submarine cables.[11]

"I am of the opinion," wrote the Acting Attorney General in 1898, "that the President has the power, in the absence of legislative enactment, to control the landing of foreign submarine cables." But "the Executive permission to land a cable is, of course, subject to subsequent congressional action."

The President as Chief Executive, Commander-in-Chief and the representative organ, seems to have sufficient power to make all political decisions in foreign affairs not exclusively vested in Congress or the treaty-making power and not conflicting with international law, treaty or existing act of Congress.

Congress, on the other hand, can make political decisions in foreign affairs so far as it can bring them under its express, implied or resultant powers, the most important of which in this connection are the powers to declare war, to annex territory, to naturalize aliens, to regulate commerce and means of conveyance and communication with foreign nations, and to regulate immigration and exclude or expel aliens. When Congress has validly acted, its act binds the President except in so far as it encroaches upon his constitutional discretion to receive and commission diplomatic officers and to act as Commander-in-Chief.

The courts have no power to make political decisions whatever. Their functions are purely judicial and when confronted with a political question they accept the decision of the political departments of the government.[12] It results that judicial precedents are not of great assistance in determining the constitutional line separating the powers of the President from those of Congress in this field.

It must be added that the distinction between "constitutional power" and "ability to effect certain results" is one often difficult to draw in practice, though doubtless valid in theory. If, for instance, the President has the "ability to effect certain results" for which Congress is given express power, through the exercise of his own undoubted constitutional powers, it would not seem far

---

[11] Moore, Digest, 2: 463; *infra*, sec. 219. See also *infra*, secs. 245–248.
[12] *Supra*, sec. 107.

from the truth to state that the constitutional powers of Congress and the President overlap. The same end may often be attained by different means.

A. *The Power to Recognize Foreign States, Governments, and Belligerency.*

192. *The Power of Recognition.*

The President as the representative organ has the power to recognize facts in international relations. He has recognized foreign states by receiving diplomatic officers or granting exequators to consuls from them, and by sending diplomatic officers or commissioners to them.[13] He has, by diplomatic correspondence through the Department of State, recognized acquisitions of territory and the establishment of protectorates by existing states.[14] Likewise, beginning with the recognition of the French revolutionary government through reception of Citizen Genet in 1793, the President has recognized new governments and he has refused to recognize *de facto* governments, thereby contributing to their ultimate downfall, as was the case with the Huerta government in Mexico and the Tinoco government in Costa Rica.[15] The President has recognized the existence of foreign war through proclamation of neutrality. Though the first such proclamation, issued in 1793 by Washington, was vigorously attacked by Jefferson and Madison, who considered it beyond his powers and contrary to the French alliance treaty of 1778, the precedent has been followed in all subsequent foreign wars, both international and civil.[16] The President has also held himself competent to recognize the termination of foreign wars and the consequent termination of American neutrality.[17] He has recognized the existence of insurgency and domestic violence in foreign

---

[13] Moore, Digest, 1: 74–119.
[14] Williams *v.* Suffolk Ins. Co., 13 Pet. 415.
[15] Moore, Digest, 1: 164; Moore, Principles of Am. Diplomacy, 213–225.
[16] Moore, Digest, 1: 164; Corwin, *op. cit.*, pp. 7–28.
[17] Mr. Seward, Sec. of State, to Mr. Goñi, Spanish Minister, July 22, 1868, Moore, Digest, 7: 337, *supra* sec. 213.

countries by proclamation and by diplomatic correspondence through the Department of State, and the courts have held that such action creates a status covered by special principles of international law. Thus in the case of the Three Friends the court distinguished between "war in the material sense" and "war in the legal sense."[18]

"Here," it said, "the political department has not recognized the existence of a *de facto* belligerent power engaged in hostility with Spain, but has recognized the existence of insurrectionary warfare prevailing before, at the time and since this forfeiture is alleged to have been incurred."

After describing two presidential proclamations calling attention to "serious civil disturbances" and "insurrection" in Cuba, the court continues:

"We are thus judicially informed of the existence of an actual conflict of arms in resistance of the authority of a government with which the United States are on terms of peace and amity, although acknowledgment of the insurgents as belligerents by the political department has not taken place."

With respect to the President's power of recognition, two questions have been raised: What are its limits? and, Is it exclusive?

193. *Limits of Recognition Power.*

The courts have taken cognizance of the President's recognition of states, governments, belligerency, insurgency and foreign acquisitions of territory on numerous occasions and they have never held that the President exceeded his powers.[19] It is clear, however, that if unlimited, the power of recognition could be used to usurp the power to declare war. Thus recognition of a foreign revolting state, if premature, would furnish a *casus belli*. This possibility was envisaged by Secretary of State Adams when occasion arose for recognizing the revolting South American Republics and he stated:[20]

---

[18] *Ibid.*, 1: 242; The Three Friends, 166 U. S. 63–66 (1897).
[19] *Ibid.*, 1: 247.
[20] Mr. Adams, Sec. of State, to the President, Aug. 24, 1818, *ibid.*, 1: 78. For discussion of circumstances justifying recognition, see Dana, Notes to Wheaton, Elements of International Law, pp. 35, 41.

"There is a stage in such contests when the parties struggling for independence have, as I conceive, a right to demand its acknowledgment by neutral parties, and when the acknowledgment may be granted without departure from the obligations of neutrality. It is the stage when independence is established as a matter of fact so as to leave the chances of the opposite party to recover their dominion utterly desperate. The neutral nation must, of course, judge for itself when this period has arrived; and as the belligerent nation has the same right to judge for itself, it is very likely to judge differently from the neutral and to make it a cause or pretext for war, as Great Britain did expressly against France in our Revolution, and substantially against Holland."

Secretary Adams' distinction seems to indicate the limits of the President's power. He may recognize a fact. To do so is not a just cause of war. A recognition before the fact is, however, intervention and practically war, the declaration of which belongs to Congress. Thus when the line has been close, as in the recognitions of the South American Republics and Texas, the President has "invoked the judgment and cooperation of Congress" before recognition[21] and where "recognition" would clearly be premature, the President has not acted at all but has turned the question over to Congress. Thus President McKinley, in his message of April 11, 1898, turned over the "solemn responsibilty" of the Cuban question to Congress with a recommendation for intervention.[22]

194. *Exclusiveness of President's Recognition Power.*

In practice, recognition has always been by authority of the President, though in a few cases the President has gained the approval of Congress or the Senate before acting.[23]

"In the preceding review," writes Moore, "of the recognition, respectively, of new states, new governments and belligerency, there has been made in each case a precise statement of facts, showing how and by whom the recognition was accorded. In every case, as it appears, of a new government and of belligerency the question of recognition was determined solely by the Executive. In the case of the Spanish-American republics, of Texas, of Hayti, and of Liberia, the President, before recognizing the new state, invoked the judgment and cooperation of Congress; and in each of these cases provision was made for the appointment of a minister, which, when made in

---

[21] *Infra,* sec. 194.
[22] Richardson, Messages, 10: 67.
[23] Moore, Digest, 1: 244.

POLITICAL DECISIONS IN FOREIGN AFFAIRS. 271

due form, constitutes, as has been seen, according to the rules of international law, a formal recognition. In numerous other cases the recognition was given by the Executive solely on his own responsibility."

The Congressional Resolution of April 20, 1898, which asserted that "the people of the Island of Cuba are and of right ought to be free and independent" has been cited as an exception but the resolution went on to "direct and empower" the President to use the army, navy and militia to "carry these resolutions into effect." It was in fact and was understood at the time to be a declaration of intervention and not a recognition.[24] As Senator Morgan of Alabama said, it was "not a historical declaration of the existing facts or situation, but it is a high political decree, . . . a basis of political action."[25]

195. *Claim of Congress to Recognition Power.*

On several occasions, the power of recognition has been claimed for Congress. Thus said Henry Clay in the House of Representatives:[26]

"There are three modes under our Constitution in which a nation may be recognized: By the Executive receiving a minister; secondly, by its sending one thither; and, thirdly, this House unquestionably has the right to recognize in the exercise of the constitutional power of Congress to regulate foreign commerce. . . . Suppose, for example, we passed an act to regulate trade between the United States and Buenos Ayres; the existence of the nation would be thereby recognized, as we could not regulate trade with a nation which does not exist."

However, Clay's original motion which provided salary for a minister to the "independent provinces of the River Plata in South America" was withdrawn and even his substitute, omitting the term "independent" and adding that the salary was to commence "when-

---

[24] Richardson, Messages, 10: 72. See also Latané, *Am. Jl. Int. Law*, 12: 899 (Oct., 1918), criticizing statement in Corwin, *op. cit.*, p. 80.
[25] *Cong. Rec.*, 55th Cong., 2d sess., Appdx., p. 290; Corwin, *op. cit.*, p. 81.
[26] Sen. Doc. 56 (cited *supra*, note 8), p. 32; Corwin, p. 76. See also notes of Secretaries of State Buchanan and Clay, Moore, Digest, 1: 245-246.

ever the President shall deem it expedient to send a minister to the said United Provinces," failed to pass.[27]

On this occasion, as later, the better opinion held that the power to recognize was vested exclusively in the Executive. Thus John Quincy Adams, then Secretary of State, writes of a meeting of President Monroe's cabinet, on January 1, 1819.[28]

"As to impeachment, I was willing to take my share of risk of it for this measure whenever the Executive should deem it proper. And, instead of admitting the Senate or House of Representatives to any share in the act of recognition, I would expressly avoid that form of doing it which would require the concurrence of those bodies. It was, I had no doubt, by our Constitution an act of the Executive authority. General Washington had exercised it in recognizing the French Republic by the reception of Genêt. Mr. Madison had exercised it by declining several years to receive, and by finally receiving Mr. Onis; and in this instance I thought the Executive ought carefully to preserve entire the authority given him by the Constitution, and not weaken it by setting the precedent of making either House or Congress a party to an act which it was his exclusive right and duty to perform. Mr. Crawford said . . . that there was a difference between the recognition of a change of government in a nation already acknowledged as sovereign, and the recognition of a new nation itself. He did not, however, deny, but admitted, that the recognition was strictly within the powers of the Executive alone, and I did not press the discussion further."

The same position has been taken by Mr. Seward and other Secretaries of State,[29] by the Senate on several occasions[30] and by the Supreme Court.[31]

"The Executive," said the latter, "having recognized the existence of a state of war between Spain and her South American colonies, the courts of the union are bound to consider as lawful those acts which war authorized and which the new Governments in South America may direct against their enemy."

---

[27] Moore, Digest, 1: 82. A later resolution passed the House of Representatives, *ibid.*, 1: 84.

[28] Memoirs of J. Q. Adams, 4: 205–206; Moore, Digest, 1: 244.

[29] Mr. Seward, Sec. of State, to Mr. Dayton, Minister to France, Apr. 7, 1864, Moore, Digest, 1: 246.

[30] Memorandum on the method of "Recognition" of foreign governments and foreign states by the Government of the United States, 1789–1897, Sen. Doc. No. 40, 54th Cong., 2d sess.; memorandum upon the power to recognize the independence of a new foreign state, Sen. Doc. No. 56, 54th Cong., 2d sess.

[31] The Divina Pastora, 4 Wheat. 32; Moore, Digest, 1: 247.

Although the President may seek the opinion of Congress before recognition; and doubtless should do so if the state or government or war in question does not have a clear *de facto* existence, yet the law is that stated by the Senate Foreign Relations Committee in 1897:[32]

"The executive branch is the sole mouthpiece of the nation in communication with foreign sovereignties. Foreign nations communicate only through their respective executive departments. Resolutions of their legislative departments upon diplomatic matters have no status in international law. In the department of international law, therefore, properly speaking, a congressional recognition of belligerency or independence would be a nullity."

Finally we may notice a practical consideration adverted to by Professor Corwin after a comprehensive survey of the subject. Concluding that "recognition, as it is known to international law, belongs to the President alone, or to the President in conjunction with the Senate" he adds:[33]

"Even if we should admit that Congress, incidentally to discharging some legislative function like that of regulating commerce, might in some sense 'recognize' a new state or government, the question still remains how it would communicate its recognition, having the power neither to dispatch nor to receive diplomatic agents. As was said of the States of the Confederation, Congress is as to other governments 'both deaf and dumb.' Why, then, claim for it a power which it could not possibly use save in some roundabout and inconclusive fashion?"

B. *The Power to Determine National Territory and Citizenship.*

196. *Judicial Recognition of Territorial Limits.*

International law recognizes that territory may be acquired by accretion and prescription; discovery and occupation; cession and conquest.[34] The courts in applying international law recognize small acquisitions by accretion and prescription. Thus mud islands formed at the mouths of rivers and gradual changes in boundary

---

[32] Sen. Doc. 56, 54th Cong., 2d Sess., p. 22.
[33] Corwin, *op. cit.*, p. 82.
[34] Wilson and Tucker, International Law, 7th ed., p. 108.

river courses have been recognized as extending the jurisdiction.[35] The courts have held general acceptance of certain marks as the boundary for a long space of time will establish it, even though such marks are ascertained to be incorrect by later surveys,[36] and they have also recognized bays with headlands more than six miles apart, such as Chesapeake and Delaware bays, as territorial waters from long assertion by the United States and tacit acceptance by other powers of that status.[37] In general, however, the courts regard the determination of boundaries as a political question.[38]

197. *Recognition of Territorial Limits by the President.*

The President is competent to recognize the acquisition of territory by discovery and occupation. Thus shall uninhabited islands in the Pacific have been taken possession of by naval commanders.[39] The President has also applied the Guano Island act passed by Congress in 1856 and as therein provided has registered islands, discovered and worked by American citizens, as within American jurisdiction and protection. In Jones *v.* United States the Supreme Court held that the jurisdiction of the United States was thus legally extended.[40]

198. *Power to Annex Territory by Treaty and Executive Agreement.*

Most of the acquisitions of territory have been by cession, though the competence of the treaty-making power was at first ques-

---

[35] Cushing, Att. Gen., 8 Op. 175 (1856); Ocean City Assoc. *v.* Shriver, 46 Atl. 690 (N. J., 1900), and English case, The Anna, 5 Rob. 373 (1805); Moore, Digest, 1: 269–273, 747.

[36] As to interstate boundaries, R. I. *v.* Mass., 4 How. 591, 639 (1846); Ind. *v.* Ky., 136 U. S. 479 (1890); Va. *v.* Tenn., 148 U. S. 503 (1893); Moore, Digest, 1: 295, 747.

[37] The Grange, Randolph, Att. Gen., 1 Op. 32; Manchester *v.* Mass., 139 U. S. 240; Moore, Digest, 1: 735–743; The Alleganean, Alabama Claims Commission, 1885, 32 Albany L. J. 484; Moore, Int. Arb. 4333, 4675; Scott, Cases on Int. Law, p. 143.

[38] Foster *v.* Neilson, 2 Pet. 253; Moore, Digest, 1: 743–745, *supra*, sec. 107.

[39] For acquisition of Midway and Wake Islands, see Moore, Digest, 1: 555.

[40] Jones *v.* U. S., 137 U. S. 202 (1890); Moore, Digest, 1: 556–580.

tioned.[41] Louisiana, Florida, Oregon, California and New Mexico, the Messila Valley, Tutuila in the Samoan group, Porto Rico, the Philippines, Guam, and the Virgin Islands have been thus acquired, as has the permanent lease of the Panama Canal Zone, and of a naval base on the Gulf of Fonseca. Reef Island near the outlet of Lake Erie and a lease of a naval base at Guantanamo, Cuba, were acquired by executive agreement.[42]

199. *Power of Congress to Annex Territory.*

Texas and Hawaii were acquired by joint resolution of Congress. Commentators have had difficulty in locating the clause on which the power of Congress to annex territory is founded. Chief Justice Marshall implied the power to annex territory from the powers to make treaties and to declare war,[43] but the former does not apply to Congress nor the latter to these cases, and as Willoughby comments after citing the cases:[44]

"It is to be observed that in none of these cases is there any argument to show just why, and in what manner, the acquiring of the foreign territory is a necessary or proper means by which war may be carried on, or treaties entered into. In fact, it will be seen that the acquiring of foreign territory has been treated as a result incidental to, rather than as a means for, the carrying on of war and the conducting of foreign relations."

It has been argued that the power to annex territory is implied in the powers to admit new states to the Union.[45] That clause might apply to Texas which was immediately admitted as a state but hardly to Hawaii; and Gouverneur Morris who drafted the Constitution, replied to Livingston's query, "whether Congress can admit as a new state territory which did not belong to the United States when the Constitution was made":[46]

[41] Willoughby, *op. cit.*, pp. 328 *et seq.* See also Wright, *Columbia Law Rev.*, 20: 141, note 100.
[42] Moore, Digest, 1: 433–554.
[43] Am. Ins. Co. *v.* Canter, 1 Pet. 511.
[44] Willoughby, *op. cit.*, p. 340.
[45] 55th Cong., 2d sess., Sen. Report, No. 681; Willoughby, *op. cit.*, p. 346.
[46] Morris, Life and Writings (Sparks), 3: 185, 192; Willoughby, *op. cit.*, p. 328.

"In my opinion they cannot. I always thought, when we should acquire Canada and Louisiana, it would be proper to govern them as provinces and allow them no voice in our councils. In wording the third section of the fourth article, I went as far as circumstances would permit to establish the exclusion. Candor obliges me to add my belief that had it been more pointedly expressed, a strong opposition would have been made."

If Congress has the power at all, as it doubtless has, it has it as a resultant of the various powers connected with foreign relations which together confer all sovereign powers necessary for national defense.[47]

The Supreme Court has admitted the power of Congress to acquire territory by conquest but has denied such power to the President:[48]

"The genius and character of our institutions are peaceful, and the power to declare war was not conferred upon Congress for the purposes of aggression or aggrandizement, but to enable the general government to vindicate by arms, if it should become necessary, its own rights and the rights of its citizens. A war, therefore, declared by Congress, can never be presumed to be waged for the purpose of conquest or the acquisition of territory; nor does the law declaring the war imply an authority to the President to enlarge the limits of the United States by subjugating the enemy's country. The United States, it is true, may extend its boundaries by conquest or treaty, and may demand the cession of territory as the condition of peace, in order to indemnify its citizens for the injuries they have suffered, or to reimburse the government for the expenses of the war. But this can only be done by the treaty-making power or the legislative authority, and is not a part of the power conferred upon the President by the declaration of war."

We conclude that the courts in applying international law and the President in the exercise of his diplomatic powers may recognize minor acquisitions of territory by operation of international law, and that more considerable bodies of territory may be acquired by treaty or by joint resolution of Congress.

200. *Power of Congress to Naturalize Aliens and Establish Criteria of Citizenship.*

The Constitution provides that " all persons born or naturalized in the United States, and subject to the jurisdiction thereof, are

---

[47] Willoughby, *op. cit.*, p. 340.
[48] Fleming *v.* Page, 9 How. 603.

citizens of the United States." [49] Congress has exclusive power "to establish an uniform rule of naturalization," [50] and it has by implication the power to determine, within the constitutional provision, who are natural born citizens. Thus it has provided that: [51]

"All children heretofore born or hereafter born out of the limits and jurisdiction of the United States, whose fathers were or may be at the time of their birth citizens thereof, are declared to be citizens of the United States; but the rights of citizenship shall not descend to children whose fathers never resided in the United States."

Congress may also naturalize persons by special act, as it has many Indian tribes[52] and the Porto Ricans.[53]

From its power to naturalize is deduced the power to determine criteria of expatriation. An act of 1868 "recognizes the natural and inherent right of expatriation" and enacts that: [54]

"Any declaration, instruction, opinion, order, or decision of any officers of this Government which denies, restricts, impairs, or questions their right of expatriation is hereby declared inconsistent with the fundamental principles of this Government."

Laws have also stated presumptions of expatriation of naturalized citizens, such as two years residence in the country of origin or five years residence in other foreign country.[55]

201. *Power of Executive to Recognize Citizenship.*

Within the limits of these laws, the Executive, actually the Department of State, must recognize the citizenship or alienage of persons, in offering protection or responding to claims of foreign governments in behalf of their citizens. The Executive may make requirements with reference to passports and registration at con-

---

[49] U. S. Constitution, Amendment XIV; U. S. *v.* Wong Kim Ark, 169 U. S. 649.
[50] *Ibid,* Art. I, sec. 8, cl. 4; Chirac *v.* Chirac, 2 Wheat. 259.
[51] Rev. Stat., sec. 1993; Comp. Stat., 3947.
[52] Rev. Stat., sec. 2312, Act Feb. 8, 1887, sec. 6, 24 Stat. 390, as amended in 1901 and 1906; Comp. Stat., sec. 3951.
[53] Act March 2, 1917, sec. 5, 39 Stat. 953; Comp. Stat., sec. 3803bb.
[54] Rev. Stat., sec. 1999; Comp. Stat., sec. 3955.
[55] Act March 2, 1907, sec. 2, 34 Stat. 1228.

sulates in the place of residence and the evidence necessary to prove citizenship.[56] Within the United States the question of citizenship is ordinarily one for judicial determination, but immigrants claiming citizenship may, under present laws, have the fact of citizenship decided adversely and finally by administrative officials without appeal to the courts. According to the Ju Toy case these laws do not violate constitutional guarantees.[57]

C. Power to Determine Foreign Policy.

202. Congressional Resolutions on Incidents in Foreign Affairs.

Declarations of foreign policy may be made by Congress in the form of joint resolutions, but such resolutions are not binding on the President. They merely indicate a sentiment which he is free to follow or ignore. Yet they are often couched in mandatory terms and in defense of his independence the President has frequently vetoed them. Thus in 1877, President Grant vetoed two resolutions extending appreciation to Pretoria and Argentine Republic for the "complimentary terms in which they had referred to the first centennial":[58]

"Sympathizing as I do in the spirit of courtesy and friendly recognition which has prompted the passage of these resolutions, I cannot escape the conviction that their adoption has inadvertently involved the exercise of a power which infringes upon the constitutional rights of the Executive. . . . The Constitution of the United States, following the established usage of nations, has indicated the President as the agent to represent the national sovereignty in its intercourse with foreign powers, and to receive all official

---

[56] Borchard, *op. cit.*, p. 488.
[57] U. S. *v.* Ju Toy, 198 U. S. 253; Willoughby, *op. cit.*, p. 1290.
[58] Richardson, Messages, 7: 431. See also Sen. Rep., quoted *supra*, sec. 191. President Harding is reported to have opposed Senator Borah's amendment to the naval appropriation bill of 1921, authorizing a conference on disarmament with Great Britain and Japan, on the ground that it "might embarrass executive action, or appear to carry a congressional recommendation on international policies within the jurisdiction of the executive." (Press Report, May 3, 1921, *Cong. Rec.*, May 17, 27, 1921, 61: 1508, 1857.) These objections were, however, later withdrawn (Letter to Representative Mondell, June 25, 1921), and the bill with the amendment was approved July 12, 1921, two days after President Harding had announced his intention to call a conference on limitation of armament.

communications from them, . . . making him, in the language of one of the most eminent writers on constitutional law, 'the constitutional organ of communication with foreign states.' If Congress can direct the correspondence of the Secretary of State with foreign governments, a case very different from that now under consideration might arise, when that officer might be directed to present to the same foreign government entirely different and antagonistic views or statements."

Similar objection has sometimes been raised in Congress itself. Thus Webster said of an item in the appropriation bill for the Panama mission of 1826, which attempted to attach conditions:[59]

"He would recapitulate only his objections to this amendment. It was unprecedented, nothing of the kind having been attempted before. It was, in his opinion, unconstitutional, as it was taking the proper responsibility from the Executive and exercising, ourselves, a power which, from its nature, belongs to the Executive, and not to us. It was prescribing, by the House, the instructions for a Minister abroad. It was nugatory, as it attached conditions which might be complied with, or might not. And lastly, if gentlemen thought it important to express the sense of the House on these subjects, or any of them, the regular and customary way was by resolution. At present it seemed to him that we must make the appropriation without conditions, or refuse it. The President had laid the case before us. If our opinion of the character of the meeting, or its objects, led us to withhold the appropriation, we had the power to do so. If we had not so much confidence in the Executive as to render us willing to trust to the constitutional exercise of the Executive power, we have power to refuse the money. It is a direct question of aye or no. If the Ministers to be sent to Panama may not be trusted to act, like other Ministers, under the instructions of the Executive, they ought not to go at all."

203. *President Not Bound by Congressional Resolutions on Foreign Affairs.*

The Executive has never hesitated to ignore resolutions or acts

---

[59] Benton, Abridgment of Debates in Congress, 9: 91. Congressional resolutions on incidents in the control of foreign affairs have sometimes been defeated in Congress from an apprehension that they might be unconstitutional encroachments upon the President's powers. See Clay's resolution of 1818 for recognition of United Province of Rio de la Plata (Moore, Digest, 1: 182); Benton's resolution of 1844 criticizing President Tyler's treaty for annexation of Texas (*Cong. Globe*, 13, Appdx., 474); Sumner's resolut:on of 1871 criticizing President Grant's effort to annex Santo Domingo (*Cong. Globe*, 42d Cong., 1st sess., pt. 1, p. 294); McLemore's resolution of March, 1916, " to warn all citizens of the United States to refrain from traveling on armed vessels" (*Cong. Rec.*, 1916, pp. 3700–4).

of this kind, even when passed. Thus a resolution of 1864 declared, with reference to the Maximillian Government of Mexico, that:

"It does not accord with the policy of the United States to acknowledge a monarchical government, erected on the ruins of any republican government in America, under the auspices of any European power."

Secretary of State Seward explained to the minister in France:

"This is a practical and purely Executive question, and the decision of its constitutionality belongs not to the House of Representatives nor even to Congress, but to the President of the United States. . . . While the President receives the declaration of the House of Representatives with the profound respect to which it is entitled, as an exposition of its sentiments upon a grave and important subject, he directs that you inform the Government of France that he does not at the present contemplate any departure from the policy which this Government has hitherto pursued in regard to the war which exists between France and Mexico. It is hardly necessary to say that the proceeding of the House of Representatives was adopted upon suggestions arising within itself, and that the French Government would be seasonably apprised of any change of policy upon this subject which the President might at any future time think it proper to adopt."

Congress promptly resolved upon receipt of this communication that:

"Congress has a constitutional right to an authoritative voice in declaring and prescribing the foreign policy of the United States, as well in the recognition of new powers as in other matters, and it is the constitutional duty of the President to respect that policy, not less in diplomatic negotiations than in the use of the national forces when authorized by law; and the propriety of any declaration of foreign policy by Congress is sufficiently proved by the vote which pronounces it; and such proposition, while pending and undetermined, is not a fit topic of diplomatic explanation with any foreign power."

Mr. Blaine criticized this resolution in the House:

"To adopt this principle is to start out with a new theory in the administration of our foreign affairs, and I think the House has justified its sense of self-respect and its just appreciation of the spheres of the coordinate departments of government by promptly laying the resolution on the table."

But after changing the term "President" to "Executive Department" the House passed the resolution, which, however, failed to come to a vote in the Senate.[60]

---

[60] McPherson, History of the Rebellion, pp. 349–354; Sen. Doc. No. 56 (cited *supra,* note 30), p. 47. See also President Wilson's refusal to carry

Though congressional resolutions on concrete incidents are encroachments upon the power of the Executive Department and are of no legal effect, yet they may be of value as an index of national sentiment.

"They have," says Professor Corwin, "often furnished the President valuable guidance in the shaping of his foreign policy in conformity with public opinion. Thus the resolutions which were passed by the Senate and House separately in the second session of the Fifty-third Congress, warning the President against the employment of forces to restore the monarchy of Hawaii, probably saved the administration from a fatal error. Again, the notorious McLemore resolution, requesting the President 'to warn all citizens of the United States to refrain from traveling on armed merchant vessels,' though ill-judged enough as to content, did nevertheless furnish the administration a valuable hint as to the state of the public mind, and one which it was quick to take. For the President, even in the exercise of his most unquestioned powers, cannot act in a vacuum. He must ultimately have the support of public sentiment." [61]

204. *Congressional Declarations of General Policy.*

Congressional resolutions on foreign relations have often been of a more general character, avoiding reference to specific incidents, though doubtless suggested by such incidents. Thus a Senate resolution of 1858 asserted that American vessels on the high seas are not subject to visit and search in time of peace,[62] a law of 1868 asserted the right of expatriation to be "a natural and inherent right of all people"[63] and resolutions at various times have suggested the negotiation of arbitration treaties.[64] A section of the naval appropriation act of 1916 declared it to be:[65]

out provisions of the Jones Merchant Marine Act of June 5, 1920, directing the termination of certain treaty provisions, and President Lincoln's failure to terminate the Great Lakes disarmament agreement of 1817 in accord with a resolution of 1865, *supra,* secs. 174, 184.

[61] Corwin, *op. cit.,* p. 45.
[62] Moore, Digest, 2: 946.
[63] Rev. Stat., sec. 1999; Comp. Stat., sec. 3955.
[64] See A League of Nations (World Peace Foundation), I, No. 1 (Oct., 1917).
[65] Act Aug. 29, 1916, 39 Stat. 618; Comp. Stat. 7686b. In the Spring of 1921 President Harding is reported to have opposed the Borah amendment on disarmament (*supra,* sec. 56). In his message to Congress of April 12, 1921,

282   THE CONTROL OF AMERICAN FOREIGN RELATIONS.

"The policy of the United States to adjust and settle its international disputes through mediation or arbitration, to the end that war may be honorably avoided. It looks with apprehension and disfavor upon a general increase of armament throughout the world, but it realizes that no single nation can disarm, and that without common agreement upon the subject every considerable power must maintain a relative standing in military strength."

Negotiation of reciprocal agreements with Canada on the use of boundary waters has also been suggested.[66] A Senate resolution of 1912, though suggested by the Magdalena Bay incident, was expressed as a general policy related to the Monroe Doctrine.[67] Treaty reservations have sometimes offered the Senate an opportunity for the expression of general policies. The Hague Conventions on the Pacific settlement of international disputes were signed with a reservation: [68]

"Nothing contained in this convention shall be so construed as to require the United States of America to depart from its traditional policy of not intruding upon, interfering with, or entangling itself in the political questions of policy or internal administration of any foreign state; nor shall anything contained in the said convention be construed to imply a relinquishment of the United States of America of its traditional attitude toward purely American questions."

The Senate appended a similar reservation to the Algeciras Convention of 1906.[69]

205. *Power of President to Determine Foreign Policy.*

It is believed that resolutions expressing general policies or principles on most subjects connected with foreign relations may be

---

he said with reference to the proposed peace resolution: "It would be unwise to undertake to make a statement of future policy with respect to European affairs in such a declaration of a state of peace (with Germany). In correcting the failure of the Executive, in negotiating the most important treaty in the history of the nation, to recognize the constitutional powers of the Senate, we would go to the other extreme, equally objectionable, if Congress should assume the functions of the Executive. (*Cong. Rec.*, 61: 95. See also remarks of Senator Hitchcock, April 29, 1921, *ibid.*, 61: 745.)

[66] Act June 13, 1902, 32 Stat. 373, Comp. Stat. 9984; Act June 29, 1906, 34 Stat. 628, Comp. Stat. 9989d.

[67] *Cong. Rec.*, Aug. 2, 1912, 48: 10046, A League of Nations, I, No. 5, p. 298 (June, 1918); Hart, The Monroe Doctrine, p. 235.

[68] Malloy, Treaties, etc., pp. 2032, 2047.

[69] *Ibid.*, p. 2183.

POLITICAL DECISIONS IN FOREIGN AFFAIRS 283

constitutionally passed by Congress,[70] and may furnish useful guides to the President. Congressional expressions of opinion on particular issues, however, and attempts to direct the President thereon encroach upon the executive field and may embarrass the President's action.[71] In practice foreign policy has developed by executive precedent, practice and declaration. The farewell address of Washington and the Monroe Doctrine, both purely executive in origin and future interpretation, have been the most important expressions of foreign policy.[72] In recent years, however, Congress and especially the Senate have tended to express permanent policies more freely, by resolution. Though the Monroe Doctrine was stated in 1823 and on several occasions efforts were made to gain for it legislative endorsement, the first statement referring to it, accepted by either House of Congress, appears to be the reservation to the Hague Convention of 1899 accepted by the Senate, and on this occasion the doctrine was not referred to by name.[73]

---

[70] The constitutional authority of Congress may be traced to the power to declare war. According to Rawle, "the right to qualify, alter or annul a treaty being of a tendency to produce war, is an incident to the right of declaring war." (*Supra,* sec. 187.) The declaration of a foreign policy doubtless has a similar tendency toward the production or avoidance of war.

[71] The power of Congress to declare general foreign policies does not confer a power to direct the details of their execution any more than the power to declare war confers a power to direct the details of military campaigns (*infra,* sec. 221), or the power to make laws on certain subjects confers a power to direct their administration (*infra,* sec. 230). The first would encroach upon the President's power to receive and commission diplomatic officers and to negotiate treaties, as the second would upon his power as commander-in-chief and the third upon his power as chief executive.

[72] Richardson, Messages, 1: 221–224; 2: 209, 218–219; Moore, Digest, 6: 370, 401; see also Taft, *op. cit.,* p. 113; Foster, Century of Am. Diplomacy, p. 438.

[73] *Supra,* note 6. The joint resolution of Feb. 20, 1895, endorsing the suggestion in President Cleveland's annual message that the British-Venezuelan boundary dispute be submitted to arbitration (28 stat. 971) and the act authorizing and appropriating for a commission to investigate this dispute in accordance with the recommendation of his special message of Dec. 17, 1895 (29 stat. 1), are considered by J. W. Foster to evidence "formal approval" of the Monroe Doctrine by Congress (*op. cit.,* p. 477). These Congressional acts refer to a particular situation rather than to the Monroe Doctrine as a whole though doubtless they implied an endorsement of that Doctrine since it had been put forth as the grounds for action in President Cleveland's messages.

CHAPTER XVI.

The Power to Make Political Decisions in Foreign Affairs: War and the Use of Force.

A. The Power to Make War.

206. The Power to Make War.

Congress is given power "to declare war, grant letters of marque and reprisal and make rules concerning captures on land and water," and "to provide for calling forth the militia to execute the laws of the union, suppress insurrection and repel invasions." "The President shall be commander-in-chief of the army and navy of the United States and of the militia of the several states, when called into the actual service of the United States" and "he shall take care that the laws be faithfully executed."[1]

War has been defined as "the relation which exists between states when there may lawfully be a properly conducted contest of armed public forces."[2] It is thus to be distinguished from the use of military force. Battles may be fought, vessels captured and commerce embargoed without war, and on the other hand war may exist without a gun fired or a vessel captured or a trade route disturbed. The Supreme Court has distinguished the recognition of "war in the material sense" from "war in the legal sense."[3] We may thus regard war as a definite period of time within which the abnormal international law of war and neutrality has superseded normal international law. What authority in the United States has power to begin and end this period of time?

207. The Causation of War.

We have noticed the distinction between "the existence of a constitutional power and the existence of an ability to effect certain

---

[1] U. S. Const., I, sec. 8, cl. 11, 15; II, sec. 2, cl. 1, sec. 3.

[2] Wilson and Tucker, *op. cit.*, p. 233. See also Grotius, De Jure Belli ac Pacis, liv. I, c. 1, par. 2; Vattel, Droit des gens, liv. III, c. 1, sec. 1.

[3] The Three Friends, 166 U. S. 1, *supra*, sec. 192, and Nelson, J., dissent in the Prize Cases, 2 Black 635, 690.

results." [4] Now the ultimate causation of war may have nothing to do with the war powers of organs of the government. An act of a state legislature discriminating against aliens or a judicial decision depriving foreign nations of rights under international law may be a *casus belli*. Yet neither states nor courts have any war powers at all. The President especially is endowed with powers which in their exercise may lead to war.

"The President," says Pomeroy, "cannot declare war; Congress alone possesses this attribute. But the President may, without any possibility of hindrance from the legislature, so conduct the foreign intercourse, the diplomatic negotiations with other governments, as to force a war, as to compel another nation to take the initiative; and that step once taken, the challenge cannot be refused. How easily might the Executive have plunged us into a war with Great Britain by a single dispatch in answer to the affair of the Trent. How easily might he have provoked a condition of active hostilities with France by the form and character of the reclamations made in regard to the occupation of Mexico." [5]

But the President's powers go even beyond this. As Commander-in-Chief, he may employ the armed forces in defense of American citizens abroad, as he did in the bombardment of Greytown, the Koszta case and the Boxer rebellion, and thereby commit acts of war, which the government they offend may consider the initiation of a state of war. Thus on April 23, 1914, after the occupation of Vera Cruz by American marines, the Huerta government handed Chargé d'affaires O'Shaughnessy his passports with the comment: [6]

"According to international law, the acts of the armed forces of the United States, which I do not care to qualify in this note out of deference to the fact that your honor personally has observed toward the Mexican people and Government a most strictly correct conduct, so far as has been possible to you in your character as the representative of a government with which such serious difficulties as those existing have arisen, must be considered as an initiation of war against Mexico."

Such presidential acts, though perhaps a *casus belli,* do not necessarily initiate a state of war, as the intention to do so does not exist.[7] If war results it is one recognized or declared by the foreign power, though in the absence of a treaty requiring a formal declaration of war, it may antedate to the first act of war.

---
[4] *Supra,* sec. 191.
[5] Pomeroy, Constitutional Law, p. 65.
[6] *Am. Year Book,* 1914, p. 235.
[7] *Supra,* sec. 210, note 20.

208. The Recognition of War by Congress.

Suppose a foreign government commits such acts against the United States. What authority can recognize them as in fact the initiation of war? The power of Congress to declare war unquestionably embraces the power to recognize war. In fact all of the foreign wars to which the United States has been a party have been not declarations of war, but recognitions of war, if we are to judge by the terms of the initiating act of Congress. Thus on June 18, 1812,[8] Congress enacted "that war be and the same is hereby declared to exist between the United Kingdom of Great Britain and Ireland and the dependencies, thereof, and the United States of America and their territories." The act of May 13, 1846, recited:[9]

"Whereas, by the act of the Republic of Mexico, a state of war exists between that Government and the United States: Be it enacted by the Senate and the House of Representatives of the United States of America in Congress assembled, That, for the purpose of enabling the government of the United States to prosecute said war to a speedy and successful termination, the President be, and he is hereby, authorized to employ the militia, naval and military forces of the United States, etc."

War resolutions of April 25, 1898, April 6, 1917, and December 7, 1917, were of similar character.[10]

209. The Recognition of War by the President.

But does the President also have power to recognize war? President Jefferson thought not in 1801 but was not deterred from authorizing defensive measures. Read his message of December 8, 1801:[11]

"Tripoli, the least considerable of the Barbary States, had come forward with demands unfounded either in right or in compact, and had permitted itself to denounce war on our failure to comply before a given day. The style of the demand admitted but one answer. I sent a small squadron

---

[8] 2 Stat. 755. A declaration that war "exists" is the usual form in all countries. See British Proclamation of War, August 4, 1914, Naval War College, Int. Law Docs., 1917, p. 117, and other declarations in that volume. According to J. B. Moore, "the co-existence of the two phrases may be ascribed to motives of political strategy rather than to any belief or supposition that they denoted different legal conceptions." Proc. Am. Phil. Soc., Minutes, 60: xvii.

[9] 9 Stat. 9.
[10] *Infra*, notes 18, 19.
[11] Richardson, Messages, 1: 326.

of frigates into the Mediterranean, with assurances to that power of our sincere desire to remain in peace, but with orders to protect our commerce against the threatened attack. The measure was seasonable and salutary. The Bey had already declared war. His cruisers were out. . . . One of the Tripolitan cruisers having fallen in with and engaged the small schooner Enterprise, commanded by Lieutenant Sterret, which had gone as a tender to our larger vessels, was captured, after a heavy slaughter of her men, without the loss of a single one on our part. . . . unauthorized by the Constitution, without the sanction of Congress, to go beyond the line of *Defense,* the vessel, being disabled from committing further hostilities, was liberated with its crew. The legislature will doubtless consider whether, by authorizing measures of *offense* also, they will place our force on an equal footing with that of our adversaries."

Congress made the requisite authorization by resolution of February 6, 1802,[12] but Hamilton, as " Lucius Crassus," could not restrain a comment on the message:[13]

"The first thing in it, which excites our surprise, is the very extraordinary position, that though *Tripoli had declared war in form* against the United States, and had enforced it by actual hostility, yet that there was not power, for want of *the sanction of Congress,* to capture and detain her crews. . . . When analyzed it amounts to nothing less than this, that *between* two nations there may exist a state of complete war on the one side—of peace on the other. . . .

"The principle avowed in the Message would authorize our troops to kill those of the invader, if they should come within reach of their bayonets, perhaps to drive them into the sea, and drown them; but not to disable them from doing harm, by the milder process of making them prisoners, and sending them into confinement. Perhaps it may be replied, that the same end would be answered by disarming, and leaving them to starve. The merit of such an argument would be complete by adding, that should they not be famished, before the arrival of their ships with a fresh supply of arms, we might then, if able, disarm them a second time, and send them on board their fleet, to return safely home. . . .

"Who could restrain the laugh of derision at positions so preposterous, were it not for the reflection that in the first magistrate of our country, they cast a blemish on our national character? What will the world think of the fold when such is the shepherd?"

President Polk approached the position of Hamilton when he met the Mexican "invasion" of disputed American territory by authorizing the battles of Palo Alto and Resaca de la Palma. Following these engagements he said in his message of May 11, 1846:

---

[12] 2 Stat. 129.
[13] Hamilton, Works, Hamilton, ed., 7: 745-748.

"After reiterated menaces, Mexico has passed the boundary of the United States, has invaded our territory and shed American blood upon the American soil. She has proclaimed that hostilities have commenced and that the two nations are now at war.

"As war exists, and, notwithstanding all our efforts to avoid it, exists by the act of Mexico herself, we are called upon by every consideration of duty and patriotism to vindicate with decision the honor, the rights and the interests of our country.

"In further vindication of our rights and defense of our territory, I invoke the prompt action of Congress to recognize the existence of the war, and to place at the disposition of the Executive the means of prosecuting the war with vigor, and thus hastening the restoration of peace." [14]

The Supreme Court accepted the views of Hamilton and Polk, when in the prize cases, it held that President Lincoln had properly recognized the southern rebellion as war.[15]

"If a war be made by invasion of a foreign nation, the President is not only authorized but bound to resist force by force. He does not initiate the war, but is bound to accept the challenge without waiting for any special legislative authority. And whether the hostile party be a foreign invader, or States organized in rebellion, it is none the less a war, although the declaration of it be 'unilateral.' Lord Stowell (1 Dodson 247) observes, 'It is not the less a war on that account, for war may exist without a declaration on either side. It is so laid down by the best writers on the law of nations. A declaration of war by one country only is not a mere challenge to be accepted or refused at pleasure by the other.' . . .

"This greatest of civil wars was not gradually developed by popular commotion, tumultuous assemblies, or local unorganized insurrections. However long may have been its previous conception, it nevertheless sprung forth suddenly from the parent brain, a Minerva in the full panoply of war. The President was bound to meet it in the shape it presents itself, without waiting for Congress to baptize it with a name; and no name given to it by him or them could change the fact. . . .

"Whether the President, in fulfilling his duties as Commander-in-Chief in suppressing an insurrection, has met with such armed hostile resistance, and a civil war of such alarming proportions, as will compel him to accord to them the character of belligerents, is a question to be decided by him, and this Court must be governed by the decision and acts of the political department of the government to which this power was intrusted. 'He must determine what degree of force the crisis demands.' The Proclamation of blockade is itself official and conclusive evidence to the Court that a state of war existed which demanded and authorized a recourse to such a measure, under the circumstances peculiar to the case."

---

[14] Richardson, Messages, 4: 442–443
[15] The Prize Cases, 2 Black 635, 638. Approved Matthews *v* McStea, 91 U. S. 7 (1875).

WAR AND THE USE OF FORCE. 289

President McKinley accepted this opinion and applied it to foreign war when on April 22, 1898, he recognized the Spanish rejection of the congressional ultimatum of April 20,[16] as a declaration of war and authorized a blockade of Cuba.[17] Three days later, on April 25, Congress passed a resolution declaring:[18]

> "That war be, and the same is hereby, declared to exist, and that war has existed since the twenty-first day of April, *Anno Domini* eighteen hundred and ninety-eight, including said day, between the United States of America and the Kingdom of Spain."

In his war message of April 2, 1917, President Wilson asked "Congress to declare the recent course of the German government to be in fact nothing less than war against the United States." Nevertheless, he admitted that it belonged to Congress to "formally accept the status of belligerent which has thus been thrust upon it." Congress did so by a resolution signed by the President 1:18 p.m., April 6, 1917, which asserted "that the state of war between the United States and the Imperial German Government which has thus been thrust upon the United States is hereby formally declared."[19]

210. *The Power to Recognize War.*

Practice and opinion indicate that the President concurrently with Congress has power to recognize the existence of civil or foreign war against the United States. It is believed, however, that such power could not properly be exercised unless the fact of war against the United States was so patent as to leave no doubt. Acts of war, such as those committed by Germany from 1915 to 1917, would not justify presidential recognition of war. In fact it is believed that with the general acceptance of the III Hague Convention of 1907,

---

[16] 30 Stat. 738; Moore, Digest, 6: 226.
[17] Message April 25, 1898, Moore, Digest, 6: 229.
[18] 30 Stat. 364.
[19] Comp. Stat., p. 17, Naval War College, Int. Law Doc., 1917, p. 225. A resolution of Dec. 7, 1917, stated: "Whereas the Imperial and Royal Austro-Hungarian Government has committed repeated acts of war against the Government and the people of the United States of America: Therefore be it Resolved . . . That a state of war is hereby declared to exist between, etc." *Ibid.*, 1917, p. 230.

by which "the contracting powers recognize that hostilities between themselves must not commence without previous and explicit warning, in the form either of a declaration of war, giving reasons, or of an ultimatum with conditional declaration of war," the President could not consider any act by a foreign power, short of such declaration or ultimatum, as a justification for recognition of war on his own responsibility. The commencement of war implies not only "acts of war" but also the intention to make war.[20] Thus where acts of violence or reprisal alone are in question, Congress is the only authority that can put the country in a state of war, though the President may take defensive measures, and doubtless with a wider scope than President Jefferson's message of 1801 indicated.

211. *The Power to Declare War.*

Where no war exists in fact, Congress is the only authority in the United States that can declare one, and Congress cannot delegate this power.

"The Constitution," said Senator Stone, of Missouri, "vests the war-making power alone in the Congress. It is a power that Congress is not at liberty to delegate. Moreover, I am personally unwilling to part with my constitutional responsibility as a Senator to express my judgment upon the issue of war, whenever and however it may be presented."[21]

However, this does not mean, as Senator Stone was contending when he made this unimpeachable statement, that Congress cannot delegate power to the President to use force for protective purposes.[22] Nor does it mean that the treaty-making power may not create an obligation upon Congress to declare war or to refrain from declaring it under given circumstances.[23]

212. *The Power to Terminate War.*

Though war may be begun by one nation, it takes two to end it. The President can make an armistice which suspends or terminates

---

[20] The Ekaterinoslav, The Argun, Takahashi, International Law Applied to the Russo-Japanese War, pp. 573, 761; Cobbett, Leading Cases on International Law, pp. 78.

[21] *Cong. Rec.*, 64th Cong., 2d Sess., p. 5895; Corwin, *op. cit.*, p. 153.

[22] In the Federal Convention, Aug. 17, 1787, "declare" war was substituted for "make" war on motion of Madison and Gerry so as to "leave the executive the power to repel sudden attacks." Farrand, *op. cit.*, 2: 318.

[23] *Supra,* secs. 37, 59, 151, 173.

hostilities but the treaty-making power must ordinarily act to terminate the war.

> "I have yet to learn," wrote Secretary of State Bayard, "that a war in which the belligerents, as was the case with the late Civil War, are persistent and determined, can be said to have closed until peace is conclusively established, either by treaty when the war is foreign, or when civil by proclamation of the termination of hostilities on one side and the acceptance of such proclamation on the other. The surrender of the main armies of one of the belligerents does not of itself work such termination." [24]

However, as the quotation suggests, war may be terminated in two other ways, by complete conquest, causing annihilation of one belligerent, or by cessation of hostilities and tacit acceptance of peace by both parties.[25] The South African and American civil wars illustrate the first method; the wars between Spain and her revolting American colonies the second.

213. *The Power to Recognize the Termination of War.*

What authority in the United States can determine the exact date at which a war terminates in these circumstances? The question is one of fact and the recognition of facts in international relations is normally a function of the President. Thus President Johnson proclaimed the end of the Civil War and the courts recognized these proclamations as authoritative.[26] Secretary of State Seward seems to have assumed likewise that the Executive could recognize the end of a war between two foreign states, when in 1868 he informed the Spanish minister that "the United States may find itself obliged to decide the question whether the war still exists between Spain and Peru, or whether that war has come to an end." [27]

The question of terminating a war by proclamation, made by one side and acquiesced in by the other, was raised by the Knox

---

[24] Moore, Digest, 7: 337. Jefferson thought "general letters of mark and reprisal" might be preferred to a formal declaration of war, "because, on a repeal of their edicts by the belligerent, a revocation of the letters of mark restores peace without the delay, difficulties and ceremonies of a treaty." Letter to Mr. Lincoln, 1808, *ibid.*, 7: 123.
[25] Wilson and Tucker, *op. cit.*, pp. 281-282.
[26] 14 Stat. 811, 13 Stat. 814, The Protector, 12 Wall. 700.
[27] Moore, Digest, 7: 337.

resolution of May 21, 1920, for repealing the declarations of war against Germany and Austria. This resolution was vetoed by President Wilson on May 27,[28] because it "does not seek to accomplish any of these objects" for which the United States entered the war, but when again introduced by the Senate Foreign Relations Committee, April 25, 1921, it passed both Houses and was signed by President Harding, July 2, 1921. The Resolution was defended on the ground that what Congress could pass it could repeal. This assumption fails to recognize the distinction between an act of legislation and a resolution creating a status or condition. Congress cannot, in general, repeal resolutions of the latter class, of which resolutions admitting states to the Union, incorporating territory, admitting nationals to citizenship, etc., are examples. An act of Congress can undoubtedly terminate war legislation and bring war to an end so far as domestic law is concerned,[28a] but its international effect, whatever its wording, depends upon the attitude of the enemy. This was recognized by President Harding when he submitted to the Senate draft treaties by which the enemy powers accepted the resolution of July 2, 1921:[28b]

"Formal Peace," he wrote to Senator Lodge on September 21, 1921, "has been so long delayed that there is no need now to emphasize the desirability of early action on the part of the Senate. It will be most gratifying if you and your colleagues will find it consistent to act promptly so that we may put aside the last remnant of war relationship and hasten our return to the fortunate relations of peace."

We have noticed that the power of recognizing foreign states, governments and belligerency is vested exclusively in the Presi-

---

[28] See note by C. P. Anderson, *Am. Jl. Int. Law*, 14: 384 (July, 1920). Text of Resolution, *ibid.*, p. 419; legislative history, *ibid.*, p. 438; veto message, Cong. Rec., 59: 7747. See also Corwin, *Mich. Law Rev.*, 18: 669 (May, 1920).

[28a] This was accomplished in part by a Resolution of March 3, 1921 (41 Stat. 1359), and in full by that of July 2, 1921. See remarks of Senator Lodge, Cong. Rec., Sept. 24, 1921, 61: 6434.

[28b] Cong. Rec., Sept. 24, 1921, 61: 6434. In presenting the treaties from the Committee on Foreign Relations Senator Lodge remarked: "Where would the failure to ratify leave us? It would leave us where we are today—in a technical state of war with Germany, Austria, and Hungary." *Ibid.*, September 26, 1921, 61: 6458.

dent.[29] The power to recognize the existence of war to which the United States is a party is vested concurrently in the President and Congress, the latter having the power by implication from its express power to declare war.[30] No constitutional clause has been cited from which congressional power to recognize the termination of war can be implied. On the contrary a resolution vesting Congress with power to "make peace" was voted down in the Federal Convention of 1787.[31]

The President's power to recognize the termination of war may be clearly deduced from his power as the representative organ and has been admitted by the Supreme Court in the case of the Civil War.[32] His proclamation or his reception or dispatch of diplomatic representatives from or to a former enemy therefore seems the proper method for recognizing peace in the absence of treaty, though, as in the case of recognizing new states, he is of course free to solicit the advice of Congress, which action would usually be desirable. This was the course actually followed in terminating the wars with Germany, Austria, and Hungary. By his proclamation, issued on November 14, 1921,[32a] after exchange of ratifications of the treaty with Germany of August 25 (and similar treaties with the other powers) President Harding recognized that the war terminated on July 2, 1921, the date on which Congress had passed a resolution declaring the war "at an end." The antedating of the proclamation indicates that the war terminated, not by express treaty, but by tacit agreement, recognized in the United States by the President, when, in his opinion, there was sufficient evidence that Germany had concurred in the opinion expressed by the United States on July 2.

B. The Power to Use Force in Foreign Affairs.

214. Diplomatic Pressure.

Force, coercion, or pressure may assume a number of forms in the conduct of foreign relations. The sending of notes, the making

---
[29] *Supra,* sec. 194.
[30] *Supra,* sec. 210.
[31] Debate, Aug. 17, 1787, Farrand, *op. cit.,* 2: 319.
[32] The Protector, 12 Wall. 700.
[32a] Treaty Series No. 658.

of formal protest, the withdrawal of a minister or ambassador, or the complete severance of diplomatic relations are milder forms of pressure, although all may carry implications of more serious action, and the last is seldom resorted to except as a preliminary to war. These acts are within the exclusive power of the President.[33]

215. *Display of Force.*

A more material means of bringing pressure is the display of force. This measure may be designed to bring pressure upon a foreign government by intimidation; to bring protection to merchant vessels on the high seas; or to bring order on the high seas through the intimidation of pirates, slave traders, etc. The President as Commander-in-Chief has power to move the navy. President Roosevelt's dispatch of a naval vessel to Colon, Panama, in 1903 illustrates the effectiveness of such methods. His dispatch of the fleet around the world in 1903 furnishes another illustration.[34] Display of force is useless as an agency of intimidation unless the party to be intimidated believes the force has power to act. Hence this method of bringing pressure can hardly be separated from such methods as the occupation of territory, reprisals, and the seizure of private property. Consequently the use of the navy for intimidation should be authorized by the President only after due consideration and never by a subordinate except in extreme emergency. Thus in 1887 Secretary of State Bayard wrote the Chargé in Peru:[35]

"It is always expected that the agents of this Department abroad will exercise extreme caution in summoning national war vessels to their aid at critical junctures, especially if there be no practical purpose to be subserved by their presence."

Congress has on several occasions authorized the display of force for protecting merchant vessels. Such authority was given by several acts of 1798 to defend them against French privateers. On February 25, 1917, President Wilson asked Congress to authorize

---

[33] Moore, Digest, 7: 103.

[34] *Supra,* sec. 145, Thayer, Life of John Hay, 2: 351. President Roosevelt's threat to employ force if Germany refused to arbitrate the Venezuela question in 1904, may also be mentioned, *Ibid.,* 2: 287.

[35] Moore, Digest, 7: 109, see also Mr. Adee to Mr. Sill, 1895, *ibid.,* 2: 401.

the arming of merchant vessels as a defense against German submarines but added: [36]

"No doubt I already possess that authority without special warrant of law, by the plain implication of my constitutional duties and powers, but I prefer in the present circumstances not to act upon general implication. I wish to feel that the authority and the power of the Congress are behind me in whatever it may become necessary for me to do."

The proposed measure passed the House of Representatives but was defeated by a Senate filibuster. Several Senators attacked it as an unconstitutional delegation of the power to declare war. However, on March 12th, Secretary of State Lansing gave out a statement to the foreign legations in Washington that: [37]

"The government of the United States has determined to place upon all American merchant vessels sailing through the barred areas, an armed guard for the protection of the vessels and the lives of the persons on board."

President John Adams had no doubt of his power to authorize the arming of merchant vessels, although he asked Congress to make detailed regulations for this purpose as it did in 1798.[38] The neutrality laws appear expressly to recognize the President's power by requiring armed merchant vessels leaving American ports to give bond "until the decision of the President is had thereon."[39] It should be noticed, however, that international law, as interpreted in American courts, authorizes the condemnation by a belligerent of merchant vessels resisting visit and search,[40] and an act of 1819, still in effect, expressly prohibits resistance to "a public armed vessel of some nation in amity with the United States."[41] The President's power to authorize arming is, however, clear, as is his power to authorize protection by naval convoys.[42]

---

[36] Corwin, *op. cit.*, p. 152.

[37] Naval War College, Int. Law Docs., 1917, p. 225.

[38] Message, May 16, 1797, Richardson, Messages, 1: 237.

[39] Criminal Code of 1910, sec. 17.

[40] The Bermuda, 3 Wall. 514; The Jane, 37 Ct. Cl. 24; The Rose, 37 Ct. Cl. 240; Moore, Digest, 7: 485–487; Naval War College, Int. Law Topics, 1903, p. 110; 1907, p. 61.

[41] Act March 3, 1819, 3 Stat. 513, made permanent Jan. 30, 1823, 3 Stat. 721. See also remarks of J. Q. Adams, Moore, Digest, 7: 492.

[42] *Ibid.*, 7: 492; Corwin, *op. cit.*, p. 156.

Congress has sometimes authorized the use of the navy for police purposes on the high seas, as to enforce neutrality and the suppression of piracy and the slave trade as required by treaty, but the President would seem to have power even in the absence of such acts, though seizures could not be made except of American vessels, pirates, or vessels liable under treaties.[43]

Forces may also be displayed on land frontiers by authority of the President as a defensive measure. An illustration is furnished by the mobilization on the Mexican border in 1914.[44]

216. *Occupation and Administration of Territory.*

The President doubtless has power to order the occupation of foreign territory to defend the territory of the United States against an "instant and overwhelming" menace.[45] Thus the Amelia Island pirates were destroyed in 1817 and General Pershing's expedition was sent into Mexico in pursuit of Villa in 1916.[46] An "instant and overwhelming" menace to American citizens abroad would give similar justification. The bombardment of Greytown, Nicaragua, in 1852 and the dispatch of troops to Peking in 1901 are illustrations.[47] The President may similarly dispatch troops in fulfilment of treaty guarantees. Thus several Presidents dispatched troops to Panama in pursuance of the guarantee treaty of 1846 and President Roosevelt sent troops to Cuba in 1906 in pursuance of the treaty of 1903.[48]

Where foreign territory is occupied in order to bring pressure upon a foreign government, the action is very likely to lead to war and an authorizing resolution of Congress would seem necessary. However, such occupations have occurred without express authorization, as for example President Taft's dispatch of troops to Nicaragua and San Domingo, and President Wilson's dispatch of troops to

---

[43] *Supra*, secs. 125, 126, 151.

[44] *Am. Year Book*, 1914, p. 303.

[45] The legitimacy of self-help in the presence of "a necessity of self-defense, instant, overwhelming and leaving no choice of means and no moment for deliberation" was recognized in the Caroline controversy of 1840, Moore, Digest, 2: 412.

[46] For other instances see Moore, 2: 402-408.

[47] *Ibid.*, 2: 400-402, 414-418; 5: 476-493.

[48] *Supra*, sec. 145, Taft, *op. cit.*, p. 87.

San Domingo, Haiti, and Vera Cruz, Mexico.[49] In such cases ratifying resolutions have frequently been passed after the act, or treaties have been made with the occupied state.[50]

Occupation of enemy territory is, of course, a legitimate method of warfare, and a declaration of war, *ex propria vigore,* authorizes the President to both occupy and militarily govern enemy territory, although it does not authorize him to annex it.[51]

217. *Capture and Destruction of Foreign Military Forces.*

The dispatch of military or naval forces to capture or destroy the forces of a foreign government would seem to bear such a close resemblance to war that it could hardly be authorized by the President alone. However, as we have seen in the case of the Tripolitan "war" of 1801, President Jefferson took such action, which was subsequently ratified by Congress. President Polk did the same in the Mexican war, though according to his theory the battles of Palo Alto and Resaca de la Palma were fought on United States territory in repelling invasion. Commodore Perry seems to have been authorized to use force to open Japan in 1852 and the Wyoming had similar authority to aid in the opening of the Straits of Shiminoseki, Japan, in 1864.[52] In fact in most cases of display of force, undoubtedly an ultimate use of force was authorized. Naval officers have often been sent on diplomatic missions by authority of the President alone, to semi-civilized states, with the evident intention that force should not only be displayed but used if necessary.[53]

Use of military force against foreign powers has often been authorized by Congress without declaration of war. This was true of resolutions relating to France in 1798, to Tripoli in 1801,

---

[49] Corwin, *op. cit.,* p. 162, *supra,* sec. 207.

[50] Thus a ratifying resolution was passed after the Vera Cruz incident of 1914, and a treaty authorizing the exercise of a police power by the United States was made with Haiti after the intervention had begun.

[51] Cross *v.* Harrison, 16 How. 164; Santiago *v.* Nogueras, 214 U. S. 260; Fleming *v.* Page, 9 How. 603.

[52] Moore, Digest, 7: 112–118.

[53] *Infra,* sec. 239. See also Paullin, Diplomatic Negotiations of American Naval Officers, Baltimore, 1912.

to Algiers in 1816, to Paraguay in the Water Witch incident of 1858, to Venezuela in 1890.[54]

A declaration or recognition of war of course automatically gives full power to the President to authorize an attack upon the military forces of the enemy.

218. *Seizure and Destruction of Private Property.*

Congress is expressly given power to "grant letters of marque and reprisal, and make rules concerning captures on land and water."[55] The President has no power to direct the capture of private property without express authorization of statute, treaty, or international law. Congress may authorize the grant of letters of marque and reprisal in time of peace, but has never done so.[56] During the war of 1812 privateering commissions were issued and in the Civil War they were authorized but not issued. Privateering is prohibited by the Declaration of Paris of 1856, and though the United States has never acceded, yet it has not resorted to the practice in subsequent wars.[57] Congress may authorize naval forces to make reprisal upon private property at sea in time of peace. Thus President Jackson asked Congress to authorize him to make reprisals against French vessels in view of the non-execution of the claims treaty of 1831:[58]

"The laws of nations," said President Jackson, "provide a remedy for such occasions. It is a well settled principle of the international code that where one nation owes another a liquidated debt, which it refuses or neglects to pay, the aggrieved party may seize on the property belonging to the other, its citizens or subjects, sufficient to pay the debt, without giving just cause of war. This remedy has been repeatedly resorted to, and recently by France herself towards Portugal, under circumstances less unquestionable."

Clay, in his report from the Senate Committee on Foreign Relations, wrote:[59]

"Reprisals do not of themselves produce a state of public war but they are not unfrequently the immediate precursor of it. . . . The authority

---

[54] Moore, Digest, 7: 109–112.
[55] U. S. Constitution, I, sec. 8, cl. 11.
[56] Mr. Sanford to Mr. Cass, Aug. 16, 1857, Moore, Digest, 7: 122.
[57] *Ibid.*, 7: 544, 558, 558.
[58] *Ibid.*, 7: 124.
[59] *Ibid.*, 7: 126–127.

to grant letters of marque and reprisal being specially delegated to Congress, Congress ought to retain to itself the right of judging of the time when they are proposed to be actually issued. The committee are not satisfied that Congress can, constitutionally, delegate this right."

Congress has, in fact, never authorized reprisals upon private property in time of peace, though reprisals and military expeditions against foreign territory both with and without congressional authorization have often resulted in the destruction of private property, as did the Greytown, Nicaragua, bombardment of 1852, and the Vera Cruz occupation of 1914. By a declaration of war, Congress authorizes general reprisals against enemy property at sea so far as permitted by international law.

Treaties may provide for making captures of private property, as in suppressing the slave trade and seal poaching. The President has power to employ the navy and revenue cutter service to enforce treaties without other authority, though Congress has usually given him express authority.[60]

International law authorizes the capture on the high seas of pirates at all times and of enemy and certain neutral private property in time of war. The President's powers in this regard derive from international law and are limited by it. He can authorize the capture of enemy and neutral private property at sea only as permitted by that law, which is enforced by prize courts before which captures must be brought for condemnation. Before the courts, an order of the President contrary to international law, unless authorized by express statute, will not justify the captor.[61]

Private property on land, even of the enemy, is exempt from seizure under international law, except when "military necessity" permits its requisition, sequestration, contribution, or destruction.[62] The President, it has been held, cannot authorize a general confiscation of enemy property. Thus, said the Supreme Court in Mitchell v. Harmony:[63]

---

[60] *Supra,* secs. 118, 119, 125, 126.
[61] Little v. Barreme, 2 Cranch 170.
[62] IV Hague Conventions, 1907, Arts. 46–56.
[63] Mitchell v. Harmony, 13 How. 115 (1851).

"There are, without doubt, occasions in which private property may lawfully be taken possession of or destroyed to prevent it from falling into the hands of the public enemy; and also where a military officer, charged with a particular duty, may impress private property into the public service or take it for public use. Unquestionably, in such cases, the government is bound to make full compensation to the owner; but the officer is not a trespasser.

"But we are clearly of opinion, that in all of these cases the danger must be immediate and impending; or the necessity urgent for the public service, such as will not admit of delay, and where the action of the civil authority would be too late in providing the means which the occasion calls for. It is impossible to define the particular circumstances of danger or necessity in which this power may be lawfully exercised. Every case must depend on its own circumstances. It is the emergency that gives the right, and the emergency must be shown to exist before the taking can be justified."

Congress, however, under its power to make rules concerning capture on land and water may authorize seizures contrary to international law.[64] In Brown v. United States, during the War of 1812, Chief Justice Marshall refused to permit the confiscation of British property on land since Congress had not expressly acted.[65]

"Does that declaration (of war), by its own operation, so vest the property of the enemy in the government, as to support proceedings for its seizure and confiscation, or does it vest only a right, the assertion of which depends on the will of the sovereign power? The universal practice of forbearing to seize and confiscate debts and credits, the principle universally received, that the right to them revives on the restoration of peace, would seem to prove that war is not an absolute confiscation of this property, but simply confers the right of confiscation. . . . It appears to the court, that the power of confiscating enemy property is in the legislature, and that the legislature has not yet declared its will to confiscate property which was within our territory at the declaration of war."

In view of these decisions, and considering the Emancipation Proclamation of January 1, 1863, as a general confiscation of a particular type of enemy property by proclamation of the President, there is serious ground for doubting the constitutionality of that proclamation.[66] The doubt, however, was very soon removed

---

[64] Miller v. U. S., 11 Wall. 268; Willoughby, *op. cit.*, p. 1220.

[65] Brown v. U. S., 8 Cranch 110 (1814). It is doubtful whether international law at present confers a "right of confiscation" even upon the sovereign authority. *Supra*, note 62.

[66] Richardson, Messages, 6: 85, 96, 157; Burgess, Civil War and Reconstruction, 2: 117; Rhodes, History of U. S., 4: 70, *supra*, sec. 47, note 59.

by passage of the thirteenth amendment. During the Civil War, Congress authorized the confiscation of many kinds of enemy property on land, and during the World War it authorized sequestration of such property in the United States by an alien property custodian.[67]

219. *Commercial Pressure and Retaliation.*

Through its power to regulate foreign commerce, the postal service and by implication all means of conveyance and transmission of intelligence with foreign nations, Congress may bring pressure by means of retorsion, retaliation, non-intercourse and embargoes.

Measures of retorsion and retaliation have been frequent. Thus by an act of 1818, " the ports of the United States were closed, after September 30, 1818, against British vessels arriving from a British colony which, by the ordinary laws, was closed against American vessels."[68] The general revenue act of September 8, 1916, provides for retaliation against British commercial restrictions, the black list and mail seizures although that country was not specifically referred to.[69] An act to protect American oil investors abroad by retorsion was thus referred to in a note of November 10, 1920, protesting against the Allied policy in Asia Minor:[70]

"The General leasing law of February 25, 1920, has not always been thoroughly understood. It proposes to treat the citizens of any foreign country precisely as that foreign country treats our citizens. It is no more restrictive than the golden rule. It is a purely defensive provision. . . . At the same time the United States must be prepared to meet promptly and effectively any unwelcome developments or any kind of competition that may fall to our lot with the purpose of safeguarding, so far as may be in our power, the future security of this country."

Non-intercourse measures and general embargoes were used during the French Revolutionary and Napoleonic wars to bring pressure upon the belligerents and on March 14, 1912, an act was

---

[67] *Supra,* note 64. Trading with the Enemy Act, Oct. 6, 1917, secs. 6, 7, 40 Stat. 415–416; Comp. Stat., sec. 3115½cc, d.

[68] 3 Stat. 432; Moore, Digest, 7: 106.

[69] 39 Stat. 799, secs. 805, 806; Comp. Stat., sec. 8830qr; *Am. Year Book,* 1916, pp. 68, 69, 73.

[70] This act (Feb. 25, 1920, sec. 1) was also referred to in a note to the Netherlands government on April 19, 1921, protesting against exclusion of American interests from oil development in the Djambi fields in the Dutch East Indies.

passed authorizing the President to embargo arms and munitions bound to American countries in a condition of domestic violence.[71] In all of these acts power has been delegated to the President to decide when the circumstances contemplated by the act exist and by proclamation to put it into effect. This delegation has been justified on the same theory as delegation in reciprocity acts, that it is delegation to find on a fact and not to determine a policy.[72] The general power of Congress to prohibit importations or exportations has been sustained under the commerce clause.[73] Congress also has power under this clause to regulate cables, radio and telegraph used in foreign commerce[74] but in this field the President has been held to have concurrent powers:[75]

"The President has charge of our relations with foreign powers. It is his duty to see that, in the exchange of commodities among nations, we get as much as we give. He ought not to stand by and permit a cable to land on our shores under a concession from a foreign power which does not permit our cables to land on its shores and enjoy *there* facilities equal to those accorded its cable *here*. For this reason President Grant insisted on the first point in his message of 1875.

"The President is not only the head of the diplomatic service, but commander in chief of the Army and Navy. A submarine cable is of inestimable service to the Government in communicating with its officers in the diplomatic and consular service, and in the Army and Navy when abroad. The President should, therefore, demand that the Government have precedence in the use of the line, and this was done by President Grant in the third point of his message.

"Treating a cable simply as an instrument of commerce, it is the duty of the President, pending legislation by Congress, to impose such restrictions as will forbid unjust discriminations, prevent monopolies, promote competition, and secure reasonable rates. These were the objects of the second and fourth points in President Grant's message.

"The President's authority to control the landing of a foreign cable does not flow from his right to permit it in the sense of granting a franchise, but

---

[71] Moore, Digest, 7: 142-151; 37 Stat. 630; Comp. Stat., sec. 7677.

[72] The Brig Aurora, 7 Cranch 382, 388, approved in Field *v.* Clark, 143 U. S. 649 (1892); *supra*, sec. 60.

[73] U. S. *v.* The William, 28 Fed. 614 (1808).

[74] Pensacola Tele. Co. *v.* Western Union, 96 U. S. 1 (1878).

[75] Richards, Acting Att. Gen., 22 Op. 13; Moore, Digest, 2: 462. An act of May 27, 1921, requires Presidential license for the landing and operation of cables connecting the United States with foreign countries and authorizes the President to withhold or revoke licenses in pursuance of stated objects similar to those referred to in this opinion. See Wilson, Am. Jl. Int. Law, 16: 78.

from his power to prohibit it should he deem it an encroachment on our rights or prejudicial to our interests. . . . I am of the opinion, therefore, that the President has the power, in the absence of legislative enactment, to control the landing of foreign cables."

Prohibition by Congress of the importation of particular goods, such as lottery tickets, obscene literature, low grade teas, prize fight films, etc., has also been resorted to as a protective measure and has been sustained by the courts.[76] Similarly the XVIII Amendment has provided for the prohibition of the import or export of alcoholic beverages.

Treaties may require the prohibition of commerce in certain articles but ordinarily legislation is necessary to execute such provisions.[77] Thus the commerce in opium with Corea is prohibited by article VII of the treaty of 1882 but express provision is made that it " shall be enforced by appropriate legislation on the part of the United States and of Chosen."

According to international law, as applied by American courts, trading with the enemy automatically becomes illegal by the declaration of war, unless licensed by authority of Congress or the President. Congress has, however, usually passed express acts prohibiting such trade.[78]

220. *Exclusion, Expulsion and Internment of Aliens.*

Finally as a defensive measure Congress has authorized the exclusion and internment of alien enemies in time of war and the exclusion and expulsion of aliens of defined classes and nationalities in time of peace.[79] The power of Congress to pass such acts has

---

[76] Buttfield *v.* Stranahan, 192 U. S. 470 (1904); Weber *v.* Freed, 239 U. S. 325.

[77] *Supra*, sec. 59; *infra*, sec. 256.

[78] Trading with the Enemy Act, Oct. 6, 1917, 40 Stat. 411; Comp. Stat. 3115½a.

[79] Alien enemies, Rev. Stat., 4067, amended April 16, 1918; Comp. Stat., sec. 7615; Chinese Exclusion and Expulsion, May 6, 1882, 22 Stat. 58, amended 1884, Comp. Stat., sec. 4290, and act Sept. 13, 1888, 25 Stat. 479, Comp. Stat., 4313; exclusion and expulsion of undesirable aliens, act Feb. 5, 1917, secs. 3, 18, 19, 39 Stat. 875, 887, 889, and act Oct. 16, 1918, 40 Stat., c. 186, sec. 1, Comp. Stat., 4289¼ amended May 10 and June 5, 1920, 41 stat. 593, 1009. An act of May 19, 1921, excluded all aliens beyond 3 per cent. of the number from that country resident in the United States.

been sustained, in part under the commerce clause[80] and in part as resulting from numerous powers in foreign relations which together constituted the usual powers of "sovereign and independent states."[81] These laws have delegated wide powers of enforcement, often with a minimum of judicial review, to executive officers but this delegation has been sustained.[82] The temporary alien act of June 25, 1798, provided:[83]

"That it shall be lawful for the President of the United States at any time during the continuance of this act to *order* all such *aliens* as he shall judge dangerous to the peace and safety of the United States, or shall have reasonable grounds to suspect are concerned in any treasonable or secret machinations against the government thereof, to depart out of the territory of the United States within such time as shall be expressed in such order."

Hardly less broad is the act of October 16, 1918, providing that:

"Aliens who are anarchists, . . . who are members of or affiliated with any organization that entertains a belief in, teaches or advocates the overthrow by force or violence of the government of the United States or of all forms of law, or that entertains or teaches disbelief in or opposition to all organized governments . . . shall be excluded from the United States," and if such alien is found in the United States, he "shall upon the warrant of the Secretary of Labor be taken into custody and deported."

During the World War many alien enemies were interned by order of the President under authority of the alien enemy act of July 6, 1798, as amended to include women in April, 1918.[84]

221. *Power to Employ Various Methods of Coercion.*

Of the seven types of measures discussed, the President can, in pursuance of his constitutional duties, authorize diplomatic pressure, or display of force on national territory or on the high seas without express authority of Congress. He has, in pursuance of such duties, authorized the occupation of foreign territory and the capture and destruction of foreign military forces without express authority, though generally Congress has ratified his act by later resolution. It would seem that the President in such cases ought to await an authorizing resolution unless an immediate necessity demands promptness. Finally authority to seize or destroy private

---

[80] Head Money Cases, 112 U. S. 580.

[81] Chinese Exclusion Cases, 130 U. S. 581; Fong Yue Ting *v.* U. S., 149 U. S. 398.

[82] U. S. *v.* Ju Toy, 198 U. S. 253.

[83] 1 Stat. 576. Limited to two years by its own terms.

[84] *Supra*, note 77.

property, to enforce commercial discriminations, restrictions or prohibitions and to exclude, expel or intern aliens must be given by act of Congress, treaty or international law, but much discretion may be delegated the President. The existence of war, whether by declaration of Congress or recognition by the President, *ex propria vigore,* authorizes the President, as Commander-in-Chief, to enforce such of these measures of coercion as are permitted by the international law of war, and Congress cannot interfere with him in the direction of military and naval forces:

"Congress," said the Supreme Court, "has the power not only to raise and support and govern armies but to declare war. It has, therefore, the power to provide by law for carrying on war. This power necessarily extends to all legislation essential to the prosecution of war with vigor and success, except such as interferes with the command of forces and the conduct of campaigns. That power and duty belong to the President as commander-in-chief. Both these powers are derived from the Constitution, but neither is defined by that instrument. Their extent must be determined by their nature, and by the principles of our institutions. The power to make the necessary laws is in Congress, the power to execute in the President. Both powers imply many subordinate and auxiliary powers. Each includes all authority essential to its due exercise. But neither can the President, in war more than in peace, intrude upon the proper authority of Congress, nor Congress upon the proper authority of the President. Both are servants of the people, whose will is expressed in the fundamental law. Congress can not direct the conduct of campaigns." [84a]

222. *Purposes for Which the President May Employ Force under the Constitution.*

However, we cannot distinguish the respective powers of the President and Congress merely by considering the method of coercion. The purposes or ends in view are even more important. The Constitution requires the President to "take care that the laws be faithfully executed."[85] Though this imposes a responsibility and is not a grant of power, yet it indicates certain purposes for which the President must use the constitutional powers elsewhere granted. What does the term "laws" embrace? In the Neagle case, the court held that it should be broadly interpreted.[86]

[84a] *Ex parte* Milligan, 4 Wall. 2 (1866). See also Willoughby, *op. cit.,* 2: 1207; Taft, *op. cit.,* pp 94–99; Wright, Col. Law Rev., 20: 134.

[85] U. S. Constitution, II, sec. 3; *supra,* sec. 93.

[86] *In re* Neagle, 135 U. S. 1; Willoughby, *op. cit.,* p. 1135.

306 THE CONTROL OF AMERICAN FOREIGN RELATIONS.

"Is this duty limited to the enforcement of Acts of Congress or of treaties of the United States according to their *express terms,* or does it include the rights, duties and obligations growing out of the Constitution itself, our international relations and the protection implied by the nature of the government under the Constitution?"

The Constitution guarantees the "privileges and immunities of citizens of the United States" and these were held in the Slaughter House cases to include the right to protection abroad.[87] Consequently the President's duty to execute the laws includes a duty to protect citizens abroad and in pursuance of this duty he may utilize his powers as Commander-in-Chief. Thus the court justified the President in authorizing the bombardment of Greytown, Nicaragua, in 1854:[88]

"As respects the interposition of the Executive abroad, for the protection of the lives or property of the citizen, the duty must, of necessity, rest in the discretion of the President. Acts of lawless violence to the citizen or his property cannot be anticipated and provided for; and the protection, to be effectual or of any avail, may, not unfrequently, require the most prompt and decided action. Under our system of Government, the citizen abroad is as much entitled to protection as the citizen at home. The great object and duty of Government is the protection of the lives, liberty, and property of the people composing it, whether abroad or at home; and any Government failing in the accomplishment of the object, or the performance of the duty, is not worth the preserving."

In the Neagle case the Supreme Court referred to and endorsed executive action in 1853 in protecting Martin Koszta, a Hungarian revolutionist who had not completed his American naturalization. Captain Ingraham, in command of the American sloop-of-war St. Louis arrived in Smyrna as Koszta was being abducted, "demanded his surrender to him, and was compelled to train his guns upon the Austrian vessel before his demands were complied with." The court notes that Secretary of State Marcy's defense of this action and insistence upon the liberation of Koszta who had been

---

[87] U. S. Constitution, Amendment XIV; Slaughter House Cases, 16 Wall. 36.

[88] Durand *v.* Hollins, 4 Blatch 451, 454; Corwin, *op. cit.,* p. 144. J. B. Moore notes that President Pierce and Secretary Marcy justified this action on the ground that "Greytown was a community claiming to exist outside the bounds of any recognized state or political entity." (Proc. Am. Phil. Soc., Minutes, 60: xvii.) This, however, does not apply to many other instances in which force has been used abroad under authority of the President and in this case the court rests the power on broader grounds.

placed in charge of the French consul at Smyrna "met the approval of the country and Congress, who voted a gold medal to Captain Ingraham for his conduct of the affair." Yet says the court, "upon what act of Congress then existing can any one lay his finger in support of the action of the government in this matter."[89] In view of these incidents and judicial endorsements, we may accept Borchard's statement; with the sole qualification that "the manner" must not amount to a making of war:[90]

"Inasmuch as the Constitution vests in Congress authority 'to declare war' and does not empower Congress to direct the President to perform his constitutional duties of protecting American citizens on foreign soil, it is believed that the Executive has unlimited authority to use the armed forces of the United States for protective purposes abroad in any manner and on any occasion he considers expedient."

The Constitution also guarantees the States a Republican form of government and protection against invasion.[91] Furthermore the right of national self-defense is recognized at international law and the corresponding duty of the government has been asserted by the Supreme Court:[92]

"To preserve its independence and give security against foreign aggression and encroachment is the highest duty of every nation, and to attain these ends nearly all other considerations are to be subordinated."

Thus, if he considers such action essential for the enforcement of acts of Congress and treaties and for the protection of the citizens and territory of the United States, the President is obliged by the Constitution itself to use his power as commander-in-chief to direct the forces abroad, and this duty resting on the Constitution itself cannot be taken away by act of Congress. Thus says President Taft:[93]

---

[89] *In re* Neagle, 135 U. S. 1.

[90] Borchard, *op. cit.*, p. 452. See also Root, address in Senate, Aug. 14, 1912, *Cong. Rec.*, 48: 10929; Military and Colonial Policy of the United States, 1916, p. 157.

[91] U. S. Constitution, Art. IV, sec. 4.

[92] Chinese Exclusion Cases, 130 U. S. 581 (1889).

[93] Taft, *op. cit.*, pp. 128–129. See also Wright, *Col. Law Rev.*, 20: 135–136, and *Am. Jl. Int. Law,* 12: 77; *supra*, secs. 125, 126, 151. By reduction of the army and navy or refusal of supplies, Congress might seriously impair the *de facto* power of the President to perform these duties, but it can not limit his legal power as Commander-in-Chief to employ the means at his disposal for these purposes. See *Ex parte* Milligan, 4 Wall. 2, *supra*, sec. 221.

"The President is made Commander-in-Chief of the Army and Navy by the Constitution, evidently for the purpose of enabling him to defend the country against invasion, to suppress insurrection and to take care that the laws be faithfully executed. If Congress were to attempt to prevent his use of the army for any of these purposes, the action would be void."

223. *Purposes for Which the President May Employ Force under Statute.*

Aside from the purposes defined by the Constitution itself, for which the President may utilize the forces, other purposes have been defined by act of Congress. It is true, the general delegations of power to use the militia and the similar delegation to use the army and navy "to execute the laws of the union, suppress insurrection and repel invasions" have been given an interpretation confining such use to the territory.[94] Laws in this phrase has been held to mean laws of territorial application and says Pomeroy:[95]

"Insurrection and invasion must be internal. We do not repel an invasion by attacking the invading nation upon its own soil. Still there can be no question that the militia may be called out before the invaders set foot upon our territory. It is a fair construction of language to say that one means of 'repelling' an invasion is to have a force ready to receive the threatened invaders when they shall arrive."

Attorney-General Wickersham, however, makes the qualification:[96]

"If the militia were called into the service of the General government to repel an invasion, it would not be necessary to discontinue their use at the boundary line, but they might (within certain limits, at least) pursue and capture the invading force, even beyond that line. . . . This may well be held to be within the meaning of the term 'to repel invasion.'"

The expatriation act of July 27, 1868, however, authorizes the President to demand the release of American citizens unjustly deprived of liberty and:[97]

---

[94] Act of Jan. 21, 1913 (Dick Act), 32 Stat., 776, sec. 4; 35 Stat. 400; 38 Stat. 284, based on Acts of May 2, 1794, and Feb. 28, 1795, 1 Stat. 264, 424. Judge Ad. Gen. Davis held in 1908 that the term "laws" might apply to any congressional resolution of extraterritorial effect (*Cong. Rec.*, 42: 6943), but this was not sustained by the Attorney General, *infra*, note 96.

[95] Pomeroy, Constitutional Law, 9th ed., p. 387.

[96] Wickersham, Att. Gen., 29 Op. 322 (1912).

[97] Rev. Stat., sec. 2001; Comp. Stat., sec. 3957.

"If unreasonably delayed or refused, the President shall use such means, not amounting to acts of war, as he may think necessary and proper to obtain or effectuate the release."

Aside from such general acts,[98] Congress may authorize a broad use of force by acts or resolutions applying to particular incidents and by declarations of war.[99]

According to Justice Story in Martin *v.* Mott, it belongs to the President himself to interpret the exigencies in which a use of force is justifiable:[100]

"He is necessarily constituted the judge of the existence of the exigency in the first instance and is bound to act according to his belief of the facts. . . . Whenever a statute gives a discretionary power to any person, to be exercised by him upon his own opinion of certain facts, it is a sound rule of construction that the statute constitutes him the sole and exclusive judge of the existence of those facts."

This case applied to the act of 1795 delegating the President power to call forth the militia, but the same principle would seem valid whatever the source of his authority, whether statute, treaty or the Constitution itself.

224. *Conclusion.*

Thus in practice the President has an exceedingly broad discretion to authorize the use of the forces. Under the Constitution he can use the military and naval forces to defend the territory and to protect American citizens abroad and on the high seas. The use of force to protect inchoate citizens, such as Martin Koszta, and inchoate territory such as San Domingo in 1871 is more questionable.[101] For the meeting of responsibilities under international law and treaty the President likewise has authority to use the army and navy on the high seas and in foreign territory.[102] To meet responsibilities under inchoate international law, such as the Monroe

---

[98] For legislation authorizing the use of force to meet international responsibilities, see Chap. XII, A.
[99] Moore, Digest, 7: 109, 155; Wright, *Am. Jl. Int. Law,* 12: 77.
[100] Martin *v.* Mott, 12 Wheat. 19.
[101] Corwin, *op. cit.,* pp. 142, 158, and debate there quoted from *Cong. Globe,* 42 Cong., 1st sess., pt. 1, p. 294.
[102] *Supra,* Chap. XII, A.

310 THE CONTROL OF AMERICAN FOREIGN RELATIONS.

Doctrine, the power, though often exercised, is more questionable,[103] and for the use of forces within the territory, even to meet international responsibilities, statutory authorization is generally advisable, though apparently not strictly necessary.[104] Finally, for the purpose of bringing pressure upon foreign governments for political objects, it is doubtful whether the President has constitutional power to use force, although he may bring diplomatic pressure. For political intervention, authorization by special resolution of Congress seems proper and has been the usual practice.

---

[103] Corwin, *op. cit.*, p. 162.
[104] *Supra*, sec. 126.

CHAPTER XVII.

The Power to Establish Instrumentalities for Conducting Foreign Relations.

A. Constitutional Principles.

225. The Power of Congress to Create Offices and Agencies.

The establishment of an instrumentality for conducting public affairs involves two processes, (1) the creation of an office or agency, by definition of its functions, procedure and privileges, (2) the nomination, appointment and commissioning of a person or persons to fill such office or agency. Since Chief Justice Marshall's decision in McCulloch *v.* Maryland there has been no question but that Congress has power to create instrumentalities "necessary and proper" to give full effect to the powers delegated to any of the departments of the government.[1]

"Let the end be legitimate, let it be within the scope of the Constitution, and all means which are appropriate, which are plainly adapted to that end, which are not prohibited, but consist with the letter and spirit of the Constitution, are constitutional."

This power extends not only to the creation of corporations but also to the organization of the executive and judicial departments of government. Congress has exclusive power to create "offices" under the United States aside from those established by the Constitution itself, "to raise and support armies" and "to provide and maintain a navy."[2] It also has power, concurrent in part with that of the President, "to make rules for the government and regulation of the land and naval forces";[3] and power, concurrent in part with that of the states, though supreme when exercised, to organize the

---

[1] McCulloch *v.* Md., 4 Wheat. 316.
[2] U. S. Constitution, Art. II, sec. 2, cl. 2; I, sec. 8, cl. 12, 13.
[3] *Ibid.*, I, sec. 8, cl. 14; *Ex parte* Milligan, 4 Wall. 2.

militia.[4] Thus Congress has adequate power to create any instrumentality which may be "necessary and proper" for the exercise of executive power.

Hardly less complete is its power to create courts. It may "constitute tribunals inferior to the Supreme Court" for exercising the judicial power of the United States outlined in Article III of the Constitution and may regulate their jurisdiction and the appellate jurisdiction of the Supreme Court.[5] But it may also organize courts in the territories[6] or abroad[7] and administrative courts in the United States which hear and decide cases but do not exercise the judicial power described in Article III.[8]

Practically the only legal limitation upon the power of Congress to create and organize instrumentalities not defined by the Constitution itself, for the exercise of national powers, is (1) that it may not itself exercise judicial or executive power, (2) that it may not delegate legislative power, (3) that it may not vest non-judicial power in the federal courts, though it may in administrative courts, and (4) that it may not burden state officers, though it may vest in them powers exercisable at discretion.[9]

226. *The Power to Create Offices and Agencies by Treaty.*

The treaty-making power may provide instrumentalities convenient for carrying out powers in the legitimate scope of treaties, such as diplomatic and consular offices, consular courts for exercising American jurisdiction abroad or foreign jurisdiction in the United States, and international courts, councils, and administrative unions. Doubtless in many cases Congress would have to create and provide for the necessary "offices" under the United States before such treaty-established organs could become effective, but such a need of congressional cooperation is not a legal limitation

---

[4] *Ibid.*, I, sec. 8, cl. 16; Houston *v.* Moore, 5 Wheat. 1.
[5] *Ibid.*, I, sec. 8, cl. 9; III, sec. 2, cl. 2; *Ex parte* McCardle, 7 Wall. 506.
[6] Am. Ins. Co. *v.* Canter, 1 Pet. 511.
[7] *In re* Ross, 140 U. S. 453.
[8] Gordon *v.* U. S., 2 Wall. 561; Willoughby, *op. cit.*, p. 1277.
[9] *Supra*, sec. 60; Gordon *v.* U. S., 2 Wall. 561; Ky. *v.* Dennison, 24 How. 66; Willoughby, Am. Constitutional System, p. 123.

INSTRUMENTALITIES FOR FOREIGN RELATIONS.   313

upon the treaty power. Legally the treaty power seems to be limited in its power to create and organize instrumentalities not defined by the Constitution itself, only by the condition that the instrumentality be *bona fide* of international interest and by the conditions stated above applicable to the power of Congress.[10]

227. *The Power of the President to Create Offices and Agencies.*

The President and the courts are not specifically endowed with power to create new instrumentalities for exercising national powers. In the Neagle case, the Supreme Court went far toward recognizing a power in the President to delegate executive authority to persons not occupying a congressionally established "office." This, however, should probably be interpreted no farther than a recognition that the President may create subordinate agencies, not strictly "offices" necessary for performing executive functions.[11] The President's authorization of personal "agents" for conducting diplomatic negotiations and representing the United States in international conferences is justified under the same inherent power. Legislative bodies and courts seem to have a similar inherent power to create subordinate positions by merely making appointments thereto. In most cases the nature and necessity of such subordinate positions has been established by practice and tradition, the issue being raised rather as to the inherent power to make appointments thereto, than as to the inherent power to create the position.[12]

In addition to such essential subordinate positions, the President, as representative authority of the nation, has recognized and applied international law to determine the grades of "ambassadors, public ministers and consuls" to be sent by the United States. These offices being established by the Constitution itself, congressional action is not necessary.[13] As Commander-in-Chief, the President has exercised much discretion in organizing the Army and Navy. He may provide administrative agencies and courts for governing

[10] *In re* Ross, 140 U. S. 453.
[11] *In re* Neagle, 135 U. S. 1; Willoughby, Constitutional Law, 1155.
[12] *Infra*, sec. 228 (3).
[13] *Infra*, sec. 236.

territory under military occupation, even after conclusion of war and annexation of the territory,[14] but he cannot vest such courts with prize jurisdiction.[15] This power is, of course, superseded by acts of Congress organizing the territory.

228. *The Appointment of Officers and Agents.*

Quite different is the situation with reference to the filling of such offices or agencies once created. It is often said that the appointing power is essentially executive in character, and doubtless constitutional understandings have tended toward presidential dominance in this field, but as a matter of federal constitutional law, it seems that the President has no more inherent power in this regard than do the other departments. All power to make appointments seems to be derivable (1) from express delegation by the Constitution, (2) from act of Congress, (3) from inherent powers of the departments under the principle of separation of powers. Strictly speaking, the making of an appointment involves three processes: nomination, appointment and commissioning. The first and last have for the most part been vested in the President alone, and undoubtedly the sole power of initiation and absolute veto upon appointments thus implied makes his will paramount in appointments. It should be noticed that the courts have held that the granting of a commission is a ministerial duty after the appointment has been made but they admit there is no power to compel the President to sign a commission (except threat of impeachment) and without the commission no person is an "officer" with legal powers.[16]

1. The Constitution provides that the President " shall nominate, and by and with the advice and consent of the Senate, shall appoint Ambassadors, other public Ministers and Consuls, Judges of the

---

[14] Cross *v.* Harrison, 16 How. 164; Santiago *v.* Nogueras, 214 U. S. 260.

[15] Jecker *v.* Montgomery, 13 How. 498, but Congress may retroactively confer such jurisdiction on presidential courts. The Grapeshot, 9 Wall. 129.

[16] Marbury *v.* Madison, 1 Cranch 137. If a commission has been signed and is in the hands of an officer, other than the President, its delivery may be mandamused, *ibid.*

Supreme Court, and all other officers of the United States, whose appointments are not herein otherwise provided for, and which shall be established by law." "The President shall have power to fill up all vacancies that may happen during the recess of the Senate, by granting commissions which shall expire at the end of their next session." To the states is "reserved . . . respectively, the appointment of the officers" of the militia even when called forth into national service.[17]

2. "But the Congress may by law vest the appointment of such inferior officers, as they think proper, in the President alone, in the courts of law, or in the heads of departments."[18]

3. Finally, an inherent power of appointment exists in each of the departments as an implication of the doctrine of separation of powers. "If any one of the departments," says Goodnow, "is to be expected to be independent of the others, it must have the power to appoint its subordinates. The legislature may thus appoint all its subordinate officers, while courts may appoint such officers as criers and others who are necessary in order that the courts may perform their duties properly."[19] It may be added that the President exercises such an inherent power in appointing personal agents for conducting diplomatic intercourse without congressional authorization and without consent of the Senate, a practice which the Senate has often objected to but never with success.[20] It may also be noticed that in the National Government Congress has in fact conferred power on the courts to appoint such essential subordinates as clerks, criers, reporters, etc., under the constitutional clause referred to, but doubtless in the absence of such statutes the courts could make such appointments as they have done in the states.

229. *Limitations upon the Appointing Power.*

Apparently the only constitutional limitation upon the appointing power is that which provides:[21]

---

[17] U. S. Constitution, II, sec. 2, cl. 2, 3; I, sec. 8, cl. 16.
[18] *Ibid.,* II, sec. 2, cl. 2.
[19] Goodnow, *op. cit.,* pp. 37–38.
[20] *Infra,* secs. 238–240.

"No Senator or Representative shall, during the time for which he was elected, be appointed to any civil office under the authority of the United States which shall have been created or the emoluments whereof shall have been increased during such time; and no person holding any office under the United States shall be a member of either House during his continuance in office."

It should be noticed, however, that the incompatibility of congressional membership with the holding of an "office" does not apply to service as an agent. Senators have often been sent on special diplomatic missions, under presidential appointment. The occupancy of a judicial office is not incompatible with the holding of another office. John Jay and Oliver Ellsworth were each sent on diplomatic missions by appointment of the President, consented to by the Senate, while justices of the Supreme Court, and on other occasions justices have been appointed by the President to serve on courts of arbitration.[22] The Senate held that Gallatin's position as Secretary of the Treasury was incompatible with his appointment as commissioner to conclude the Peace Treaty of Ghent and forced his withdrawal from the former position. The grounds of this incompatibility, however, were never precisely stated and do not seem to be sustained by analogy or subsequent practice. Thus while Civil Governor of the Philippines, Mr. Taft was appointed on a special mission to the Pope, and while Secretary of State, Mr. Lansing was appointed upon the mission to conclude the Peace Treaty of Versailles. In neither of these cases, however, was the appointment to a regular office, nor was it submitted to the Senate.[23]

230. *Powers of Removing and of Directing Officers and Agents.*

In the United States Government, though not in the states, the removal power seems to belong inherently to the Chief Executive. This was decided in the debate of the first Congress on a bill for organizing the Department of State and has been consistently admitted since, with exception of the period of the tenure of office acts, 1867–

---

[21] U. S. Constitution, I, sec. 6, cl. 2.

[22] Corwin, *op. cit.*, p. 66; *supra*, sec. 176.

[23] Moore, Digest, 4: 447. For facsimile reproduction of Mr. Lansing's commission, see Lansing, The Peace Negotiations, 1921, p. 28.

1887. These acts, originating in political hostility to President Johnson, were virtually held to have been unconstitutional by the Supreme Court after their repeal.[24]

Through the power of removal the President has the power to direct administrative officials with no practical restraint, as was illustrated by President Jackson's action in the bank controversy. By successive removals of Secretaries of the Treasury, he was able to direct the removal of government deposits from the Second United States Bank, although by law discretion in this matter belonged to the Secretary.[25]

> "I think," wrote Attorney General Cushing in 1855, "the general rule to be ... that the head of department is subject to the direction of the President. (This was said in relation to duties imposed by statute upon a head of a department.) I hold that no head of department can lawfully perform an official act against the will of the President and that will is, by the Constitution, to govern the performance of all such acts." [26]

As Commander-in-Chief, the President has complete power of directing the military and naval services of the national government.[27]

B. *Application of Principles to Foreign Affairs.*

231. *The Types of Agencies Conducting Foreign Relations.*

The instruments used for conducting foreign relations may be classified as (1) national, military, naval, administrative, and judi-

---

[24] Parsons *v.* U. S., 167 U. S. 324. The power to remove has usually been considered an implication of the power to appoint. (*Ex parte* Hennen, 13 Pet. 230, 1839; U. S. *v.* Perkins, 116 U. S. 143; Shurtleff *v.* U. S., 189 U. S. 311; President Wilson's veto of National Budget Bill, June 4, 1920.) This derivation of the power, however, would seem to leave Congress discretion to determine the authority to remove "inferior officers" for whose appointment they may provide, a discretion it has never successfully exercised as to executive and administrative officers and which is inconsistent with the recognized practice whereby the President alone removes, even when the appointing power is the President acting with advice and consent of the Senate. See Powell, *National Municipal Review*, 9: 538–545, and *supra,* secs. 52, 53.

[25] Goodnow, *op. cit.,* pp. 77–82.
[26] Cushing, Att. Gen., 7 Op. 453, 470.
[27] *Ex parte* Milligan, 4 Wall. 2, *supra,* sec. 221.

cial officers; (2) national and international political officers and agents; (3) international administrative and judicial agencies. Officers of the first kind are clearly national. They are the product of national law alone and are accountable to national law alone. Agencies of the last kind are just as clearly international. They can be founded only by the agreement of nations, and can exercise authority only in matters, as to which nations have agreed to be bound by them. Officers and agencies of the second class, however, occupy a twilight zone. We may distinguish the offices in the group which are primarily national from the agencies primarily international. Thus a diplomatic officer or consul, though enjoying certain rights, privileges and powers under international law, is primarily a national officer, bound primarily by his national law and policy. He can act only under express instructions. He is in fact a delegate. On the other hand, the representative of a nation sitting in a general congress or conference, such as the Hague or Algeciras conferences, the Berlin or Versailles congresses or the Assembly of the League of Nations, though theoretically occupying a status similar to that of a diplomatic officer,[28] bound by his national laws and subject to instructions, tends to be in fact a *representative* rather than a *delegate*. His judgments tend to be founded upon an international point of view, developed by the discussions of the conference itself, rather than by the instructions of his home state. In the Senate discussion upon the character of the representatives to the Panama congress in 1825, Senator Benton recognized this distinction.[29]

"The Ambassadors and Ministers here intended (that is, by the Constitution) are such only as are known to the law of nations. Their names, grades, rights, privileges, and immunities are perfectly defined in the books which treat of them, and were thoroughly understood by the framers of our Constitution. They are, Ambassadors—Envoys—Envoys Extraordinary—Ministers—Ministers Plenipotentiary—Ministers Resident. . . . Tried by these tests, and the diplomatic qualities of our intended Ministers fail at

[28] Scott, ed., Reports to the Hague Conferences, Intro., XIX.
[29] Benton, Abridgment of Debates, 8: 463-464. We do not intend to endorse Senator Benton's implication with reference to the power of the Senate to consent to the appointment of such representatives.

every attribute of the character. Spite of the names which are imposed upon them, they turn out to be a sort of Deputies with full powers for undefinable objects. They are unknown to the law of nations, unknown to our Constitution; and the combined powers of the Federal Government are incompetent to create them. Nothing less than an original act, from the people of the States, in their sovereign capacity, is equal to the task. Had these gentlemen been nominated to us as *Deputies* to a *Congress*, would not the nominations have been instantly and unanimously rejected? And shall their fate be different under a different name? The delicacy of this position was seen and felt by the administration. The terms 'Deputy' and 'Commissioner' were used in the official correspondence up to near the date of the nomination, but as these names could not pass the Senate, a resort to others became indispensable. The invitations and acceptance were in express terms, for '*Deputies* and *Representatives*' to a Congress." The nominations to the Senate are wholly different."

It is true, Senator Benton's view did not prevail in the Senate, and, according to American constitutional theory as well as to the theory of international law, representatives in an international conference or congress are no different from diplomatic officers.[30] The distinction has existed, however, as a psychological fact and will necessarily be emphasized if such conferences or congresses sit periodically.

Count Beust remarked in 1870, upon finding it impossible to call together the Concert of Europe to prevent the Russian violation of the Treaty of Paris and the impending Franco-Prussian War, "Il ne vois pas d'Europe."[31] He thus emphasized that by its periodic meetings before that time, the Concert had in fact constituted a European organ and not a mere group of national delegates. It was because of its confidence in this psychological effect of periodic conferences that the Hague Conference of 1907 recommended a third conference[32] and the actual play of this psychological factor is emphasized by the remarks of M. Nelidow of Russia, president of the conference, in his closing remarks:[33]

"We are the agents of our governments and act by virtue of special instructions, based before all other considerations upon the interests of our respective countries. The higher considerations of the good of mankind in

---

[30] Corwin, *op. cit.,* p. 57; *supra,* note 28.

[31] Von Beust, Memoires, Trans. H. de Worms, London, 1887, 2: 222.

[32] Scott, ed., Reports to Hague Conferences, pp. 216, 222. See also Instruction of Secretary of State Root to American delegates to the Second Hague Conference, 1907, Scott ed., Instructions to the American Delegates to the Hague Conferences and their Official Reports, 1916, p. 72.

[33] *Ibid.,* p. 200.

general should no doubt guide us, but in applying them we must have uppermost in our minds the intentions of those who direct our Governments. But the direct interests of different States are often diametrically opposed. It was in endeavoring to bring them into agreement with the theoretical requirements of absolute law and justice, that the spirit of good understanding, which I have just mentioned, came into play."

A similar thought in the Congress of Versailles led to the establishment of the League of Nations and in this institution the problem of, to a certain extent, merging national official delegates with true representatives in an international institution was consciously confronted. Thus said President Wilson in presenting the first draft of the Covenant to the Peace Conference on February 14, 1919: [34]

"When it came to the question of determining the character of the representation in the Body of Delegates (Assembly), we were all aware of a feeling which is current throughout the world. Inasmuch as I am stating it in the presence of the official representatives of the various governments here present, including myself, I may say that there is a universal feeling that the world can not rest satisfied with merely official guidance. There has reached us through many channels the feeling that if the deliberating body of the League of Nations was merely to be a body of officials representing the various Governments, the peoples of the world would not be sure that some of the mistakes which preoccupied officials had admittedly made, might not be repeated."

232. *National Military, Naval and Administrative Offices.*

From the standpoint of foreign relations the most important national agencies are the Army, Navy and Department of State. The Constitution puts the organization of the Army, Navy and militia in the hands of Congress. The President, however, exercises considerable independent power as Commander-in-Chief in the detailed organization of the military forces and in the organization of military governments for occupied territory, and territory annexed by treaty but not yet organized by Congress.[35]

"Theoretically," said the Supreme Court, "Congress might prepare and enact a scheme of civil government to take effect immediately upon the

---

[34] League of Nations, II, special No., p. 17.
[35] Santiago *v.* Nogueras, 214 U. S. 260.

cession, but practically, there always have been delays and always will be. Time is required for the maturing and enacting of an adequate scheme of civil government. In the meantime, pending the action of Congress, there is no civil power under our system of government, not even that of the President as civil executive, which can take the place of the government which has ceased to exist by the cession. Is it possible that, under such circumstances, there must be an interregnum? We think clearly not. The authority to govern such ceded territory is found in the laws applicable to conquest and cession. That authority is the military power, under the control of the President as Commander-in-Chief, . . . But whatever may be the limits of the military power, it certainly must include the authority to establish courts of justice which are so essential a part of the government."

The authority of such officers and courts is, however, confined to the locality. They cannot exercise a prize jurisdiction.[36]

233. *Appointment of Military and Civil Officers.*

The states are guaranteed the privilege of appointing militia officers, but the President may delegate his authority as Commander-in-Chief of the militia when " in the actual service of the United States " to an officer of his own appointment.[37] The appointment of army and navy officers, as well as of civil officers, is vested in the President acting by and with the advice and consent of the Senate, except insofar as Congress may have vested the appointment of inferior officers " in the President alone, in the courts of law, or in the heads of departments." The President may make interim appointments during a recess of the Senate.[38]

Congress has actually vested the appointment of warrant officers of the Navy and Marine Corps in the President alone and temporarily in the Secretary of the Navy.[39] Petty officers in the Navy and non-commissioned officers in the Army are appointed by commissioned officers. Commissioned officers are generally appointed by the President with the advice and consent of the Senate but

---

[36] *Supra*, sec. 227.
[37] Secretary of War Monroe, 1812, Am. State Pap., Mil. Aff., 1: 604; Att. Gen. Butler, 2 op. 711 (1835).
[38] *Supra*, sec. 228.
[39] Rev. Stat., sec. 1405, Act May 22, 1917, sec. 5, 40 Stat. 86; Comp. Stat., secs. 2554, 2555.

emergency appointments below the rank of colonel have been vested in the President alone.[40] Promotion and retirement are provided for by detailed acts of Congress. All military officers are commissioned by the President and he has the power of removal, though in the Army and Navy this power is exercised only through courts-martial. As Commander-in-Chief, the President exercises the power of directing all the military and naval services.[41]

234. *Organization of the Department of State.*

The Department of State is peculiarly under control of the President. It was organized by an act of 1789 and, differing from other departments, is not required to make any reports to Congress.

"It is," says Senator Spooner, of Wisconsin, "a department which from the beginning the Senate has never assumed the right to direct or control, except as to clearly defined matters relating to duties imposed by statute and not connected with the conduct of foreign relations. We *direct* all the other heads of departments to transmit to the Senate designated papers or information. We do not address directions to the Secretary of State, nor do we direct requests, even to the Secretary of State. We direct requests to the real head of that department, the President of the United States, and, as a matter of courtesy, we add the qualifying words: 'if in his judgment not incompatible with the public interest.'"[42]

Though Senate confirmation of the appointment of the Secretary of State is required, yet, as in the case of other cabinet officers, it is never withheld. As "real head of that department" the President has never tolerated a lack of political harmony with the Secretary of State. Thus in 1800 after President Adams had requested Timothy Pickering to tender his resignation and no response had been forthcoming he addressed him a note which "discharged him from any further service as Secretary of State." President Wilson promptly accepted Secretary of State Lansing's resignation in 1920 when a divergence in policy became evident.[43]

---

[40] Act May 18, 1917, sec. 8, 40 Stat. 81, as amended April 20, 1918; Comp. Stat., sec. 2044b.

[41] *Ex parte* Milligan, 4 Wall. 2.

[42] Senate Debate, Feb. 6, 1906, *Cong. Rec.*, 40: 1419; Reinsch, Readings in Am. Fed. Govt., p. 85; Corwin, *op. cit.*, p. 176; Hunt, The Department of State of the United States, 1914, pp. 84, 105.

[43] Foster, A Century of Am. Diplomacy, p. 180; Lansing, The Peace Negotiations, 1921, p. 3.

INSTRUMENTALITIES FOR FOREIGN RELATIONS. 323

Negotiations are ordinarily conducted primarily by the Secretary of State, but the President may act personally. Thayer, in his Life of Hay, thus indicates the relation between Presidents and Secretaries of State: [44]

"Mr. Hay used to tell his friends that often President McKinley did not send for him once a month on business, but that he saw President Roosevelt every day. That statement illustrates the difference in initiative between the two Presidents; or, at least, the ratio of their interest in foreign relations. From the moment of Mr. Roosevelt's accession, the State Department felt a new impelling force behind it. The Secretary still conducted the negotiations, but the origination and decisions of policy came to rest more and more with the President. In no other case was this so true as in that of the Panama Canal. In the earlier stages Mr. Roosevelt gave directions which Mr. Hay carried out; before the end, however, the President took the business into his own hands; and has always frankly assumed entire responsibility for the decisive stroke."

235. *National and International Political Officers and Agents.*

The Constitution itself recognizes the offices of "ambassadors, other public ministers and consuls" and specifically vests power to appoint their occupants in the President acting with advice and consent of the Senate. The exact definition of the grades, powers and privileges of these officers is determined by international law and treaty. As has been noticed, each of the three departments of government is held to have inherent power to appoint subordinates necessary for carrying out its functions. The President's power to negotiate, implied from his power to receive foreign ambassadors and ministers, and from his power in the making of treaties, undoubtedly makes it necessary for him to employ special, sometimes secret, agents to conduct negotiations. These powers, however, have given rise to controversy.

Congress, and particularly the Senate, has questioned the power of the President (a) to interpret international law and treaty with reference to the grades, functions and privileges of diplomatic officers, (b) to decide when and where occasion has arisen for dispatching such officers, and (c) to act through agents appointed by himself alone and holding no "office" established either by the Constitution or by act of Congress.

[44] Thayer, Life of John Hay, 2: 297. See also Hunt, *op. cit.*, p. 91.

236. *Power to Determine Grades in Foreign Service.*

Until 1855 there appears to have been no question but that the President had exclusive power to decide, according to international law and treaty, upon the grades of diplomatic and consular officers.[45] Jefferson, as Secretary of State, expressed the opinion that the Senate had "no right to negative the grade" in advising and consenting to appointments.[46] Congress passed no laws on the subject, and appropriation acts were drawn so as to impose no limitations upon the President's discretion in this respect.[47]

By an act of March 1, 1855, Congress provided:

"From and after the 30th of June, next, the President of the United States shall, by and with the advice and consent of the Senate, appoint representatives of the grade of envoys extraordinary and ministers plenipotentiary," with a specified annual compensation for each, "to the following countries, etc. . . . The President shall appoint no other than citizens of the United States who are residents thereof, or abroad in the employment of the Government, at the time of their appointment."

Attorney-General Cushing held that the provisions of this act "must be deemed directory or recommendatory only, and not mandatory."[48]

"The limit of the range of selection," he continued, "for the appointment of constitutional officers depends on the Constitution. Congress may refuse to make appropriations to pay a person unless appointed from this or that category; but the President may, in my judgment, employ him, if the public interest requires it, whether he be a citizen or not, and whether or not at the time of the appointment he be actually within the United States. . . . For Congress can not by law constitutionally require the President to make removals or appointments of public ministers on a given day, or to make such appointments of prescribed rank, or to make or not make them at this or that place. He, with the advice of the Senate, enters into treaties; he, with the advice of the Senate, appoints ambassadors and other public ministers. It is a constitutional power to appoint to a constitutional office, not a statute power nor a statute office. Like the power to pardon, it is not limitable by Congress."

---

[45] The rules of the Treaty of Vienna, 1815, with reference to the grades of diplomatic officers have been applied as international law, Moore, Digest, 4: 430.

[46] *Ibid.*, 4: 450; Jefferson, Writings (Ford, ed.), 5: 161; Hunt, *op. cit.*, p. 105.

[47] Madison to Monroe, 1822, *Ibid.*, 4: 451; Corwin, *op. cit.*, p. 67.

[48] Cushing, Att. Gen., 7 Op. 214.

In spite of this reasoning, Congress has continued such legislation. The revised statutes specified the salaries of diplomatic officers at various countries but did not specify the grade individually except for a few of the less important countries such as Hayti, Liberia, Egypt, etc.[49] They refused compensation to diplomatic and consular officers not citizens of the United States and provided that they take bonds for good behavior.[50] The latter provision has been sustained in the Court of Claims.[51] An act of March 3, 1893, "authorized" the President to appoint "ambassadors" in certain cases, and an act of March 2, 1909, provided "hereafter no new ambassadorship shall be created unless the same shall be provided for by an act of Congress."[52] Since then Congress has specifically authorized new grades as an Ambassador to Spain, 1913; to Argentine, 1914; to Chile, 1914; an Envoy Extraordinary and Minister Plenipotentiary to Paraguay, 1913; and to Uruguay, 1913.[53] An act of 1915 provided grades and salaries for secretaries of legation, consuls-general and consuls, and provided that appointments be hereafter to the grade and not to a specific country. The consular service was reorganized in detail by an act of April 5, 1906.[54]

Thus Congress has, in fact, organized the permanent diplomatic and consular services and through its control of appropriations it seems able to compel acceptance of its organization. It has not usually authorized special or temporary missions or representation on international conferences and congresses. The President himself has designated the grade of such officers, and provided compensation from the contingent fund at his own disposal. However, Congress has recently attempted to prevent such action.[55]

---

[49] Rev. Stat., sec. 1675; Comp. Stat., sec. 3117.
[50] Rev. Stat., secs. 1744, 1697; Comp. Stat., secs. 3149, 3150.
[51] Williams v. U. S., 23 Ct. Cl. 46; Moore, Digest, 4: 457.
[52] 27 Stat. 496; 35 Stat. 672; Comp. Stat., 3121.
[53] 38 Stat. 110, 241, 378.
[54] 34 Stat. 99; 38 Stat. 805.
[55] Act March 4, 1913, 37 Stat. 913; Comp. Stat., sec. 7686. See Report on the Foreign Service, National Civil Service Reform League, N. Y., 1911, p. 65. As to the value of legislation on the subject, see *Ibid.*, 220–223, and as to methods of Congressional control, *Ibid.*, 227–228.

237. *Power to Determine Occasion for Appointments in Foreign Service.*

During the early days of the government it was customary to send special missions for the conclusion of treaties and on several of these occasions the President appointed commissioners without consulting the Senate. On other occasions, as in the appointment of John Jay to negotiate a treaty with Great Britain and later in the appointment of two successive missions of three commissioners sent to negotiate with France, he consulted the Senate and they did not question his authority to decide that the occasion required a diplomatic mission.[56]

In March, 1813, during the recess of the Senate, President Madison appointed Gallatin, J. Q. Adams, and Bayard as "Envoys Extraordinary and Ministers Plenipotentiary" to negotiate a treaty of peace with Great Britain. When the Senate reassembled, Senator Gore, of Massachusetts, introduced a resolution. It recited the constitutional provision authorizing the President "to fill up all vacancies that may happen during the recess of the Senate by granting commissions which shall expire at the end of the next session" and then asserted that "no such vacancy can happen in any office not before full" and consequently the President's act was not "authorized by the Constitution, inasmuch as a vacancy in that office did not happen during such recess of the Senate and as the Senate had not advised and consented to their appointment."

Senator Gore assumed that the existence of an "office" in the foreign service could only be determined by the President acting with the Senate and consequently there having been no "office" there was no "vacancy." Senator Bibb, of Georgia, however, took the position in reply that the President alone decided whether an "office" in the foreign service existed and might decide that it did during a recess in which case he could fill the vacancy.[57]

"Sir," he said, "there are two descriptions of offices altogether different in their nature, authorized by the Constitution—one to be created by law, and the other depending for their existence and continuance upon con-

---

[56] Crandall, *op cit.*, pp. 75–76.
[57] Benton Abridgment, 5: 86, 91.

tingencies. Of the first kind are judicial, revenue, and similar offices. Of the second are Ambassadors, other public Ministers and Consuls. . . . They depend for their original existence upon the law, but are the offspring of the state of our relations with foreign nations, and must necessarily be governed by distinct rules. . . . I say, then, that whether the office of a Minister exists or does not—how and when it exists are questions not particularly and precisely settled by the Constitution; but that the Executive authority to nominate to the Senate foreign Ministers and Consuls, and to fill vacancies happening during the recess, necessarily includes the power of determining those questions."

The Senate ultimately ratified all of these appointments and those of two additional commissioners, Clay and Russel, though it insisted that Gallatin should first resign the office of Secretary of the Treasury.

On December 25, 1825, President J. Q. Adams sent to the Senate the names of three men "to be envoys extraordinary and ministers plenipotentiary to the assembly of American Nations at Panama." Senator Benton, of Missouri, contended that these persons were in reality "Deputies and Representatives to a Congress" and were not Ambassadors and Public Ministers in the meaning of the Constitution at all. However, his view did not prevail and the appointments were eventually ratified though the appointees arrived at Panama too late to take part in the Congress.[58]

In result, these two cases seem to demonstrate the power of the President to decide when occasion for appointment to an office in the foreign service exists and this has been since sustained in the opinions of many Attorneys-General.[59] In spite of this admission of his power, on subsequent occasions, the President has usually sent special missions without reference to the Senate at all, perhaps because recollection of the Senate opposition in these two instances lurked in his mind. In this way, peace missions following the Mexican, Spanish and World Wars and the American representation at the Hague, Algeciras and other international conferences were constituted. The President alone has decided that the occasion existed, sent the mission and compensated it out of the contingent

---

[58] *Ibid.*, 8: 463-464.
[59] 1 Op. 631; 2 Op. 535; 3 Op. 673; 4 Op. 532; 7 Op. 190, 223; 10 Op. 357; 11 Op. 179; 12 Op. 32; 19 Op. 261; Corwin, *op. cit.*, p. 55.

fund or relied upon a subsequent appropriation.[60] Here also the Congress has sought to intervene, though its power is less than in the case of permanent missions, requiring steady appropriations. By an act of March 4, 1913, it provided:[61]

"Hereafter the Executive shall not extend or accept any invitation to participate in any international congress, conference, or like event without first having specific authority of law to do so."

Congress has undoubtedly gone beyond its powers in thus attempting to control the President's foreign negotiations and the President has ignored the act, notably at the Versailles Peace Congress. The actual influence of Congress in this field depends upon the necessity for appropriations. If international conferences become frequent, this necessity would doubtless be controlling.[62]

238. *Power of President to Appoint Diplomatic Agents.*

Finally, the Senate has often criticized the President's practice of appointing agents, sometimes with the titles of diplomatic officers, without gaining its consent. This practice began almost immediately after ratification of the Constitution when President Washington by a letter of October 13, 1789, requested Gouverneur Morris, then in Paris, to go to London as private agent, and "on the authority and credit" of the letter to "converse with His Britannic Majesty's Ministers as to certain matters affecting the relations between the two countries." In 1792 John Paul Jones, then an admiral in the United States Navy, was appointed as commissioner to treat with Algiers. In 1816 President Monroe sent three commissioners to investigate affairs in the revolting Spanish-American colonies and in the same year he sent Isaac Chauncey, a naval captain, to act with Consul William Shaler to negotiate a treaty with Algiers.[63]

---

[60] Crandall, *op. cit.*, p. 76. This was also true of the conference on limitation of armament, 1921, though provisions in the Naval appropriation acts of 1916 and 1921 authorized the calling of such a conference, *supra*, sec. 204.

[61] 37 Stat. 913; Comp. Stat., 7686.

[62] Report on Foreign Service, *supra*, note 55, pp. 225-228

[63] Moore, Digest, 4: 452-453.

INSTRUMENTALITIES FOR FOREIGN RELATIONS. 329

239. Practice of Sending Presidential Agents.

Since that time the practice has become exceedingly common. Among the more notable appointments have been Charles Rhind, Commodore Biddle, and Consul David Offley to negotiate a treaty with Turkey in 1829; Colonel Roberts, special agent to China, Siam and other eastern states in 1832; A. Dudley Mann, special agent to various German states in 1846, confidential agent to revolting Hungary in 1849, and special agent to Switzerland in 1850; Nicholas Trist, commissioner to conclude a treaty of peace with Mexico in 1847; Commodore Perry, commissioner to conclude a treaty with Japan in 1852. During the Civil War a number of special and confidential agents were sent to England for purposes of investigation and propaganda as well as negotiation. Commodore R. W. Shufeldt was sent as special envoy to conclude a treaty with Corea in 1881; Secretary of State Bayard with William Putnam of Maine and J. B. Angell of Michigan were vested with power to treat with Great Britain on the North East Fisheries question in 1887. James H. Blount was sent as special commissioner to Hawaii in 1893. Secretary of State Day and Whitelaw Reid, associated with Senators Cushman K. Davis, William P. Frye and George Gray, were sent to Paris to conclude a treaty of peace with Spain in 1898. Missions were sent to the Hague conferences in 1899 and 1907 and W. W. Rockhill was sent as "commissioner of the United States to China with diplomatic privileges and immunities" in 1900. Henry White and Samuel R. Gummere were commissioned by President Roosevelt to represent the United States at the Algeciras conference of 1906. Governor Taft, of the Philippines Commission, was sent to negotiate with the Pope in 1902. John Lind was sent as confidential agent to Mexico in 1913, Colonel House was sent to Germany in 1916 and to France in 1917, and Elihu Root at the head of a special mission of nine was sent to Russia in 1917, with the title of Ambassador Extraordinary. President Wilson constituted himself, with Secretary of State Lansing, Colonel House, Henry White and General Tasker Bliss, a commission to conclude a treaty of peace with Germany in 1919, and in 1921, after failure of the Senate to consent to the ratification of the treaty of Versailles, President Harding authorized Ellis Loring Dresel to negotiate a separate peace treaty with Germany. In the same year President Harding appointed Secretary of State Hughes, Elihu Root, Senators Lodge and Underwood American delegates to the Conference on Limitation of Armament.[64]

A minority of the Senate Foreign Relations Committee reported in 1888:[65]

"The whole number of persons appointed or recognized by the President, without the concurrence or advice of the Senate, or the express authority of Congress, as agents to conduct negotiations and conclude treaties (prior to June 25, 1887) is four hundred and thirty-eight. Three have been appointed by the Secretary of State and thirty-two have been appointed by the President with the advice and consent of the Senate."

Apparently the only appointments to special missions which have been confirmed by the Senate since 1815 are the commissioners to the Panama Congress of 1825, those to negotiate with China in 1880, and the five commissioners to negotiate the Treaty of Washington with Great Britain in 1871.[66]

240. *Controversies with Respect to Presidential Agents.*

In spite of the habitual practice, the Senate has often protested. Its objection to the interim appointments by President Madison in 1813 would extend *a fortiori* to purely presidential commissioners. President Jackson's mission appointed to treat with Turkey in 1829 was criticized in the Senate in 1831, though Senator Tazewell, of Virginia, the principal critic, admitted "the power of the President to appoint *secret* agents when and how he pleases."[67]

"But," he continued, "as a Senator, I do claim for the Senate, in the language of the Constitution, the right of advising and consenting to the appointment of any and every officer of the United States, no matter what

---

[64] *Ibid.*, 4: 440, 446, 456; Crandall, *op. cit.*, p. 78; Foster, Diplomatic Practice, chap. X; Corwin, *op. cit.*, pp. 62, 64; Henry Adams, Education, p. 146; J. M. Forbes, Letters and Recollections, 1899, 2: 32; Paullin, Diplomatic Negotiation of American Naval Officers, *passim;* Gerard, My Four Years in Germany, p. 197; Lansing, The Peace Negotiations, Chap. II; Root, The United States and the War, 1918, p. 92; Lodge, Remarks in the Senate, September 26, 1921, Cong. Rec., 61: 6458.
[65] Fiftieth Cong., 2d Sess., Sen. Doc. No. 231, VIII, 332.
[66] Crandall, *op. cit.*, p. 77.
[67] Benton, Abridgment, 11: 207.

INSTRUMENTALITIES FOR FOREIGN RELATIONS. 331

may be his name, what his duties, or how he may be instructed to perform them. And it is only because secret agents are not officers of the United States, but the mere agents of the President or of his Secretaries, or of his military or naval commanders, that I disclaim all participation in this appointment."

Senator Livingston answered: [68]

"Sir, there are grades in diplomacy which give different ranks and privileges—from an ambassador to a secret agent. . . . Ambassadors and other public Ministers are directed to be appointed by the President by and with the advice and consent of the Senate; because public missions required no secrecy, although their instructions might. But the framers of the Constitution knew the necessity of missions, of which not only the object but the existence should be kept secret. They therefore wisely made co-operation of the Senate ultimately necessary in the first instance, but left the appointment solely to the President in the last. . . . On the 30th March, 1795, in the recess of the Senate, by letters patent under the great broad seal of the United States, and the signature of their President (that President being George Washington), countersigned by the Secretary of State, David Humphreys was appointed commissioner plenipotentiary for negotiating a treaty of peace with Algiers. . . .

"I call the attention of the Senate to all the facts of this case with the previous remark, that the construction which it gives to the Constitution was made in the earliest years of the Federal Government, by the man who presided in the convention which made that Constitution, acting with the advice and assistance of the leading members of that body, all fresh from its discussion; men who had taken prominent parts in every question that arose. . . .

"By those men, with this perfect and recent knowledge of the Constitution, acting under the solemn obligation to preserve it inviolate and without any possible motive to make them forget their duty, was this first precedent set; without a single doubt on the mind that it was correct; without protest, without even remark. A precedent going the full length of that which is now unhesitatingly called a lawless, unconstitutional usurpation; bearing the present act out in all its parts, and in some points going much beyond it."

Although futilely, the Senate continued to protest. In 1882, in consenting to ratification of the treaty with Corea it resolved that it: [69]

"does not admit or acquiesce in any right or constitutional power in the President to authorize or empower any person to negotiate treaties or carry on diplomatic negotiations with any foreign power, unless such person shall have been appointed for such purpose or clothed with such power by and

---

[68] *Ibid.*, 11 : 220–222.
[69] Malloy, Treaties, etc., p. 340.

with the advice and consent of the Senate, except in the case of a Secretary of State or diplomatic officer appointed by the President to fill a vacancy occurring during the recess of the Senate, and it makes the declaration in order that the means employed in the negotiation of said treaty (with Corea) be not drawn into precedent."

In 1888 the Senate Foreign Relations Committee in reporting adversely upon the proposed fisheries treaty with Great Britain held in "reserve, for the time being, those grave questions touching usurpations of unconstitutional powers or the abuse of those that may be thought to exist on the part of the Executive." The minority report, however, sustained the President's appointments in this case by citation of precedents, and in the debate Senator Sherman, chairman of the Foreign Relations Committee, who had concurred in the majority report, admitted:[70]

"The President of the United States has the power to propose treaties, subject to ratification by the Senate, and he may use such agencies as he chooses to employ, except that he can not take any money from the Treasury to pay those agents without an appropriation by law. He can use such instruments as he pleases. . . . I suppose precedents have been quoted by the Senator from Alabama (Mr. Morgan, who prepared the minority report) to sustain that position. I do not disagree with him, nor does this controversy turn upon that point."

Senate criticism was directed against the commissioning of J. H. Blount to Hawaii in 1893 with "paramount" authority in all matters affecting the relationship of the United States to the Islands. The majority report of the Foreign Relations Committee, however, held:[71]

"Many precedents could be quoted to show that such power has been exercised by the President on various occasions, without dissent on the part of Congress. These precedents also show that the Senate of the United States, though in session, need not be consulted as to the appointment of such agents."

This position was endorsed by Senator Lodge in presenting the German peace treaty to the Senate in 1921:[71a]

"It is the unquestioned right of the President to appoint personal agents to gather information for him, as was done in a rather famous case when Ambrose Dudley-Mann was sent to Hungary at the time of Kossuth's rebel-

---

[70] Moore, Digest, 4: 455; *Cong. Rec.*, Aug. 7, 1888, pp. 7285, 7287.
[71] *Cong. Rec.*, 53d Cong., 2d Sess., p. 127; Corwin, *op. cit.*, p. 64.
[71a] Cong. Rec., September 26, 1921, 61: 6458.

INSTRUMENTALITIES FOR FOREIGN RELATIONS. 333

lion, or the President, of course, can appoint anyone he chooses to represent him in a negotiation, because the power of initiating and negotiating a treaty is in his hands.

"We have an example at this moment in the treaty with Germany now before us. As I stated on Saturday, the Gentleman who represented us in Berlin had been sent there by President Wilson, taken from the diplomatic service and charged to represent the United States as far as it could be done as a commissioner. He was simply a personal agent of the President. He could not officially represent the United States. We could not have an ambassador because we were technically at war with Germany. Therefore he was sent there, and he represented the President in negotiating the treaty with Germany now before us and signed it."

Finally notice may be taken of the 7th proposed Senate reservation to the Treaty of Versailles. As considered on November 19, 1919, it provided:

"No citizen of the United States shall be selected or appointed as a member of said commisssions, committees, tribunals, courts, councils, or conferences except with the approval of the Senate of the United States."

Later this sentence was omitted, and, as considered on March 19, 1920, reservation seven retained merely the requirement that the United States should only be represented in the League of Nations, and, on the agencies established by the treaty, by persons authorized thereto by "an act of the Congress of the United States providing for his appointment and defining his powers and duties." [72]

241. *Presidential Agent Not an Officer.*

The power of the President independently to dispatch diplomatic agents seems to be considered a proper implication from the President's diplomatic powers and is well established in practice. Such an agent, however, is not an officer of the United States. This is evidenced by the fact that Senators who, according to the Constitution, cannot at the same time hold offices under the United States, have occasionally served on special missions and also by express statement of the Attorney-General. He is not, under the law, en-

---

[72] The League of Nations, III, no. 4, pp. 179, 196 (Aug., 1920). A reservation of similar effect was made by the Senate in consenting to ratification of the German peace treaty of August 25, 1921, Cong. Rec., Oct. 18, 1921, 61: 7194.

titled to compensation. Thus the President is limited in the use of such missions by the size of the contingent fund.[73]

242. *International Administrative and Judicial Agencies.*

The third class of instrumentalities for conducting foreign relations are international in character and rest on treaty or agreement alone. Arbitration courts for hearing particular questions have been set up by executive agreement alone, by executive agreement authorized by general treaties and by treaties. The Bureau of the Universal Postal Union is authorized, so far as the United States is concerned, by executive agreement under an act of Congress. The Bureau of other international unions and of the Hague Permanent Court of Arbitration as well as the panel of arbitrators of the court are set up by treaty. International courts were established for trial of slave traders by the treaty of 1863–1870 with Great Britain and by the XII Hague Convention of 1907 an international prize court was provided for, but the latter treaty, though consented to by the Senate, has never been ratified.

The President has usually appointed representatives in such bodies on the authority of the agreement or treaty alone, though if the body is permanent, the need of appropriation makes congressional action necessary. Congress has provided by law for participation of the United States in the Pan-American Union,[74] the Bureau of the Hague Permanent Court of Arbitration,[75] the International Prison Commission,[76] and other organs. It has not attempted to control the organization or method of appointing representatives on such bodies, though the proposed seventh reservation to the Peace Treaty of Versailles would have done so for organs set up by that treaty. In general the congressional acts seem to have assumed that the power to appoint commissioners to such bodies is vested in the President alone, and that such commissioners are not "officers" of the United States, since Senators

---

[73] The U. S. Constitution, I, sec. 6, cl. 2; Knox, Att. Gen., 23 Op. 533 (1901); Moore, Digest, 4: 440; Corwin, *op. cit.,* pp. 65–66.

[74] Act July 14, 1890, 26 Stat. 275.

[75] Act March 22, 1902, 32 Stat. 81.

[76] Act Feb. 22, 1913, 37 Stat. 692; Act *re* International Waterways Commission, June 13, 1902, 42 Stat. 373; Comp. Stat., sec. 4984.

INSTRUMENTALITIES FOR FOREIGN RELATIONS. 335

have frequently served, especially on courts of arbitration. In 1913, however, Congress attempted to forbid presidential participation in any "international congress, conference or like event, without first having specific authority of law to do so."[77]

Congress through its control of appropriations has been gaining an increasing influence in regulating the grade, location and number of offices in the permanent foreign service, and the President's constitutional discretion in these matters has been seriously impaired. The President has, however, retained his independence both of Congress and of the Senate in the sending of special missions, and the appointment of representatives on international organs. Although the consular service has to a considerable extent been brought under civil service regulations, the diplomatic service has not for positions above that of Secretary. Appointments are regarded as political and the President exercises discretion, limited by the legislation establishing the office and the need of senatorial advice and consent. These services are subject to the direction of the President, enforceable through his independent removal power.[78]

243. *Conclusion on Power to Conduct Foreign Relations.*

We conclude that under the Constitution the control of foreign relations is given almost exclusively to the national government, but it extends only so far as expressly or impliedly delegated. In fact, this delegation has been almost, if not entirely complete, and the constitutional limitations upon its exercise in defense of individual rights, states rights and the rights and privileges of national organs of government are comparatively unimportant. Adequate powers exist in the President, the treaty-making power, Congress and the courts to meet all international responsibilities, to make agreements of a genuinely international character, to make decisions of international importance, and to carry out national policies. But these powers have been distributed among independent organs. Is there a single principle underlying this distribution? We believe there is. The President initiates, controls and concludes, checked by the possibility of a Senate veto on permanent

---

[77] *Supra,* notes 61, 72.

[78] Report on the Foreign Service, *supra,* note 55, pp. 21-31, 45, 65; *supra,* sec. 230.

international agreements and by a congressional veto upon national decisions calling for positive action.

For meeting the ordinary responsibilities and exercising the ordinary powers of states in the family of nations, guided by international law, the President alone is competent, and his powers, being in the main derived from the Constitution itself, he is not subject to the detailed direction of Congress, as he is in exercising his powers in domestic administration. For departures from the normal, whether by way of international agreement or national policy, though the President initiates, the Senate or Congress must consent. While the powers upon which these organs are able to insist go little beyond a discretionary veto upon consummations, yet the President ought to understand that to avoid the possibility of this contingency he should consider their advice during the course of negotiations and diplomacy.

The dominating position of the President in foreign relations results from his initiative, and this is a necessary consequence of the position he occupies as the representative authority of the United States under international law. His office is the only door through which foreign nations can approach the United States. His voice is the only medium through which the United States can speak to foreign nations. Moreover the fathers appear to have intended him to occupy this position and subsequent history has shown his exercise of the initiative and essential control. On occasions when foreign affairs have not pressed he has subordinated his initiative to congressional policies but always when crises have arisen he has met them with a prompt decision and adequate resources of power. Only rarely has the veto of coordinate departments destroyed his achievements.

PART V.

THE UNDERSTANDINGS OF THE CONSTITUTION.

CHAPTER XVIII.

Understandings Concerning the Relations of the Independent Departments.

244. *Reason for Constitutional Understandings.*

The various organs of the national government are together vested with sufficient power to conduct foreign affairs and meet international responsibilities, but, according to the doctrine of separation of powers, each of the three departments of government exercises an independent discretion, legally uncontrolled by any other authority. Three difficulties may arise from this situation:

(*A*) The powers of two departments may overlap, giving rise to contrary action on the same occasion.

"The existence," said a Senate Foreign Relations Committee report of 1898, "of the same power for the same purposes in both the legislative and executive branches of the Government might lead to most unfortunate results. For instance, if the legislative and executive branches both possessed the power of recognizing the independence of a foreign nation, and one branch should declare it independent, while the other denied its independence, then, since they are coordinate, how could the problem be solved by the judicial branch?"[1]

(*B*) An independent department may lack sufficient power to achieve a desired end without the cooperation of another independent department.

"A treaty," said the Circuit Court, "is the supreme law of the land in respect of such matters only as the treaty-making power, without the aid of Congress, can carry into effect. Where a treaty stipulates for the payment of money for which an appropriation is required, it is not operative in the sense of the Constitution."[2]

(*C*) Organs properly adapted to meeting certain international responsibilities may not exist. The general principle which ought

---

[1] Sen. Doc. 56, 54th Cong., 2d sess., p. 4; Corwin, *op. cit.*, p. 36, *supra*, sec. 191.

[2] Turner *v.* Am. Baptist Missionary Union, 5 McLean 347; Wharton, Digest, 2: 73; Moore, Digest, 5: 222.

to govern the discretion of the departments in the presence of such difficulties has been thus expressed by the Supreme Court of North Carolina:[3]

"While the executive, legislative, and supreme judicial powers of the government ought to be forever separate and distinct, it is also true that the science of government is a practical one; therefore, while each should firmly maintain the essential powers belonging to it, it cannot be forgotten that the three coordinate parts constitute one brotherhood, whose common trust requires a mutual toleration of what seems to be a 'common because of vicinage' bordering on the domains of each."

A. The Overlapping of Powers of Independent Departments.

245. *Constitutional Understanding Respecting the Overlapping of Powers.*

The difficulty arising from the overlapping of the powers of two independent and coordinate departments of the government has been met in part by the legal principle that the most recent exercise of power prevails and in part by the understanding that each department should so exercise its concurrent powers as not to impair the validity of action already taken by the other department without that department's consent.

246. *Concurrent Powers of President and Congress.*

The powers of the President or of the courts cannot conflict with those of Congress or the treaty-making power, because the constitutional acts of the latter are declared the supreme law of the land. Consequently, a conflicting act of the President or the courts would be contrary to law and void. The President and courts, however, have certain powers concurrent with congressional powers in the sense that they may validly act, until Congress has acted. Thus the Supreme Court could determine its appellate jurisdiction upon the basis of Article III of the Constitution alone,[4] and the President could organize and conduct military government in newly acquired territory, regulate the landing of cables, and issue regulations for branches of the civil service before Congress

---
[3] Brown *v.* Turner, 70 N. C. 93, 102.

[4] *Ex parte* McCardle, 7 Wall. 506, 513, and Marshall, C. J., in Durousseau *v.* U. S., 6 Cranch 307, 313, and U. S. *v.* Moore, 3 Cranch 159, 170, 172.

had acted.[5] But once Congress, or the treaty-making power, has acted, if its act is constitutional, there is no doubt but that it is the supreme law of the land, and the President and courts are henceforth bound by it.[6] An act either of Congress or of the treaty-making power which encroaches upon the constitutional powers of the President or courts is of course unconstitutional and void. The courts may so declare it, but it has been generally held that the President is confined to the veto to invalidate unconstitutional legislation. If an act has been signed by a predecessor, is passed over his veto, or is signed by himself inadvertently, it is held that he must obey it, even though the act is clearly unconstitutional, until such time as the courts may declare it void.[7] This principle is not, however, extended to congressional acts affecting the inherent powers and the foreign relations powers of the President. Such acts, if encroachments upon presidential powers, even though mandatory in terms and formally valid, have been interpreted as merely advisory and as leaving the President discretion to ignore them. Thus, the President has ignored congressional acts and resolutions prescribing conditions for the removal of administrative officers,[8] defining the grades of diplomatic officers,[9] directing the negotiation or modification of treaties,[10] and formulating foreign policy.[11]

[5] Santiago *v.* Nogueras, 214 U. S. 260; Richards, Acting Att. Gen., 22 Op. 13; Moore, Digest, 2: 452–463; *supra,* sec. 219.

[6] Where two organs enjoy concurrent powers to produce a status, the one acting first, of course, effects the result. Thus a presidential recognition of war would be effective irrespective of subsequent acts of Congress. "In short, it frequently happens that the same legal result may be produced by very different powers of government; nor need the fact lead to confusion, since, as soon as any of the competent powers has acted, the result is produced." Corwin, *Mich. Law Rev.,* 18: 672, but see his President's Control of Foreign Relations, p. 36.

[7] Willoughby, *op. cit.,* pp. 1306–1309.

[8] As President Johnson's refusal to accept the tenure of office act, for which he was impeached, but not convicted. See also President Cleveland's action in the Duskin case, Presidential Problems, 1904, p. 56, and Parsons *v.* U. S., 167 U. S. 324.

[9] Cushing, Att. Gen., 7 Op. 186; *supra,* sec. 236.

[10] Crandall, *op. cit.,* p. 74; *supra,* sec. 174.

[11] *Supra,* sec. 203.

247. *Concurrent Powers of the President and the Courts.*

The power of the President to settle international controversies may, however, overlap the jurisdiction of the courts to settle private controversies. The understanding that the authority taking prior action should govern, has usually been applied in such cases. Thus a German prize crew brought the British vessel Appam into an American port, while the country was neutral. The original owner promptly libelled the vessel in the United States District Court and while the case was pending the German government sought, through the Department of State, to have their claim submitted to arbitration. Secretary Lansing replied in a note of April 7, 1916:[12]

"Moreover, inasmuch as the *Appam* has been libeled in the United States District Court by the alleged owners, this government, under the American system of government in which the judicial and executive branches are entirely separate and independent, could not vouch for a continuance of the *status quo* of the prize during the progress of the arbitration proposed by the Imperial Government. The United States Court, having taken jurisdiction of the vessel, that jurisdiction can only be dissolved by judicial proceedings leading to a decision of the court discharging the case—a procedure which the executive cannot summarily terminate."

On this statement two comments may be made. Unquesionably, the President, through the Secretary of State, had power to settle the controversy with Germany by arbitration or otherwise, irrespective of the results of the District Court's decision. The fact that the United States could not vouch for a continuance of the *status quo* of the vessel was no reason for refusing to arbitrate the international issue. In the second place, even if constitutional difficulties did prevent the President meeting responsibilities under international law, such difficulties would not be a valid defense against claims by foreign nations. Foreign nations are entitled to expect satisfaction of their claims through the President, according to the measure of international law alone. However, the case illustrates the operation of the constitutional understanding whereby the President refuses to consider controversies already in process of consideration by the courts.

---

[12] Department of State, White Book, European War, No. 3, p. 344.

Conversely, the courts ordinarily refuse to pass on controversies in process of diplomatic settlement. Thus, in the case of Cooper, the Supreme Court was asked to issue a writ of prohibition to restrain the United States District Court of Alaska from enforcing a sentence of forfeiture of a British vessel alleged illegally to have taken seal in American jurisdictional waters fifty-seven miles from shore. Discussion was going on between Great Britain and the Department of State as to whether this point was in American jurisdiction and the court expressed the opinion that the President had power to settle the controversy.

> "If this be so, the application calls upon the court, while negotiations are pending, to decide whether the Government is right or wrong, and to review the action of the political departments upon the question contrary to the settled law in that regard."

The court dismissed the suit on finding that there had been no definite facts found as to the place of seizure, but its opinion indicates the feeling that it ought not to prejudice the results of the controversy pending before the Department of State. The court, however, seemed to regard this feeling as an understanding rather than a legal requirement, for it said: [13]

> "We are not to be understood, however, as underrating the weight of the argument that in a case involving private rights the court may be obliged, if those rights are dependent upon the construction of acts of Congress or of a treaty, and the case turns upon a question, public in its nature, which has not been determined by the political departments in the form of a law specifically settling it, or authorizing the Executive to do so, to render judgment, since we have no more right to decline the jurisdiction which is given than to usurp that which is not given."

This latter power seems to have been exercised in the case of Pearcy v. Stranahan, where the Supreme Court decided upon the status of Pine Island off Cuba, although the matter was and had been for seven years pending in the State Department. Where a decision has actually been given by the political departments on such questions as the limits of jurisdiction, the status of governments and states, etc., the courts follow such decisions implicitly.[14]

---

[13] *In re* Cooper, 143 U. S. 472; Moore, Digest, 1: 744; Willoughby, *op. cit.,* p. 1010.

[14] Pearcy *v.* Stranahan, 205 U. S. 257 (1907); Jones *v.* U. S., 137 U. S. 202; *supra,* sec. 107.

248. *Concurrent Powers of Treaty Power and Congress.*

The most notable overlapping of power, however, occurs in the case of Congress and the treaty-making power. Treaties may require the payment of money, establish customs duties, regulate foreign commerce, fix a standard of weights and measures, provide for international postal service and international copyright, provide courts for the trial of seamen on foreign vessels sojourning in the United States, define and provide for punishing offenses against the law of nations, require the meeting of guarantees by armed force or declaration of war, regulate declarations of war or forbid them in certain circumstances, prohibit the granting of letters of marque and reprisal, make rules concerning captures on land and water, limit the size or disposition of military forces, make rules for the conduct of land and naval forces in war, annex or dispose of territory, in fact there are very few of the enumerated powers of Congress which have not been the subject of treaty. It has been suggested that the treaty power lacks "constitutional competency" to act on these subjects. To this the answer of Calhoun seems adequate:[15]

"If this be the true view of the treaty-making power, it may be truly said that its exercise has been one continual series of habitual and uninterrupted infringements of the Constitution. From the beginning and throughout the whole existence of the Federal Government it has been exercised constantly on commerce, navigation, and other delegated powers."

The court has often recognized this overlapping and considering that acts of Congress "made in pursuance of" the Constitution, and treaties "made under the authority of the United States" are both the supreme law of the land, has regarded them of equal validity and applied the most recent in date in case a conflict is too definite to reconcile.[16] / Thus, according to the law neither treaty-making power nor Congress is limited by the previous exercises of concurrent power by the other. In practice, however, it has been recognized that Congress ought not to violate treaties at will and

---

[15] Moore, Digest, 5: 164.
[16] Head Money Cases, 112 U. S. 580; Chinese Exclusion Cases, 130 U. S. 58; U. S. *v.* The Peggy, 1 Cranch 103.

that the treaty-making power ought not to alter congressional policies at random. The fact that the President and Senate participate in both treaty-making and legislation tends to minimize such conflicts, but in some cases they have occurred. Thus the Chinese exclusion acts of 1889 were in conflict with the Burlingame treaty of 1868. Congress, however, has usually refrained from impairing treaties by legislation and if treaties were found to conflict with proposed legislative policies, has advised the President to negotiate modifications in the treaty. As such negotiation and ratification of the resulting treaty is always discretionary with the President and Senate, the practice means that changes are in fact brought about by concert of Congress and the treaty-making power.[17]

Treaties have very seldom been found to conflict with earlier acts of Congress. Perhaps the only case is a treaty with France of 1801, which required the return of uncondemned prizes and thereby divested certain captors of their rights to prize money as provided by an earlier act of Congress.[18] This is accounted for by two reasons. Many treaties which would affect established legislative policies in such matters as tariffs, commercial regulation, etc., are by their own terms made to depend for effectiveness upon congressional acceptance. Most other treaties conflicting with legislative policy are held not to be self-executing and consequently cannot be carried into effect until Congress acts. This is true of treaties requiring an appropriation, a declaration of war, criminal punishment, etc. The obligation of Congress to pass such legislation will be considered later. However, whichever reason applies, the treaty power does not in practice modify existing acts of Congress without the consent of Congress.

---

[17] See La Follette Seaman's Act of 1915 and Jones Merchant Marine Act of 1920, *supra*, secs. 184, 187.

[18] U. S. *v.* The Peggy, 1 Cranch 103. See also La Ninfa, 75 Fed. 513, applying the award of the Behring Sea Arbitration based on treaty and opposed to the earlier interpretation of an act of Congress; and also application of most-favored-nation clause in Swiss treaty of 1850 in 1898, *supra*, sec. 154.

B. Cooperation of Independent Organs.

249. Constitutional Understanding Respecting the Cooperation of Independent Organs.

The difficulty which arises from the frequent need of cooperation between independent and coordinate departments in carrying out the powers of the national government is met by a constitutional understanding which may be stated in the following words: Where action contemplated by any independent department requires the cooperation of another independent department for its carrying out, the advice of that department ought to be sought before the action is taken, but where such action has already been taken the department whose cooperation is required ought to perform the necessary acts even though its advice had not been asked or if asked had not been followed.

"Whenever," reported the Senate Foreign Relations Committee, "affirmative action of either the executive or the legislative branch of the government may involve a call upon the assistance of the other, the branch about to take action should, if possible, first obtain indications of the other's desires." [19]

"It is a general principle," says Finley-Sanderson, "that any valid act done by either the legislative, executive or judicial branches of the government is binding upon each of the others, and is not subject to be set aside by either of them." [20]

Each department of the national government may exercise powers which will require the cooperation of one or more of the other departments in carrying out. Such acts by the courts, the President, Congress and the treaty-making power will be considered in succession.

250. Decisions by the Courts.

Most decisions of the Federal Courts will be ineffective unless the President enforces them. Undoubtedly to so enforce them is a legal obligation of the President under his duty "to take care that the laws be faithfully executed" and an attitude such as that taken by President Jackson when he remarked: "John Marshall has

---

[19] Sen. Doc. 56, 54th Cong., 2d sess., p. 5. See also Hill, Present Problems in Foreign Policy, 1919, p. 171, and *infra*, sec. 256.

[20] Finley-Sanderson, The Executive, p. 217; Wright, *Am. Jl. Int. Law*, 12: 94; *supra*, sec. 69.

made his decision, now let him enforce it" is a violation of his oath to the Constitution.[21] He has no independent discretion as to whether the court's decision was really a correct interpretation of the Constitution and law. There is in this case no duty on the part of the court to consider the President's probable attitude before making its decision. On the contrary, the court ought to apply the law impartially and irrespective of the views of the political organs of government.

Decisions of the Supreme Court which involve an interpretation of the Constitution, statutes, treaties or other laws of the United States form precedents which by constitutional understanding ought to be followed in future cases by all organs of the government. The political organs of the government in performing acts within their discretionary powers may exercise independent judgment as to the meaning of the Constitution, laws and treaties. Thus, Congressmen and Senators would not be violating their oaths to support the Constitution if, honestly believing the decision erroneous, they repassed a statute which had just been declared unconstitutional nor would the President if he signed it. Likewise the treaty power and the President are not legally bound to follow judicial decisions as to the scope of their powers in conducting foreign relations and as we have seen foreign nations are entitled to regard the statements of the President on the subject as practically authoritative. However, it is believed that the other organs of government ought to regard the interpretation of law by the Supreme Court as final and to be departed from only in extreme cases.[22] But adherence to this understanding implies acceptance by the court of its converse, namely, that in making decisions on constitutional questions affecting the competence of independent organs, the court must carefully weigh the opinions of these departments and follow them if possible. This understanding has been accepted by the court in its repeated assertion that it will hold the view of the political departments, as evidenced through the

---

[21] Sumner's Jackson, p. 227.

[22] The President and Congress may, of course, adhere to stricter canons of constitutional interpretation than the court. Wright, *Col. L. R.*, 20: 140; Willoughby, *op. cit.*, p. 1306; Taft, *op. cit.*, p. 136; Finley-Sanderson, *op. cit.*, p. 218; Cushman, *Minn. Law Rev.*, 4: 275.

formal conclusion of a statute or treaty, in the highest respect and will not regard such acts as unconstitutional unless so beyond reasonable doubt.[23]

251. *Acts of the President.*

The President, as well as the courts, may need the cooperation of other organs in order to make his acts effective. In the performance of political acts within his power, the courts have considered themselves bound to give effect to his decisions. Thus the courts have held themselves bound to give effect to his decisions as to which of two contending governments in a state of the Union is legitimate, as to whether the government in a state is republican in form, as to the extent of American territory, as to the existence of a contingency requiring a calling forth of the militia, as to the existence of civil war in the United States, as to the condition of belligerency or neutrality of the United States, as to the status of foreign governments and their representatives, as to the extent of territory of foreign states, as to the existence of insurgency, civil war or international war abroad, and as to the settlement of claims of American citizens upon foreign governments. In giving effect to such political decisions the court has usually grouped the President and Congress together as the "political department of the government" and has not often discussed the relative competence of each in such matters.[24] Unquestionably, it might do so, and could properly refuse to follow a political decision of the President if on a subject beyond his competence. Thus in his dissent in the prize cases,[25] Justice Nelson, supported by three colleagues, was unwilling to accept the President's proclamation of blockade as the initiation of civil war, holding that the power to declare the existence of war, even civil war, was confined to Congress. The majority, however, thought themselves bound by the political decision of the President. The courts also consider themselves bound to apply

---

[23] Willoughby, *op. cit.*, p. 20; Cushman, Mich. Law Rev., 19: 771.
[24] *Supra*, sec. 107.
[25] The Prize Cases, 2 Black 635, 690.

executive orders of the President, if made under legal authority, in the same manner as acts of Congress.[26]

On the other hand, if acts of the President require for their carrying out cooperation by Congress or by the treaty-making power, the obligation of these organs is founded not upon law but upon a constitutional understanding. The President may make executive agreements which require action by Congress. Such was that by which Great Britain ceded Reef Island in Lake Erie on condition that the United States would erect a lighthouse thereon; that providing for the administration of San Domingan customs houses; and that providing for reciprocity with Canada. So also the President may make agreements requiring action by the treaty-making power. Such were the preliminaries of peace with Spain in 1898 and with Germany in 1918. Such also were protocols with Costa Rica and Nicaragua looking toward the conclusion of treaties providing for the construction of a Trans-Isthmian Canal.

Though Congress and the treaty-making power ought to give effect to such agreements if made within the President's power, it unquestionably is within their legal power to refuse. Such executive agreements are not supreme law of the land. Consequently before making such agreements the President ought to get the advice of these bodies if possible.[27]

Draft treaties negotiated by the President are of even less obligation than such executive agreements, and experience has shown that the Senate does not hesitate to reject or amend them.[28] Consequently it is especially important that the President keep himself informed of the attitude of that body during the course of negotiation and conform his policy thereto.[29]

The conduct of diplomatic negotiations by the President and the employment of troops for defense of American citizens abroad or defense of the territory may easily lead to military undertakings which will require either congressional appropriations or a declaration of war. Thus all so-called declarations of war by

---

[26] Goodnow, *op. cit.*, p. 85.
[27] *Supra,* secs. 166, 169, 170, 172.
[28] *Supra,* sec. 177.
[29] *Supra,* sec. 176; *infra,* sec. 266, par. 4.

Congress have in fact been declarations of the "existence of war" and the act of Congress of July 13, 1861, was a ratification of the proclamation of the President of April 19, 1861, which was held to have signified the actual beginning of war.[30] Doubtless, in each of these cases Congress was under a practical, though not a legal obligation to carry out the undertaking begun by the President, and unquestionably in such undertakings the President ought to keep himself informed of and give due consideration to the opinion of Congress.[31]

The same is true of acts under the President's authority as Commander-in-Chief in time of war. Seizures of property under military necessity in occupied areas by way of requisition and contribution require subsequent compensation according to the law of war. Also the emancipation proclamation, if indeed it was within the President's power at all, certainly required action by Congress, if not the amending power, to remain effective after the war. After the Civil War Congress actually provided for compensation in certain cases or seizure and the amending power passed the thirteenth amendment abolishing slavery.[32]

252. *Acts of Congress.*

Congress when acting within its powers makes laws which legally bind the courts and the President. The courts, as the official interpreters of the Constitution, may examine the competence of Congress and refuse to apply unconstitutional statutes. The President, in his capacity as head of the national administration, has not even this power.[33] While acting as the representative organ of the government in foreign relations, however, he has an independent constitutional position, and is not subject to the direction of Congress. Treaties are on a par with acts of Congress, consequently while conducting negotiations with a view to treaty making, the President is not bound to follow resolutions or directions of Congress even though mandatory in terms. As a matter of constitutional understanding Congress ought not to pass such resolu-

---

[30] The Prize Cases, 2 Black 635, and *supra*, sec. 208.
[31] *Supra*, sec. 209.
[32] *Supra*, secs. 216–218.
[33] *Supra*, sec. 246.

tions except with the consent of the President, and it has usually followed this understanding. If such resolutions are passed, doubtless the President ought to follow them as a matter of constitutional understanding, and he usually has. However, he is the judge of the considerations which are likely to make negotiations successful and retains his discretion in spite of congressional directions.[34]

253. *Acts of the Treaty-Making Power. Obligation of the Courts.*

The obligation of organs of government to aid in the carrying out of the undertakings of coordinate organs has been most discussed in connection with the execution of treaties. Treaties if self-executing are of the same legal effect as acts of Congress and bind the President and the courts in the same manner. The latter may declare a treaty unconstitutional and void, but has never done so. The treaty-making power covers a broader field than does the power of Congress since it is given in full to the national government while the legislative power is divided between national and state governments. Apparently the only ground on which a treaty could be declared void would be that it dealt with a subject not proper for international negotiation, a limitation so vague as to be hardly capable of judicial application, or that it violated an express or implied prohibition of the constitution.[35] Since a declaration of unconstitutionality based on constitutional prohibitions would not ordinarily relieve the United States of international responsibility, the courts have always attempted, heretofore with success, to reconcile doubtful treaty provisions with the Constitution.[36] The courts cannot consider voidable treaties void until the political departments have acted. Thus, the Supreme Court required the extradition of an American citizen to Italy under the treaty of 1871 even though Italy had repeatedly violated the treaty by refusing to extradite Italian citizens wanted by the United States. For the courts a treaty is law from the date of its proclamation by the President until announcement of its termination by the political departments of the

---

[34] *Supra,* secs. 203, 246.
[35] *Supra,* secs. 67, 68, 173.
[36] *Supra,* sec. 31.

government, or its supercession by a conflicting treaty or act of Congress.[37]

254. *Acts of the Treaty-Making Power: Obligation of the President.*

The President is legally bound by treaties the same as by acts of Congress, whether they have been made by himself or his predecessors. He cannot modify them by agreements with the other party without ratification by two-thirds of the Senate, though precedents indicate that he may upon his own authority terminate them by denunciation under the terms of the treaty itself.[38] In case the treaty directs the President in such political matters as the negotiation of another treaty, or the urging upon Congress or the States of legislation, he retains his discretion and is constitutionally competent to ignore such directions, though by an understanding of the Constitution he ought to make honest efforts to carry out the treaty.

255. *Obligation of the Treaty-Making Power Itself as to Future Action.*

The treaty power cannot bind its own future action. Clearly it can repeal one treaty by negotiating a new one with the same party. But if it concluded a conflicting treaty with a different party, a more complicated situation arises. Under constitutional law, unquestionably the more recent treaty prevails though the courts ought to reconcile the two treaties by interpretation if possible. Under international law, however, the older treaty prevails on the theory that a treaty violative of the rights of an innocent third party is against the policy of international law. Therefore, although the treaty power is not legally bound to respect its earlier treaties, it ought to do so. The obligation is an understanding which has generally been observed. The Jay treaty with Great Britain in 1794 was alleged to violate certain provisions of the French treaty of 1778; and the Panama treaty of 1903 was alleged

---

[37] *Supra*, sec. 182 *et seq.*
[38] *Supra*, secs. 172, 186.

to violate provisions of the Hay-Pauncefote treaty with Great Britain of 1901, but they were not clearly proved to do so.[39]

Treaties may require subsequent action by the treaty-making power to give them effect. Such is the case with certain general arbitration treaties which require the conclusion of a special treaty or *compromis* for submission of each particular controversy coming under the general arbitration treaty. Such would also be true of the treaty of Versailles, which urges the conclusion of treaties upon such subjects as the maintenance of fair labor conditions, the maintenance of freedom of communications and transit, the prevention and control of disease, etc. Such provisions as this do not legally bind the treaty-making power, but undoubtedly the President and Senate ought to make due efforts to conclude such treaties when the occasion arises.

256. *Acts of the Treaty-Making Powers: Obligation of Congress.*

Treaties may require action by Congress to give them effect. Where executive and judicial action alone is sufficient to give treaties effect they are said to be "self-executing," but an exact distinction between those treaty provisions which become *ex propria vigore* the supreme law of the land and those which require legislative action is not clear. In Foster *v.* Neilson (1829), Chief Justice Marshall thought the provision of the Florida cession treaty that grants of land made in Florida prior to January 24, 1818 "shall be ratified and confirmed" was not self-executing and that the courts could not recognize such titles until Congress had acted. Subsequently an examination of the Spanish text of the treaty showed that the phrase should have read "shall remain ratified and affirmed" and in United States *v.* Percheman (1833) Chief Justice Marshall held that this rendered the clause self-executing, supporting his decision also on principles of general international law.[40] However, there are many acts which the treaty power cannot itself perform or the performance of which it cannot authorize by any organ other than Congress, yet Congress is under a certain obliga-

---

[39] Wright, Conflicts between International Law and Treaties, *Am. Jl. Int. Law,* 11: 576–579.

[40] Foster *v.* Neilson, 2 Pet. 253 (1829); U. S. *v.* Percheman, 7 Pet. 51 (1833); see also *supra,* sec. 137.

tion to perform them itself when necessary for carrying out a treaty. The obligation may seem absolute in view of the statement of Article VI that treaties are the supreme law of the land, but in practice, and in view of the equal constitutional power of Congress itself to make supreme law superseding treaties, the constitutional duty of Congress must be considered as an understanding of the Constitution, rather than a law.[41]

Practice indicates that treaty provisions dealing with matters which for historical and practical reasons have been placed by the Constitution peculiarly within legislative competence,[42] require congressional cooperation for their execution. Of this character are treaty provisions dealings with finances, whether (1) requiring appropriations of money, or (2) altering revenue laws and commercial regulations. While even in these cases Congress ought to act so as to give effect to a ratifed treaty, yet the treaty-making power is under an equal obligation to consider, in connection with its view of international policy, the views on domestic policy of Congress, before finally ratifying the instrument. In these matters foreign and domestic policy are connected with extraordinary intimacy, and a complete collaboration of the treaty power and the legislative power is appropriate. An opportunity for Congress to pass upon treaties of this character before ratification would seem generally expedient though not legally necessary.[43]

---

[41] Hamilton, however, wrote in a draft for Washington's message to the House of Representatives on the Jay treaty: "The House of Representatives have no moral power to refuse the execution of a treaty which is not contrary to the Constitution, because it pledges the public faith; and have no legal power to refuse its execution, because it is a law, until at least it ceases to be a law by a regular act of revocation of the competent authority." Works, Hamilton ed., 7: 566.

[42] The Constitution not only gives the financial powers to Congress, but it gives them especially to the House of Representatives. The terminology of Art. 1, sec. 7, cl. 1, and sec. 9, cl. 7, is a different sort of delegation from the powers given by Art. 1, sec. 8. This is a recognition of the historical connection between control of the purse and the rise of the House of Commons in England. See the Federalist No. 58; Magoon, Reports, p. 151.

[43] The objection brought in the Federal Convention of 1787 against such submission to Congress, that it would make secrecy impossible (Farrand, *op. cit.*, 2: 538), would probably have less weight at present. See also *supra*, secs. 59, 149, 154. Sir Cecil Hurst reported to the 6th committee of the First Assembly of the League of Nations that "at the time when the convention of

Other treaty provisions require for their performance detailed supplementary legislation or specific acts which the Constitution directs to be performed by Congress. In this category are treaty provisions requiring (3) the incorporation and administration of territory,[44] (4) the organization of courts and creation of offices and (5) a declaration of war in certain contingencies, or abstention from war.[45] In these cases Congress is bound to act and carry out in good faith the obligations which the treaty power has undertaken. These matters are ones upon which a proper decision might be expected from a comprehensive view of international relations, and hence the treaty power enjoys a greater freedom of action than in those of the former category.

Another class of treaty provisions are by nature self-executing, but because of historical traditions and constitutional interpretation, require legislation to be executable. Here are included treaties (6) defining crimes and extending criminal jurisdiction. The common law has been traditionally assiduous in protecting the individual against arbitrary criminal punishment, and this spirit, especially in reference to criminal procedure, has been embodied in Article 3, Section 2, Clause 3, the Fifth and Sixth Amendments, but federal courts are not denied a general criminal jurisdiction by any specific clause of the Constitution, and in some early cases they actually assumed jurisdiction of crimes defined by customary international law. This view has, however, changed, and it is now held that

---

Saint Germain (for control of arms trade) was drawn up it was realized that in certain countries the complete execution of its provisions might necessitate legislation" (First Assembly Document, No. 199) and the Temporary Mixed Commission on Armaments attributed the failure of the United States to ratify this convention to the failure of Congress to pass the necessary legislation (Second Assembly Document, No. 81, p. 15). Congress failed to respond to the President's request for legislation in execution of similar provisions of the Brussels act of 1890. (Moore, Digest, 2: 468-474.) *Supra*, sec. 118.

[44] The terminology of Art. 4, sec. 3, cl. 2, indicates that the power is supplementary in character.

[45] That the power of Congress to declare war is directory, rather than a peculiar congressional prerogative, is indicated by the incorporation in the same clause of the power to "make rules concerning captures," which is clearly shared with the treaty power. *Supra*, sec. 151.

the criminal jurisdiction of federal courts it entirely statutory.[46] Hence, treaty crimes must be incorporated in acts of Congress before they become cognizable in federal courts.[47]

In general it may be said that where the cooperation of Congress is necessary to carry out a treaty, Congress ought to act, exercising discretion only as to the means most suitable for attaining the ends contemplated by the treaty, and the duty is none the less binding in international law and constitutional understanding from the fact that the Constitution furnishes no power to compel it. The entire system of the Constitution demands that each department accept in good faith and cooperate in carrying out the undertakings of the other departments. But such cooperation cannot be relied upon unless the treaty power has given due consideration to the attitude of Congress before making the commitment.

"There is force, no doubt," says David Jayne Hill, "in the contention that the Congress of the United States is under a moral obligation to maintain the honor of the nation, which implies the strict fulfillment of all pledges made by the treaty-making power, but there is even more weight in the affirmation that the treaty-making power is under a moral obligation not to pledge the honor of the nation in doubtful conditions, as well as under a legal obligation not to destroy the freedom of a coordinate branch of the government by pledging it to a performance beyond the intentions of the Constitution from which all its authority is derived." [48]

---

[46] *Supra*, secs. 128, 129.

[47] Congress has passed laws giving courts jurisdiction over many offenses against international law, *supra*, secs. 112–122. Although State courts must regard treaties as the supreme law of the land, they appear to be excluded from jurisdiction of treaty crimes by the Judicial Code, sec. 256, cl. 1, which gives the Federal courts exclusive jurisdiction "of all crimes cognizable under the authority of the United States." A treaty crime would probably be considered in this category, even if, because of the failure of Congress to act, the Federal courts could not exercise jurisdiction.

[48] Hill, Present Problems in Foreign Policy, 1919, p. 171. Secretary of State Hughes has spoken to the same effect: "The extent to which Congress would regard itself as bound, as a matter of good faith, to enact legislation for the purpose of carrying out treaties has been the subject of debate, from time to time, since the days of Washington. Despite these debates, and notwithstanding its power to frustrate the carrying out of treaties, Congress in a host of instances has passed the necessary legislation to give them effect; and the disposition has frequently been manifested to avoid any basis for the charge of bad faith through a disregard of treaty stipulations. . . . Foreign

C. Duty of the Departments to Act.

257. *Constitutional Understanding Respecting the Establishment of Necessary Instrumentalities.*

The difficulty which arises from the lack of constitutional instrumentalities for meeting all international responsibilities is met in part by the legal duty of the President " to take care that the laws be faithfully executed " and in part by an understanding requiring Congress to supply the instrumentalities necessary for meeting international responsibilities. Story pointed out that Congress was under an obligation to establish inferior federal courts in order to carry out the purposes of the Constitution.[49]

"If Congress may lawfully omit to establish inferior courts, it might follow that in some of the enumerated cases the judicial power could nowhere exist. . . . Congress is bound to create some inferior courts, in which to vest all that jurisdiction which, under the Constitution, is exclusively vested in the United States, and of which the Supreme Court cannot take original cognizance."

We have noticed that Congress, under the necessary and proper clause, has power to provide for meeting international responsibilities.[50] It is believed that it is under a constitutional duty to exercise these powers.

258. *Duty of All Organs to Aid in Meeting International Responsibilities.*

The traditional conceptions of American statesmen has been that all organs of government were bound to aid in the meeting of international responsibilities.

---

nations might be expected to take the view that they were not concerned with our internal arrangements, and that it was the obligation of the United States to see that the action claimed to have been agreed upon was taken. If that action was not taken, although Congress refused to act because it believed it was entitled to refuse, we should still be regarded as guilty of a breach of faith. It is a very serious matter for the treaty-making power to enter into an engagement calling for action by Congress unless there is every reason to believe that Congress will act accordingly." (Address in New York, March 26, 1919, on the League of Nations Covenant, International Conciliation, Special Bulletin, April, 1919, pp. 689–691.) See also *supra,* sec. 39.

[49] Martin *v.* Hunter, 1 Wheat. 304 (1816).
[50] *Supra,* sec. 225.

"The statesmen and jurists of the United States," says Sir Henry Maine, "do not regard international law as having become binding on their country through the intervention of any legislature. They do not believe it to be of the nature of immemorial usage of which the memory of man runneth not to the contrary. They look upon its rules as a main part of the conditions on which a state is originally received into the family of civilized nations. . . . If they put it in another way, it would probably be that the state which disclaims the authority of international law places herself outside the circle of civilized nations." [51]

In accordance with this conception of international law, Duponceau has written: [52]

"The law of nations is to be carried into effect at all times under the penalty of being thrown out of the pale of civilization or involving the country in war. Every branch of the national administration, each within its district and its particular jurisdiction, is bound to administer it. . . . Whether there is or not a national common law in other respects, this *universal common law* can never cease to be the rule of executive and judicial proceedings until mankind shall return to the savage state."

The exercise by each organ of all constitutional powers necessary to assure the meeting of international responsibilities is a constitutional understanding which each organ of the government ought to observe. The United States has insisted upon this principle in its dealings with other nations.[53] Foreign nations have diplomatically and judicially asserted it.[54] The Senate, the courts, the President and text writers have maintained it at different times.[55] It is difficult to see on what other principle the meeting of international responsibilities in good faith can be assured in a government of divided powers, and if these responsibilities are not met it would seem that the objects of the Constitution as stated in its preamble to which all officers of the government are pledged under oath would be in peril. Organs of government, says Pillet, must observe the more

---

[51] Maine Int. Law, p. 37, *supra*, sec. 33.

[52] Duponceau, *op. cit.*, p. 3.

[53] Mr. Livingston, Sec. of State, to Mr. Serrurier, June 3, 1833, Wharton, 2: 67; *supra*, sec. 3.

[54] French Conseil d'Etat, Dalloz, Juris. Gen., Rept. t. 42, s. v. Traité Int., No. 131, Wright, *Am. Jl. Int. Law*, 12: 94.

[55] *Supra*, secs. 11, 39, 69.

fundamental obligations of international law "on penalty of exposing the state to a responsibility which may paralyze its sovereignty and put obstacles to the reign of its national law."[56]

[56] Pillet, *Rev. Gen. de Droit Int. Pub.,* 5: 87.

CHAPTER XIX.*

THE CONTROL OF FOREIGN RELATIONS IN PRACTICE.

259. *The Position of the President.*

Our study of the international and constitutional law governing the conduct of foreign relations has brought out two facts. First, that the President is the dominating figure. As the representative authority under international law and as the authority with exclusive power under constitutional law to communicate with foreign nations he has the initiative in conducting foreign affairs. No less significant, however, is the fact that the President does not have constitutional power to perform many acts essential to a proper conducting of foreign relations. Many of these powers are vested in other departments of the government, coordinate with the President. In such cases he is obliged to rely on persuasion and the operation of understandings of the Constitution in order to carry out foreign policies successfully, and to meet international responsibilities. Has this proved a practically effective system for conducting foreign relations?

260. *Friction in the American System.*

That it has often developed friction is unquestionable. "A treaty entering the Senate," wrote John Hay, "is like a bull going into the arena; no one can say just how or when the final blow will fall—but one thing is certain, it will never leave the arena alive."[1] When the Secretary of State put this in his diary he had seen seventeen treaties borne from the Senate lifeless or so mutilated by amendments that they could not survive. We can pardon his earlier statement: "The fact that a treaty gives to this country a great, lasting advantage seems to weigh nothing whatever in the minds of about half the Senators. Personal interest, personal spites, and a con-

---

* The major portion of this chapter was published in the American Political Science Review, February, 1921.

[1] Thayer, The Life of John Hay, 2: 393.

tingent chance of petty political advantage are the only motives that cut any ice at present."[2] Numerous illustrations of strained relations between the Executive and the Legislature at Washington might be cited. Thus in "The Education," Henry Adams records the reply of a cabinet officer to his plea for patience and tact in dealing with Congress: "You can't use tact with a Congressman! A Congressman is a hog! You must take a stick and hit him on the snout."[3]

Going back even farther we find in John Quincy Adams's Diary comment on a very early incident:[4]

> "Mr. Crawford told twice over the story of President Washington's having at an early period of his administration gone to the Senate with a project of a treaty to be negotiated, and been present at their deliberations upon it. They debated it and proposed alterations so that when Washington left the Senate Chamber he said he would be damned if he ever went there again. And ever since that time treaties have been negotiated by the Executive before submitting them to the consideration of the Senate."

Senator Maclay, who was present at the time, records the same incident in his journal on August 22, 1789.[5]

> "I cannot now be mistaken. The President wishes to tread on the necks of the Senate. . . . He wishes us to see with the eyes and hear with the ears of his Secretary only. The Secretary to advance the premises, the President to draw the conclusions, and to bear down our deliberations with his personal authority and presence. Form only will be left to us."

261. *Criticisms of the American System.*

The prevalence of such incidents suggests that the difficulties which arose between President Wilson and the Senate in considering the Peace Treaty of Versailles were not wholly due to personalities. It suggests that institutions may have been partly to blame. Indeed, Viscount Grey, in his letter to the *Times* of January 31, 1920, said that the American Constitution "not only makes possible, but, under certain conditions, renders inevitable conflict between the Executive and the Legislature."

---
[2] *Ibid.*, 2: 274.
[3] The Education of Henry Adams, 1918, p. 261.
[4] Memoirs, 6: 427.
[5] Journal of William Maclay, N. Y., 1890, p. 132.

American commentators have often deplored this situation. Frequently they have urged reform, usually in the direction of the British cabinet system, but their attention has been centered upon *domestic affairs*. It is an extraordinary fact that, with respect to the control of *foreign affairs,* the reverse is true. British writers have looked hopefully to the United States as a model for reform. Thus, in his American Commonwealth, Lord Bryce says:[6]

"The day may come when in England the question of limiting the present all but unlimited discretion of the executive in foreign affairs will have to be dealt with, and the example of the American Senate will then deserve and receive careful study."

This opinion has been acted upon, and features of the American system have been endorsed by the British union for democratic control of foreign relations founded in 1914.[7]

262. *Need of Popular Control in Foreign Relations.*

Two things seem to be needed in an institution designed to conduct foreign relations with success—concentration, or the ability to act rapidly and finally in an emergency, and popular control giving assurance that permanent obligations will accord with the interests of the nation. The subordination of national interests to dynastic and personal ends, prominent in sixteenth and seventeenth century diplomacy, showed the vice of an irresponsible concentration of power. The natural remedy seems to be parliamentary participation in treaty-making and war-making and this has in part been provided for in most continental European Constitutions during the nineteenth and twentieth centuries.[8] In England alone, the Crown

---

[6] American Commonwealth, 2d ed., p. 104.

[7] "The Morrow of the War," first pamphlet issued by the Union of Democratic Control, 1914, printed in Ponsonby, Democracy and Diplomacy, London, 1915, p. 21.

[8] See Myers, Legislatures and Foreign Relations, *Am. Pol. Sci. Rev.,* 11: 643 *et seq.* (Nov., 1917), and British report on Treatment of International Questions in Foreign Governments, Parl. Pap., Misc. No. 5 (1912), Cd. 6102, printed in Appdx. II, Ponsonby, Democracy and Diplomacy, p. 128 *et seq.,* and Heatley, Diplomacy and the Study of Foreign Relations, 1919, p. 270 *et seq.* See also Methods and Procedure in Foreign Countries Relative to the Ratification of Treaties, 66th Cong., 1st Sess., Sen. Doc. 26.

preserves its ancient prerogative in these matters and although in practice Parliament is sometimes consulted before ratification of important treaties, Lord Bryce and others have urged a more certain method of popular control, suggesting study of the American process of Senate participation.[9] But why labor the point! Democracy is convinced of the merits of democratic diplomacy. There is greater need to emphasize the importance of concentration.

263. *Need of Concentration of Authority.*

This need of concentration of power for the successful conduct of foreign affairs was dwelt upon in the works of John Locke,[10] Montesquieu,[11] and Blackstone,[12] the political Bibles of the constitutional fathers. It was emphasized by many speakers in the federal

---

[9] *Supra,* notes 6, 7. For relations of Crown and Parliament in treaty-making in England, see Anson, Law and Custom of the Constitution, 3d ed., II, pt. 2, p. 103 *et seq.*

[10] *Supra,* sec. 83.

[11] " By the (executive power, the prince or magistrate) makes peace or war, sends or receives embassies, establishes the public security, and provides against invasions. . . . The Executive power ought to be in the hands of a monarch; because this branch of government which has always need of expedition is better administered by one than by many; whereas, whatever depends on the legislative power is oftentimes better regulated by many than by a single person. But if there was no monarch, and the executive power was committed to a certain number of persons selected from the legislative body, there would be an end of liberty; by reason the two powers would be united, as the same persons would actually sometimes have, and would moreover always be able to have, a share in both." (Montesquieu, L'Esprit des lois, l. xi, c. 6, ed. Philadelphia, 1802, 1: 181, 186.)

[12] " With regard to foreign concerns, the king is the delegate or representative of his people. It is impossible that the individuals of a state, in their collective capacity, can transact the affairs of that state with another community equally numerous as themselves. Unanimity must be wanting to their measures, and strength to the execution of their counsels. In the king, therefore, as in a centre, all the rays of his people are united, and form by that union a consistency, splendor, and power that make him feared and respected by foreign potentates; who would scruple to enter into any engagement that must afterwards be revised and ratified by a popular assembly. What is done by the royal authority, with regard to foreign powers, is the act of the whole nation; what is done without the king's concurrence is the act only of private men." (Blackstone, Commentaries, 1: 252.)

convention,[13] by the authors of the Federalist,[14] and by President Washington in his message on the Jay treaty.[15] The same opinion

[13] See remarks by Hamilton and Gouverneur Morris, Farrand, *op. cit.,* I: 290, 513.

[14] " It seldom happens in the negotiation of treaties, of whatever nature, but that perfect *secrecy* and immediate *dispatch* are sometimes requisite. There are cases where the most useful intelligence may be obtained, if the persons possessing it can be relieved from apprehension of discovery. Those apprehensions will operate on those persons whether they are actuated by mercenary or friendly motives; and there doubtless are many of both descriptions who would rely on the secrecy of the President, but who would not confide in that of the Senate, and still less in that of a large popular assembly. The convention have done well, therefore, in so disposing of the power of making treaties that although the President must, in forming them, act by the advice and consent of the Senate, yet he will be able to manage the business of intelligence in such a manner as prudence may suggest.

"They who have turned their attention to the affairs of men must have perceived that there are tides in them; tides very irregular in their duration, strength and direction and seldom found to run twice exactly in the same manner or measure. To discern and to profit by these tides in national affairs is the business of those who preside over them; and they who have had much experience on this can inform us that there frequently are occasions when days, nay, even when hours, are precious. . . . So often and so essentially have we heretofore suffered from the want of secrecy and dispatch that the Constitution would have been inexcusably defective if no attention had been paid to those objects. Those matters which in negotiations usually require the most secrecy and the most dispatch are those preparatory and auxiliary measures which are not otherwise important in a national view than as they tend to facilitate the attainment of the objects of negotiation. For these the President will find no difficulty to provide; and should any circumstance occur which requires the advice and consent of the Senate, he may at any time convene them." (The Federalist, Jay, No. 64, Ford, ed., pp. 429-430.) See also Hamilton, No. 70, Ford, ed., p. 467.

[15] " The nature of foreign negotiations requires caution and their success must often depend on secrecy; and even when brought to a conclusion a full disclosure of all the measures, demands, or eventual concessions which may have been proposed or contemplated would be extremely impolitic; for this might have a pernicious influence on future negotiations, or produce immediate inconveniences, perhaps danger and mischief, in relation to other powers. The necessity of such caution and secrecy was one cogent reason for vesting the power of making treaties in the President, with the advice and consent of the Senate, the principle on which that body was formed confining it to a small number of members." (Washington's Message to the House of Representatives, March 30, 1796, Richardson, *op. cit.,* p. 194.)

was restated by De Tocqueville, who, because he doubted the ability of democracy to achieve this concentration, doubted its capacity to cope with foreign affairs.

"As for myself," he said, "I have no hesitation in avowing my conviction, that it is more especially in the conduct of foreign relations that democratic governments appear to me to be decidedly inferior to governments carried on upon different principles. Foreign politics demand scarcely any of those qualities which a democracy possesses, and they require on the contrary the perfect use of almost all those faculties in which it is deficient. . . . Democracy is unable to regulate the details of an important undertaking, to persevere in a design, and to work out its execution in the presence of serious obstacles. It cannot combine its measures with secrecy and it will not await their consequences with patience. These are qualities which more especially belong to an individual or to an aristocracy and they are precisely the means by which an individual people attains to a predominant position." [16]

But lest the apologist of the "Ancient Regime" be thought biased, let us hear a recent writer of a different school. Mr. Walter Lippmann thus discusses the uses of a king: [17]

"The reason why we trust one man, rather than many, is because one man can negotiate and many men can't. Two masses of people have no way of dealing with each other. . . . The American people cannot all seize the same pen and indite a note to sixty-five million people living within the German Empire. . . . The very qualities which are needed for negotiation—quickness of mind, direct contact, adaptiveness, invention, the right proportion of give and take—are the very qualities which masses of people do not possess."

264. *Practice in American History.*

As practice is the best evidence of what Constitutions are, so history is the best evidence of what institutions must become, if

[16] Democracy in America, N. Y., 1862, 1 : 254.
[17] The Stakes of Diplomacy, 2d ed., 1917, pp. 26, 29. See also remarks of Senator Spooner, of Wis., in Senate, January 23, 1906: "The conduct of our foreign relations is a function which requires quick initiative, and the Senate is often in vacation. It is a power that requires celerity. One course of action may be demanded tonight, another in the morning. It requires also secrecy; and that element is not omitted by the commentators on the Constitution as having been deemed by the framers of the most vital importance. It is too obvious to make elaboration pardonable." (*Cong. Rec.*, 40: 1420; quoted Corwin, *op. cit.*, p. 176.) See also Sen. Doc. No. 56, 54th Cong., 2d Sess., pp. 6–18; Reinsch, World Politics, 1900, p. 334; Heatley, *op. cit.*, p. 71.

they are to perform their functions. "Even democratic countries like France and England," says Bryce, "are forced to leave foreign affairs to a far greater degree than home affairs to the discretion of the ministry of the day." [18] The Greek city states in which diplomacy by mass meeting led to disaster when confronted by the astuteness of Philip of Macedon are the exception which proves the rule.[19] Thus, in the United States *when foreign problems have come to the front, concentrated authority has been developed to cope with them.* In the first period from 1789 to 1829 foreign relations were complex. Presidents were chosen because of their experience in diplomacy, and they displayed competence and leadership. There was friction but in all cases until the last,—John Quincy Adams's policy with reference to the Panama congress,—the President's policy prevailed. In the second period which extended from 1829 to 1898 our problems were mainly domestic. In these Congress assumed a leadership and though Presidents continued to assert their prerogative in foreign affairs, opportunities were only occasional and defeats were frequent. Presidents were chosen for political availability, not for ability or experience, and the Senate's power of vetoing treaties was strengthened by frequent exercise. In his "Congressional Government," presented as a doctor's thesis in 1885, Woodrow Wilson generalized the progress of this period as follows:[20]

"In so far as the President is an executive officer he is the servant of Congress; and the members of the Cabinet, being confined to executive functions, are altogether the servants of Congress.

"Party government can exist only when the absolute control of administration, the appointment of its officers as well as the direction of its means and policy is given immediately into the hands of that branch of the government whose power is paramount, the representative body.

"No one, I take it for granted, is disposed to disallow the principle that the representatives of the people are the proper ultimate authority in all matters of government and that administration is merely the clerical part of government. Legislation is the originating force. It determines what shall

---

[18] American Commonwealth, 2d ed., 1: 218. See also Reinsch, World Politics, p. 329.
[19] Ibid., 1: 217.
[20] Congressional Government, 15th ed., pp. 266, 273–274.

be done; and the President, if he cannot or will not stay legislation by the use of his extraordinary power as a branch of the legislature, is plainly bound in duty to render unquestioning obedience to Congress. . . . The principle is without drawback and is inseparably of a piece with all Anglo-Saxon usage; the difficulty, if there be any, must lie in the choice of means whereby to energize the principle. The natural means would seem to be the right on the part of the representative body to have all the executive servants of its will under its close and constant supervision, and to hold them to a strict accountability; in other words, to have the privilege of dismissing them whenever their service became unsatisfactory."

The third period began with the Spanish War of 1898. Our foreign relations have increased in complexity and with them the President's power and influence; but because of the enlarged sense of senatorial prerogative, developed through three-quarters of a century of comparative diplomatic isolation, friction has been extreme.[21] Woodrow Wilson, now professor of politics at Princeton University, wrote a preface for the 15th edition of his book in 1900.[22]

" Much the most important change to be noticed is the result of the war with Spain upon the lodgment and exercise of power within our federal system; the greatly increased power and opportunity for constructive statesmanship given the President, by the plunge into international politics and into the administration of distant dependencies, which has been that war's most striking and momentous consequence. When foreign affairs play a prominent part in the politics and policy of a nation, its Executive must of necessity be its guide; must utter every initial judgment, take every first step of action, supply the information upon which it is to act, suggest and in large measure control its conduct.

" It may be, too, that the new leadership of the Executive, inasmuch as it is likely to last, will have a very far-reaching effect upon our whole method of government. It may give the heads of the executive departments a new influence upon the action of Congress. It may bring about, as a consequence, an integration which will substitute statesmanship for government by mass meeting. It may put this whole volume hopelessly out of date."

Where the President has acted in domestic administration, he has acted within limits, narrowly defined by Congress, and as time has gone on, his discretion in this field has become less and less. Where, on the contrary, he has acted in foreign affairs, his discretion has been very wide, and Congress has generally followed his

[21] Reinsch, American Legislatures, p. 95; Willoughby, *op. cit.*, p. 460.
[22] Congressional Government, pp. xi–xiii.

lead. "The Senate," says Carl Russell Fish, speaking of the period since 1898, "has been confined to checking or modifying the policy of the administration. The direction of policy has been with the executive."[23] Can we not assume that the result of over a century of experience under the Constitution illustrates certain necessities in an adequate control of foreign affairs?[24]

265. *Constitutional Change Not Necessary.*

Our system for controlling foreign relations has been copied in its main outlines on the continent of Europe, and its adoption has been suggested as a reform worth considering in England. It has in it elements making for concentration of authority in an emergency, yet it assures control by the people's representatives of permanent obligations. More than all we are used to it. Remembering Montaigne's warning that "all great mutations shake and disorder a state,"[25] we may question the advisability of radical change in the Constitution.

266. *Need of Constitutional Understandings.*

Improvement lies not in structural change in our organs for control of foreign relations,[26] but in the development of understandings

---

[23] American Diplomacy, N. Y., 1916, p. 428; see also Reinsch, World Politics, p. 337.

[24] Corwin, *op. cit.*, p. 207.

[25] Montaigne, Essays, Cotton, ed., 2: 760.

[26] The writer is inclined to believe that a change in the treaty power from two-thirds of the Senate to a majority of both houses would be an improvement. This would be in accord with the practice of most continental European governments. It would obviate the complaint of the House of Representatives and eliminate the ever present possibility of inability to execute a treaty, valid at international law, because of refusal of the House to agree to appropriations or necessary legislation. It would also make deadlocks less frequent. One party is much more likely to control a majority of both houses than two-thirds of the Senate. The main objection of the fathers to submission to the House was on the score of secrecy, and this has frequently been abandoned by the Senate in recent years. This change, which would, of course, require a constitutional amendment, would make the treaty-making power the same as the legislative power, except that the President would have the sole initiative, and retaining an ultimate decision on ratification, would have an absolute veto. See also J. T. Young, The New American Movement, N. Y., 1915, p. 25, and former Representative and Governor of Massachusetts, S. W. McCall, "Of the Senate" and "Again the Senate," *Atlantic Monthly,* Oct., 1903, and Sept., 1920.

for the smooth interaction of the independent departments of government.[26a] Lord John Russell remarked that "political constitutions in which different bodies share the supreme power are only enabled to exist by the forbearance of those among whom this power is distributed."[27] It is a familiar thought and has been developed in detail by Professor Dicey, who distinguishes the conventions or understanding from the law of the British Constitution. The former explain how the independent organs of the supreme power, King, Lords and Commons, shall exercise their discretion, *i.e.*, how the Crown shall exercise its prerogative and the Houses of Parliament their privileges. He believes that in England these conventions have grown up so as to assure the ultimate triumph of the will of the political sovereign, *i.e.*, the majority of the voters for members of the House of Commons.[28]

In the eighteenth century the British Constitution, though perhaps organized to preserve liberty, as Montesquieu, De Lolme and Blackstone thought, was a jarring and jangling instrument. There was little of smoothness in the relations of George III, his ministers and his parliaments. The United States Constitution is now in that condition. We have good institutions but we have not yet developed constitutional manners which will make them work like a well-ordered dinner party. The crudity of Jefferson's pell mell banquet and Jackson's Peggy O'Neil cotillion persists in the relations of the departments of government.

Our conventions will not be those of England. In the conduct of domestic affairs, our system of legally enforceable limitations upon power rather than the English system of unlimited power, subject to immediate political responsibility for its exercise, is likely to persist. We will continue to rely upon legal responsibility, rather than political responsibility as in England, or administrative responsibility as on the continent of Europe. In short, the object of the conventions and understandings which we will develop will be the ultimate triumph of the people acting through the constitution-amending process, not as in England, the people acting through an election to the House of Commons.

[26a] See Appendix B, p. 375.
[27] Quoted, Wilson, Cong. Govt., 15th ed., p. 242.
[28] Dicey, The Law of the Constitution, 8th ed., Chap. XIV.

In the conduct of foreign affairs, however, there will probably be a closer approximation in the two countries. At present parliamentary control does not exist in the British foreign office[29] any more than constitutional limitations check the President's control of foreign relations.[30] In foreign affairs neither a daily questioning under threat of ousting from office, nor a judicially interpreted confinement to constitutional powers has proved feasible. Until international organization is much further developed, great discretion must be vested in a single head. Acts involving assumptions of national responsibility must be final. Under present conditions we must frankly recognize executive leadership in foreign affairs. But we must attempt to develop understandings so that the President's wide discretion will only be exercised after the most careful consideration possible, and in a way which will make the employment of a senatorial or congressional veto an extreme rarity, and an impeachment a virtual impossibility. Such understandings might develop through:

1. Declaration by Congress of permanent policies, not in any way restricting executive methods, but pointing the general ends toward which the President should direct his effort;[31]

2. Development by treaty of international organization and arbitration so as to bring as large a portion of diplomacy as possible under the control of recognized principles of international law, an atmosphere in which democratic institutions, and particularly American institutions, have always thriven;[32]

---

[29] See remarks of A. J. Balfour and Premier Asquith to Select Committee of the House of Commons on Procedure, 1914 (Report 378), printed in Ponsonby, *op. cit.*, Appdx. 1, p. 121 *et seq.* See also *ibid.*, p. 45 *et seq.*, Heatley, *op. cit.*, pp. 68–70, 265, and *supra*, note 18.

[30] See H. J. Ford, "The War and the Constitution," and "The Growth of Dictatorship," *Atlantic Monthly*, Oct., 1917, and May, 1918, and *supra*, sec. 68.

[31] *Supra*, sec. 204.

[32] "Democracies are absolutely dependent for their existence upon the preservation of law. Autocracies can give commands and enforce them. Rules of action are a convenience, not a necessity, for them. On the other hand, the only atmosphere in which a democracy can live between the danger of autocracy on one side and the danger of anarchy on the other is the

3. Observance by the independent departments of government of the understanding that toleration, consideration, and respect should grace the exercise of powers which may collide with the powers of other departments, which may need supplementing by the action of other departments, or which may be indispensable for the meeting of international responsibilities.[33] Finally, as a necessary condition of such observance;

4. Maintenance of close informal relations between the agencies of the government having to do with foreign affairs. Such relations now exist between the President and the administrative departments represented in the Cabinet. Why should not the Cabinet be enlarged so as to include representatives of the legislative branch? The Vice-President, who is closely in contact with the Senate, has been added by President Harding. But a more genuine congressional point of view could be gained by admitting also the Speaker of the House, President pro tem. of the Senate, and perhaps the Chairman of the House Committee on Foreign Affairs and the Senate Committee on Foreign Relations. The President, sitting with these five officials, together with the Secretaries of State, Treasury, War, Navy, Commerce and the Attorney-General, would form a Cabinet capable of reaching decisions on foreign affairs likely to secure cooperation from all departments of the government and yet not too large to do business.[34]

Closer relations might also be established by the President with Congress and especially with the Senate through personal delivery of messages and explanations of his policy, but always at his initiative.[35] The present practice, whereby Congress does not " direct " the Secretary of State to submit papers and information as it

---

atmosphere of law. . . . The conception of an international law binding upon the governments of the world is, therefore, natural to the people of a democracy, and any violation of the law which they themselves have joined in prescribing is received with disapproval, if not with resentment." E. Root, The Effect of Democracy on International Law, *Proc. Am. Soc. Int. Law*, 1917, pp. 7–8.

[33] *Supra*, sec. 244.

[34] The writer owes this suggestion to Professor John A. Fairlie.

[35] " Rule XXXVI of the Standing Rules of the Senate still provides the manner in which the President is to meet the Senate in executive session. Henry Cabot Lodge, in referring to the recognition in this rule of the right

does other cabinet officers but requests the real head of the department, the President of the United States, "to submit matters if, in his judgment, not incompatible with the public interest," must be maintained.[36]

Finally, close informal relations between the President and congressional committees on foreign affairs should exist, here again at the President's initiative. President Madison was right, as Senator Lodge pointed out in 1906, in refusing to receive a Senate committee sent on *command* of that body to interview him with reference to an appointment of a minister to Sweden.[37] But the President should often *invite* such committees to discuss with him.[38] Thus, without limiting the President's power in foreign relations, or in any way impairing his capacity to take speedy action when necessary, we might develop understandings which would show him how he ought to exercise his discretion—understandings sanctioned in last analysis by the possibility of Senate or congressional veto of his measures, defeat of his party in the next election, or even impeachment.

Though this essay has dealt with constitutional law and constitutional understandings, it must be emphasized that the system is not the most important part of government. Any system will work with big men.[39] It is the merit of the British system that it throws

of the President to meet with the Senate in consideration of treaties, said in the United States Senate, January 24, 1906: 'Yet I think we should be disposed to resent it if a request of that sort was made to us by the President.' *Cong. Rec.*, 59th Cong., 1st sess., 1470" (Crandall, *op. cit.*, p. 68, note 5). But see remarks of Senator Bacon, *supra*, sec. 176. President Wilson revived the custom in abeyance since the time of John Adams of appearing in person before Congress for the delivery of formal messages.

[36] *Supra*, sec. 234.

[37] "In the administration of Mr. Madison the Senate deputed a committee to see him in regard to the appointment of a minister to Sweden, and he replied that he could recognize no committee of the Senate, that his relations were exclusively with the Senate." Senator Lodge of Massachusetts, Jan. 23, 1906, *Cong. Rec.*, 40: 1420, quoted Corwin, *op. cit.*, pp. 174–175.

[38] *Supra*, sec. 176. A recent illustration is President Wilson's offer to discuss the treaty of Versailles with the Senate Foreign Relations Committee, an offer which resulted in several conferences in the White House during the summer of 1919. See 66th Cong., 1st sess., Sen. Doc. 106, p. 499 *et seq.*

[39] "Constitute government how you please, infinitely the greater part of it must depend upon the exercise of powers which are left at large to the

big men to the top. The United States must develop political traditions and methods that will do the same.[40] The people and parties must insist on men of experience and tried capacity as candidates. For the conduct of foreign relations, the personnel of the Presidency, the Secretaryship of State and the Senate are especially important. The Senate might well have more members with executive and administrative experience as did the Senate of ancient Rome. Why not retain the services of ex-Presidents and Secretaries by electing them to the Senate?[41] Conversely, Secretaries of State might well be chosen from men of legislative, especially senatorial, experience.[42] Finally, the President on whom falls final responsibility for leading the separated and often antagonistic agencies of government to the goal of a successful foreign policy should not be a dark horse. Why not develop traditions of advancement, as from a governorship to the Senate, then to the Vice-Presidency, or to the Cabinet, and finally to the Presidency. It was done in the first forty years of our national history.[43] It would lead bigger men to the Senate and Cabinet. It would insure capacity and popular confidence in the President.

---

prudence and uprightness of ministers of state. Even all the use and potency of the laws depends upon them. Without them your Commonwealth is no better than a scheme upon paper; and not a living, active, effective organization." Edmund Burke.

[40] Reinsch, World Politics, pp. 340-346.

[41] There have been some notable examples of this in recent years, such as Senators Root and Knox.

[42] "From Monroe's Secretaryship of State in 1811, down to the resignation of Mr. Blaine, that position was held constantly by men who had been United States Senators, with the exception of brief interregna, covering altogether less than one and a half years, and with the exception of William M. Evarts, who became a Senator later in his career. Since the resignation of Mr. Blaine an entirely new system has come into use, Senators Sherman (and Knox) being the only Secretaries of State who had also been members of the Senate. Under these circumstances, it is not surprising that there should have been more friction between the President and the Senate on foreign matters than existed during the earlier years of our nation's life." (Reinsch, Am. Legislatures, p. 95, quoted in Willoughby, *op. cit.*, p. 460.)

[43] For table showing the experience of American Presidents, see *Am. Pol. Sci. Rev.*, 15: 25. Wilson (Congressional Government, pp. 251-256) refers to the tendency of the governorship rather than membership in the Senate or House to be in the line of promotion to the presidency.

APPENDIX A.

Congressional Delegation of Power to Make International Agreements.[1]

The above heading may occasion criticism. Thus Professor J. B. Moore is inclined to think that "no 'delegation' of power whatever is involved in the matter."

> "As Congress possess no power whatever to make international agreements," he continues, "it has no such power to delegate. All that Congress has done in the cases referred to is to exercise beforehand that part of the function belonging to it in the carrying out of a particular class of international agreements. Instead of waiting to legislate until an agreement has been concluded and then acting on the agreement specifically, Congress has merely adopted in advance general legislation under which agreements, falling within its terms, become effective immediately on their conclusion or their proclamation."[2]

It is true that Congress has no agreement making power to delegate,[3] but it is also true that in fields covered by Congressional legislation the President can not make an agreement until Congress has passed an authorizing act.[4] Treaties will supersede earlier legislation, but this force has never been attributed to executive agreements. In the type of subject matter here involved an agreement is necessarily both an international bargain and a national regulation. Now, while Congress has no power to make an international bargain, it does have power to regulate postal service, copyrights, tariffs, etc. Strictly it is this power to make regulations within the scope of general laws which it delegates to the President and not the power to make bargains with foreign nations, but since in dealing with matters of domestic administration within the power of Congress the two are inextricably connected, the result in this field is the same as though the power to make the agreement flowed wholly from the Congressional act. It has therefore seemed least misleading to adhere to the usage suggested both by custom and the language of Congressional acts.

---

[1] See section 61.
[2] Proc. Am. Phil. Soc., Minutes, 60: XV.
[3] *Supra,* sec. 159.
[4] *Supra,* sec. 162.

APPENDIX B.

Constitutional Understandings.[1]

Professor J. B. Moore has pointed out that "so-called constitutional understandings are logically much more of the essence of things under the British system than under the American system," noting the analogy of the former constitution to the common-law system of private rights established by gradually developing judicial precedents and of the latter constitution to the civil-law system established by formal code.[2] "Just as the British Constitution," said Gladstone, "is the most subtle organism which has proceeded from progressive history, so the American Constitution is the most wonderful work ever struck off at a given time by the brain and purpose of man."[3] The same contrast has been noted by Bryce in his contrast of "rigid" and "flexible" constitutions.[4] Without questioning the value of this contrast many writers have, however, dwelt upon the "flexibility" of the "rigid" American Constitution due to "constitutional understandings."[5]

---

[1] See section 266.
[2] Proc. Am. Phil. Soc., Minutes, 60: XIV.
[3] Fisk, Critical Period of American History, p. 264.
[4] Bryce, Studies in History and Jurisprudence, 1: 139 et seq.
[5] Wilson, Congressional Government, 1885, pp. 7-9, Constitutional Government, in the United States, 1908, p. 57; Bryce, American Commonwealth, ed. 1891, 1: 390; Beard, American Government, ed. 1910, p. 60; Munro, Government of the United States, 1919, p. 57; Wright, The Understandings of International Law, Am. Journ. Int. Law, 14: 578–580.

INDEX

Abrogation of treaty. (See Treaty.)
Act of Congress:
   Authority of President to use force under, 308.
   Construed in accord with international law, 165.
   Enforcement of international law by, 186-187.
   Ignored by President, 341.
   Insufficiency of, to meet all international responsibilities, 185-189.
   Limitation of state powers by, 74.
   Provisos in deference to international law and treaty, 163-164.
   Publication of, 31.
   Source of Federal criminal jurisdiction, 199.
   Subject to international cognizance, 30, 32, 40.
   Supersedes customary international law, 174.
   Supersedes earlier treaty, 162, 345.
   Superseded by later treaty, 164.
   Superseded by arbitration award, 110.
   Vetoed by President because violative of treaty, 164-165.
   When effective, 31, 199.
Acts of Congress referred to:
   Alien enemies, 86, 303.
   Alien exclusion and expulsion, 83, 188, 303, 304.
   Alien landholding, 163-164.
   Annexation of territory, 275.
   Anti-trust, 165.
   Appreciation of foreign compliments, 278.
   Appropriation for international claims, 66, 226.

Arming of merchant vessels, 294-295.
Arms trade, 184.
Authorizing arbitration, 281, 283.
Authorizing armament limitation conference, 278, 282.
Authorizing executive agreements, 105, 106.
Authorizing intervention, 271, 297.
Authorizing participation in international organization, 228, 334.
Authorizing President and Courts to meet international responsibilities, 100.
Authorizing treaty negotiation, 248.
Authorizing use of force, 167, 186, 192, 296, 297.
Cable landing, 302.
Canal tolls, 163.
Chinese exclusion, 83, 261, 345.
Citizenship, 277.
Copyrights, 105.
Declaration of war, 286, 289.
Diplomatic immunities, 163, 167.
Draft, 163.
Enforcement of consular awards, 185.
Enforcement of treaties, 74.
Embargo and non-intercourse, 301-302.
Expatriation, 277-281.
Extradition, 184, 194.
Forbidding Presidential participation in international conferences, 325, 328, 335.
Fulfillment of guarantees, 227.
Guano islands, 134, 173, 274.
International navigation rules, 181.

378 THE CONTROL OF AMERICAN FOREIGN RELATIONS.

Jurisdiction in Bering Sea, 164, 165, 174, 345.
Jurisdiction of Federal courts, 170, 198.
Migratory birds, 87.
Militia, 94.
Navigation and shipping, 84, 163, 258, 281, 345.
Neutrality, 74, 181, 295.
Offenses against diplomatic officers, 180.
Offenses against foreign currency, 182.
Offenses against international boundaries, 183.
Offenses against international law, 87, 179–184, 356.
Offenses against resident aliens, 180.
Offenses against treaties, 184–186.
Offenses at sea, 165.
Offenses in foreign countries, 183.
Oil leases, 301.
Organization of diplomatic and consular services, 167.
Organization of military and naval services, 167.
Patents, 105.
Piracy, 180.
Postal service, 105.
Presentation of claims, 22, 29.
Prize money, 345.
Prizes, 164, 167.
Rank of diplomatic officers, 324, 325.
Recommending state enforcement of international law, 177, 179, 180.
Release from state jurisdiction of person exempt under international law, 161, 171, 180, 229.
Return of deserting seamen, 184.
Retaliation, 301.
Sedition and espionage, 188.
Tariff, 106, 164.
Tenure of office, 316.
Termination of treaties, 256, 281.
Trademarks, 105.
Trading with the enemy, 303.

Treatment of enemy property, 301.
War power, 74.
White slavery, 87.
Acts of government organs, responsibility for, 151.
Acts of parliament, when void, 210.
Adams, Charles Francis:
  On President's power to terminate treaty, 39.
  On American accession to Declaration of Paris, 47.
Adams, Henry, On relations of Congress and the President, 361.
Adams, John:
  Dismissal of Secretary of State, 322.
  On power to arm merchant vessels, 295.
Adams, John Quincy:
  On duty to ratify treaties, 43, 252.
  On recognition, 270, 272.
  On relations of President and Senate, 361.
Admiralty jurisdiction of federal courts, 200.
Administrative Agreements. (See Executive Agreements.)
Advice, meaning of, in League of Nations Covenant, 114.
Agents, power of President to appoint, 249, 315. (See also Diplomatic Agents.)
Agreement:
  Determination of obligations by, 218.
  National Obligations founded on, 206, 208.
Agreements, international, conclusiveness of President's statements condemning, 41.
Alabama, arbitration on "due diligence," 176, 177.
Alabama, case of, 18.
Alabama claims court, 222.
Algeciras general act. (See Treaty.)
Alien enemies, expulsion and internment of, 85, 304.
Aliens:

# INDEX.

Congressional power to protect, 88.
Exclusion of, constitutional, 83, 130, 303.
Expulsion of constitutional, 83, 303.
Indemnity for injury of, 225.
Insufficiency of legislation to protect, 187.
International law applied in cases regarding status of, 172.
Jurisdiction of federal courts in cases affecting, 201–203.
Offenses against punished, 180.
Rights of, 170, 201.
Source of power to exclude and expel, 133.
State legislation discriminating against, 162.
State power to protect, 154, 179. (See also Treaties.)
Ambassador, power to appoint, 325. (See also Diplomatic Officers.)
Amelia Island Case, 193, 296.
Amendment to constitution. (See Constitution of United States.)
Amendment to treaty. (See Treaties.)
Amends in reparation, 229.
American Civil War:
Commencement of, 288.
Termination of, 291.
Anarchy, offense against international law, 188.
Annexation. (See Act of Congress, Territory, Treaties.)
Appam, case of, 24, 342.
Apology, amends by, 229.
Appointment of officers, power to make, 314.
Appropriations, power to make, 225.
Arbitration, International:
Authority to submit cases to, 62, 222, 223.
Awards binding, 61, 224.
Awards self executing as to boundary settlements, 226.
Awards supreme law of the land, 174, 224, 245.
Duty to submit cases to, 222.
Effect of fraud, 223, 224.
Grounds for rejecting award, 224.

Number of cases settled by, 244.
Submission of cases to, constitutional, 110.
Types of cases submitted to, 215. (See also Treaty.)
Arbitration court, establishment of, 334.
Arbitration Treaties, 109, 223.
Definition of justiciable questions, 211–212.
Not applicable to third parties, 166.
Senate rejection of, 252.
Suggested by Congress, 248.
Arguelles, case, 78, 190, 195, 237.
Armament limitation:
Provisions of League of Nations Covenant, 114.
Treaties on, suggested by Congress, 248.
Armies, power to raise, 85.
Armistice, 240. (See also Executive Agreement.)
Arms trade, 184, 191.
Aroostook war, 230.
Arthur, Chester A., President, Veto of Chinese exclusion act, 165, 261.
Articles of Confederation, 21.
Control of Foreign Relations under, 61, 138.
Legislation enforcing international law under, 177, 179, 180.
National powers under, 145.
Treaty power under, 43, 246.
Assassination, not a political offense, 189.
Asylum, not permitted, 168.
Austin, John, on Nature of International law, 210.
Austria:
Protest on President's comment on Kossuth revolution, 36.
Termination of war with, 293. (See also Treaties.)
Austria-Hungary, declaration of war against, 289.

Bacon, Senator, of Georgia:
On legislative nature of treaty-making power, 139, 140.
On Senate participation in treaty negotiation, 250.

Baldwin, Simeon E., On power of President to conclude *compromis* of arbitration, 108.
Barnett, James F., on power of states to make agreements, 232.
Bayard, T. F., Secretary of State:
  On display of force, 294.
  On international responsibilities, 18.
  On power to interpret political treaties, 215.
  On powers of Congress and President to determine obligations, 216.
  On Senate amendments to treaty, 47.
  On termination of war, 291.
Belligerency:
  Distinguished from insurgency, 200, 269.
  Recognition of, a political question, 172.
Benton, Thomas Hart, Senator from Missouri:
  On Diplomatic Officers.
  Resolution on Texan annexation, 279.
Bering Sea fisheries case, 110, 164, 165, 174, 343.
Bering Sea fisheries treaty, suggested by Congress, 248. (See also Treaties.)
Bernstorff, Count, German Ambassador, rebuked, 29.
Beust, Count, Austrian Chancellor, on Concert of Europe, 319.
Beveridge, A. J., Senator from Indiana:
  On executive nature of foreign relations power, 137.
  On nature of treaty-making power, 139.
Bibb, Senator, of Georgia, on appointment of diplomatic officers, 326–327.
Bills of rights, reason for, 172.
Blackstone, Sir William, on control of foreign relations, 363.
Blaine, James G., on Congressional resolutions on foreign policy, 280.
Blockade proclamation, effect of, 38, 288.

Borchard, E. M.:
  On international court of claims, 225.
  On making of contracts, 41.
  On power of government to abandon claims, 82.
  On power of officers to bind the state, 26.
  On President's power to use force abroad, 307.
  On responsibilities of states, 151.
Boundaries:
  Demarkation of, 232.
  Executive agreements regarding, 239.
  Offenses relating to punished, 183.
  Recognition of changes in, 274.
Boxer rebellion, 241, 285, 296.
Brazil, recognition of insurgent navy of, 40.
Breaking diplomatic relations. (See Diplomatic relations.)
Brewer, Justice:
  On nature of national powers, 131.
  On political questions, 83.
British Empire, International responsibilities of, 15. (See also Great Britain.)
Bryan, William J., Secretary of State:
  On irregularity of diplomatic communications to the people, 22.
  On responsibilities of German Government for Prussian treaty, 16.
  Peace treaties by. (See Treaties.)
Bryce, James:
  On cognizability of acts of Congress, 32.
  On control of foreign relations, 366.
  On influence of Senate in foreign affairs, 362.
  On rigid and flexible constitutions, 375.
Burke, Edmund, on discretion in the conduct of government, 372.

INDEX. 381

Burlingame treaty. (See Treaties, China.)
Burton, Senator, on Arbitration treaties, 112.

Cabinet, relation to President, 371.
Cable, power to regulate, 302. (See also Treaties, Submarine cable.)
Calhoun, John C.:
  On treaty-making power, 101, 103, 121–122, 344.
  On unitary responsibility under international law, 25.
California-Japanese controversies. (See Japan.)
Canadian Waterway Commission, 183, 219.
Capitulations, 240.
Caroline case, 206.
Cartel, 235, 240. (See also Executive agreement.)
Ceremonials, obligation of, 209.
Cherokee Indians. (See Treaties.)
China:
  Dispatch of troops to, by President, 227.
  Reservation to treaty of Versailles, 49. (See also Treaties.)
Chinese exclusion acts:
  Protected by China, 17, 162.
  Subject to international cognizance, 32. (See also Acts of Congress.)
Citizens of the United States, definition, 276.
Citizenship:
  Determination by courts, 278.
  Recognition by Department of state, 277.
Civil services, observance of international law by, 167.
Civil war, authority to use force in, 193. (See also American Civil War.)
Claims:
  Delegation of power to settle, 220.
  International, 82, 209.
  Law applied in settling, 222.
  May be compromised, 82.
  May be presented to President, 222.
  Mode of presentation, 23, 35, 65, 217.
  Number settled by treaty and arbitration, 244.
  War, settlement of, by treaty, 220.
Claims court. (See Court of Claims.)
Claims treaty. (See Treaties.)
Clay, Henry:
  On recognition power of Congress, 271.
  On right of Senate to refuse ratification of treaties, 44.
  On reprisals, 298.
  Resolution of recognition, 279.
Clayton-Bulwer treaty. (See Treaties, Great Britain.)
Cleveland, President Grover:
  On Monroe Doctrine, 39, 283.
  On obligation to indemnify injured aliens, 225.
  Urges legislation to enforce arms trade treaty, 191.
Colombia. (See Treaties, Colombia.)
Colonial governor, power of, 145.
Comancho case, 99, 162.
Commander-in-chief, power of President to make arrangements as, 240. (See also President.)
Comity of nations, international understandings, 8, 212.
Commerce, power to control, 302.
Commercial treaties. (See Treaties.)
Commission of inquiry, power of President to submit controversies to, 219.
Commissioners, appointment of, 326. (See also Diplomatic agents.)
Common law:
  Certain principles of, 209–211.
  Obligations under, 213.
  Jurisdiction of federal courts under, 196–198.

Compromis of arbitration:
  Power to make, 108, 223, 236.
  Senate participation in, 216–217.
  (See also Executive agreement.)
Concert of Europe, nature of, 319.
Concurrent resolution, ineffective to denounce treaty, 34.
Confederate states of America, unofficial reception of mission by England, 35.
Confiscation of property, 169.
Congress:
  Can not be deprived of powers by treaty, 101.
  Can not bind President in foreign affairs, 350.
  Can not delegate legislative power, 312.
  Can not delegate power to authorize reprisals, 209.
  Can not delegate war power, 290.
  Can not exercise judicial or executive functions, 312.
  Can not make treaties, 233.
  Checks upon disregard of international law by, 164.
  Concurrent resolution not subject to international cognizance, 33.
  Consent of, to state agreements, 230.
  Control of federal administration, 235.
  Control of Indian relations, 234.
  Control of diplomatic officers, 61.
  Delegation of power to President, 302.
  Delegation of power to make international agreements, 105, 233, 236, 374.
  Duty of courts to apply acts of, 350.
  Duty of President to enforce acts of, 350.
  Duty to carry out Executive agreements, 237, 349.
  Duty to carry out military undertaking of President, 349.
  Duty to execute treaties, 191, 207.
  Incompatibility of membership in, with public office, 316.
  Influence in foreign relations, 366, 370.
  Initiative in domestic affairs, 148.
  May be deprived of discretion by treaty, 103.
  National obligations to be determined by, 216.
  Observance of international law by, 162.
  Powers concurrent with President, 340, 341.
  Powers concurrent with treaty-making power, 344, 345.
  President's official communications to, subject to international cognizance, 36.
  Privileges and immunities of, 96.
  Recognition of international responsibilities, 18.
  Rejection of resolutions affecting foreign relations, 279.
  Relation to President, 371.
  Resolution of single house, not subject to international cognizance, 33.
  Veto on war declaration, 149.
  (See also Act of Congress; Congress, powers; House of Representatives, Senate.)
Congress, powers of, 96.
  Abrogation of treaty, 260.
  Annexation of territory, 275–276.
  Appropriations, 225.
  Cable landing, 267.
  Commerce, 302.
  Commercial pressure, 301.
  Conduct of war, 305.
  Confiscation of enemy property, 300.
  Creation of offices, 311.
  Criteria of expatriation, 277.
  Declaration of war, 227, 290, 248.
  Interpretation of constitution, 347.
  Intervention, 310.
  Meeting of international responsibilities, 18, 100, 159.
  Naturalization, 277.

INDEX. 383

Denunciation of treaty, 258.
Enforcement of treaty, 185, 228.
Extradition, 190, 195.
Foreign relations, 138, 139, 266, 267.
Government of territory, 134.
Imports prohibition, 303.
Initiation of treaties, 233–234.
Organization of army and navy, 221, 320.
Participation in international organization, 334.
Protection of resident aliens, 88, 187.
Rank of diplomatic officers, 324–325.
Recognition, 270, 271, 273, 286.
Reprisals, 298.
Resolutions on foreign policy, 278–283.
Termination of executive agreements, 236.
Termination of voidable treaties, 356.
Termination of war, 292.
Treaty making, 261
Use of force, 305.

Conquest:
Acquisitions of territory by, 276.
Termination of war by, 291.

Conspiracy against foreign states, 188.

Constitution of United States:
Amendments to, when effective, 31.
Appeals from Supreme Court to international tribunal not permitted by, 118.
Compared with British constitution, 375.
Compared with European constitutions, 369.
Controls conduct of foreign relations, 4.
Courts can not exercise non-judicial powers, 117.
Delegation of legislative power, prohibited, 99, 103, 312.
Extent to which knowledge of, by foreign nations is presumed, 38, 41.

Fundamental principles of, 71–75.
Importance of able men to administer, 372, 373.
International law to be enforced under, 179.
International responsibilities recognized by, 18.
Interpretation of, in accordance with international law, 162.
Motives for forming, 145.
Need of modification in foreign relations control, 368.
Protects powers of each department, 98.
Reasons for friction in its operation, 369.
Supersedes customary international law, 174.
Validity of consent to treaty determined by, 26. (See also Congress, Courts, President, Separation of Powers, States of United States, Treaty-making power.)

Constitutional limitations:
Do not affect international responsibilities, 17.
Mainly of territorial application, 124.
On foreign relations power, 121, 125.
On national powers, 76.
On state powers, 73.

Constitutional provisions referred to:
Abolition of slavery, 80, 301, 350.
Administration of territory, 355.
Admission of new states, 130, 275.
Appointing power, 98, 101, 119, 314–316.
Appropriations, 104, 354.
Citizenship, 276.
Compulsory process for obtaining witnesses, 56, 79, 81, 162.
Creation of courts, 99, 103, 312.
Creation of offices and agencies, 103, 311.
Declaration of war, 104, 355.
Diplomatic officers, 14, 243, 323.
Division of power between states and nation, 73, 132.

Due process of law, 78, 170, 196, 202.
Duty to execute laws, 146, 157, 235, 305, 357.
Executive power vested in President, 95, 135, 155.
Foreign commerce, 302, 303.
Grand jury, 85.
Guaranteed rights of individuals, 77.
Guarantees of criminal procedure, 355.
Independence of judiciary, 202.
Inviolability of state territory, 55, 57, 89, 307.
Judicial power, 95, 116, 158.
Jurisdiction of federal courts, 202.
Legislative power vested in Congress, 95, 96.
Letters of marque and reprisal, 298.
Maintenance of courts, 15.
Militia, 94, 304.
Naturalization, 277.
Necessary and proper clause, 80, 87, 155, 179, 311, 357.
Non-suability of states by individuals, 205.
Offenses against law of nations, 79, 87, 155, 179.
Organization of army and navy, 320.
Organization of courts, 355.
Powers of President, 141, 146.
Power to conduct foreign relations, 71.
Power to meet international responsibilities, 159.
Preamble, 358.
President's use of force, 305.
Privileges and immunities of citizens, 306.
Procedure for acts of Congress, 107.
Prohibition of alcoholic beverages, 79, 162, 303.
Raising of armies, 94.
Republican form of government in states, 57, 307.
Revenue laws, 354.

Rules of capture, 85.
Separation of powers, 76, 95.
States' rights, 76, 86.
Supreme law of the land, 5, 32, 344.
Treaty-making power, 53, 246.
Treaty supersedes state laws, 162.
Treaties supreme law of land, 57, 73, 104, 172, 196, 354.
Veto power, 141.
War powers of national government, 284.
War powers of states, 264.
Constitutional understandings:
  Importance of, 8, 126, 368, 369, 375.
  Meaning of, 7, 8.
  Protect exercise of powers by each department, 98.
  Reason for, 339.
  On consideration in exercise of powers, 371.
  On coöperation of independent organs, 346.
  On duty of departments to act, 357.
  On overlapping of powers, 340.
  On reserved powers of states, 75, 92.
  On treaty negotiations, 251.
  Sanctions of, 372.
  Suggestions for development of, 370.
Constitutions, limitations upon, by, international law, 14.
Consular courts:
  Do not exercise judicial powers of United States, 116.
  Need not accord jury trial, 78, 84.
Consular regulations, 168.
Consular service, appointments to, 325, 335.
Consuls:
  International law applied in cases affecting, 172.
  Legislation enforcing awards of foreign, 185.
Contract:
  National obligations based on, 206.
  State obligations based on, 205.

INDEX.   385

Contractual obligations, responsibility for, 153.
Continental Congress, recognition of international responsibilities, 18.
Contributions of enemy property, 299.
Controversies, international, settlement of. (See Arbitration, Executive agreements, Permanent Court of International Justice, Treaties.)
Convoys, power to authorize, 295.
Cooley, T. M., on popular sovereignty, 72.
Copyright agreements. (See Acts of Congress.)
Corwin, E. S.:
  On concurrent powers of departments, 341.
  On Congressional resolutions on foreign policy, 281.
  On President's power to make executive agreements, 240.
  On recognition power, 273.
  On representative powers of President, 23.
Council of conciliation, power of President to submit controversy to, 219.
Courtesy, international, duty of, 209, 212.
Court of Cessation, France, on interpretation of treaties, 218.
Court of Claims:
  Jurisdiction of, 221.
  Suability of states in, 205.
Court of International Justice. (See Permanent Court of International Justice.)
Court, Supreme. (See Supreme Court.)
Courts of claims, special, 222.
Courts, extra-territorial. (See Extra-territorial courts.)
Courts, federal. (See Federal courts.)
Courts martial:
  Jurisdiction of, 168.
  Not affected by constitutional limitations, 84.
Courts of United States:
  Bound by arbitral awards, 174, 245.
  Bound by written law, 174.
  Can not make international agreements, 234.
  Constitutional powers of, 96.
  Determination of citizenship by, 278.
  Decisions do not affect international responsibility, 18.
  Do not investigate political questions, 172, 269.
  Duty to apply Acts of Congress, 351.
  Duty to apply reservations to treaty, 253.
  Duty to apply treaties, 172, 257.
  Enforcement of executive agreements, 236, 242.
  Establishment of, required by international law, 14.
  Foreign relations powers of, 266, 267.
  Observance of executive agreements, 239.
  Observance of international law, 170.
  Power to meet international responsibilities, 158.
  Recognition of termination of treaty, 256.
  Recognition of territorial accretions, 273. (See also Court of Claims, Federal courts, Supreme Court.)
Courts, Prize. (See Prize courts.)
Crandall, S. B.:
  On Congressional initiative of treaties, 248.
  On duty to know treaty power of foreign states, 41.
  On negotiators of treaties, 249.
Crawford, Secretary of the Treasury, on power of recognition, 272.
Criminal judgments, not executable in foreign courts, 189.
Criminal jurisdiction of federal courts. (See Federal courts.)
Crown, British, powers of, 143.
Cuba, dispatch of troops to, by President, 227. (See also Treaties.)
Cuban insurgents, status of, 173.
Cullom, Shelby E., Senator from Illinois, on arbitration treaties, 112.

Cushing, Caleb, Attorney-General:
  On duty of Congress to execute treaties, 63
  On President's power of direction, 317.
  On President's power to determine rank of diplomatic officers, 324.
Czar's ambassador, case of, 178.

Dana, H. W., on obligation of Congress under treaties, 63.
Davis, acting Secretary of State, on methods of presenting international claims, 23.
Davis, Judge Advocate General, on use of militia, 308.
Declaration of London. (See Treaties.)
Declaration of Paris. (See Treaties.)
Declaration of War. (See War.)
Declaratory judgments on boundaries, 213.
De Facto Government:
  Treaty making power of, 57.
  Unofficial reception of missions from, 35.
Delegate distinguished from representative, 318.
Delegation of legislative power. (See Constitution of United States.)
Democracies:
  Capacity to conduct foreign relations, 365.
  Dependence on law, 370.
Denial of justice, 152, 170.
Denunciation of treaty. (See Treaties.)
Department of State. (See State, department of.)
Derby, Lord, on obligation of guarantee treaty, 214.
Destruction of enemy property, 299.
De Tocqueville, Alexis, on control of foreign relations, 365.
Dicey, E. V., on constitutional understandings, 369.
Dillon, French consul, case of, 17, 55–56, 79, 81, 116.

Diplomatic relations, grounds for breaking, 20.
Diplomatic service, appointments to, 325, 335.
Diplomatic agent:
  Appointment of, 316, 328, 329.
  Position compatible with judicial or legislative office, 316.
Diplomatic agreements, 243. (See also Executive agreements.)
Diplomatic etiquette, breach of, in Senate amendment to treaty, 45.
Diplomatic immunities, 79, 162, 168, 173, 177.
Diplomatic instructions, 168.
Diplomatic mission:
  By naval officers, 297.
  Self constituted, forbidden, 34.
Diplomatic officers:
  Communicate only with executive, 29.
  Communications to people improper, 29.
  Duty to exchange, 209.
  Grades established by international law, 323.
  Immunities of, 79, 162, 163, 168, 173, 177.
  International law applied in cases affecting, 171.
  Jurisdiction in cases affecting, 170, 202.
  Nature of, 318.
  Offenses against, punished, 179, 180.
  Power to determine grades of, 324.
  Power to determine occasion for appointing, 326.
  Powers fixed by international law, 14.
  Protection of, by President, 194.
  Reception of, political question, 172.
  Unofficial reception of, from de facto government, 35.
Diplomatic pressure, power to bring, 293.
Diplomatic protection of citizens abroad, 15, 16.

INDEX. 387

Disarmament. (See Armament limitation.)
Discovery, acquisition of territory by, 274.
Display of force, 294.
Domestic affairs distinguished from foreign affairs, 150, 263, 264.
Dominions, British self governing:
    Foreign relations power of, 16.
    Representation in League of Nations, 16.
Drago doctrine, 153.
Draft acts, constitutionality of, 85, 94. (See also Acts of Congress.)
Dubois, Dutch minister, case of, 79, 162.
Due diligence, 152, 176, 177.
Due Process of Law. (See Constitution of United States.)
Duponceau, Peter, on obligation of international law, 58, 358.

Embargo:
    On arms to insurgents, 183.
    Power to authorize, 301.
Emancipation proclamation, constitutionality of, 86, 300, 350.
England. (See Great Britain.)
Exchange of Notes, 235. (See also Executive agreement.)
Exchange of ratifications. (See Treaties.)
Exclusion. (See Aliens, Chinese Exclusion.)
Executive:
    Danger of excessive influence in foreign relations, 5.
    Usually representative organ, 26.
    (See also President.)
Executive agreement:
    Annexation of territory by, 275.
    Congressional execution of, 237.
    Duty of President to accept if made within instructions, 44.
    Extradition by, 237.
    License to trade, 240.
    Military agreements, 240.
    National obligations based on, 206.
    Number claims settled by, 244.
    Obligation of, 234.
    Power to make, 54, 237, 243.
    Preliminary to treaty negotiation, 228, 243.
    Submission of private claims to arbitration by, 223.
    Termination of, 236, 262.
    Transit of foreign troops, 242.
    Under authority of Congress, 105, 374.
    Under authority of Treaty, 106-110, 236.
    Validity of, 239.
Executive agreements referred to:
    Boxer protocol, 1901, 241.
    Canadian reciprocity, 349.
    Copyrights, 105.
    Costa Rica, transisthmian canal, 349.
    Gentlemen's agreement, with Japan, 243.
    Germany, 1918, armistice, 54.
    Germany, 1918, peace preliminaries, 54, 216, 241, 349.
    Great lakes disarmament, 1817, 242.
    Guantanamo lease, 107, 236.
    Hay open door notes, 243.
    Horse-shoe reef cession, 236, 349.
    Lansing-Ishii agreement with Japan, 235, 243.
    Mexican boundary marauders, 187, 217, 242.
    Nicaragua canal, 349.
    North Atlantic Fisheries, 240.
    Patents, 105.
    Postal service, 105.
    Reciprocity, 106.
    Root-Takahira agreement with Japan, 235, 243.
    San Juan island occupation, 239.
    Santo Domingan customs, 156, 349.
    Spain, 1898, peace preliminaries, 54, 241, 349.
    Trade marks, 105.
Executive message as means of international communication, 36.
Executive orders:
    Regulating military and civil services, 167.
    Supersede customary international law, 174.
Executive power, nature of, 140.

Executive regulations and instructions, how enforced, 168.
Expatriation, right of, 277.
Expulsion. (See Aliens, Alien enemies.)
Extradition:
  Based on treaty, 189.
  By authority of President, 190, 194.
  By state authority, 153, 178, 231.
  Constitutionality, 78.
  Jurisdiction of federal courts over, 198.
  Political assassins liable to, 189.
  Statutes regarding, 184.
Extra-territorial courts:
  Establishment of, 15.
  Criminal jurisdiction of, 191.

Family of nations:
  Admission to, 20.
  Organization of, 214.
  States members of, bound by international law, 58.
Federal Courts:
  Creation of, 312.
  Decision on political questions, 173.
  Duty of President to execute decisions of, 346, 347.
  May not exercise non-judicial functions, 312.
  Powers concurrent with President, 342, 343.
  Power to determine national obligations, 221. (See also Courts of United States, Supreme Court.)
Federal Courts jurisdiction:
  Admiralty, 200, 201.
  Cases affecting aliens, 170-171, 201-203.
  Cases affecting diplomatic officers, 202.
  Cases affecting military and naval officers, 169.
  Cases brought by foreign states, 23.
  Claims, 221-222.
  Criminal, 196-199, 355, 356.
  Exclusive, 178.

Enforcement of international law, 196.
Enforcement of neutrality, 182.
Enforcement of treaties, 190, 191.
Extradition, 198.
Prize, 169, 200, 221.
Release of persons claiming immunity under international law, 171.
Federal governments:
  Treaty-making power may be distributed, 15.
  Unitary responsibility of, 15.
Federalist:
  On Articles of Confederation, 21.
  On control of foreign relations, 364.
  On inapplicability of constitutional limitations to foreign relations power, 124.
  On nature of foreign relations power, 140, 147.
  On obligation of treaties, 6.
Field, David Dudley, on conspiracy against foreign nations, 185.
Field, Justice:
  On sovereign powers of national government, 130.
  On treaty-making power, 121.
Fillmore, Millard, President:
  Executive agreement by, 237.
  On war powers of President, 192.
Finley, J. H., and Sanderson, J. F., on coöperation of departments, 346.
Fish, Carl Russel, on control of foreign relations, 368.
Fish, Hamilton, Secretary of State:
  On Dillon case, 17.
  On relation of legislation to treaty, 17.
  On Senate amendments to treaty, 47.
Fisheries:
  Executive agreement regarding, 239.
  Senate rejection of treaty concerning, 252.
  State agreements on, 232.
Florida invasion, 193. (See also Treaties, Spain.)

INDEX. 389

Foreign relations:
　Control of, in American history, 366.
　Control of, in European countries, 362.
　Control of, under constitution, 335, 336.
　Classification of agencies for conducting, 317–318.
　Criticism of American system of control, 361.
　Distinguished from domestic affairs, 150, 263, 264.
　Friction in control of, 360.
　Need of concentration in control of, 363.
　Need of popular control, 362.
　Need of Presidential leadership, 370.
　Need of secrecy in control of, 364–365.
Foreign relations power:
　Constitutional point of view, 6.
　Danger of executive control, 5.
　Difficulty of developing legal theory, 3.
　Dual position of, 4.
　Elements of, 71.
　Executive nature of, 135.
　International point of view, 4.
　Law and understandings of, 7.
　Legislative nature of, 137.
　National government, 129.
　Nature of, 3, 134, 148.
　Not judicial, 135.
　Overlapping of, 266.
　Political question, 124.
　Practical control of, 148.
　Relation to constitutional and international law, 4.
　States of United States, 129. (See also Recognition, Treaty-making power, War.)
Fortification of Horseshoe Reef, forbidden, 237.
Foster, J. W.:
　On congressional approval of Monroe Doctrine, 283.
　On Control of Foreign Relations under Articles of Confederation, 61.
　On power of President to conclude *compromis* of arbitration, 108.
France:
　Inability to execute claims treaty, 66.
　Protest at President Jackson's threat of reprisals, 36.
　Treaty-making power, 53. (See also Treaties, France.)
French spoliation claims, 82, 219, 222.
Freund, Ernst, on inapplicability of constitutional limitations to foreign relations power, 124.
Frye, William P. (See William P. Frye.)
Full powers, effect of exchange of, 42.

Garfield, James, President, opinion on President's powers, 157.
Geffcken, on duty to know treaty power of foreign states, 41.
Gênet, Citizen, French Minister, recall of, 29.
Geneva arbitration. (See Alabama case.)
Gentleman's agreement. (See Executive agreements.)
Germany:
　Foreign relations power, 16.
　Controversy on tonnage dues, 32.
　Declaration of war against, 289.
　International responsibility of national government, 15.
　Preliminaries of peace with. (See Executive agreements.)
　Termination of war with, 293. (See also Treaties, Germany.)
Gladstone, W. E., on nature of British and American constitutions, 375.
Goodnow, Frank J.:
　On administrative powers in American colonies, 145.
　On appointment of agents, 315.
　On powers of President, 156.
Gore, Senator of Massachusetts, on appointment of diplomatic officers, 326.

Governments, recognition of, 268.
(See also Federal Governments.)
Grant, U. S., President:
    Message on cable landing, 302.
    On representative powers of President, 22, 30.
    Veto of Congressional resolutions affecting foreign relations, 30, 278.
Gray, Justice:
    On extradition power of President, 195.
    On foreign relations power of national government, 130.
    On judicial applicability of international law, 171.
    On President's power to permit transit of troops, 242.
Great Britain:
    Creation of executive departments, 144.
    Distribution of powers, 143–145.
    Nature of constitution, 369, 375.
    Powers of crown, 143.
    Powers of Parliament, 143.
    Treaty-making power, 53, 55. (See also British Empire, Treaties.)
Great Lakes Disarmament agreement. (See Executive agreements, Treaties.)
Greece, control of foreign relations in, 366.
Gresham, Secretary of State:
    On duty of states to know foreign constitutions, 41.
    On termination of executive agreements, 236.
Grey, Sir Edward, on American Constitution, 361.
Greytown incident, 285, 296, 299, 306.
Griggs, Attorney-General, on treaty-making power, 123.
Guaranteed rights of individuals. (See Constitution of United States.)
Guarantee, International:
    Interpretation of, 60, 217.
    Obligation of, 214.
    Power to fulfill, 227.
    Under League of Nations, 115.

Guarantee Treaties. (See Treaties.)
Guadaloupe-Hidalgo, treaty of. (See Treaties, Mexico.)
Guano Islands, 134, 274.

Habeas Corpus, suspension of writ, 85.
Hague Conference, 1907, recommendations as to future conferences, 319.
Hague Conventions, 1899, 1907:
    Deposit of ratifications, 50.
    Not applicable to third parties, 166.
    Reservations to, 48, 51, 282.
Hague Conventions, 1907, referred to:
    I, Settlement of international disputes, 108, 110, 210, 228, 334.
    II, Public contract debts, 153, 223, 247.
    III, Declaration of war, 289.
    IV, Rules of land warfare, 299.
    V, Neutrality on land, 177, 191, 196.
    X, Geneva Convention at Sea, 185.
    XII, International Prize Court, 110, 117, 224, 334.
    XIII, Neutrality at Sea, 177, 191.
Hague Permanent Court of Arbitration, bureau, participation of United States in, 228, 334.
Hall, James Parker, power of states of United States to make agreements, 230.
Hall, W. E.:
    On basis of international law, 13.
    On independence of states, 264.
Hamilton, Alexander:
    Conception of presidency, 145.
    Instructions for neutrality enforcement, 196.
    On Articles of Confederation, 21.
    On duty of Congress to execute treaties, 354.
    On inapplicability of constitutional limitations to foreign relations power, 124.
    On nature of foreign relations power, 136, 147.

On President's power to meet international responsibilities, 155.
On Tripolitan war, 287.
Harding, Warren Gamaliel, President:
On Congressional resolutions on foreign policy, 278, 281–282.
On termination of war, 292.
Harlan, Justice, on power of Congress to enforce treaties, 185.
Harley, J. E., on obligation to ratify treaties, 42.
Harrison, Benjamin, President, urges legislation to protect aliens, 229.
Hartford convention, 93.
Hawaii:
Congressional resolution regarding, 281.
Annexation treaty rejected by the Senate, 252. (See also Treaties, Hawaii.)
Hay, John, Secretary of State:
Arbitration treaties, 109.
Conference with Senators on treaty negotiation, 251.
On Senate's attitude toward treaties, 360.
Relations with President, 323.
Hay open door notes. (See Executive agreements.)
Hay-Pauncefote Treaty. (See Treaties, Great Britain.)
Hayes, Rutherford B., President:
On good faith of treaties, 261.
On termination of treaty, 257, 258.
Veto of Chinese exclusion act, 17, 164.
Hayti, dispatch of troops to, by President, 227. (See also Treaties, Hayti.)
"Helvidius" (Madison), 136.
High seas, offenses on, punished, 180.
Hill, David Jayne:
On duty of treaty-making power to consider attitude of Congress, 356.
On necessity of separation of powers, 5.

Hitchcock, Senator of Nebraska, proposed reservation to Treaty of Versailles, 60.
Hoadley, Bishop, on power to interpret law, 63.
Hoar, Senator of Massachusetts, on appointment of Senators to negotiate treaties, 251.
Hobbes, Thomas, on nature of international law, 210.
Hohfeld, W. M., on fundamental legal conceptions, 214.
Holland, T. E., definition of obligation, 213.
Holmes, Oliver Wendell, Justice:
On law-making power of judges, 64.
On power of Congress to enforce treaties, 186.
On non-suability of sovereign, 210.
On validity of treaties, 87–88.
Holy Alliance, sympathy for absolute governments, 14.
Horseshoe reef, cession of, 237.
House of Representatives:
Advisability of participation in treaty-making, 246, 368.
No treaty-making power, 62, 233.
On Congressional resolutions on foreign policy, 280.
Resolution on obligation to appropriate for treaty, 6, 226.
Resolution on Maximillian government in Mexico, 33. (See also Congress.)
Huerta, Victoriana, Defacto President of Mexico:
Non-recognition of, 20, 268.
Note on United States intervention, 215.
Hughes, Charles Evans, on duty of treaty-making power to consider attitude of Congress, 356, 357.
Hungary, termination of war with, 293.
Hyde, Charles Cheney, on executive agreements submitting claims against United States, 244.

Immigration laws. (See Act of Congress Aliens.)
Imperfect obligation. (See Obligation.)
Imperfect rights under international law, 8.
Independence:
  Of nations, 13, 263, 264.
  Questions of, non-justiciable, 29.
Indians:
  Control of, by Congress, 234.
  Naturalization of, 277. (See also Treaties.)
Insurgency:
  Distinguished from belligerency, 200, 269.
  International law applied in cases affecting, 172.
  Neutrality laws applied to, 200.
  Recognition of, political question, 172, 268, 269.
Insurgents:
  Acts in behalf of, violation of neutrality laws, 182.
  Embargo on arms to, 183.
  Internment of, 196.
Insurrection against foreign governments, punished, 183.
International administration, 247.
International agencies, creation of, 334.
International agreements, power of states to make, 230–232. (See also Executive agreements, Treaties.)
International claims. (See Claims.)
International conferences:
  Nature of delegates to, 318.
  Participation in, authorized, 228, 334.
  Presidential participation in, forbidden, 325, 328, 335. (See also Hague Conferences.)
International coöperation, duty of, 209.
International court, determination of national obligations by, 222. (See also Hague Permanent Court of Arbitration, International Prize Court, Permanent Court of International Justice.)

International court of claims, proposal for, 224–225.
International law:
  Acquisition of territory under, 134, 173.
  Acts of Congress interpreted by, 165.
  Applied by courts, 158, 171, 221, 222.
  Applied in claims settlement, 223.
  Based on agreement of states, 208.
  Can not be altered by municipal law, 16.
  Codified in executive regulations, 168.
  Conclusiveness of acts and utterances of national organs under, 38.
  Conditions favoring observance of, 161.
  Confiscation of enemy property under, 300.
  Constitution interpreted in accordance with, 162.
  Defines rank of diplomatic officers, 318, 323.
  Definition of, 13, 212.
  Does not require withdrawal of claim, 66.
  Enforcement of, 176–179, 196.
  Governs foreign relations power, 4.
  Immunities under, 79, 242.
  Imposes limitation upon national organs, 14.
  Imposes moral obligations, 210.
  Interpreted by national organs in first instance, 213.
  Interpretation of, by President, 245.
  Limits of jurisdiction defined by, 165.
  Nature of, 13.
  Naval forces bound by, 168.
  National obligations founded on, 206, 209.
  Obligation of, 58, 212.
  Observance of, by Congress, 162.
  Observance of, by Courts, 170.

INDEX. 393

Observance of, by military and civil services, 167.
Observance of, by President, 166.
Observance of, by treaty-making power, 166.
Offenses against, 79, 159.
Offenses against, punished in federal courts, 196, 197.
Offenses against, punished in state courts, 154, 180.
Power to seize property under, 299.
President bound by, in exercise of war powers, 169.
Principles of state responsibility, 151.
Prohibits trading with the enemy, 303.
Release from states of persons claiming immunity under, 171.
Representative authority under, 15.
Respect for, in acts of Congress, 163.
Self defense under, 307.
Sources of 208.
Supersedes British Order in Council, 170.
Tacit acceptance of, 58.
Termination of treaty by operation of, 256.
Treaties codifying, 247.
Types of cases in which applied, 159, 171.
Validity of treaty under, 57.
Value of, for democracies, 370.
Written law interpreted in accord with, 175.
International organization:
Advisability of development of, 370.
Power to participate in, 228.
Delegation of power to, 110.
International Prison Commission, participation in, by United States, 334.
International Prize Court, 110, 224, 334.
Constitutionality of, 117.
International responsibilities. (See Responsibilities, international.)

International understandings:
Do not require withholding of claims, 66.
Meaning, 7, 8.
International unions, participation in, 334.
Internment:
Of alien enemies, 304. (See also Alien enemies.)
Of troops—
Constitutionality, 78.
Obligation, 209.
Under executive authority, 196.
Intervention distinguished from recognition, 270.
Invasion, power to repel, 308.
Iredell, Justice, on power to terminate voidable treaties, 256.
Irish independence, congressional resolutions on, 34.
Italian lynching cases, 18, 25, 60, 67, 206, 225, 229.
Italy:
Claims in regard to Louisiana lynchings, 18.
Withdrawal of minister from United States, 21. (See also Treaties.)

Jackson, Andrew, President:
On enforcement of judicial decisions, 346.
On reprisals, 298.
Recommendation of reprisals, 25, 36, 66.
Removal of bank deposits, 317.
Seeks Senate advice to treaty, 250.
Japan:
Land ownership controversy, 24, 90, 265.
Protests at anti-alien legislation, 30.
School children controversy, 90, 265. (See also Treaties.)
Jay, John:
On control of foreign relations, 364.
On duty to ratify treaties, 43.

On obligation of treaties, 6.
On Senate discretion in treaty-making, 252.
Jefferson, Thomas:
Attitude toward neutrality proclamation, 268.
Initiation of Tripolitan war, 297.
On effect of general reprisals, 291.
On grades of diplomatic officers, 324.
On nature of foreign relations power, 137, 138.
On President's foreign relations powers, 22, 28, 36, 38.
On Treaty-making power, 102, 123.
On Tripolitan war, 286.
Johnson, Andrew, President, proclamation of termination of Civil War, 291.
Jones merchant marine act, 258, 281, 345.
Judge in own case, 112, 209–210.
Judgments, execution of foreign, 189.
Judges, law-making power of, 63.
Judiciary. (See Courts.)
Judiciary, federal, privileges and immunities of, 97. (See also Federal courts.)
Jurisdiction:
Armed forces to respect foreign, 168.
International law applied in cases regarding limits of, 172.
Of federal courts. (See Federal courts, jurisdiction.)
Justiciable questions, 211, 212.
Justinian Digest, on making of contracts, 41.

Kent, James, Chancellor, on treaty-making power, 55.
King can do no wrong, 210.
Knox, Philander C.:
On international cognizability of Acts of Congress, 32.
On League of Nations Covenant, 113.
Resolution for termination of war, 292.

Kocourek, on distinction of obligation and responsibility, 214.
Kossuth revolution, 36.
Koszta case, 285, 306, 309.

La Abra and Wyle claims, 223.
La Follette Seaman's act, 84, 258, 345.
Land Warfare, rules of, 168.
Lansdowne, Lord, British foreign minister, on Senate amendment to treaty, 45.
Lansing, Robert, Secretary of State:
On Appam case, 342.
On arming of merchant vessels, 295.
On diplomatic communications to the people, 29.
On international responsibilities of representative organ, 19, 24.
On Lansing-Ishii agreement, 243.
Lansing-Ishii agreement. (See Executive agreements.)
Latin-American states, attitude toward diplomatic protection of citizens, 16.
Law, relation to understandings, 7, 8. (See also Acts of Congress, Constitution, International law.)
League of Nations:
Appointment of representatives in, 333.
Arbitration under, 113, 210, 223.
Article 10, 60, 61, 114, 214, 241.
Conciliation by, 219.
Domestic affairs under, 263.
Exercises no legislative power, 114.
Guarantees under, 115.
Justiciable questions under, 212, 214.
Limitation of Armament by, 114.
Mandates under, 114.
Nature of delegates to, 320.
Permanent International Court of. (See Permanent court.)
Powers of, 113.
Powers of Council, 60.
Representation of British dominions in, 16.
Respect for earlier treaties, 166.
Settlement of disputes by, 114.

INDEX. 395

Treaties to be concluded under, 228.
    Unanimity required, 113. (See also Reservations to Treaty of Versailles, Versailles treaty.)
Lee, Attorney-General:
    On duty of diplomatic officers to communicate with executive only, 29.
    On foreign relations power of Secretary of State, 22.
Legal obligations. (See Obligations.)
Legislation. (See Acts of Congress, State statutes, Congress.)
Legislative acts, do not affect international responsibilities, 17.
Legislative omissions, do not affect international responsibilities, 17.
Legislative power, delegation of. (See Constitution of United States.)
Legislature, difficulty of exercising foreign relations power, 7.
Lenin, defacto head of Russian government, non-recognition of, 20.
Letters of marque. (See Repristas.)
Letters rogatory. (See Rogatory.)
Liability, synonymous with responsibility, 213, 214.
Libels against foreign states, not punishable by federal statute, 187, 188.
License to trade, 240.
Lincoln, Abraham, President:
    Blockade proclamation by, 38.
    Extradition of Arguelles, 190, 195, 237.
    Recognition of civil war, 288.
    Refusal to carry out congressional resolution on foreign affairs, 281.
    Refusal to denounce treaty, 258.
    Repudiation of armistice made by General Sherman, 44, 240.
    Use of force to suppress rebellion, 193.
Lippmann, Walter, on control of foreign relations, 5, 365.
Liquor trade punished, 184. (See also Constitutional provisions.)

Livingston, Edward:
    On fulfillment of treaties, 4.
    On President's power as sole agent of international communication, 28.
    On President's power to appoint diplomatic agents, 331.
Locke, John:
    On delegation of legislative power, 104.
    On nature of foreign relations power, 141.
Lodge, Henry Cabot, Senator from Massachusetts:
    On personal meetings of President with Senate, 371–372.
    On Presidential agents, 332.
    On President's relations to Senate foreign relations committee, 372.
    On termination of war, 292.
    Proposed reservations to treaty of Versailles, 61.
Logan, Dr. George, self-constituted mission to France, 34.
Logan act, 22, 34.
London, Declaration of. (See Treaties.)
London Naval Conference, 117, 118.
London protocol, 1871. (See Treaties.)
Louisiana lynchings. (See Italian lynching cases.)
"Lucius Crassus" (Hamilton), 287.
Lusitania, warning in respect to, 29.

Maclay, William, Senator:
    On relation of President to Senate, 361.
    On Washington's appearance in Senate, 250.
McLean, Justice, on discretion of Congress in execution of treaties, 66.
McLemore, Representative from Texas, resolution warning Americans from travelling on armed merchant vessels, 279, 281.
McLeod case, 18, 59, 161, 180, 229.
McKinley, William, President:
    Initiation of Spanish war, 289.

Unofficial reception of mission from South Africa, 35.
Recommends intervention in Cuba, 270.
Urges legislation to protect resident aliens, 187.
Madison, James:
Attitude toward neutrality proclamation, 268.
On duty to ratify treaties, 43.
On nature of foreign relations power, 138.
On nature of executive power, 145.
On treaty making, 246.
Practice in recognition, 272.
Magdalena Bay incident, 282.
Maine, Sir Henry Sumner, on American attitude toward international law, 358.
Mandates, 114.
Marcy, William, Secretary of State:
On constitutionality of treaties, 81.
On Greytown incident, 306.
Maritime law, power of federal courts to enforce, 200.
Marshall, John:
On confiscation of enemy property, 300.
On power to annex territory, 275.
On self-executing treaties, 207.
On extradition power of President, 194.
On interpretation according to international law, 165.
On representative powers of President, 21.
On resultant powers of national government, 133.
Mason and Slidell, unofficial reception in England, 35.
Maximilian government in Mexico, Congressional resolution on, 33, 280.
Meade's claim, 82.
Mediation, power to President to accept offer of, 219.
Medley, D. J., on beginning of cabinet responsibility in England, 144.
Metzger case, 27, 41.

Mexican boundary commission, 183, 184.
Mexican war, 297.
Declaration of, 286.
Initiation of, 287, 288.
Mexico:
Boundary marauders. (See Executive agreements.)
Mobilization of troops on border, 296. (See also Treaties.)
Migratory birds. (See Acts of Congress, Treaties.)
Militia:
Power of President to call forth, 192, 193.
Use of, in Civil War, 193.
Miller, Justice, on power of Congress to enforce treaties, 186.
Miller, David Hunter:
On unitary responsibility of British Empire under League of Nations, 16.
On reservations to treaty, 48.
Military agreements, power of President to make, 240. (See also Executive agreements.)
Miltary commissions, jurisdiction of, 168.
Military forces:
International law applied in cases affecting, 172.
President's power to use, 186, 192.
Use of, by President in Civil War, 193.
Use of, regulated by Congress, 167.
Military government, power to establish, 320–321.
Military officers, appointment of, 320–321.
Military services:
Control of, by courts, 169.
Observance of international law by, 167.
Ministers. (See Diplomatic officers.)
Modus vivendi, 235, 239. (See also Executive agreements.)

INDEX.   397

Monroe Doctrine, 282, 283.
   Congressional approval of, 283.
   Use of force in pursuance of, 309.
Monroe, James, President, appointment of diplomatic agents, 328.
Montaigne, on Constitutional changes, 368.
Montesquieu, on foreign relations power, 142, 363.
Moore, John Bassett:
   On "apprehensive interpretation" of the Constitution, 162.
   On arbitration treaties, 112.
   On congressional delegation of power to make international agreements, 374.
   On constitutional understandings, 375.
   On declaration of war, 286.
   On Greytown incident, 306.
   On method of settling international claims, 244.
   On power of recognition, 270.
   On treaty-making power, 102.
Moral obligations. (See Obligations.)
Morgan, Senator from Alabama, on Cuban intervention resolution, 271.
Morris, Gouverneur:
   Conception of Presidency, 145.
   On power of Congress to admit new states, 276.
   On treaty making, 246.
Most-favored-nation clause, 32. (See also Treaties.)
Municipal law:
   Can not alter international responsibilities, 16.
   International law applied as part of, 158, 171, 221, 222.

National decisions, conclusiveness of President's statements in reference to, 38.
National government of United States:
   Distribution of foreign relations powers, 266.
   Foreign relations power of, 130, 265, 266.
   International responsibility of, 15.
   Power to make international agreements, 233.
   Power to meet international responsibilities, 154.
   Responsibility of, for violations of international law within the states, 206. (See also Constitution of United States.)
National honor, questions involving, non-justiciable, 211.
National obligations. (See Obligations.)
Natural rights, 80.
Navassa island, status of, 173.
Naval officers, appointment of, 297, 320–321.
Naval warfare, rules of, 168.
Navigation rules, offenses against, punished, 181.
Navy:
   Use of, for intimidation, 294.
   Use of, as marition police, 296.
Necessity:
   Military, justifies capture of enemy property, 299.
   Use of self help in, 296.
Negotiation of treaties. (See Treaties.)
Negotiations, conduct of, 219.
Nelidow, President of Second Hague Conference, on nature of delegates to international conferences, 320.
Neutrality:
   Enforcement by executive, 196.
   Enforcement by federal courts, 200.
   International law applied in cases affecting, 172.
   Offenses against, punished, 179, 181.
   Panama Canal Zone, 239.
   President's proclamation of, conclusive, 39.
   Proclamation by President, 268.
   Proclamation, effect of, 199, 200.
Non-intercourse, power to authorize, 301. (See also Embargo.)
Non-justiciable question, definition of, 211.
North Atlantic fisheries arbitration, on sovereignty, 215.
North Atlantic fisheries case, 109.

North Atlantic fisheries *modus vivendi*, 240.
North German Confederation. (See Treaties.)

Obligations:
  Definition of, 213.
  Conditions under which they exist, 214.
  Distinguished from responsibilities, 213, 214.
  Responsibility for fulfillment, 152.
  Imperfect, 212.
  Legal contrasted wth moral, 211, 215.
  Moral, 210.
  National—
    Determination of, 220–222.
    Difficulty of determining, 209–210.
    Nature of, 206.
    Power to interpret, 215.
    Power to perform, 225.
    Presumed to be moral, 211.
    Presumed to be non-justiciable, 211.
    Responsibility for performance of, 205.
Occupation of foreign territory, 296.
Office under United States, incompatibilities of, 316.
Oil investments, diplomatic discussion regarding, 301.
Olney, Richard, Secretary of State:
  Interpretation of Monroe Doctrine, 39.
  On obligation to indemnify injured aliens, 225.
Opium trade, 303. (See also Treaties.)
Oppenheim, L., on representative organ, 20.

"Pacificus" (Hamilton), 136.
Panama, recognition of, 218. (See also Treaty.)
Panama Canal:
  Dispatch of troops to, 227.
  Guarantee of. 218.
  Senate rejection of treaties concerning, 252.

Panama Canal tolls act, 32, 163.
  Controversies concerning, 60, 163, 165.
Panama Canal Zone, executive agreement regarding, 238, 239.
Panama Congress, appointment of delegates to, 279, 327.
Pan-American Union, participation in, by United States, 334.
Passport regulations, 277.
Patent agreements. (See Acts of Congress.)
Pennsylvania, Attorney-General of, on letters rogatory, 189.
Permanent Court of International Justice:
  Compulsory jurisdiction on protocol, 224.
  Establishment of, 224.
  Jurisdiction of, 113, 223, 224.
  Justiciable questions, 212.
Perry, Matthew C., Commodore, opening of Japan, 297.
Pershing, John, General, punitive expedition to Mexico, 296.
Pierce, Franklin, President, on Greytown incident 306.
Pillet, on observance of international law, 358, 359.
Pine Island controversy, 173, 343.
Pious Fund and case, 65, 108.
Piracy, 180, 184.
  Defined by international law, 201.
  Suppression of, 296, 299.
Phillimore, Sir Robert, on duty of belligerents to establish prize courts, 15.
Philippines, independence of, 253.
Police power, exercise of, by United States in Panama, 218.
Policy:
  Power to decide on, not affected by constitutional guarantees, 82.
  Power to decide on, not affected by states' rights, 93.
  Power to decide on, not limited by separation of powers, 120.
  Pronouncements on, by President, subject to international cognizance, 39.

Political questions, 232, 348.
  Acquisition of territory, 134.
  Boundary determination, 274.
  Classification of, 172.
  Determined by political departments, 215.
  Includes most foreign relations powers, 124.
  Not considered by courts, 83, 172, 267, 343.
  Termination of treaty, 257.
Polk, James K., President:
  Initiation of Mexican war, 297.
  On effect of executive interpretation of treaty, 217.
  On Mexican war, 287.
Pomeroy, J. N.:
  On repelling invasion, 308.
  On war powers of President, 285.
Porto Ricans, naturalization of, 277.
Postal agreements. (See Acts of Congress, Executive agreements.)
Prescriptive bays, recognition of, 274.
Presidency:
  Analogy to British Crown, 145.
  Conception of, in Federal Convention, 145.
  Development of administrative powers of, 146.
President of United States:
  Agreement to urge foreign claims upon Congress, 244.
  Bound by act of Congress and treaty, 341.
  Can not acquire territory by conquest, 276.
  Can not authorize reprisals, 298.
  Can not be deprived of power by treaty, 119.
  Can not confiscate enemy property on land, 299.
  Can not determine obligations within power of Congress, 216.
  Can not establish prize courts, 221, 321.
  Capacity to start war, 285.
  Classification of powers, 235.
  Communications to Congress subject to international cognizance, 35.
  Conclusiveness of acts and utterances of, under international law, 38, 58, 59.
  Concurrent powers with Congress, 340, 341.
  Concurrent powers with federal courts, 342, 343.
  Constitutional basis of representative powers, 23.
  Constitutional powers of, 96.
  Dominance in conduct of foregn relations, 137, 336, 360.
  Duty of Congress to carry out political undertakings of, 349.
  Duty of courts to follow political decisions of, 348.
  Duty of treaty-making power to carry out political undertakings of, 349.
  Duty to enforce treaties, 352.
  Duty to execute acts of Congress, 350.
  Enforcement of executive agreements, 236.
  Exclusiveness of recognition power, 270.
  Extent of power in making armistices, 241.
  Extent to which he can bind the nation, 244.
  Final authority in treaty denunciation, 258.
  Foreign relations powers distinguished from administrative powers, 147.
  Foreign states may bring claims before, 24.
  Impeachment of, 167.
  Independent of Congress in conducting foreign relations, 149, 258, 278–281, 341.
  Leadership in foreign affairs, 149, 366–368.
  Need of traditions for advancement to, 373.
  Neutrality proclamation by, 199.
  Observance of international law by, 166.
  Official acts of, subject to international cognizance, 25, 28, 35.
  Personal delivery of messages by, 371, 372.

Practice in conducting foreign relations, 136.
Presumed to speak for the nation, 25, 36, 37.
Privileges and immunities of, 25, 97.
Purposes for which he may use force abroad, 306.
Purposes for which he may use force in American territory, 193, 194.
Recognition of international responsibilities, 18.
Recommendation of amendments to treaty, 254.
Refusal to submit treaty to Senate, 254.
Relations with cabinet, 371.
Relations with Congress, 371.
Relations with Congressional committees on foreign affairs, 372.
Relations with Secretary of State, 322, 323.
Relations with Senate, 360, 361.
Representative organ, 21, 26.
Requests for Senate advice during treaty negotiations, 250.
Sole agency of international communication, 28.
Unofficial reception of mission from defacto governments, 35.
Use of veto in defense of international law, 164.
War powers limited by international law, 85–86, 169.
Why given treaty-making power, 246.
Withdrawal of treaty from Senate, 254.
President, powers of, 146.
Appointment of officers, 314.
Appointment of diplomatic agents, 249, 328, 329.
Appointment of diplomatic officers, 325.
Appointment of military and naval officers, 321.
Appointment of peace missions, 327.
Appointment of treaty negotiators, 119, 249.
Arming of merchant vessels, 295.
Cable landing, 267, 302.
Commissioning military and civil officers, 322.
Conclusion of *compromis* of arbitration, 223.
Conclusion of executive agreements, 53, 233–236, 243.
Confiscation of property in war, 85.
Control of foreign relations, 141, 266, 267.
Creation of offices, 313.
Denunciation of treaties, 259.
Determination of foreign policy, 64, 282.
Determination of national obligations, 217.
Determination of occasions for using military force, 193.
Direction of administration, 141, 148, 194, 317.
Direction of military forces, 305.
Enforcement of awards of foreign consuls, 195.
Enforcement of international law, 192.
Enforcement of neutrality, 176, 182.
Enforcement of treaties, 190.
Exchange of ratifications of treaty, 52, 254.
Extradition under treaty, 194.
Extradition without treaty, 195.
Formal amends, 229.
Fulfillment of guarantee, 227.
Government of unorganized territory, 320–321.
Initiate treaties, 248.
Interim appointments, 119.
Internment of foreign troops, 196.
Interpretation of constitution, 347.
Interpretation of international law, 245.
Interpretation of national and state laws, 40.
Interpretation of treaty, 47, 245.

INDEX.

Meeting of international responsibilities, 100, 158.
Movement of military and naval forces, 119, 186, 227, 304, 309.
Movement of military and naval forces abroad, 296.
Movement of military forces in United States territory, 193.
Negotiation of treaties, 44, 249.
Organization of army and navy, 320.
Proclamation of treaties, 255.
Radio censorship, 196.
Ratification of treaties, 52, 254.
Reception of diplomatic officers, 242.
Recognition, 39, 268.
Recognition of citizenship, 277.
Recognition of termination of treaty by international law, 256.
Recognition of termination of war, 291, 293.
Recognition of territorial acquisitions, 274.
Recognition of war, 286.
Removal of officers, 146, 194, 316, 322.
Repudiation of acts by subordinates, *ultra vires,* 40, 44.
Return of deserting seamen under treaty, 195.
Signature of treaties, 251.
Suppression of boundary incidents, 184.
Treaty making, 261–262.
Veto, 119.
Presidential agent, not an officer of United States, 333.
Presidential agreements. (See Executive agreements.)
Prize courts:
  Apply international law, 19, 171, 221.
  Cases settled by, 221.
  Duty of, 299.
  Duty of belligerents to establish, 15, 173.
  Effect of municipal law limitations upon, 19.
  Power to establish, 221, 314.

Prize jurisdiction. (See Federal courts, Jurisdiction.)
Prizes, restoration of, 182, 200. (See also Acts of Congress.)
Proclamation of neutrality. (See Neutrality.)
Proclamation of treaties. (See Treaties.)
Property, private, power to authorize seizure, 85, 298.
Protectorates, recognition of, 268.
Protocol, 235. (See also Executive agreements.)
Public vessels, international law applied in cases affecting, 172.
Privateering, power to authorize, 298.

Radio, power to regulate, 196, 302.
Ratification of treaty. (See Treaties.)
Rawle, William:
  On abrogation of treaties, 260.
  On powers of President, 149.
  On termination of treaties, 283.
Reasonable doubt, acts must be unconstitutional beyond, 348.
Rebus sic stantibus, 256.
Reciprocity treaties, Senate rejection of, 252. (See also Executive agreements, Treaties.)
Recognition:
  By subordinate does not bind President, 40.
  Distinguished from intervention, 270.
  Exclusiveness of President's power, 39, 270.
  Grounds for withdrawing, 20.
  Method of, 268.
  Of foreign states and governments, 39, 268–273.
  Of termination of war, 291, 293.
  Of war, 286, 289.
  Political question, 172.
  Power of, 266, 268.
  Relation of, to war, 269.
  Resolutions on, by states of United States, 265.
  Source of power, 133.
Reinsch, Paul S., on experience of Secretaries of State, 373.

Removal power, 316. (See also President.)
Renault, L., on inexpediency of treaty reservations, 49.
Reparation:
  By formal amends, 229.
  By punishment of individual, 178, 229.
  By release of prisoner, 229.
  Obligation of, 153, 209.
Repentigny claim, 222.
Representative distinguished from delegate, 318.
Requisition of enemy property, 299.
Representative organ of government, 13.
  Attributes of, under international law, 15, 28.
  Constitutional restrictions on, 19.
  Duty of states to maintain, 21.
  Form of, 26.
  May be altered by constitutional amendment, 26.
  Must be free of municipal law restrictions, 19.
  President of the United States as, 21.
  Sole agency of international communication, 28.
Reprisals:
  Effect of, 291.
  Power to authorize, 298.
Res adjudicata, 64, 235.
Reservations to treaty:
  Express consent to, 45.
  Made at exchange of ratifications, 255.
  Made at signature, 251.
  Must be agreed to by President and Senate, 46.
  Not permitted, to Declarations of Paris and London, 49.
  Number of cases of, 253.
  Occasions for presenting, 48, 50.
  Refusal of foreign state to accept, 254, 255.
  Senate's power, 253.
  Statements of policy in, 282.
  Tacit consent to, 48.

Reservations to treaty referred to:
  African Slave Trade general act, 51.
  Algeciras convention, 282.
  Corea-United States, 1882, 331.
  France-United States, 1801, 50, 255.
  Great Britain-United States, 1794, Jay treaty, 253.
  Hague Conventions, 51, 111, 282.
  Monroe Doctrine, 282.
  Sanitary convention, 1903, 52.
  Spain-United States, 1819, Florida purchase, 49.
  Spain-United States, 1898, 253.
Reservations to Versailles treaty proposed by United States Senate, 49, 107.
  Appointment of representatives in League of Nations, 119.
  Constitutionality, 119.
  Power to use military force, 119.
  Presidential agents, 333.
  Withdrawal from League of Nations, 34, 107, 119.
Reserved powers of states of United States:
  Classification of, 89.
  Constitutional understandings regarding, 86.
  Do not limit treaty-making power, 89.
Responsibilities:
  Distinguished from obligations, 213–214.
  Powers not deducible from, 154.
  Social conditions under which they exist, 214.
Responsibilities, international, 13.
  Based on consent, 58.
  Classification of, 213.
  Definition of, 213.
  For domestic disturbances, 264.
  Duty of government organs to meet, 358.
  Instrumentalities for meeting, defined by treaty, 99.
  Meeting of, distinguished from making agreements, 62.
  Not affected by municipal law, 16.

INDEX.   403

Of President under international law, 27.
Power of Congress to meet, 100, 159.
Power of courts to meet, 100, 158.
Power of President to meet, 100, 157.
Power of states of United States to meet, 153.
Power of treaty-making power to meet, 160.
Power to meet, not affected by constitutional limitations, 78, 87, 99.
Power to meet, not an inherent executive power, 155.
Power to meet through enforcement of international law, 176.
Principles of, 151.
Recognition of, by Continental Congress, 18.
States judges of their own, 14.
To perform national obligations, 205.
Understandings with respect to, 9.
Unitary under international law, 15, 25.
Resultant powers of national government, 132.
Retaliation, power to authorize, 301.
Retorsion, power to authorize, 301.
Rio Grande, boundary commission, 184.
Richards, Acting Attorney General, on power to land cables, 267, 302.
Rivier, on the representative organ, 20.
Rogatory, letters, not applicable in criminal cases, 189.
Roman law, ogligations under, 213.
Roosevelt, Theodore:
  Dispatch of troops, 296.
  Influence in foreign affairs, 323.
  Interpretation of Panama Canal Guarantee, 217, 218.
  Negotiation of Algeciras Convention, 136.
  On anarchy as offense against international law, 188.
  On executive agreement with Santo Domingo, 237.
  On President's powers, 156.
  Submission of Pious funds case to arbitration, 108.
  Unofficial reception of mission from South Africa, 35.
  Urged legislation to protect resident aliens, 187.
  Use of navy, 294.
  Withdrawal of treaties from Senate, 109, 254.
Root, Elihu:
  Arbitration treaties, 109, 112.
  On constitutionality of international prize court, 117.
  On obligation of Congress under treaties, 62.
  On responsibility of national government for protecting resident aliens, 18.
  On value of international law for democracies, 370.
Root-Takahira agreement. (See Executive agreements.)
Russell, Lord John:
  On constitutional understandings, 369.
  On effect of Blockade proclamation, 38.
Russia:
  Claim to jurisdiction in Bering Sea, 174.
  Treaty protecting citizens suggested by Congress, 248. (See also Treaties.)
Russo-Japanese war, commencement of, 290.

Sackville, Lord, British minister, recall of, 29.
Salmong, John W., on responsibility, 214.
Salisbury, Lord, British Premier, discussion of Monroe Doctrine, 39.
Salutes:
  Amends by, 229.
  Exchange of, 168, 209.
Sanitary Convention. (See Treaties.)
San Juan Island, agreement regarding, 239.

Santo Domingo:
  Annexation treaty, Senate rejection, 252.
  Executive agreement regarding, 156, 238.
Scott, James Brown, on reservation to treaties, 51.
Scrap of Paper incident, 212, 261.
Seamen:
  May be compelled to fulfill contracts, 84.
  Return of deserting, 195.
Secrecy. (See Foreign relations.)
Secret agents, power to appoint, 330.
Secretary of State:
  Appointment of, 322.
  Conferences with Senators on treaty negotiation, 251.
  Recognition of citizenship, 277.
  Removal of, 322.
  Relations with President, 323.
Secretary of War, power to settle certain claims, 220.
Sedition against foreign sovereigns, punishable in states, 178.
Self executing treaties. (See Treaties.)
Sequestration of enemy property, 299.
Senate:
  Advice to treaty negotiation, 250.
  Conception of, in Federal Convention, 145.
  Consent to ratification of treaties, 252.
  Consent to treaty reservations, 50.
  Duty to carry out preliminaries of peace, 241.
  Duty to ratify treaty in accord with executive agreement, 243.
  Duty to ratify treaty in accord with instructions, 43.
  Influence in foreign affairs, 368.
  Participation in appointment of treaty negotiators, 249, 330, 331.
  Participation in claims settlement, 224.
  Participation in *compromis* of arbitration, 223.
  Participation in instruction of treaty negotiators, 250.
  Power in treaty making, 261.
  Power to determine national obligations, 216.
  Number of treaty reservations by, 253.
  Protests against Presidential agents, 330–332.
  Refusal to reject or consent to treaty, 253.
  Rejection of treaties, 44, 238, 252.
  Relations with President, 360, 361.
  Reservation, amendment and interpretation of treaty, 253.
  Veto of treaties, 149.
  Why given participation in treaty making, 93.
  Withdrawal of treaty from, by President, 254.
Senate Committee on Foreign Relations:
  Conferences with President, 250, 372.
  On arbitration treaties, 111.
  On coöperation of departments, 346.
  On denunciation of treaties, 259.
  On executive nature of foreign relations power, 137.
  On overlapping of powers of departments, 339.
  On power of recognition, 273.
  On power of states of United States in foreign relations, 265.
  On Presidential agents, 119, 249, 330, 332.
  On reason for President's initiative in treaty making, 248.
  On representative powers of President, 21.
Senate resolutions:
  Foreign acquisition of neighboring naval bases, 282.
  Interpretation of treaty by, ineffective, 33, 34, 46.
  Visit and search of vessels, 281.
Senators:
  Appointment as treaty negotiators, 251, 316, 333.
  Conference of Secretary of State with, on treaty negotiations, 251.

Separation of Powers:
  Does not limit power to make decisions on national policy, 120.
  Limitations derived from, 95.
  Limitations on treaty-making power, 101.
  Most important limitation on foreign relations power, 125.
  Origin of theory, 172.
  Should not be too rigidly applied, 126. (See also Constitution of United States.)
Seward, William H., Secretary of State:
  On House resolutions affecting foreign policy, 33, 280.
  On practice in international communication, 23.
  On termination of foreign wars, 291.
Sherman, William T., General, armistice by, repudiated, 44, 240.
Sherman, John, on Presidential agents, 249, 332.
Sherman anti-trust act, 165.
Signature of treaty. (See Treaties.)
Slave trade, suppression of, 184, 295. (See also Treaties.)
Slavery, prohibition of, in accord with international law, 80. (See also Constitutional provisions, Emancipation Proclamation.)
South Africa, unofficial reception of mission from, 35.
South African war, termination of, 291.
Sovereign powers, not vested in national government, 130-132.
Sovereigns:
  International law applied in cases affecting, 171.
  Sedition against, punishable in states, 178.
Sovereignty:
  Nature of, 134.
  Questions involving, non-justiciable, 214.
  Theory of, divided, 72.
Spain:
  Controversies on obligation of preliminaries of peace, 54.
  Controversies on ratification of treaties, 42, 43. (See also Treaties.)
Spanish-American war:
  Effect on control of foreign relations in United States, 367.
  Initiation of, 289.
  Preliminaries of peace. (See Executive agreements.)
Spanish colonial wars, termination of, 291.
Spanish-Peruvian war, termination of, 291.
Spanish treaty claims commission, 222, 245.
Spooner, Senator of Wisconsin:
  On control of foreign relations, 365.
  On Department of State, 322.
  On executive nature of foreign relations power, 137.
Stanton, Commodore, recognition of Brazilian insurgents, repudiated by President, 40.
Stare Decisis, application to international decisions, 64, 65.
State, Department of:
  Agency of communication, 21.
  Negotiation by, 219.
  Organization of, 322.
State, Secretary of. (See Secretary of State.)
States of the United States:
  Admission to the union, 275, 276.
  Anti-alien legislation by, 90-91.
  Consent to alienation of territory, 89.
  Consent to treaty, 55.
  Contracts by, 205, 232.
  Exempt from taxation, 86.
  Guaranteed rights of, 76.
  Jurisdiction of courts, in cases affecting aliens, 202.
  Limitations on powers of, 73.
  Limitations on foreign relations powers, 265.
  No extradition power, 190, 231.
  No power to perform national obligations, 205.
  Not internationally responsible, 25.
  Not judge in own case, 210.

Officers of, may not be burdened with national duties, 312.
Release from, of persons claiming immunity under international law, 161, 171, 180, 229.
Remedies by, will not relieve national government of responsibility, 206.
Republican form of government guaranteed, 86.
Resolutions by, recommending recognition, 265.
Suability of, 205, 206.
Territory of, guaranteed, 86.
Territory of, may not be ceded, 88. (See also Constitution of United States.)

States of the United States, powers:
Agreement making, 230–232, 261.
Appontment of militia officers, 321.
Criminal legislation concurrent with Congress, 178.
Diplomatic, 264.
Enforcement of international law, 177.
Foreign relations, 129.
Meeting of international responsibilities, 153.
Protection of resident aliens, 179.
Regulation of alien property holding, 91.
Reserved, 75.
War, 264.

States of the United States, statutes:
Publication, 30.
Subject to international cognizance, 30, 40.
Void if contrary to treaty, 91, 161, 175.
When effective, 30, 161.

States' rights, limit national powers, 86.

States, sovereign:
Bound by international law, 55.
Consent to suit in justiciable controversies, 211.
Definition of, 15.
May bring suits in United States courts, 23.
Non-suability, 210.
Offenses against punished, 182.

Recognition of, 20, 268.
Recognition of, political question, 172.
Stone, Senator of Missouri, on war powers of Congress, 290.
Story, Joseph, Justice:
On criminal jurisdiction of federal courts, 198.
On duty of Congress to establish inferior federal courts, 357.
On interpretation of treaties, 218.
On President's discretion, 309.
On President's power to carry out awards of foreign consuls, 195.
On treaty-making power, 234.
Stowell, Lord, on initiation of war, 288.
Submarine cable convention. (See Treaties.)
Succession, law of, 80.
Sumner, Charles, Senator from Massachusetts:
On denunciation of treaty, 259.
Resolution on proposed Santo Domingan annexation, 279.
Supreme Court of the United States:
Appellate jurisdiction of, 203.
Effect of decisions as precedents, 347.
Original jurisdiction of, 202.
Suspension of arms, 240.
Sutherland, George:
On arbitration treaties, 112.
On war powers of President, 84, 170.
Switzerland:
Controversy on application of most-favored-nation clause, 33, 228.
International responsibility of national government, 15.
Official commentary on League of Nations covenant, 60, 114. (See also Treaties.)

Taft, William Howard:
Dispatch of troops, 296.
On arbitration treaties, 111, 112.
On denunciation of treaties, 259.
On executive agreements, 238.

INDEX. 407

On powers of President, 156.
On power to interpret laws, 64.
On President's power to determine foreign policy, 64, 245.
On President's power to direct forces, 119, 308.
On responsibility of nation for protection of resident aliens, 25.
Proclamation of Japanese treaty of 1911, 45.
Urges legislation to protect resident aliens, 187.
Withdrawal of treaties from Senate, 254.

Taney, Chief Justice:
On foreign relations powers of national government, 134.
On nature of foreign relations powers, 131.
On powers of states of United States to make agreements, 230.

Taylor, Zachary, President, communication on Kossuth revolution protested by Austria, 25, 36.

Tazewell, Senator from Virginia, on President's power to appoint diplomatic agents, 330.

Telegraph, power to regulate, 302.

Termination of executive agreements. (See Executive agreements.)

Termination of Treaties. (See Treaties.)

Termination of war. (See War.)

Territory:
Annexation of, political question, 172.
Conquest of, 276.
International law applied to determine rights in newly acquired, 172.
Methods of acquiring, 273–275.
Military government of, constitutional, 83, 85.
Power to annex, 83, 130, 274, 275.
Power to cede, 226.
Recognition of acquisitions, 268, 274.
Source of power to annex, 133.

Texas annexation treaty, Senate rejection, 252.

Thayer, W. R., on relations of President and Secretary of State, 323.

Tinoca, de facto President of Costa Rica, non-recognition of, 20, 268.

Trademark agreements. (See Acts of Congress.)

Treaties:
Abrogation of, 260–261.
Amendments to, 46.
Annexation of territory by, 274–275.
Applied by courts, 162, 172, 222.
Appointment of negotiators of, 249.
Authorizing executive and judicial action 190.
Authorizing executive agreements, 106, 236.
Authorizing extradition by state authority, 178.
Can not deprive Congress of powers, 101.
Can not deprive courts of inherent powers, 116.
Can not vest courts with non-judicial functions, 117.
Capture of property under authority of, 299.
Change in character of, during 19th century, 206–207.
Claims settled by, 244.
Classification of subject matter, 247.
Conclusion of, may be national obligation, 228.
Conflict with acts of Congress, 164, 175, 305, 345.
Conflict with another treaty, 166, 175, 352.
Conflict with customary international law, 174.
Conflict with state law, 91, 175.
Congress deprived of full discretion by, 103.
Congressional execution of, 103, 226, 354–356.
Courts can not make, 234.
Delegation of judicial power by, 112, 116.
Delegation of power by, to international organs, 110, 112.

Delegation of power by, to President, to conclude *compromis* of arbitration, 108.
Denunciation on notice, 258.
Deposit of ratifications, 50.
Designating special organs to execute, 26, 99.
Duty to ratify, 42, 252, 253.
Exchange of ratifications, 48, 50, 52, 254.
Imposes moral obligation, 210.
Initiation of, 248.
International obligation of, not affected by congressional abrogation, 260, 261.
Interpretation of, 63, 112, 218.
Interpretation by President, 25, 245.
Interpretation of law by, 115–116.
Interpretation of, requires full treaty power, 48, 65, 217.
Interpretation by national organs in first instance, 213.
Interpreted in accord with international law, 166.
Interpretive resolutions by Houses of Congress, 253.
Making of, distinguished from meeting responsibilities, 62.
May deal with subjects in power of Congress, 102, 103, 344.
Most-favored-nation clause, application to Switzerland, 46.
Must deal with subjects of international scope, 123.
National claims submitted to arbitration under, 223.
National obligations based on, 206.
Negotiation under authority of President, 44.
Never declared unconstitutional, 80, 247.
Number concluded by United States, 246, 247.
Number rejected by Senate, 252.
Objection of foreign states to Senate amendment, 44.
Obligation of, 6, 59, 212.
Obligation of Congress to enforce, 191.
Obligation to ratify, 42.

Offenses against, punished, 179, 184–186.
Offenses created by, may be punished, 79.
Organs for interpreting, 210.
Power of Congress to pass laws in execution of, 87.
Power to conclude, under national constitution, 53.
President's refusal to submit to Senate, 254.
Proclamation of, 255.
Protocols postponing exchange of ratifications, 47.
Provisions dependent on state legislation, 26, 30, 31.
Publication of, 31.
Qualified ratification of, must be consented to, 45.
Ratification of, 42, 52, 252, 254.
Recognition of, in act of Congress, 163.
Rejection of, by foreign government, 255.
Repudiation of, 6, 260.
Requiring legislative execution, 208.
Requiring subsequent treaty, 353.
Reservations to. (See Reservations to Treaty.)
Respect for earlier treaties by, 166.
Secrecy in negotiation of, 354.
Secret, 255.
Self executing, 207, 228, 353.
Senate participation in interpretation of, 48, 217.
Senate refusal to ratify, 44, 238.
Settlement of controversy by, 219.
Signature of, 48, 249, 251.
States of United States forbidden to make, 230.
Steps in conclusion of, 41, 42.
Subject matter of, 246.
Supreme law of land, 158, 255.
Termination of, 39, 107, 256–262, 351, 352.
Termination of, political question, 172.
Ultra vires provisions, 53–56.
Validity if made by de facto government, 57.

INDEX.

Validity if made under necessity, 57, 89.
Voidable, 256.
War, effect on, 256.
When effective, 31, 42, 52, 255.
Withdrawal from Senate by President, 245. (See also Executive agreements.)
Treaties concluded by United States, referred to:
Austria, 1921, termination of war, 293.
Cherokee Indians, 1790, 43.
China, 1868 (Burlingame), **immi**gration, 164, 257, 345.
    1894, protection of citizens, 191.
Colombia, 1846, guarantee, 217, 227, 247, 296.
Corea, 1882, commerce, 249, 303, 331.
Cuba, 1903, protection, 217, 296.
    1903, reciprocity, 106.
Denmark, 1917, cession of Virgin Islands, 252.
France, 1778, alliance, 247, 256, 257.
    1778, commerce, 90, 166.
    1788, consuls, 43.
    1801, commerce and claims, 45, 47, 50, 219, 220, 345.
    1803, Lousiana purchase, 102.
    1831, claims, 66, 219, 220.
    1852, consuls, 56.
    1853, alien land ownership, 31, 90.
    1898, commercial reciprocity, 33.
    1919, proposed guarantee, 253.
Germany, 1844, commerce, 102.
    1921, termination of war, 293.
Great Britain, 1783, peace, 31, 162, 191.
    1794 (Jay), commerce and claims, 62, 102, 226, 255, 266, 352.
    1803 (King-Hawksbury), proposed boundary, 44.
    1814 (Ghent), peace, 326, 327.

    1817, Great Lakes disarmament, 39, 242, 247, 258.
    1818, fisheries, 215.
    1842 (Webster-Ashburton), Maine boundary, 55, 89, 220, 226, 227, 230.
    1846, Oregon boundary, 220.
    1850, Isthmian canal (Clayton-Bulwer), 25, 45, 47, 48, 65, 255, 258.
    1854, use of state canals, 31, 90.
    1871 (Washington), neutral duties, 177.
    1892, Bering sea arbitration, 164.
    1900 (Hay-Pauncefote), proposed Isthmian canal, 45.
    1901 (Hay-Pauncefote), Isthmian canal, 163, 258.
    1908, arbitration, 47, 99, 109, 210–211.
    1910, claims, 224.
    1911, Canadian boundary commission, 183, 219.
    1918, migratory birds, 87, 185.
Hawaii, 1884, reciprocity, 47.
Hayti, 1915, intervention and guarantee, 217, 247, 297.
Hungary, 1921, termination of war, 293.
Indian tribes, 43, 234.
Italy, 1871, extradition and rights of citizens, 67, 351.
Japan, 1911, rights of citizens, 45, 90.
Mexico, 1848 (Guadaloupe Hidalgo), peace, 25, 47, 48, 65, 109, 217, 220, 255.
    1889, boundary commission, 184.
North German Confederation, 1868, naturalization, 46.
Panama, 1903, guarantee, 247, 352.
Russia, 1832, commerce, 259.
    1867, Alaska purchase, 102, 245.
Santo Domingo, 1907, customs administration, 238.

Spain, 1795, embargoes, 245.
   1819, Florida purchase, 49.
   1898, peace, 46, 220, 251.
Switzerland, 1855, most-favored-nation clause, 33, 46, 48, 228, 260.
Turkey, 1874, extradition, 47.
Treaties, general, referred to:
  Algeciras convention, Morocco, 50, 136, 282.
  Alien rights, 89.
  Arbitration. (See Arbitration treaties.)
  Arms trade, 354, 355.
  Bering sea sealing, 185, 228.
  Brussels general act, 1890, African slave trade, 45, 50, 51, 191, 227.
  Bryan, peace, 219, 247.
  Commercial, 228.
  Consular jurisdiction, 185.
  Declaration of London, maritime capture, 49.
  Declaration of Paris, maritime warfare, 47, 49, 245, 298.
  Geneva convention, Red Cross, 185, 191, 247.
  Guarantee, 247, 253.
  Hague conventions. (See Hague conventions.)
  International administration, 247.
  International organization, 228.
  League of Nations Covenant. (See League of Nations Covenant.)
  London, 1871, obligation of treaties, 212.
  Maritime salvage, 185.
  Pan-American pecuniary claims, 1910, 99, 222.
  Radio telegraph, 185.
  Sanitary convention, 1903, 52.
  Submarine cable, 1885, 47, 185, 216, 228.
  Vereiniging, 1902, end of Boer war, 35.
  Versailles. (See Versailles, treaty of.)
  Vienna, 1815, classification of diplomatic officers, 14.
  White slavery, 1904, 87.

Treaty-making power, 53, 55, 233, 246.
  Can not be delegated, 104.
  Can not bind its own future action, 352.
  Capacity to meet international responsibilities, 160.
  Concurrent powers of Congress, 344–345.
  Constitutional limitations upon, 121, 248, 351.
  Constitutional provisions on, 55.
  Creation of offices by, 312.
  Delegation to international organ, 111.
  Denunciation of treaty by, 259.
  Duty to carry out executive agreements, 349.
  Duty of Congress to carry out acts of, 353–356.
  Duty of courts to enforce acts of, 351.
  Duty of President to enforce acts of, 352.
  Limited by guarantees of private right, 80.
  Limited by separation of powers, 101.
  Limited by states' rights, 55, 88.
  May create courts, 104.
  Observance of international law by, 166.
  Opinion of text writers on, 92.
  Should respect states' reserved powers, 93.
  Suggested modification of, 368.
  Termination of voidable treaty by, 256.
  Under Articles of Confederation, 246.
Tripolitan war, 286, 297.
Trumbull case (Chile vs. U. S., 1892), 27, 41.
Tucker, H. St. George, on conflicts of state legislation with treaty, 162.
Turkey. (See Treaties.)

Ulpian, on making of contract, 41.
Understandings, relation to law, 7, 8. (See also Constitutional understandings, International understandings.)

INDEX.

United States. (See National government, States of United States, Constitution, House of Representatives, Senate, Congress, President, Courts.)
Vattel, E.:
 On imperfect obligations, 8.
 On legal and moral obligations, 211.
 On obligation of international law, 67.
 On organ to interpret treaty, 210.
Venezuela claims cases, 109.
Vera Cruz incident, 205, 297, 299.
Versailles treaty:
 Compatibility with preliminaries of peace, 54.
 Deposit of ratifications, 50.
 League of Nations Covenant. (See League of Nations Covenant.)
 Obligation to ratify, 216.
 Reservation proposed by China, 49.
 Reservations proposed by Senate. (See Reservations to treaty of Versailles.)
 Senate rejection of, 252.
Veto. (See President.)
Vicarious responsibility, 152.
Vice President, participation in cabinet meetings, 371.
Vienna, Treaty of. (See Treaties.)
Villa, pursuit of, 193, 296.
Virgin islands, annexation treaty rejected by Senate, 252.
Vital interests, questions involving, non-justiciable, 211.

Walsh, T. J., Senator from Montana, on termination of treaty, 108.
War:
 Causation of, 284, 285.
 Declaration authorizes general reprisals, 299.
 Declaration, effect of, 256, 297, 298, 299.
 Declaration, power, 227, 266, 286, 290.
 Declaration, prohibits trading with enemy, 303.
 Definition, 284.
 Fact of, subject to international cognizance, 39.
 International law applied in cases affecting, 172.
 Obligation to make, under treaty, 62.
 Power to make, 284.
 Powers, subject to constitutional limitations, 84.
 Recognition of, 39, 268, 286, 289.
 Termination of, 39, 268, 290, 291, 293.
 Termination of, political question, 173. (See also Belligerency, Civil war.)
War of 1812, declaration of, 286.
Wars referred to:
 American civil, 288, 291.
 Mexican, 286–288, 297.
 Russo-Japanese, 290.
 South African, 291.
 Spanish-American, 289, 367.
 Spanish Colonial, 291.
 Spanish-Peruvian, 291.
 Tripolitan, 286, 297.
 War of 1812, 286.
 World war, 280, 293.
 Declaration, proposed amendment, regarding, 93.
Washington, George, President:
 Appointment of diplomatic agents, 328, 331.
 Farewell address, 67, 283.
 On control of foreign relations, 364.
 On international favors, 67.
 On treaty-making power, 5, 233.
 On power of House of Representatives in treaty making, 62, 246.
 Neutrality proclamation, 196.
 Personal discussion with Senate, 361.
 Practice in recognition, 272.
 Recognition of France, 136.
 Seeks Senate advice to treaty, 250.
Washington, treaty of. (See Treaties, Great Britain.)
Water Witch incident, 298.

Webster, Daniel:
  On congressional resolutions on foreign affairs, 279.
  On duty of states to maintain courts, 14.
  On obligation of international law, 58.
  On treaty-making power, 55.
Webster-Ashburton treaty. (See Treaties, Great Britain.)
Westlake, John, on recognition, 20.
White slavery. (See Acts of Congress, Treaties.)
Wickersham, George, Attorney General, on repelling invasion, 308.
William P. Frye, case of, 24.
Willoughby, W. W.:
  On adoption of international law by United States, 59.
  On denunciation of treaty, 260.
  On extradition power, 195.
  On Neagle case, 157.
  On power to annex territory, 275.
  On power of states to make agreements, 232.
  On power to meet international responsibilities, 154.
  On President's powers, 146.
  On sovereign powers of national government, 131.
  On treaty-making power, 56.
  On war powers of President, 169, 170.
Wilson, G. G., and Tucker, G. F.:
  Definition of state, 15.
  Powers of Department of State, 22.
Wilson, James, proposal for treaty-making power, 246.
Wilson, Woodrow:
  Dispatch of troops, 296.
  Fourteenth point of, 241.
  On American entry into World War, 289.
  On experience of Presidents, 373.
  On legal and moral obligations, 211.
  On nature of delegates to League of Nations Assembly, 320.
  On obligation of preliminaries of peace, 54.
  On Panama Canal Tolls controversy, 60, 163.
  On power to arm merchant vessels, 295.
  On President's leadership in foreign relations, 367.
  On relation of President to Congress, 366.
  On termination of treaty, 108.
  On unitary responsibility of British Empire in League of Nations, 16.
  Personal conference with Senate Committee on Foreign Relations, 372.
  Refusal to carry out congressional resolution on foreign affairs, 280.
  Removal of Secretary of State, 322.
  Sympathy for democratic form of government, 14.
  Termination of treaties, 258.
  Veto of war termination resolution, 292.
Woodbury, Justice, on jurisdiction of federal courts, 199.
World War:
  American entry into, 289.
  Declaration of, 280.
  Preliminaries of peace. (See Executive Agreement.)
  Termination of, 293. (See also Versailles treaty.)

Yrujo, Spanish minister, case of, 29.